Cambridge Studies in French

THE SEDUCTIONS OF PSYCHOANALYSIS

Cambridge Studies in French

General editor: MALCOLM BOWIE

Recent titles in this series include:

MITCHELL GREENBERG
Corneille, Classicism, and the Ruses of Symmetry

HOWARD DAVIES
Sartre and 'Les Temps Modernes'

ROBERT GREER COHN
Mallarmé's Prose Poems: A Critical Study

CELIA BRITTON
Claude Simon: Writing the Visible

DAVID SCOTT
*Pictorialist Poetics: Poetry and the
Visual Arts in Nineteenth-Century France*

ANN JEFFERSON
Reading Realism in Stendhal

DALIA JUDOVITZ
*Subjectivity and Representation in Descartes
The Origins of Modernity*

RICHARD D.E. BURTON
*Baudelaire in 1859
A Study in the Sources of Poetic Creativity*

MICHAEL MORIARTY
Taste and Ideology in Seventeenth-Century France

A complete list of books in the series is given
at the end of the volume.

THE SEDUCTIONS OF PSYCHOANALYSIS

FREUD, LACAN AND DERRIDA

JOHN FORRESTER
Department of History and Philosophy
of Science, University of Cambridge

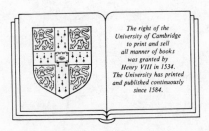

The right of the
University of Cambridge
to print and sell
all manner of books
was granted by
Henry VIII in 1534.
The University has printed
and published continuously
since 1584.

CAMBRIDGE UNIVERSITY PRESS

CAMBRIDGE

NEW YORK   PORT CHESTER

MELBOURNE   SYDNEY

Published by the Press Syndicate of the University of Cambridge
The Pitt Building, Trumpington Street, Cambridge CB2 1RP
40 West 20th Street, New York, NY 10011, USA
10 Stamford Road, Oakleigh, Melbourne 3166, Australia

© Cambridge University Press 1990

First published 1990
Printed in Great Britain at
the University Press, Cambridge

British library cataloguing in publication data

Forrester, John
The seductions of psychoanalysis. Freud,
Lacan and Derrida. – (Cambridge studies in French)
1. Psychoanalysis
I. Title
150.19′5

Library of Congress cataloguing in publication data

Forrester, John.
The seductions of psychoanalysis. Freud, Lacan, and
Derrida / John Forrester.
p.   cm. – (Cambridge studies in French)
Bibliography.
Includes index.
ISBN 0–521–37243–7
1. Psychoanalysis.   2. Freud, Sigmund, 1856–1939.   3. Lanan,
Jacques, 1901–1981.   4. Derrida, Jacques.   I. Title   II. Series
RC504.F63   1989
150.19′5 – dc20   89–7209   CIP

ISBN 0 521 37243 7

CE

*In memory of my mother and father
and of Rosemary*

CONTENTS

Contents

ACKNOWLEDGEMENTS

Some of the chapters in this book have previously appeared in a similar form in books or journals. I would like to thank the following for granting permission to reprint them (with alterations, in some cases major ones): *Social Research*, New School for Social Research, New York, for 'The true story of Anna O.', *Social Research 53* 1986 pp. 327–47; Tavistock Publications for 'Contracting the disease of love: authority and freedom in the origins of psychoanalysis', in W.F. Bynum, Roy Porter and Michael Shepherd, eds., *The anatomy of madness, Essays in the history of psychiatry. Vol. I. People and ideas*, London: Tavistock, 1985, pp. 255–70; ICA Publications for 'Freud, Dora and the untold pleasures of psychoanalysis', in Lisa Appignanesi, ed., *Desire*, London: ICA Documents, 1984, pp. 4–9; Basil Blackwell for 'Rape, seduction, psychoanalysis', in Sylvana Tomaselli and Roy Porter, eds., *Rape*, Oxford: Basil Blackwell, 1985, pp. 57–83; Free Associations Books for 'In place of an introduction: *The Seminar of Jacques Lacan. Books I and II*', *Free Associations*, nos. 10 and 11, 1987 and 1988; Routledge and Kegan Paul for 'Who is in analysis with whom? Freud, Lacan, Derrida', *Economy & Society 13* 1984 pp.153–77; The Macmillan Press Ltd for 'Psychoanalysis: gossip, telepathy and/or science?', in James Donald, ed., *Psychoanalysis and culture*, London: Macmillan, 1990; Oxford University Press for 'Transference and the stenographer: on Dostoevsky's *The gambler*', *Paragraph 3* 1984 pp. 48–82; Science History Publications and ICA Publications for 'Michel Foucault and the history of psychoanalysis', *History of Science 18* 1980 pp. 286–303. I would like to thank Sigmund Freud Copyrights Ltd, The Institute of Psycho-analysis and The Hogarth Press for permission to quote from *The Standard Edition of the Complete Psychological Works of Sigmund Freud*, translated and edited by James Strachey, and S. Fischer Verlag for permission to quote from Sigmund Freud, *Gesammelte Werke*, 18 vols., Frankfurt am Main: S. Fischer,

Acknowledgements

1940–68 and *Studienausgabe*, 11 vols., Frankfurt am Main: S. Fischer, 1969–75.

This book was written in spurts over a period of some ten years. During that time I have accumulated many debts, both personal and intellectual, both individual and institutional, whose traces are visible, at least to me, in the pages that follow. For part of this time, I was first a Junior, then a Senior, Research Fellow at King's College, Cambridge: to that generous institution, and to the many friends there with whom I worked and discussed ideas, I would like to offer my thanks. Since 1984, I have been a Lecturer in the History and Philosophy of Science in the University of Cambridge. To my colleagues, my fellow students of science in the Department of History and Philosophy of Science, in particular to Nicholas Jardine, David Papineau and Simon Schaffer, I would like to offer my thanks for creating the friendliest of intellectual communities over the last five years.

When the preparation of this book was in its final stages, I spent three weeks in Brazil, where I delivered versions of several of the chapters to a number of institutions, both analytic and academic; I would like to thank my audiences and hosts, especially Osmyr Gabbi (UNICAMP) and Jurandir Costa (UFRJ), for all the helpful comments I received, which led to some last-minute changes and clarifications of the arguments.

Several of the chapters were read in various draft forms by Sylvana Tomaselli, from whose meticulous, generous and sceptical intelligence they benefited greatly. In addition, I would like to thank the following for the aid they have given to my work over the years: Sheelagh Barnard, John Barrell, Malcolm Bowie, Teresa Brennan, Danièle Brun, Terry Counihan, Madeleine Davis, Jacques Derrida, Olivier Flournoy, Marie Frapin, Bernadette Gallagher, Stephen Gaukroger, Anthony Giddens, Wladimir Granoff, Gail Grayson, André Green, Ilse Hellmann, Andrew Hislop, Louise Holland, Michael Ignatieff, Suzanne Kappeller, Frank Kermode, Gregorio Kohon, Claire Laudet, Colin MacCabe, René Major, Juliet Mitchell, Toril Moi, Ian Noble, Pascal and Gisèle Petit, J.-B. Pontalis, Roy Porter, Chris Prendergast, Jacqueline Rose, Alison Sajovic, Colin Sparrow, Gareth Stedman Jones, Conrad Stein, Tony Tanner, Cathy Urwin, Marina Warner, Bob Young. Much of what I have written would not have been thinkable without the extended conversations I enjoyed with M. Eglé Laufer; to her I

Acknowledgements

offer especial thanks. My greatest pleasure is to acknowledge my indebtedness to Lisa Appignanesi, an indebtedness which is ample even when I consider only her intellectual and editorial aid, yet extends to so much else.

ABBREVIATIONS

SE   Freud, *The standard edition of the complete psychological works of Sigmund Freud* (24 volumes), ed. James Strachey in collaboration with Anna Freud, assisted by Alix Strachey and Alan Tyson, London: The Hogarth Press and the Institute of Psycho-analysis, 1953–74

GW   Freud, *Gesammelte Werke* (18 volumes), Frankfurt am Main: S. Fischer Verlag, 1940–68

Stud   Freud, *Studienausgabe* (10 volumes with an unnumbered *Ergänzungsband* [abbreviated as Erg]), Frankfurt am Main: S. Fischer Verlag, 1969–75

Origins   Freud, *The origins of psychoanalysis. Letters to Wilhelm Fliess, drafts and notes 1887–1902*, ed. Marie Bonaparte, Anna Freud and Ernst Kris, authorised translation by Eric Mosbacher and James Strachey, introduced by Ernst Kris, London: Imago, 1954

Letters   Freud, *Letters of Sigmund Freud, 1873–1939*, ed. Ernst L. Freud, trans. Tania and James Stern, London: The Hogarth Press, 1970

E   Lacan, *Ecrits*, Paris: Seuil, 1966 [Where there are two numbers, separated by / , the first number refers to the page number in the French edition, the second to the page number in *Ecrits: a selection*, trans. by Alan Sheridan, London: Tavistock, 1977.]

Sem   Lacan, *Le Séminaire*, Paris: Seuil, 1973– (25 volumes). [Where there are two numbers, separated by / , the first number refers to the page number in the French edition, the second to the page number in the English translation.]

OT   Foucault, *The order of things* (1966), London: Tavistock, 1970

VS   Foucault, *La Volonté de savoir*, Paris: Gallimard, 1976

HS I   Foucault, *The history of sexuality. Vol. I: An introduction*, trans. Robert Hurley, London: Allen Lane, 1979

INTRODUCTION

I

There are some hosts and hostesses who have an unexpectedly light touch in the way of introductions, and succeed in bringing their guests together.[1] They know everybody's names, and tell their guests interesting stories about one another; they treat the proper name as if it were, despite its intrinsic meaningless anonymity, despite its lacking the cosy associations that all other words possess, a palimpsest, ready to be covered over with some version or other of our life-histories – whom we work for, whom we share our privacy with, who are our parents and children, what we believe in, what we read, and so forth. If I tell you some stories about where the following chapters came from, if I introduce them to you one by one, like guests at a party we shall be joining for a while together, my duties and pleasures as host will be discharged – to each of our satisfactions, if all goes well.

But before I do so, I should tell you in whose house we will be spending our time. Whoever the master is whose plans one is following, the rooms of the mansion always end up being do-it-yourself. From where did the bits and pieces of my bricolage come? An extended love-affair with physical chemistry; the discovery of science's history, and the beginnings of an awareness of the complexity of the history of our civilisation's thought in general; a bracing and bewildered encounter with the sceptical and constructive strands of philosophy, with Hume and Kant; a turn away to the social and political foundations of scientific thought, and the intuition that psychoanalysis must be the point where the biological metaphors of late-nineteenth-century thought met the genuinely modern demand for a science of man; the discovery that the Freud I had read, the master of the symbol, was nowhere to be found in the voluminous literature devoted to him, even in the books on him that I valued most, such as Wollheim and Rieff; a reluctant,

1

growing intimacy with the works of Jacques Lacan, who at least shared that fundamental perception with me, if in a style and intellectual world that I found alien and discomforting; the intermittent and crucial encounters with Foucault's œuvre, which, over the years, tracked across my own path, always ahead of me, always moving in surprising directions. These are the cornerstones of the house that you and the other guests, the chapters that follow, will be staying in together. But you may well ask: why *continue* to be interested in psychoanalysis beyond the recognition of its nodal point in the history of man's thought about himself, beyond the recognition of its centrality to any account of turn-of-the-century thought and the advent of modernism?[2]

Psychoanalysis challenges the various philosophies of the human subject on a number of different levels – at the level of theory, through its theories of action, its models of the mind and its insistence on the textuality of experience; and, in its practice, whilst mediating between the man of care and the subject of knowledge,[3] it challenges both – the philanthropic motives of the former and the absolute mastery of the latter. Certainly, to lie on the couch, seeking wisdom by talking nonsense, is a challenge, perhaps even an insult, to the well-defined routines of 'analytic' philosophy.

Yet Ellenberger's suggestion that Freud revived a more ancient mode of philosophical practice – together with the arcane religious institutions that went with it in Greece[4] – does not encompass the cultural importance of psychoanalysis. In France, in the last thirty-odd years, analysis came to dominate the easy gossip of weekend conferences, intellectual salons, psychiatric hospitals and cafés. As a cultural phenomenon, its presence cannot be overlooked; on the shorter view, its rise to fashionable prominence in intellectual circles is often linked to the decline of the varieties of Marxism and the events of May 1968.[5] On a longer view, however, the years of intellectual brilliance and expansionist enthusiasm predated such wider political events: the heyday of innovation was more truly the 1950s than any later date.[6] From this brilliant innovative phase stems the Freudianisation of France and the insinuation of analytically inclined professionals and intellectuals into many unlikely corners, of which the psychiatric profession was only one.

Whatever one might surmise as to France's repeating, in her own inimitable way, the victory that Freud's followers had earlier had in the United States, in Britain, in contrast, analysis was a well-established if slightly eccentric national institution by the end of the Second World War, and it has managed to retain its cultural marginality. The new interest in analysis of more recent years, felt in intellectual circles beyond the descendants of Bloomsbury, stemmed from curious temporary alliances amongst the intellectual sects of the time: political theory of a post-Marxist, Althusserian persuasion and 'French theory'; cinema and the theory of mass media; feminism and the question of gender in sociology, anthropology and psychology. Anyone working in a culture encounters these movements and is transformed by them, even if he or she swims against the current. In my case, I found myself working in an idiosyncratic direction in relation to these movements: from science to its history, from a sociology of science to the history of psychoanalysis, and from there to 'French theory'. These facts of individual biography leave their traces in many of my opinions and preoccupations. The Derrida with whom I conduct a dialogue is the psychoanalytic critic, the reader of Freud's texts without equal anywhere today, whether in circles analytic or non-analytic.[7] The Lacan I read is as much an analyst who demonstrates how to interpret, to intervene, to *act*, in the analytic sense, by reading Freud, as he is the founder of a new theory of culture, a new world view encompassing the relations between individual destiny and social law.

No matter how rich the writings of Freud, of Lacan, of Derrida may be, the justification for interest in analysis is to be found on the level on which Foucault finally placed it: as a new form of discourse. Although I sincerely believe, and act on the belief, that Freud's writings are an extraordinary resource, they are so and will continue to be so only as long as the practice of analysis preserves and develops the form of discourse that Freud invented. And this form of discourse has become even more vital and fundamental insofar as other disciplines, from the theory of cinema to the philosophy and sociology of science, have looked to a general theory of discourse. The specific theory of the psychoanalytic discourse pre-exists all the other post-modern general theories of discourse; it challenges them to justify the very project of their generality, it offers them an example, maybe even a template, and it incites the question that is antecedent to any possible treatment of discourse. Freud did *invent* a new form of discourse whose extraordinary laws and possibilities are still being investigated; he did invent a form of discourse whose capacity for fascination, whose ability to hypnotise (rather than analyse) and whose power are each inseparable from the truth it creates. These essays are dedicated to an investigation of some of the resources of that practice; the gamble is that these resources are not yet exhausted.

II

Telling the story of the origins of psychoanalysis, as some of these chapters do, necessarily involves questioning the truth of history and the very concept of truth itself. The first chapter, 'The true story of Anna O.', is an ironic reflection on the requirement on the historian to find an objective truth. Psychoanalysis, in its guise as an archaeology of the living past – the past as it lives in the patient, in monuments, in archival documents, in semantic evolution, in traditions, in traces, as a famous passage from Lacan puts it[8] – poses serious questions to any historical practice that goes beyond Augustine's 'present time of past things'.[9] Yet within this critique, psychoanalysis has discovered a distinctive articulation of past, present and future – the structure of deferred action, of causality after the event (*après coup*, *Nachträglichkeit*). This deferred action has been exhaustively referred to in much French analytic literature (though whether it has been sufficiently developed is another question). This does not prevent it from being important; nor does it conceal its very deep affinities with the Derridean concept of *différance*, of difference and deferral, and with Derrida's meditations upon the origin and end of all things. Telling the true story of Anna O., the 'first' patient of psychoanalysis, who was treated some dozen years before psychoanalysis came into existence, we rediscover the very structure of psychoanalytic explanation itself: an event that is understood only after some other event or events acquired a causative function.

Psychoanalysis thus permeates its own history – not just in the sense that its practitioners are repeatedly retelling the story in the way that it needs to be told if it is to function as the founding myth, but in the sense that to make sense of the historical event 'itself', even to perceive that the historical event in question exists, one must give the account psychoanalytically. The same problem of the relation of past and present to future emerges in chapter 5, '. . . a perfect likeness of the past'. I had for long been intrigued by the final paragraphs of *The interpretation of dreams*, in which Freud's dialectical twists and turns are, if anything, more agile and surprising than at any other point in the book. Amongst the many topics he addresses in these final pages, there is the final, eminently appropriate question: the relation of dreams, of Freud's dreams, to the future, to his future – *sous entendu*, the future of psychoanalysis. However abstemious Freud aimed to be in his claims as to the ability of psychoanalysis to read the future, let alone write it, and however sceptical, in an Enlightenment tradition, he might have been, he was well aware that psychoanalysis owed its vitality to its epistemic neighbours – the occult, the prophetic, the promisers of all kinds. As he said to his daughter Anna, when she asked how he could promise a patient 'relief from his symptoms, an increase in working capacity, and an improvement of his personal and social relationships', when there was reason to doubt that these promises could be kept: 'There one can see that you are not a doctor.'[10]

One of the paradoxes of the public posture of psychoanalysis, both in theory and in practice, is that it entices and withholds, seduces and says no. Freud's own writing style embodies this posture. Lacan's achieves it through antiphrasis. Psychoanalysis can only welcome any raising of the stakes in its practice: it must welcome all the storms and stresses of violent antagonism, of infatuation, of tears, laughter and forgetting. It welcomes these because it lives off the *analysis* of the immediate 'reality' of these states. An analysis that has no moments of crisis, in which reality does not impinge, or in which the analysis never threatens to invade everyday life, is hardly worth the name – not to mention its being an unlikely event. Yet all these states must be dissolved into the fictionality proper to analysis – a fictionality that is explored in a number of these essays. In chapter 2, 'Contracting the disease of love: authority and freedom in the origins of psychoanalysis', I propose a reading of the history of psychoanalysis that shows both how the means for instigating these states was discovered and how the means for containing them was put in place: the psychoanalytic contract. It is the unique way in which the analyst responds to the flow of speech, his or her unique way in responding to these speech acts, that allows the issues of love and authority to be broached so freely and so necessarily by the patient.

The subject . . . begins analysis by talking about himself without talking to you, or by talking to you without talking about himself. When he can talk to you about himself, the analysis will be over.[11]

The aim of analysis is a mutation in the speaking relations between subject and analyst, a speaking relationship that is taken to be exemplary (though not directly so) of the subject's relations to others in general. Lacanian and object-relations theorists can agree on at least this – what else does the 'relation' in 'object relations' mean? The means by which this modulation is achieved is the kernel of psychoanalytic practice. What it involves is the analyst's taking up the 'analytic position', most descriptions of which, starting with Freud's free-floating attention, are so impoverished. Many of these essays are diverse attempts to find a description which does justice to the discursive complexity of this position. For instance, the analytic position is described historically in chapter 2 by contrasting medical and hypnotic practices with Freud's analytic practice. We see that, from the beginning, his analytic practice involved transference interpretations – simply in the easy gymnastics Freud displayed whenever mention of himself cropped up in the discourse of the patient, whether through allusion, through naming or word-play (Freud the murderer, *Freude* (joy) the libertine) or through being directly addressed as 'you'. But it is also part of the historical thesis advanced in this chapter that the transference, as the dimension proper and unique to analysis, was recognised, discovered, or, I would prefer to say, carved out as a recognisable discursive silhouette, at the outset of Freud's 'analytic' practice.

It was not entirely an accident that it was the early Seminars of Lacan's that I translated. Not only are they relatively straightforward stylistically, but they also reveal how Lacan's theories of the relations of language and psychoanalysis were, at that time, in the mid 1950s, only minimally imbued with the jargon of signifier and signified. The inclination towards formalism, the love of structure and of system that drew many of the structuralists, is not very pronounced in these seminars. Indeed, it was my close reading of them in 1977, together with twin encounters with Derrida and Austin, that helped me understand the deficiences of my own account in *Language and the origins of psychoanalysis*. Chapter 7, 'What the psychoanalyst does with words: Austin, Lacan and the speech acts of psychoanalysis', redresses this imbalance. It is a Romantic argument – it looks to the sources of energy and force in linguistic utterance, rather than to the formal patterns of signification. Yet its aim is also an historical one: to show how Freud's conversational practice was both a means of structuring the analytic process and a subtle and enormously responsive instrument for the unravelling of the speech acts of the patient's so-called 'associations'. Freud's practice indicates that he had realised that *whatever* he said to the patient, be it about the weather or about all the other 'whethers', was equivalent to an interpretation. Not only that: Freud realised that his interpretations were acts and that his actions embodied interpretations. Yet, *even knowing this*, he still continued to serve his patients food when hungry, to pound the arm of his chair and berate them for thinking him too old to be worthy of love. Acts, these, no question; no danger of Freud's sidling sheepishly behind the wall of silence for fear of disturbing the analytic process.

Paying off the debt this way involves the curious ploy of showing that Jacques Lacan's theory of speech in psychoanalysis has marked affinities with the whimsical Englishness of the writing of J.L. Austin. It would be hard to imagine a more English philosopher than Austin; one might suggest Lewis Carroll. It has always intrigued me how the hostility to Lacan in the English-speaking world has taken him to be the most archetypally French of the group of theorists who have, since the 1950s, transformed, indeed re-created, the intellectual world; yet the eminently English Austin and the unspeakably French Lacan shared a conviction of the overwhelming force of speech (as opposed to 'writing', to 'constatation'); they shared a conviction that language conceived of as a mark, an inscription – that is, as if it were a record, the quintessence of the function of memory – omitted the force, the life of speech. Psychoanalysis is a pure culture of this life instinct.

When speech comes alive in analysis, when it is full speech, we are in the dimension of transference. Psychoanalysis began with transference, I have argued; with it came two other themes: seduction and responsibility. The theme of seduction is so often on the lips of those who discuss the history of psychoanalysis that it is surprising, significantly surprising, that few writers have addressed the 'logic of seduction'. That such a logic exists is testified to by the profusion of 'how to' manuals in the erotic sphere, without mentioning the classics in the genre: Casanova's *Mémoires*, Laclos's *Les Liaisons dangereuses*, Kierkegaard's *Diary of a seducer*, Mozart's *Don Giovanni*. What was the logic of seduction inherent in Freud's seduction theory? It was out of this simple question concerning the early history of psychoanalysis that two companion chapters grew: 'Contracting the disease of love' (chapter 2) and 'Rape, seduction, psychoanalysis' (chapter 4). One of these addresses the question as it arises in medicine, in the sexually tinged relation between patient and doctor, with the background theme of suggestion and the seemingly *ethical* question of the limits of the intervention of the doctor (should he seduce, if this leads to a cure?). The other addresses the no-man's-land between seduction and rape, as mapped out by primarily *legal* notions of responsibility. That these chapters can address the same question simply reflects the adjacency of medical ethics and legal responsibility and guilt to the position that Freud was carving out for his conception of the ethos of the analyst.

Yet to call it an ethos conceals the sense in which it is the construction of this ethos that propels psychoanalysis into being. The analyst behaves as an epistemological radical, by ignoring the difference between truth and lies, between truth and fiction (see my article 'Lying on the couch' and my book of the same title). The analyst also behaves as a legal subversive in bypassing the distinction between rape and seduction. The analyst refuses the common-sense ethics of the medical profession, by allowing the patient to go through the motions of seduction and betrayal and by performing the rhetorical gymnastics which Freud describes himself as having gone through, almost in slow motion, in the 'Dora' case-history – all so as to *intensify* the emotional hothouse of the consulting room, so as to *induce* a new symptom more unwieldy than any other that went before. With heavy irony, Freud called this symptom the transference-neurosis, with all that that implies as to the patient's long-term attachment to the analyst and the institutions of analysis, with all that that implies as to the *institutionalisation* of analysis (its propagation, like a plague).

However, this does not mean that Freud 'knew what he was doing' when he invented psychoanalysis. To assume that he did would be a quite unpsychoanalytic claim to make. Moreover, his blindnesses, even his ability to sleepwalk,[12] are, as he himself taught, the most educative and meaningful of acts. The case of Dora has been the centre of extraordinary interest for what we can learn from these blindnesses. Indeed, each of Freud's case-histories, incomplete, marred as they all deliberately and self-confessedly are, have been examined in this way. Chapter 3, 'The untold pleasures of psychoanalysis: Freud, Dora and the Madonna', sketches out what I have learnt from this elegant failure, this epoch-making narrative, whose flaws are like *The golden bowl*, splitting 'on lines and by laws of its own',[13] indiscernible lines along which the fracture may well soon appear. Indeed, beyond the question of femininity that has preoccupied so many commentators, including myself, this essay attempts to show how Freud's own conscious conception of the analytic situation could not contain what his actions were none-theless provoking: the eroticisation of the analytic situation itself. In Dora's case, this expressed itself in the fear that Freud's own science might become just feminine gossip: hence Freud's difficulty in perceiving the scene of two women talking together as the primal scene of Dora's analysis.

That this 'feminine' gossip may well be the cultural unconscious of psychoanalysis is explored in two further chapters: 'Who is in analysis with whom? Freud, Lacan, Derrida' (chapter 9) and 'Psychoanalysis: gossip, telepathy and/or science?' (chapter 10). What in any other field of historical research would pass as gossip has, in the particular branch of the family of Freud researches[14] concerned with the early development of his theories, become of seemingly momentous significance for the judgement and interpretation of both psychoanalysis and its founder. How is it that here, in writing the history of psychoanalysis, in thinking about how psychoanalytic institutions function, in addressing the politics – in the broadest sense – of psychoanalysis, such importance could accrue to the issues of who was sleeping with whom and who was in analysis with whom?

Every so often, books are published in which Freud's character is taken to be the prime mover of all things analytic. Turn-of-the-century psychiatrists raged against the rising tide of filth embodied in psychoanalysis and against the filth of its founder's scientific imagination. The 'philosopher' Frank Cioffi argued that Freud's work could be refuted on the grounds that he was a 'liar'. Some recent versions of this moral crusade taking Freud as its focus have adopted the seemingly more-psychoanalytic-than-thou posture of searching for sexual skeletons in Freud's closet as a means of neutralising, and thereby dismissing, his theories – an approach that amounts to a reading by *contresens* of lines from Heine that Freud quoted as an association to one of his dreams:

> Selten habt ihr mich *verstanden*,
> Selten auch verstand ich Euch,
> Nur wenn wir im *Kot* uns fanden,
> So verstanden wir uns gleich.[15]

Hence the mild furore that Swales' claim that Freud had a sexual relationship with Minna Bernays, his sister-in-law, has created.[16] Hence the controversy over Masson's claim that Freud gave up his seduction theory out of a mixture of intellectual cowardice and desire to be accepted by his scientific peers. In other historical fields, such claims are neither exceptional nor significant. The fact that the physicist Millikan systematically steered (using, amongst other techniques, censorship) his experimental results towards success in measuring the charge of the electron, an achievement for which he received the Nobel Prize, raises eyebrows only amongst those determined to idealise at least someone; whether or not he slept with his sister-in-law would not, as it does in Freud's case, make the front page of the *New York Times*.

Reflecting on this state of affairs, I became convinced that the interest in Freud's sexual life runs deeper than the feet-of-clay hypothesis, deeper than the wish for Freud to be as hypocritical[17] as the rest of us, deeper than the desire to show that Freud's sexual theories were closely allied to personal obsessions of his; it is constitutive of how we are to read Freud.

Why is this so? The answer has more to do with the details of the practice of psychoanalysis than with anything distinctively theoretical. We all know that psychoanalysis opens up all secrets. We all know that psychoanalysis shrugs off all reticences concerning our opinions of other people. We all suspect that the practice of analysis allows the airing of truths, facts, rumours, fantasies that live only a phantom-like existence elsewhere. From the outset, then, the practice of psychoanalysis involves speaking what sounds often remarkably like gossip, rumour and – that extraordinary word so close to the analytic process itself – *hearsay*.

Take a look at the dreams analysed in *The interpretation of dreams*. Stories of Dr M. (Breuer), of Fl. (Fliess), fathers, mothers, children. What Fliess, as the book's first reader *and* censor – and it is significant that these two functions could not be distinguished for Freud – expunged was a dream about Freud's fiancée's not having brought a dowry to her marriage. One can almost hear the hushed, excited tones – 'After all, he did accept her without a dowry, what can you expect?' What better topic for gossip could there be?

Take a look at the 'histories' of psychoanalysis; take, as I do in chapter 9, the biography of Ernest Jones, with its stories of the swapping of analysands between analysts, with the attendant tensions that make it seem more like wife-swapping, or its stories of husbands and wives putting their marriage, on the rocks, on the couch, with the not unexpected resolution: the analyst ends up attending the wedding of the woman, on behalf of her ex-husband, a wedding at which the groom just happens to have the same name as the man she has just left. Why be surprised, any more than one is surprised that these stories do not figure in Jones' *auto*biography? People's lives just *do* end up like that, end up sounding as if they were stories written by a witty analyst in the 'idle' moments between patients.[18]

These questions are addressed in a number of the chapters that follow. Chapter 9 is concerned with the institutional questions raised; chapter 10 addresses the more formal questions of the relation between the very structure of the psychoanalytic situation and gossip; chapter 3 shows how the theme of gossip lay at the heart of the problems Freud had with his 'handling' of Dora. But the most telling way to address these questions is by telling *stories*: stories about analysis, stories from analyses, stories told by analysts. All of which raises the general question about the most common form of story told *about* analysis (outside of Woody Allen movies and cognate genres): the case-history.

What is the story of the unconscious? One thing Freud insisted upon was that the unconscious did not obey the rules of narrative: it knows no time, no before and after, no beginning and end – no way of representing death. Yet the case-history quite often takes the form of a melding of two different yet equally traditional narratives: the narrative of a life and the narrative of an analysis. Freud's attempt at the representation of the time of the unconscious turns to the topographical and archaeological, in a famous passage from *Civilization and its discontents* in which he compares the preservative power of the mind to the fiction of a Rome where all the buildings that had ever been built there are still standing.

Let us, by a flight of imagination, suppose that Rome is not a human habitation but a psychical entity with a similarly long and copious past – an entity, that is to say, in which nothing that has once come into existence will have passed away and all the earlier phases of development continue to exist alongside the latest ones . . .

There is clearly no point in spinning our phantasy any further, for it leads to things that are unimaginable and even absurd. If we want to represent historical sequence in spatial terms we can only do it by juxtaposition in space: the same space cannot have two different contents. Our attempt seems to be an idle game. It has only one justification. It shows us how far we are from mastering the characteristics of mental life by representing them in pictorial terms.[19]

But how, we may ask, did the argument move from being about *preservation* to being about *pictorial representation*?[20] The missing leg of the syllogism pertains to endings. It is only because a given space demands the end of one object's occupation of it before a second one may move in in its place ('the same space cannot have two different contents') that we find the representation of preservation difficult. But what of the space itself? Is that not preserved in the course of the sequential substitution? Why is there no problem about the representation of this container, this space which contains the objects? Why do we have no difficulty believing that Rome exists – Rome, forever, eternally, the eternal city? Could we permanently doubt it, in the same way that Freud doubted the existence of Athens as he stood on the Acropolis?[21]

The problem is not so much spatial as temporal. Freud's analogy leads us too quickly away from the temporal aporia of his theory; it leads us away from preservation, from repetition, from 'the first time', from the relation of the repeated 'now' to the lost 'then'. The problem of preservation is much more akin to the problem of interminability than it is to the problem of the predication of identicals.

These are the aporia that Lacan probed in the most notorious area of his work: the temporality of analysis. I examine these in chapter 8, 'Dead on time: on Lacan's theory of temporality'. Here, on this topic, there is truly an intersection of gossip and logic, of theory and its limits. Lacan was evicted from the International Psycho-analytic Association over the question of his short sessions. Yet he asked questions which many analysts think are valid: Why should the analyst sell time by the clock? Why should analysis be more an advertisement for the Taylorisation of modern bourgeois society than for the liberation of the timeless unconscious? Why does the remark that Freud's major achievement was to make the psychiatrists run on time make us laugh thoughtfully? The chapter also addresses the question, how successful was Lacan in demonstrating that logic, despite its aspirations to timelessness and eternity, crucially depends upon a temporal moment, the moment of judgement?

There are other ways of attempting to disrupt the inexorable unfolding of time than entering analysis. The fate of Dostoevsky's gambler hangs upon his finding the right moment to place his bets. 'Les jeux sont faits', 'Time, gentlemen, please', 'Closing time',

> Footfalls echo in the memory
> Down the passage which we did not take
> Towards the door we never opened
> Into the rose-garden.[22]

Gambling opens up the dialectic of the instant and eternity, as did the writing of Dostoevsky's own story to a deadline which represented the definitive loss of his own authorial voice. Chapter 11, 'Transference and the stenographer: on Dostoevsky's *The gambler*', explores the relation of gambling and time, of transference and authorship, and the limits and intercalations of the life and the work: at what point does the life of the author end and the authorship of the life begin? At what point does the illusion of mastery shift over from the author to the means of communication (stenographer, publisher) and thence to reader? When do the introductions stop and the laws of reciprocity require host and guests to exchange their identities?

I

THE TEMPTATION OF
SIGMUND FREUD

. . . when a woman sues for love, to reject and refuse it is a distressing part
for a man to play; and, in spite of neurosis and resistance, an incomparable
magic emanates from a woman of high principles who confesses her
passion. It is not a patient's crudely sensual desires which constitute the
temptation. These are more likely to repel, and it will call for all the
doctor's tolerance if he is to regard them as a natural phenomenon. It is
rather, perhaps, a woman's subtler and aim-inhibited wishes which bring
with them the danger of making a man forget his technique and his medical
task for the sake of a fine experience.

Sigmund Freud, 'Observations on transference-love'

1

THE TRUE STORY OF
ANNA O.

Above all, the patient will *begin* his treatment with a repetition . . .

Sigmund Freud[1]

In 1932, Sigmund Freud wrote to his friend Stefan Zweig concerning some misleading remarks that Zweig had made in his book *Mental healers* about the prehistory of psychoanalysis. Freud wanted to correct the impression that, in his treatment of Anna O., the first patient of psychoanalysis, Breuer had brought to light certain suppressed sexual feelings. That this was not in fact what had happened could have been deduced from Breuer's own published record of the case in *Studies on hysteria*. There he had written:

The element of sexuality was astonishingly undeveloped in her; the patient, whose life became known to me to an extent to which one person's life is seldom known to another, had never been in love, and in all the enormous number of hallucinations which occurred during her illness that element of mental life never emerged.[2]

But Freud not only corrected the erroneous account Zweig had given, he added his own version of the end of the treatment of Breuer's patient, a version which forms the basis for a history of psychoanalysis – in fact can be described as locating the true point of origin of psychoanalysis, the point from which its entire later development makes sense.

What really happened with Breuer's patient I was able to guess later on, long after the break in our relations, when I suddenly remembered something Breuer had once told me in another context before we had begun to collaborate and which he never repeated. On the evening of the day when all her symptoms had been disposed of, he was summoned to the patient again, found her confused and writhing in abdominal cramps. Asked what was wrong with her, she replied: 'Now Dr. B.'s child is coming!' . . . Seized by conventional horror he took flight and abandoned the patient to a colleague. For months afterwards she struggled to regain her health in a sanatorium.[3]

17

Freud recounted how this was Breuer's lost opportunity: 'At this moment he held in his hand the key that would have opened "the doors to the Mothers", but he let it drop.'[4]The key phrase, no doubt, is '*Dr. B.'s child*'. The transference was in his grasp, but he let it go.

If this is an account of the origin of psychoanalysis, then it is couched in the form of a negative: it recounts Breuer's *failure* to found psychoanalysis, here conceived of as centred on the sexual transference. Freud, looking back in retrospect, implies that Breuer could have made the discoveries he himself later made, if only he had been able to recognise this *sexual transference*: that is, a moment in the treatment of a patient when sexuality erupted into the open in the form of a direct implication of the doctor.

For it should be remembered, despite what Freud implied in other parts of his letter to Zweig,[5] that Breuer fully recognised the importance of sexuality in the etiology of the neuroses: '*the great majority of severe neuroses in women have their origin in the marriage bed*'.[6] And Breuer was aware enough of the context of social relations in which such an 'assertion' could be made and recognised to add the following note:

It is a most unfortunate thing that clinical medicine ignores one of the most pathogenic factors or at least only hints at it delicately. This is certainly a subject in which the acquired knowledge of experienced physicians should be communicated to their juniors, who as a rule blindly overlook sexuality – at all events so far as their patients are concerned.[7]

We should note the manner in which Breuer's criticisms of his colleagues for only hinting at the importance of sexuality is repeated in his own allusion to the reason for young doctors' systematic blindness to the importance of sexuality: namely, their preoccupation with their *own* sexual desire as opposed to the sexual reality of their patients. Breuer was thus invoking in an uncannily accurate fashion precisely the perception of his 'juniors' that Freud was later to judge was true of his 'senior', Josef Breuer.[8]

Breuer was certainly aware of the ubiquity of the sexual problem. Yet we can still safely conclude, I think, that this did not guarantee that he was immune from strong personal reactions when he was implicated in this very etiology.

It is clear, then, that the overall significance of Freud's reconstruction of the denouement of the treatment of Anna O. was to show that Breuer had the key of the sexual transference in his hand and let it slip; we can add that, despite Freud's forgetting it, it was not so much the sexual aspect of this that was important but the combination of the two: sexuality which implicated the doctor.

Transference or countertransference

Another source of information concerning the end of Anna O.'s – or, more appropriately, Bertha Pappenheim's – treatment exists. It is the correspondence between Freud and his fiancée, Martha, in which conversations with Breuer and various bits of gossip are exchanged.

I know this from a colleague, the Assistant to the Chief Physician, who is well known there and who sometimes goes out there to substitute for Dr. Breslauer. He is completely enchanted by the girl, by her provocative appearance in spite of her grey hair, by her wit and her cleverness. I believe that if he as a psychiatrist did not know so well what a burden the inclination to a hysterical illness can be, he would have fallen in love with her. But, Martchen, discretion *on all sides*. And be discreet, too, about what I am about to tell you. Breuer too has a very high opinion of her, and gave up her care because it was threatening his happy marriage. His poor wife could not stand the fact that he was so exclusively devoting himself to a woman about whom he obviously spoke with great interest. She was certainly only jealous of the demands made on her husband by another woman. Her jealousy did not show itself in a hateful, tormenting fashion, but in a silently recognized one. She fell ill, lost her spirits, until he noticed it and discovered the reason why. This naturally was enough for him to completely withdraw his medical attention from B.P. Can you keep this to yourself, Martchen?[9]

Martha replied:

It has often been on the tip of my tongue to ask you why Breuer gave up Bertha. I could well imagine that those somewhat removed from it were wrong to say that he had withdrawn because he realised that he was unable to do anything for her. It is curious that no man other than her physician of the moment got close to poor Bertha, that is when she was healthy she already [had the power] to turn the head of the most sensible of men – what a misfortune for the girl. You will laugh at me, dearest, I so vividly put myself in the place of the silent Frau Mathilde that I could scarcely sleep last night.[10]

Two days later, Martha received Freud's complex response:

My beloved little angel, you were right to expect that I would laugh at you. I do so with great gusto. Are you really so vain as to believe that people are going to contest your right to your lover or later to your husband? Oh no, he remains entirely yours, and your only comfort will have to be that he

The temptation of Sigmund Freud

himself would not wish it any other way. To suffer Frau Mathilde's fate, one has to be the wife of a Breuer, isn't that so?[11]

Whereas Freud's recollected reconstruction in his letter to Zweig focused almost exclusively on the relationship between Breuer and his patient, here Sigmund and Martha are placing that treatment within a complex web of medical and familial relations. Freud is describing the position of the two men, Breuer and the assistant, who become fascinated by Bertha ('Breuer too has a very high opinion of her'). To be sure, the two men hold back from Bertha, although for different reasons: the Assistant because he cannot forget what he as a psychiatrist knows about such a woman patient, Breuer because he had it brought to his attention by his wife how exclusive his interest in his patient had become. Freud's account wavers between on the one hand attributing to Breuer the same amorous interest that the Assistant was fully aware of, but which the latter moderates given his better knowledge, and on the other denying that Breuer felt anything other than medical concern for his patient, whose demands, unhappily for her, were perceived by Mathilde Breuer as excessive and beyond the call of medical duty. To Freud, one of the doctors was clearly *amorously* inclined, with *medical* knowledge acting as the limit on his action; the other, Breuer, was *medically* concerned to the point of exclusive devotion, and the limit on his devotion was placed by an outside force, his wife's perception of a threat to her position in his affections, this *external* force thus determining the point at which his medical devotion passed over into something else. The two men shared a common response, but their different motivation and reasons for caution obscured this common element.

So it fell to Martha, momentarily identifying with Bertha's position, to separate out what would later be called the dimension of transference-countertransference. Her comment, while grammatically awkward, succinctly managed to leave in suspense whether it was transference or countertransference at issue: 'It is curious [*merkwürdig*] that no man other than her physician of the moment got close to poor Bertha, that is when she was healthy she already [had the power] to turn the head of the most sensible [*vernünftigsten*] of men – what a misfortune for the girl.'[12]

Freud's reply, however, does not address this acute observation. Instead, he picks up on the second identification manifest in Martha's letter, that with Mathilde Breuer, the abandoned doctor's wife rather than the unfortunate patient, thus focusing on the

20

doctor's relation with his spouse rather than on the doctor–patient relationship in which her friend Bertha had become embroiled. What Martha had seen, which Freud could not yet see, was the 'impersonal nature of the process', as Freud was to describe the transference, indeed this specific occasion of the transference, in his obituary of Breuer in 1925.[13] Martha could perceive it – 'It is curious . . . ' – by picking up the cues in Freud's letter describing the similar responses of both doctors to the patient; she could recognise the key element of repetition in their response, the repetition that turns it into something 'impersonal'. And in this sense her interpretation of Freud's letter was a psychoanalytic one *avant la lettre*: making explicit what he had said without knowing it. What is more, her interpretation is entirely in accord with the way in which the Aristotelian tradition has always cast this element of repetition: as the essential ingredient of tragedy, the *automaton* of fate: 'what a misfortune . . . ' Only much later was Freud to make this tragic aspect central to his conception of transference.

For the moment, though, Freud would not perceive the impersonal or 'universal'[14] nature of the Breuer–Bertha affair. He was too concerned to combat the possibility that the same thing as had happened to Mathilde Breuer might happen to Martha. Such was Freud's sophistication, though, that even in this defensive move he touched on a key aspect of this question: he discerned vanity masquerading as jealousy, implicitly invoking a notion of the projected desire of the vain woman onto her rivals as a source of the fear of loss aimed at by jealousy. The next sentence, however, switches tack, shifting from the vanity of women to the weight attaching to the masculine lover's character: 'To suffer Frau Mathilde's fate, one has to be the wife of a Breuer . . . ' Freud is implying that there was something overly complex or insufficient in Breuer's love for his wife – something, for instance, like a dissatisfaction in love, from which Freud will not suffer if Martha loves him in a spirit of humility rather than vanity.

Masson[15] concludes from this sequence of letters that Freud did not yet know of (or was not willing to mention to Martha) the phantom pregnancy, the 'event' which he was later to think prompted Breuer to terminate his treatment of her in June 1882. However, it seems more likely that this is exactly what Breuer had informed Freud of in July 1883, on the evening of the hottest day of the year, in a letter we will come to shortly; it seems likely that this is the item referred to in that letter which Breuer asked his young colleague not to speak of with Martha until after their marriage. As

Freud himself implied in his letter to Zweig of 1932, it was not so much knowing about this incident – not so much the fact of having been told of it – as knowing how to make something of it which was to be Freud's later achievement. Where Martha saw the tragedy of fate, Freud was later to see the dynamic source of therapeutic change, to see the possibility of changing one's fate rather than submitting to it.

But are we to conclude that the true discoverer of the transference was Martha Bernays? That would be foolish – precursoritis of the most flagrantly terminal kind. She may well have recognised something that Freud was both personally disinclined to ponder and professionally incapable of recognising at the same time. That is, it might well have been structurally impossible for him to make that recognition within the terms of his conception of medical practice ('To suffer Frau Mathilde's fate, one has to be the wife of a Breuer, isn't that so?'). Indeed, this argument can be taken one step further: Breuer was incapable of recognising it as well, but he was at least in a better position than either Freud or Martha, since he actually had a *practice* in which such a perception might have been put to good use. Freud's distinction was to put such a perception to good use within such a practice, later, when he became a doctor – that is, he made the perception of the transference a *theoretical element* within a *theoretical argument* that neither Martha's psychological acuity nor Breuer's, Chrobak's and Charcot's professional worldly wise acumen could achieve.[16]

However, we can offer yet another interpretation of this incident. What Freud told Martha of in his letter was perhaps not so much the germ of the transference as the distorted account of the countertransference. After all, it was the *doctors* whose interest was aroused by Bertha; it was the *doctors* and the disturbance it caused in them that formed the true subject matter of Freud and Martha's exchange of letters. Bertha figured as the poor soul who still had the power to attract her doctors' attention, the poor soul who 'had the power to turn the head of the most sensible of men'.[17] What caused consternation and required discretion was the *doctors'* reaction to their fascination for her. It seems more plausible to say that Freud and Martha were discovering the countertransference than the transference.

And that is where the story of the hysterical childbirth fundamentally alters one's understanding of what was going on. Freud's story, recounted for the first time in 1932, concentrated on this transferential 'acting out' as being the 'key to the mothers'. Yet what concerned him and Martha in 1883 was more like a key to the *fathers*, the key that Breuer was to highlight in the *Studies on hysteria* as so crucial to understanding the ignorance about feminine sexuality among doctors: the young doctors overlook the factor of sexuality precisely because they are blinded by the presence of their *own* sexuality. Does this account not fit what Freud and Martha conjectured had happened to Breuer? Breuer remarked on the absence of sexuality in the case of Anna O., only to fall victim to a sexual crisis in which he was suddenly implicated, whether we take that crisis to have primarily been his wife's chronic jealousy or the sudden advent of Bertha's scene of childbirth. Breuer was no spring chicken in 1882 when the scene with Bertha occurred (he was forty years old) but did he quite qualify as one of the experienced physicians who knew of the importance of sexuality as a pathogenic factor in the neuroses? Or was he more akin to one of the juniors, who were blind to it because of their own preoccupations?

So we are inevitably led to ask: Which came first, the transference or the countertransference? And it seems we can answer this question only with another: Does it make sense to try to separate them? Is it plausible to give an answer to this question? Might it not be, for psychoanalysis, the chicken-and-egg question *par excellence*?

But even to set sail in the uncharted waters of the transference and countertransference, Freud had to adopt a particular strategy of defence – a fruitful defence, given the future survival value of psychoanalytic technique – that enabled him to hear his patients say things like 'Dr. B.'s child is coming!' and immediately respond by affirming, 'This is not my baby, it is someone else's. Whose?'

The disclaiming of responsibility for the baby is the key to many of the levels we are dealing with here. Dr B.'s baby is quite obviously, on one level, psychoanalysis herself. Breuer fled from the scene, as if he were guilty. Freud stayed and disclaimed responsibility. It seems so utterly implausible for Freud to disclaim responsibility for psychoanalysis – and yet that is precisely what he often would do in later years. For instance, when presented in 1909, in Worcester, Massachusetts, with what he later called 'the first opportunity of speaking in public about psychoanalysis',[18] he declared:

If it is a merit to have brought psychoanalysis into being, that merit is not mine. I had no share in its earliest beginnings. I was a student and working for my final examinations at the time when another Viennese physician,

The temptation of Sigmund Freud

Dr. Josef Breuer, first (in 1880–2) made use of this procedure on a girl who was suffering from hysteria.[19]

Freud is quite unequivocal: Breuer is responsible for psychoanalysis. And it is to the examination of the theme of responsibility that we now turn.

Responsibility and irresponsibility

The interpretation of dreams is the royal road to the unconscious. Freud's first step down this royal road was taken on 24 July 1895, when he analysed the dream he had dreamed the night before: the dream of Irma's injection.[20] In this dream, Freud treated a patient who was in reality causing him some trouble, not least as a result of the disapproval for his method of treatment he sensed his colleagues felt. In alarm and anxiety in the dream, he called in a senior colleague, who is undoubtedly Breuer, and then two younger medical colleagues; each of these men, but particularly the Breuer figure, make medical fools of themselves, and, as if in response, Freud sees a chemical formula, trimethylamine, which is a direct reference to his close friend and colleague, Fliess, who offers him supportive suggestions and collaborative discussion.

The analysis of the dream led Freud to discern in the dream a complex attempt to demonstrate that he is not responsible for the failure of his treatment of Irma; if she still has pains, whatever these pains are caused by, it is clearly not Freud the dreamer's fault.

Freud dreamed the dream of Irma's injection shortly after the publication of *Studies on hysteria*, the project whose accomplishment marked the termination of his intimacy with Breuer, its co-author. That book contained Breuer's account of his treatment of Anna O. and his chapter on the theory of hysteria, together with four case histories of women hysterics by Freud and a final chapter by Freud devoted to the therapy of hysteria; the authors' 'Preliminary communication' of 1893, which Freud had, after much urging, gotten Breuer to collaborate on in 1892 following their joint treatment of Frau Cäcilie M., preceded the case histories. All of these patients were women; two of them had been treated as a result of prolonged and detailed collaboration between Freud and Breuer (Frau Emmy von N. and Frau Cäcilie M.).

The Irma dream repeated this scene: Freud's treatment of a female hysteric, his calling in Breuer for an opinion on the case. Already here, as we broach the topic of the dream, we sense how the complicated relations of Freud's life and work are being interpreted, represented and selected from by the dream.[21] The Irma dream proposes one clear solution to questions of medical responsibility: it is a disclaimer of Freud's responsibility for anything that goes wrong in the treatment of his patient, while it is also a statement of Breuer's incompetence, his ignorance of what is really going on.

The scene of the dream is thus a recapitulation of the scene of the origin of psychoanalysis itself in so far as it stages the examination of a female patient by Freud and Breuer. Yet, in the dream and its associations, there is none of the sense of close, conflict-free, harmonious collaboration that can be perceived through reading between the lines of the *Studies*:

Dr. Breuer and I knew [Frau Emmy von N.] pretty well and for a long time, and we used to smile when we compared her character with the picture of the hysterical psyche which can be traced from early times . . . The woman we came to know was an admirable one.[22]

This atmosphere of warm intimacy had been established over long years of friendship, from the early 1880s on. In a letter to his fiancée written in 1883, Freud described an evening with Breuer as follows:

Then we had supper upstairs in our shirtsleeves (at the moment I am writing in a somewhat more advanced *negligé*), and then came a lengthy medical conversation on moral insanity and nervous diseases and strange case-histories – your friend Bertha Pappenheim also cropped up – and then we became rather personal and very intimate and he told me a number of things about his wife and children and asked me to repeat what he had said only 'after you have married your Martha'. And then I opened up and said: This same Martha, who at the moment has a sore throat in Düsternbrook, is in reality a sweet Cordelia, and we are already on terms of the closest intimacy and can say anything to each other. Whereupon he said he too always calls his wife by that name because she is incapable of displaying affection to others, even including her own father. And the ears of both Cordelias, the one of 37 and the other of 22, must have been ringing while we were thinking of them with serious tenderness.[23]

As we know from the *Studies*, this atmosphere of balmy intimacy was the condition for Breuer's being persuaded to publish his case-history of Anna O. Certainly that case could never be regarded as a complete success, as we have seen: Bertha was confined to a sanatorium after the abrupt ending of her treatment, and her condition continued to deteriorate. Freud wrote to Martha some months later:

Bertha is once again in the sanatorium in Gross-Enzersdorf, I believe. Breuer is constantly talking about her, says he wishes she were dead so that the poor woman could be free of her suffering. He says she will never be well again, that she is completely shattered.[24]

All of this material reinforces the impression gained from Ellenberger's important paper[25] that Breuer's treatment of Anna O. was in large part a medical disaster, however many symptoms were disposed of through the talking cure. As can be seen from this letter, Breuer was considerably agitated over the fate of his patient – was indeed preoccupied, we may infer, with the questions of medical responsibility that pervaded Freud's work with neurotics in the 1890s.[26] However, we have already seen that in his correspondence with Martha, Freud was more intent on absolving Breuer from medically irresponsible action in Bertha's case than he was in learning the lesson that Martha could have taught him about the repetition of Bertha's amorous relation with her two doctors. 'She was certainly only jealous of the demands made on her husband by another woman.' The readiness with which Freud assured Martha of the restricted focus of Mathilde's jealousy indicates the importance of his *excluding* the possibility that any other dimension was present – for instance, the demands, implicit or otherwise, that her *husband* was making on the patient. Surely it would not have been difficult for Freud to contemplate such demands, given that he had just described a colleague and peer of his who was sorely tempted to make such demands. Freud's initial response, then, to the question of erotic tensions between doctor and patient is not reprobation, nor headshaking, but is rather one of focusing on the question of the *motives* for the doctor's actions.

In his view, Breuer's excessive interest in Bertha did not amount to an erotic demand. Martha, however, bypassed such a fine distinction, homing in instead on the interesting fact that Bertha's erotic life had twice become exclusively centred on her relationship with her doctor. Freud was more intent on absolving Breuer from medically irresponsible behaviour. And it is exactly this theme that preoccupied Freud on the night of 24/5 July 1895, in the dream of Irma's injection. The question he now posed himself was: Who is responsible for Irma's persistent pains? And the answers proved that, on three different counts, it was not her doctor who was responsible.

It is not only the dream of Irma's injection that focuses on the question of medical responsibility.[27] It would be possible to argue that this is *the* central concern of the majority of dreams of his own that Freud analysed in *The interpretation of dreams*. As we have known since Max Schur published the letters from Freud to Fliess dealing with the Emma episode of March 1895, the dream of Irma's injection dealt with Fliess' responsibility for that mishandled operation, as well as with Freud's preoccupation with his responsibility for Irma's and his other hysterics' treatment. We can extend the account, so that one of the underlying themes of the dreambook itself is revealed as: Who is responsible for psychoanalysis?[28]

There is a previously unnoticed connection between the scene of the treatment of Anna O. and the scene of the Irma dream – a connection which, if we were not dealing with the prehistory of psychoanalysis, would be regarded as a coincidence of no significance. As Freud tells us in his associations to the first element of the dream,

we were spending that summer at Bellevue, a house standing by itself on one of the hills adjoining the Kahlenberg. My dream was thus anticipating . . . it was my wife's birthday and a number of guests, including Irma, were being received by us in the large hall at Bellevue.[29]

As Ellenberger[30] has discovered, Bellevue was also the name of the hospital at which Anna O. was consigned by Breuer after his abrupt termination of her treatment.[31] This unforeseen connection backs up our hypothesis that Freud's Irma dream is repeating the founding treatment of Bertha Pappenheim. Freud is asking the question: was Breuer irresponsible in his treatment of Bertha, was Fliess irresponsible in his treatment of Emma, am I irresponsible in my treatment of Irma (Anna Hammerschlag) and all the other hysterics I am treating?[32] Yet, as I indicated above, it is only because Freud could convert this question of personal and medical ethics into one of theoretical significance that he was able to found psychoanalysis, through separating out the dimension of transference-countertransference. He avoided taking responsibility – this method of treatment is Breuer's, not mine, this patient's amorous advance is not directed to me but to someone else, these pains are not due to me but to someone else. Even, perhaps, his own child, Anna, who is in his wife's womb as he dreams the Irma dream, and is its symbolic core, its navel, belongs to someone else – to psycho*anna*lysis, maybe, the word he coined six weeks after Anna's birth, the child to which Anna Freud was to devote her life. It is also possible to venture one final piece of psychoanalytic detective work on Freud's children, so as to ascertain the interaction of theory and experience.

One of the stories Freud told in 'On the history of the psychoanalytic movement' pertained to a joint consultation with Chrobak. The patient's anxiety states could be assuaged only by information about her physician's exact whereabouts at all hours of the day. After the consultation, Chrobak mentioned to Freud that this patient was still a virgin, despite eighteen years of marriage, and that in cases like these the doctor cannot hope for a cure but must protect the husband's reputation with his own. When people talk about the doctor's inability to cure such a patient, all the doctor can do is keep silent. In such cases, Chrobak went on, the only cure was the repeated dosage of a *'penis normalis'*.

It is possible that this joint consultation was the one arranged just as Martha started labour with her first child, Mathilde (named after Mathilde Breuer).[33] And Freud was brought to remark in this context that

My consulting room is full of new faces . . . as if the birth of a daughter were equal to a certificate of qualification for the medical profession.

So we may well be entitled to treat Freud's memory of the consultation with Chrobak, as recounted in 1914, as a screen-memory of the birth of his first child (a daughter) and the advent of paternity. Jokingly, he himself equated the medical and paternal functions; we can interpret this as a flight from the responsibility of paternity into that of the doctor. We find here the same move as elsewhere: the personal function of paternity (if such exists) is replaced by the 'impersonal' function of the doctor. The *'penis normalis'* which one might well have attributed to Freud following the birth of his first child is now to be hidden behind the reputation of the doctor. 'It is not me who is the father of this child, but the doctor, maybe even my senior colleague, Chrobak.' This fantasy then reverberates in Freud's memory as the screen-memory of the consultation, whose moral is: 'It is not me who is the father of the idea that sexuality lies in the heart of the neuroses, but Chrobak, who would prescribe a *penis normalis* if he could.'

Such remarks could be made about the other stories that Freud tells of the origins of psychoanalysis – those of Breuer and Charcot, from the same pages as the Chrobak story, and also all those other precursors that Freud filled his own writings with. There is a strange dialectic at work here between Freud's continual unearthing of precursors for the discovery of psychoanalysis (his wish to disown responsibility for his child) and the quite transparent fact that only Freud was responsible for psychoanalysis, that, if anything, his followers are irremediably weighed down by the debt to Freud they incur in becoming analysts. This debt is the transference to Freud, the defining characteristic of the profession. In which case, Freud's memory of the case might well be intertwined with questions concerning his own paternal function.

The dream of Irma's injection is thus not only the moment when Freud opened up the royal road to the unconscious. It is the repetition of the founding scene of psychoanalysis, Breuer's treatment of Anna O., the analyst's confrontation with the female hysteric; and it is also an attempt to avoid repeating Breuer's flight in the face of the anxiety of responsibility, medical, marital and otherwise. But it avoids that repetition by placing the onus of responsibility for founding psychoanalysis elsewhere. In avoiding that responsibility, Freud could thus discover the sexual trans-ference: he could *rename* the moment when a patient (or his wife) said 'Dr. Freud's baby is coming!' as nothing to do with him. Someone else's responsibility. Whose?

2

CONTRACTING THE DISEASE OF LOVE: AUTHORITY AND FREEDOM IN THE ORIGINS OF PSYCHOANALYSIS

In his interesting and thought-provoking diatribe against psycho-analysis, *Le Psychanalysme*, Robert Castel bases his critique on the following considerations:

The whole of psychoanalysis is determined by the framework of a contract. If I am not mistaken, no one has paid attention to the implications that this fundamental structure has: rules of protocol, the role of money, etc. As if this contract were a simple framework which surrounds something else, something essential. However, the problem is not to open up the packet to see what there is inside, because the contractual structure is not a framework, it is the fertile matrix of all psychoanalytic effects. Through it, emotion itself is contractualised.[1]

Thirty pages on, he writes: 'The analytic relation represents the liberal assumption, its epiphany: free choice, free contract, free associations, free-floating attention, etc. – it is only the libidinal charges which are fixed.'[2] I will not be following Castel in his diatribe, but I think this perception of the analytic relation is essentially correct, and is a deep one. Not only can the twin notions of contract and the liberal ideal of freedom be claimed to pervade the Western liberal societies in which psychoanalysis originated and in which it has come to occupy a privileged if restricted corner of public mythology, these ideals and the limited realities to which they cling can also be seen to determine the very nature of the psychoanalytic situation.

However, the psychoanalytic situation is defined by a contract that is proper to the professions. Maurice's (1838) definition of the professions, to be found in the *OED*, runs as follows: 'Profession . . . is expressly that kind of business which deals primarily with men as men, and is thus distinguished from a Trade, which provides for the external wants or occasions of men.' Taking this interesting definition as our starting-point, we may ask: what does a professional contract yield to the parties? The naïve answer, 'professional advice', may well be of use; the professional offers advice, instruction, esoteric knowledge – that blend of knowledge and authoritative support that Foucault called *savoir-pouvoir*. The relations that generate it are, in the ideal case, contracts between free men, not produced by occasional need but concerned with something like the 'soul', whether it be the social, religious or medical soul. What the professional contract is above all meant to preserve is the freedom of the contracting parties, enshrined in the notion, concomitant upon the idea of professional advice, that the parties are free to act upon that advice and free to ignore it. As likely as not, one pays for the advice, and the payment ensures the freedom to ignore it. What distinguishes the prescription from the command is the interposition of the contractual dimension: the prescription an 'opinion' couched in the form of a command.

What happened when the doctor's speech became the *materia medica*? The practice of hypnotism arose within the medical profession as a scientistic development which raised crucial questions of authority, freedom and knowledge. Psychoanalysis inherited these questions from hypnotism and provided a novel form of *rapprochement* between the increasingly dominant ideal of knowledge as power and the professional ideal of freedom. Hypnotism acted as a recasting of the ancient conception of medicine as both science and art and set the scene for the twentieth-century embodiment of the doctor as 'artistic' healer – the psychoanalyst. Yet the question of 'art' – of a technique suited to the unique individual – was raised in the form of a technique of control and persuasion, and revealed the contradictions of the contract, rather than fulfilling it. Psychoanalysis was a response to this crisis of the medical contract as revealed by hypnosis, although its subsequent development aimed at supplying its own auto-critique in accordance with its own subjection to the general laws of contract. Psychoanalysis was thus always a borderline case, subject to the power relations of the medical contract but aiming at examining this contractual dimension itself as a fantasy.

The golden age of medical hypnotism lasted roughly twenty years, from 1875 to 1895.[3] Three features of this episode in medical history will retain our attention. Firstly, the therapeutic zeal of those practitioners who took up the defence of hypnotism, a zeal that was in marked contrast with the therapeutic nihilism of the teaching hospitals. Secondly, arguments concerning hypnotism raised issues regarding the fundamental basis of all medical therapeutics – what we might well call an early theory of the placebo effect. A modern medical authority has defined the placebo effect as 'what all treatments have in common'.[5] The concept of suggestion elaborated in connection with the effects of hypnotism was an antecedent of such attempts to define what all treatments have in common. Thirdly, the therapeutic effects of hypnotism revealed to the practitioners themselves features of power and authority upon which their livelihoods depended.

In defending the therapeutic uses of hypnotism, Freud drew variously upon these three factors. Both those who attacked and those who defended hypnotism argued that, while hypnotism may be new, suggestion has been employed by doctors since time immemorial. One of Freud's developments of this point was: '"we are all constantly giving suggestions", [opponents] say; and in fact a physician – even a non-hypnotist – is never better satisfied than when he has repressed a symptom from a patient's attention by the power of his personality and the influence of his words – and his authority'.[6] Hence the fact that hypnotism uses suggestion cannot legitimately be used to criticise it – such a criticism would bring down the House of Medicine together with the pillars of suggestion. The authority of medicine is already at issue, and it is only medical bad faith which will accuse hypnotism of being an abuse of such authority:

It is quite interesting to find the most positive determinists suddenly defending the imperilled 'personal free-will', and to hear psychiatrists who are in the habit of suffocating the 'freely aspiring mental activity' of their patients with large doses of bromide, morphine and chloral, arraigning suggestive influence as something degrading to both parties.[7]

However, despite this delightful piece of rhetoric, Freud was perhaps missing his own point. It was not the dubious moral side-effects that troubled these organic determinists, but rather the recognition, abundantly clear to Freud, that hypnotism implicated the doctor's authority, as well as his drugs, in any causal account of medical success. In an ideal world of drugs and surgery, the doctor's authority is conferred on him by his knowledge and skill. In hypnotism, his therapeutic success stands exposed naked, is *seen* to be dependent upon a system of authority relations. The fear of the more astute of those who attacked hypnotism was not that it was ineffective, nor that it was immoral; rather, they anticipated that the success of a psychology of hypnotism would reveal that the doctor was *always* only effective in so far as he was immoral, in so far as the real drug that was being prescribed was he himself, in one of his social incarnations.[7] Morphia and chloral would be revealed as the doctor's alibis rather than his sacraments. According to these critics – and to Freud – it was not so much that the hypnotic state of sleep rendered the doctor that much more powerful, as that the hypnotic state of sleep allowed the doctor to take advantage of his patient and employ his full authority, without rendering it decent by dressing it up as a drug, a rest cure or a spasm of electricity.

What of the social context of these relations of power that Freud and others recognised as consequent upon the uses of hypnotism? On the one hand, the great discoveries of hypnotism, those of Charcot and Bernheim, were made in the wards and lecture theatres of large hospitals for the poor. Bringing hypnotism home to a private medical practice in Vienna was to transplant it from the theatrical atmosphere of Charcot's weekly display of the arts of nosology and clinical description to expectant students and a vast public, to a private world in which the most prominent expectations of both doctor and patient alike were neither a thirst for melodrama nor a reward for servile obedience, but rather sceptical hostility and therapeutic pessimism.[8] Bernheim confessed to Freud that his private patients did not respond to hypnotism in anything like the eager and dramatic manner that the charity patients did. The picture of the venerable country doctor, Liébeault, the university professor Bernheim's pastoral mentor, hypnotising the poor of his parish one after the other, under each other's gazes, in a large barn at the back of his house, could not offer a more poignant contrast with the hushed, heavily carpeted private world of bourgeois front rooms and bedrooms in which Freud practised his art.

Yet it is not easy to tease a social history out of these facts. However, the one lengthy case-history that Freud published of a patient cured by hypnotism does reveal the ambiguous social fabric out of which his cures based on the magisterial exercise of medical charisma were woven – yet it is (already) a family affair. A young woman with whom Freud had been acquainted since she (and he) were children found herself unable to breast-feed her child, despite her wish to do so. To her astonishment, she would vomit her food and could not sleep. Her physicians 'saw to it that I was brought in professionally to employ hypnotic suggestion, since I was already personally acquainted with the patient'.[9] Two vigorous bouts of suggestion sufficed to correct the state of affairs, and the woman breast-fed her baby for eight months. Freud noted, 'I found it hard to understand, however, as well as annoying, that no reference was ever made to my remarkable achievement.'[10] A year later, with another baby, the patient again found it impossible to breast-feed.

Freud repeated his spectacular treatment, and this time was rewarded with the patient's explanation of her ungrateful behaviour: 'I felt ashamed that a thing like hypnosis should be successful where I myself, with all my will-power, was helpless.'[11] Her family had colluded in ensuring that the hypnotist was no more than a near-invisible, ghostly adjunct to her exercise in free will in overcoming her 'inhibition'.

Of course, it was Freud's distinction as an observer and writer to be able to display the ambiguous relations between sick patient, host family and the shaky self-confidence of her doctor. He was able to weigh the shame this woman felt in the scales of the prognosis and possibility of cure. Then, in following Breuer's example, he realised that what a patient had to *say* about the symptoms (her confession of shame), as well as what the doctor could impose on her from without, might well establish the conditions for removing the symptom. The patient's will-power was not simply something that was to be overridden by the superior authority and wisdom of the hypnotist, even though Freud recognised that hypnotism was founded on the existence of this authority. Right from the start, Freud recognised that hypnotism in particular, and psychotherapy in general, might also involve a battle of wills, not just the physiologically vouchsafed appropriation by the physician of his natural position to command over the hearts, minds and bodies of his flock, the procedure which had led to Liébeault's near-miraculous cures. In 1890, describing the basis of 'psychical treatment', Freud emphasised that the profound influence exerted by the hypnotist 'lies in the hypnotic subject's attitude to his hypnotist'.[12] This relation, or *rapport*, as the hypnotists called it, was distinguished by its exclusivity: the patient would obey *only* the doctor. And, Freud went on to note, it was in this respect similar both to a child's relation to its parents and to a lover's relation to the loved one – a benign mixture of 'exclusive attachment and credulous obedience'.[13] Hence:

Hypnotism endows the physician with an authority such as was probably never possessed by the priest or the miracle man, since it concentrates the subject's whole interest upon the figure of the physician; it does away with the autocratic power of the patient's mind, which, as we have seen, interferes so capriciously with the influence of the mind over the body.[14]

Once again the term 'authority' moves centre stage – with the complicating factor of being set in competition with the 'autocratic' power of the patient's mind over his body. This latter view, commonplace enough, takes on a new importance once the mental autocracy is articulated with the *social* autocracy of the doctor–patient relationship. The preconditions that might lead to the hypnotist's gaining enormous power over the patient included one interesting claim: 'if the right of a patient to make a free choice of his doctor were suspended, an important precondition for influencing him mentally would be abolished'.[15] Implicit here is the notion that a *contract* between doctor and patient, freely entered into rather than arranged by a higher authority, imposes obligations on the patient that he finds difficult to shrug off. It is this line of thought that underpins the contract to speak freely about everything (the fundamental rule of psychoanalysis).

We thus see that, via the topics of hypnotism and suggestion, three themes that were to assume great importance in psychoanalysis were brought to the fore: love (of the hypnotist), freedom (of contract, of the will) and authority (over the body, over another). In the ideal case, hypnotism worked best by the patient exercising his or her free choice in deciding upon the doctor to whom he or she would submit, in an obedience wrought out of emotions akin to love and awe. Why, then, did hypnotism often fail? Precisely because the actual, day-to-day practice of hypnotism revealed that the doctor's authority was strictly limited. Once the authority card had been played, further treatment by other methods, if necessary, was made much more difficult. In addition, if hypnotic treatment were continued for too long, the patient would simply become addicted to the doctor's treatment, exactly as he might have done if morphine were the treatment of choice. More revealingly, Freud's personal difficulties with the technique led him to remark, in 1892, that 'in the long run neither the doctor nor the patient can tolerate the contradiction between the decided denial of the ailment in the suggestion and the necessary recognition of it outside the suggestion'.[16] From the doctor's point of view, this amounted to a subjective confession of scepticism as to the extent of his own authority – a 'perhaps' has crept into the doctor's mind, alongside the imperatives he voices to the subject.

Freud gave up hypnotism partly through his own inadequacies as a hypnotist – one might say through his inadequate incarnation of the idea of medical authority – and partly through the implicit logic of the cathartic cure that he borrowed from Breuer. The cathartic cure was created when Anna O., Breuer's severely disturbed patient, insisted that he listen to *her*, rather than that *she* listen and meekly obey *him*. Employing this technique, the kaleidoscope pattern of authority relations slowly began to shift: Freud's authority as doctor was still the motor that kept the stories of traumas flowing from the patient, but it was authority in the service of an insistence that the patient knew something which the doctor did not know, something which would help him in elucidating what the symptoms meant. To be sure, the crucial shift was from the doctor telling the patient *what to do* to the patient telling *stories* that in some magical way dispelled the symptoms. The doctor, however, still provided the framework of authority: firstly, in putting the patient into an appropriate mental state in which memory was facilitated. This manœuvre, initially achieved by hypnosis, later by more subtle methods, amounted to the doctor taking command of the patient's storehouse of memories. Whereas in hypnotism the doctor's authority had been confined to forbidding the patient specific feelings, ideas, bodily expressions and so forth, or commanding these, in the new cathartic technique the doctor demanded that the patient make of him the repository of all his experiences and memories – as expressed in words. The aptly named 'pressure technique', an intermediary stage in the development of Freud's method, consisted in the doctor's placing his hand on the patient's head and assuring him that he *will* discover the appropriate idea or image as soon as the pressure of the hand is removed. The next step was the fundamental rule: say whatever comes into your head, without regard to relevance, to importance, to politeness or good taste.

While we have arrived, with this rule, at a paradigm of freedom of speech, unparalleled before or since, it might still be argued that this extreme liberalism is simply a cloak for a more insidiously intrusive domination of the patient: the incessant demand to say more, until the story makes sense – to the doctor.[17] The demand for obedience has transmuted into a demand for comprehensibility. But the difference can be delineated more subtly.

The chief novelty introduced by hypnotism was its great reliance on words. Take a case of hysteria. One physician may write down in the case-notes: 'Diagnosis: Hysteria. Treatment: Chloral'. Such a medical practice matches an ideal of clinical medicine in which a statement about the natural world (the patient's body) unequivocally corresponds to a specific pharmacological action. Another physician – let us call him Charcot, for convenience's sake – may also diagnose hysteria. And he may also agree with the first physician in meaning by this statement a specific physiological state of the nervous system. But his therapy is different. He says – rather than writes, gives or prescribes – 'You do *not* have hysteria; when you wake up you will no longer have your nervous cough.' The means by which this therapy is put into action is speech. More specifically, however, its form is that of a command expressed in speech – necessarily so, since one cannot command without speech. The therapy consists in an explicit mobilization of authority in speech. And, of course, there is a straightforward means of refusing this authority: you can retain the symptom. When the hysteric's symptom persists, the doctor's authority has been weakened in a way that a failure of chloral therapy never occasions. The reason for this lies in the nature of the different speech acts involved. The speech act of the command goes hand-in-hand with the speaker's taking up a position of authority. In refusing to obey, the subject is not saying that it is a false command, is thus not providing what a Popperian observer could take to be a refutation of the truth of the command. Commands are neither true nor false. Rather, the patient is implying that the speaker of the command is not in a position to command him or her. It is the utterer, not the bare 'factual' content (if such could be said to exist), which has been made to fail. In other circumstances, with someone else, the patient might obey the command – such, at least, might be the fear or fantasy of the rebuffed physician. Whereas, within the medical conception of chloral's action, it is assumed that it is not the doctor prescribing it who is the source of its efficacy: the prescription of chloral is not a speech act implicating the doctor as authority.

Now turn to the psychoanalytic physician. The doctor diagnoses hysteria. He then says to the patient: 'Say whatever comes into your head.' Even if the patient takes this to be a command, whatever response he gives is appropriate – even if he says 'There is nothing in my head' he will be seen to be obeying the rule – seen (eventually) even by himself to be so doing. In this way, psycho-analysis amounts to a discovery of a new form of discourse in which whatever is said complies with the wish (or the rules) of the doctor, and whatever is said implicitly bolsters his authority, in so far as saying anything falls within the domain of what the doctor ordered, thus reinforcing his position as utterer of that speech act. Even if the patient says, 'I find your rule politically suspect, I refuse to obey it', he is obeying it, thus crystallising an authority relation between the two speaking subjects, an authority relation constituted by the demand for speech. As long as he keeps talking the doctor's authority remains intact, and, indeed, is confirmed.

My argument so far has centred on the idea that the use of

hypnotism with hysterical patients exposed the authority relations underlying doctor–patient relationships. Psychoanalysis was one answer to the crisis of medical self-confidence which could and did emerge as a consequence; it was an answer which both reinforced and displaced the authority of the doctor – a double movement to which we will return. Another index of this crisis was the debate over malingering. The basic issue, from our point of view, was as follows. Although malingering was originally a matter of concern principally to the army and navy in their attempts to distinguish genuine from false physical complaints, by the end of the nineteenth century civil doctors were themselves attempting to exclude false diseases from their hospitals and practices. In as much as hysteria and malingering both exhibited symptoms that did not follow the medical laws of the possible as defined by anatomy, physiology and pathology, they were both indicative of the influence of the patient's mind over the body. The key distinction was that in malingering the patient retained responsibility for the symptoms, whereas the hysteric did not. The malingerer's 'pathology' lay primarily in his will. Hence any attempt to cure the symptoms would expose the doctor to ridicule: the central medical transaction, in which the doctor graciously accepts the gift of the symptom and takes responsibility for it, is rendered void, since the malingering patient never surrenders control of the symptom. Malingering thus signposts the fact that medical power is bounded by the patient's will. Just as the limitations of medical authority were revealed by the success and failure of hypnotism, so the doctor's impotence in the face of the patient's *responsibility* for his illness was pinpointed by malingering. In becoming pressing problems for the medical profession at the end of the century, malingering and hypnotism prompted the question: who is responsible for the failure of the treatment, the patient, the doctor – or someone else?

As we have already seen in chapter 1, Freud's invention of psychoanalysis was predicated both on asking and finding a novel answer to this question, and I now wish us to retrace our steps and consider a different aspect of this famous moment in the early history of psychoanalysis, when the question, 'Who is responsible?', became intertwined with Freud's early investigations of sexuality: the exemplary dream of Irma's injection.[18] As we may recall, in that dream of July 1895, Freud dreamed of a young woman patient of his, Irma, a hysteric, whose treatment was giving him problems. In the dream he examined her throat and called in a senior colleague, who made foolish remarks about dysentery; it then became clear that another colleague had given Irma an injection with a dirty syringe, and at the end of the dream Freud saw clearly a chemical formula in bold type – trimethylamine.

Freud's associations indicated that he was comparing Irma with two other women patients who would not have been so recalcitrant – that is, they would have allowed themselves to be cured by Freud more quickly. The various references to other doctors and colleagues in the dream had as their aim both to ridicule alternative theories as to the nature of Irma's ailments and to shift the medical responsibility for the difficulties of the treatment from Freud's shoulders to someone else's. Freud thus discovered that the main theme of the dream was a self-justification in answer to the question: who is responsible for the absence of an adequate cure?

On the one hand, he could point to another doctor who used a dirty syringe in the dream – it's not me, it's him; on the other hand, Freud had three alternative arguments proving that it was certainly not *him* (that is, Freud) who was responsible. Firstly, if Irma's illness were an organic nervous disease, it was clear why psychotherapy did not work and why Freud was not responsible for the persistence of her pains. Secondly, if her symptoms were the result of sexual frustration resulting from her widowhood, yet again, it was clear that Freud was not the guilty party. Thirdly, if she really was a hysteric, then it was her own fault that the cure did not progress, since she never opened her mouth properly; she never told him of the traumatic events that lay hidden behind her symptoms. She refused to obey the fundamental rule to say everything – so it was her own fault if she remained ill. Such recalcitrance on her part seemed to Freud very much like malingering; yet it is a much more manageable form of malingering when conceived of as Irma disobeying the fundamental rule of psychoanalysis than when it is her symptoms that are the emblems of her defiant will.

When we leave behind us the account that Freud gave in his book, the story gets a little more complicated. What did Freud expect to hear from Irma? What did he expect her to tell him which would cure her of her illness? At the time of the dream, in 1895, he was developing the seduction theory: the hypothesis that hysteria results from sexual seductions experienced by the patient when a child, the seducer usually being the father. The seducers characteristically abused their position of authority in order to colour the relation of love between child and parent with a sexual gloss that the child could neither accept nor repudiate.[19] What Freud was asking his patients to do was to indict their parents of such abuses. In the name of an authority granted him by the hope for a cure, as embodied in the fundamental rule, Freud was inciting his patients to put in doubt and bring to judgement the first authority of their lives. No wonder, we might reflect, his patients were reluctant to tell him their stories – a reluctance that he took as good evidence of their veracity.[20] From the very first, Freud was clear that the authority of his cure was set in opposition to family authority and consisted in revealing an abuse of such authority.

If you cannot trust your father not to seduce you, whom can you trust? The fundamental rule (say anything) asked Freud's patients to place trust in an extended, contractually determined relation of medical confidence and confidences. Yet, underlying the Irma dream, as he admitted in a letter written in 1908, was another theme, one in counterpoint with that confidence: 'Sexual megalomania is hidden behind it, the three women, Mathilde, Sophie, Anna, are my daughters' three god-mothers, and I have them all! There would be one simple therapy for widowhood, of course.'[21] Recall the second assumption of the dream: if Irma (in reality, Anna) and patients like her are neurotic because they are widows, there is a simple therapy: they should come to Dr Freud's consulting room for something other than telling him tales of being seduced. But if we align Freud's confession of sexual desire with the third assumption, that Irma was not obeying the fundamental rule, then the pieces fall into place in a slightly different manner. What Freud expected and hoped to *hear* were stories of paternal seduction – and this is what Irma was withholding. It looks remarkably as if Freud's desires as expressed in the dream match perfectly the seductions that he assumed had already taken place in his patients' childhoods: Freud's sexual desires to 'have' his patients mirrored perfectly a veiled desire to 'have' his daughters, the girls named after his three patients. The father (doctor) abuses his authority for sexual ends. One might say that he expected them to tell him a story whose content was what he wished, namely that they fantasised a seduction, but his wish would be recast in the form of a memory from the distant past, with the father figuring in the place of Freud. And, with the rejection of the seduction theory a couple of years later, the accent did come to fall on fantasy. And again, it is remarkable how, in the run-up to this crisis in the development of his theory, his dream-life was intertwined with his patients' narratives. In a letter to Fliess, when discussing a dream in which he had been overtly over-affectionate towards one of his own daughters, he concluded: 'The dream of course fulfils my wish to pin down a father as the originator of neurosis and put an end to my persistent doubts.'[22] We find it difficult to answer the following question: is the dream-wish a wish that his *theory* be true, or is it a wish that is intended to deny that it could be someone other than the patient's father, some other male, threatening to abuse the authority relations between man and woman, parent and child, doctor and patient? In other words, is it just a coincidence that the wish-fulfilment theory of dreams and the seduction theory mesh so neatly to exclude the question of the *doctor*'s sexual desire for his patients?

At the same time as Freud was elaborating the seduction theory and demonstrating that all dreams are wish fulfilments, he made the fundamental discovery concerning the practice of psychoanalysis. Towards the end of *Studies on hysteria*,[23] written in March 1895, Freud recounted how the chief obstacle to the patient's obeying the fundamental rule occurred when her thoughts concerned the doctor; it was then that she was most likely to be tempted into silence. He gave an example: a patient thought of receiving a kiss from him, a thought that she could not bring herself to confess. Once he had extracted this 'thought' from her, she then remembered an exactly parallel situation from the past, when she had desired to be kissed and had repudiated the thought. Freud called this phenomenon the 'transference': thoughts that in reality belonged to a forgotten event in the past were transferred to the person of the doctor. Even at this early date, while his technique was still primitive, Freud thought that the therapeutic work could just as easily be carried out in terms of the thoughts and feelings concerning the doctor as in terms of the 'true' source of these thoughts and feelings – the repressed past. Given his discovery of, and growing familiarity with, the transference, then, Freud would *expect* his patients to fall in love with him instead of telling him about the lost loves of the past; they would offer themselves to him, seduce him, repeating with him what had been thought or experienced in the past. These seductions, revengeful acts, accusations would be welcome, because they were a form of remembering. And thus much of what Freud learnt about his patients' pasts was derived from the events of the transference: the exact strategies of pleading, hostility, revenge and yearning employed by the patient with the doctor gave vital information about the past events. On the one hand, then, we find the analyst urging her to tell him these

41

fantasies (or memories). Alongside, as it were, is the shadowy figure of a man struggling with unknown desires for his patients and daughters and the urgent desire to inculpate the father.

The ruling theme is clearly seduction. And the question: Who is seducing whom? Who is responsible for, who is initiating this seduction? Seduction as the primal trauma – seduction of the patient by the beneficent authority: the aim of the treatment is to seduce her into revealing the traumatic event, either in the form of a memory or in her attempts to seduce the doctor. Let us turn to a consideration of the logic of seduction, to try to find our bearings in this new scheme of medical intervention.[24]

The first step in a seductive manœuvre might be summed up as: 'I know what you're thinking.' Whether the seductive desire is aroused by a knowing glint in the other's eyes, or whether it is generated by some accident that betrays an unforeseen opening in the bland world of objects (what is commonly known as love at first sight, the *coup de foudre*), the impulse of the seducer is predicated upon a blind conviction of the accessibility of the other. 'I know what you're thinking.' Putting it in this succinct form reveals, firstly, the assumption of authority that seduction requires. And yet seduction is to be distinguished from sexual tyranny, as it might appear in rape, through the fact that the seducer sets great store upon the speech of the other, in particular upon the 'No' of the other. However, this respect for the judgement of the other is peculiar, for the seducer will never hear a 'No' as meaning 'No'; there is no final and definitive 'No'. Following each repeated 'No', he engages in further stratagems in accordance with his fluctuating conception of the desire of the other. One stratagem consists in setting himself up as the midwife of the other's desire;[25] alternatively, he may believe in the contagion theory of desire, as Kierkegaard conceives of Don Giovanni: offering mystery to all, with more than enough to go round.[26] Whichever theory he subscribes to and puts into action, his aim will be to transform the 'No' into 'Yes'. Yet, in the very act of so doing, a doubt will arise: 'Is this a true Yes? If I did not trust the other's No, why should I trust his Yes, especially since I believe myself to have been so instrumental in engendering it?' Hence the seducer will always be prey to doubt as to the status of the other's consent, so that a seduction that is viewed from the standpoint of a questioning of the status of the consent will always be confused with rape, just as rape in which any ignorance as to the nature of the victim's desire is admitted will in retrospect be deemed to have been seduction.

It is the authority of a subject *vis-à-vis* their own desires which is brought to the fore in this discussion of rape and seduction. Yet, as Freud had already recognised in hypnosis, love may well lead to a self-abasing respect for the authority of the loved one. In a later paper on transference (1915), Freud recognised this form of love as one of the primary features of psychoanalytic practice: the analyst will 'feel certain that [the patient's] docility, her acceptance of the analytic explanations, her remarkable comprehension and the high degree of intelligence she showed were to be attributed to' her affectionate transference.[27] Inevitably, this affection turns into something more insistently demanding: it becomes an 'endeavour to assure herself of her irresistibility, to destroy the doctor's authority by bringing him down to the level of a lover'.[28] Here Freud maps out two consecutive stratagems of seduction: first, docility and respect for authority in the hope that unforeseen advantages may accrue from this collusion with the loved one; second, a frontal assault on authority in order to gain the fruits of love from the domination of the object by securing its status as an appendage to the desire of the subject. But he was quite clear, both in 1895 and in 1915, that opting for the therapy for widowhood that his dream had suggested to him would not result in a cure. Rather, he would find himself in the position of the priest who, in hoping to convert the free-thinking insurance salesman on his deathbed, failed in securing the other's soul for God and instead came away insured.[29]

What is both amusing and tragic in the story of the priest and the insurance salesman, or the patient and the analyst, is the breach of contract. If the priest is willing to insure his life, in all fairness should the salesman not allow the priest to insure his death for him by witnessing his contract with God? Similarly, in all fairness, should the psychoanalyst not be expected to take seriously the seductions of the patient? Instead, he reminds her that it is not part of the contract for him to *believe* what she says or, even if he does believe her, to act on these statements. Such an unseemly breach of the expectations of the seducer, who calculates that the other will pay more than lip-service to the charity conditions (the principles by which, according to analytic philosophers, all honest communication is generated), leads to a crisis, and it is then that the patient begins to employ speech in the mode of a command, just like a hypnotist. And this is where the different positioning of the authority relations in psychoanalysis and hypnosis is most clearly revealed: the psychoanalyst now appears as the guardian of speech which has no object or aim, for when the patient's demands appear in the guise of commands, the analyst subsumes his authority within the fundamental rule in so far as it is an implicit feature of that rule that no action should be taken on the basis of what is said. The tables have truly been turned. Where the authority of the doctor's position as speaking subject was put on the line and weakened by the refusal of the hypnotised patient to get better, the authority of speech in general is first promoted and then radically questioned by the analyst's initial willingness to elicit any and every confession, followed by his refusal to recognise and act upon the patient's passionate declarations. It is as if the fundamental rule included a hidden clause: 'Say whatever comes into your head, but you cannot *then* expect me to place any faith in what you say, or take anything you say at face value.' The transference is characterised by the patient's making a declaration that must be taken at its face value for it to have its full meaning; yet it is exactly at that moment that the analyst refuses just that. Perhaps I can clarify this with an analogy.

Suppose two people are getting married. As they stand before the officiator, one of them replies to the question with: 'I do.' As Austin pointed out,[30] it makes no sense to suppose that the person is lying at that moment or that the statement is false – though the statement may 'misfire' for various reasons, for example if the utterer is already married. But the saying of the words 'I do' *is* the act of marrying. Now imagine that one of the parties to the marriage contract has already said 'I do', but when the other is asked to reply to the question, he or she, for reasons unknown, refuses to do so. The psychoanalytic dialogue reproduces this comedy of errors, in which, on the basis of a *prior* contract, one of the parties honestly enters into promises, pledges, commands and indictments of this sort, known to philosophers as performatives. The other party, however, resolutely refuses to honour these performatives, and the means of evasion are easily described. He refuses to obey commands; he remains sceptical as to the future realisation of those events conjured into existence by promises; he declines to sign on the dotted line; he declines to plead when accused; and so on. Instead, he hides behind the iron law of free speech. As Freud put it when a patient pleaded with him to be excused from following the fundamental rule when he had broached a certain delicate topic: 'I could not grant him something which was beyond my power. He might just as well ask me to give him the moon. The overcoming of resistances was a law of the treatment.'[31]

In following the fundamental rule, which offers him free speech, the patient encounters certain forms of speech that are not effective without the co-operation of the person addressed. Our misfired marriage is a humorous instance. And many other important instances are found in the spheres of love, hate and authority. We have seen how seduction implies this dependence upon the other's 'Yes' and 'No'. One might even hazard the hypothesis that masturbation figures so prominently in psychoanalytic discourse not only because of the latter's heritage of moralistic medical intervention, but also because masturbation and rape, in an ideal world, do not require the consent of the other. Masturbation would certainly change its social status if it became normal practice for a practitioner to ask permission, or require a collective decision, before indulging. Be that as it may, in obeying the fundamental rule, one is bound to discover sooner or later that certain speech acts are not 'free', since they require the other's willingness to comply with the categories of first and second persons invoked by them.

Hence my logico-historical account runs as follows. As soon as the doctor began to dispense his speech in place of a drug, as happened in hypnosis, the implicit relations of co-operation and co-option underlying medical practice became liable to breakdown. Freud's failure as a hypnotist, and his readiness to recognise failure, forced him to concentrate his energies on the speech relations involved in *any* talking cure: commands, confessions, pleas, seductions, rebukes. With the fundamental rule and the accompanying concept of the transference, he found the ideal vehicle for turning the tables on his patients, obliging *them* to encounter the obstacle to their cure in the social relations implied by the rules their specific discourses invoked, rather than his encountering the insuperable obstacle of a failure of medical authority in a confrontation with the patient's will, his 'responsibility' for the symptoms. Freud's innovation deflected the authority that patients wished to flaunt from being that of the doctor to being the authority of language itself. As he cannily put it in 1922, 'In psychoanalysis the suggestive influence which is inevitably exercised by the physician is diverted on to the task assigned to the patient of overcoming his resistances.'[32] That is, the analyst collaborates *with* the patient in combating the resistances represented by language – the watchword is always, 'Keep talking!'

So, in psychoanalysis we find an uncannily modern commitment to a free speech that never achieves anything, that can never render its contracts valid. What is even more striking is that this commitment also supplies its own autocritique. Two examples will illustrate. Every psychoanalyst knows the patient who is a firm believer in psychoanalysis. He will offer his convictions and rationales as to the truth and importance of psychoanalysis as part of his free associations; these will receive the same neutrally evasive responses as any other discourse of belief and conviction. Psychoanalysis leaves the truth-status of all discourses in abeyance, in order to highlight whatever seductive or evangelical functions they may perform. But psychoanalysis not only treats all discursive systems as equal – equal before the law of free speech, ready to have their rules broken down and exposed by being submitted to the technique of 'take nothing at face value' – it also demands access to *all* discourses. It is the most comprehensive of the invasive discursive apparatuses discussed by Foucault in *The history of sexuality. Vol. 1*. To illustrate, one last passage from Freud: 'It is very remarkable how the task of analysis becomes impossible if a reservation is allowed at any single place . . . I once treated a high official who was bound by his oath of office not to communicate certain things because they were state secrets, and the analysis came to grief as a consequence of this.'[33] This remarkable anecdote captures much of what I have been trying to describe: the opposition between the obligatory freedom of speech demanded by the fundamental rule and any other discursive authority, as symbolised by the conflicting demands of the state and the liberal ideal of freedom of speech; the conviction that a 'No' that is allowed to subsist outside of the framework of the fundamental rule is equivalent to a residue of the 'feudal' relations between hypnotist and patient, or an element of the doctor–patient relationship that still upholds the myth of the 'No' of seduction. We can also gain a sense of how it is that the ideal of free speech can become the most arduous of all demands, to which all authority and relations of intimacy may be sacrificed as the pledges and commands that make them up are rendered empty in the name of a higher authority – that of speech itself.

To conclude: a hint of a further argument. Psychoanalysis treats money as if it truly were the universal means of exchange, and patients do behave as if they could buy love. Money is intended to dissolve any obligations other than those of a contract entered into and fulfilled – on both sides. However, even money may, on occasion, not be taken at 'face-value', as the sacred guarantee of the contract. The psychoanalyst may not trust the patient's money, precisely so as to keep psychoanalysis firmly within the domain of seduction. Take for example a problem Eissler raised in an article on the analytic fee. He pondered 'whether one should accept a fee when one analyses a call girl'. He ventured the 'surmise that the analysis has a far better chance of success if the payment of a fee is postponed until such time as the patient has made a new professional choice'.[34] The problem only arises because, when confronted by a call girl, Eissler no longer trusts the (psychoanalytic) equation, 'money = speech = freedom of contract', despite knowing full well that psychoanalysis depends upon this equation. A similar rationale lies behind a French analyst's recommendation that, when analysing a prostitute, the analyst should change his financial arrangements so that he charges by the month, rather than the standard French exchange of notes at the end of each session.

Both these arguments rely on the idea that it is only when the woman thinks the analyst is doing it for love, not money, that the seduction essential to analysis will start to unfold. The call girl is too much like the analyst to be seduced – she knows what the price of love is, she knows what an hour is worth – no ambiguity. Only when money and love no longer fully correspond with each other will the seduction start, will her words begin to fill up with ambiguity. The analyst knows too well how to weigh words, just as the call girl knows that the whore with a heart of gold is an effect of language.

Thus our analyst, member of the youngest profession, plays on the fact that patients do not know what they mean, nor do they know what money will buy. It is insofar as they do not know these things that seduction begins. And with seduction, the questioning of the contract and the calling into question of authority, whether it be the dictionary, the Bank of Italy, or the Institutes of Analysis begins. Psychoanalysis appears to be the distillation of the liberal, *laissez-faire* ethos. But it only 'works' because money and words are performatives, with effects going beyond their face-value, and not just counters in an exchange that can be limited. The original seduction is thus that offered by the contract – namely that it is *just* a contract. By offering only that, psychoanalysis subverts contractual relations in general, thus bringing to fruition what hypnosis had threatened, but failed, to accomplish. Its means of accomplishment is the free speech whereby one of the parties will contract the disease of love that the other will cure by treating the proffered seductive words as if they were simply the universal means of exchange.

The Sistine Madonna, by Raphael (courtesy Staatliche Kunstsammlungen, Dresden)

3

THE UNTOLD PLEASURES OF PSYCHOANALYSIS: FREUD, DORA AND THE MADONNA

Now I happened to know that there was also a Madonna by Raphael there and I found her at last in an equally chapel-like room and a crowd of people in silent devotion in front of her. You are sure to know her, the Sistina. My thoughts as I sat there were: Oh, if only you were with me! . . . The painting emanates a magic beauty that is inescapable, and yet I have a serious objection to raise against the Madonna herself . . . Raphael's Madonna is a girl, say 16 years old; she gazes out on the world with such a fresh and innocent expression, half against my will she suggested to me a charming, sympathetic nursemaid, not from the celestial world but from ours. My Viennese friends reject this opinion of mine as heresy . . .[1]

To *cognoscenti* of what Wladimir Granoff calls the lexicon of Freud's unconscious, this letter bears many of the trademarks of its author. He betrays longing for the presence of his fiancée, transformed into an 'Oh, if only . . .'; he manifests an ability, even though captivated by the magic beauty, to voice a serious objection, and thus reveals his capacity for sustaining contradictory responses; finally, he spots the charming nursemaid, in most unlikely garb, too real for comfort, too much of this world to allow the young lover to keep his image of love in the other world. There is even almost a note of satisfaction at finding himself a heretic.

The visit to the Dresden art gallery where Freud found the Sistine Madonna was the first occasion on which he finally 'himself began to admire' painting rather than feel that such admiration was simply 'a silent understanding among people who don't have much to do to rave about pictures painted by the famous masters'.[2] But this significant moment in the development of the young Freud's aesthetic sensibility is not the only reason for our interest in his response to the Sistine Madonna. Dora also visited Dresden and its art gallery, and her visit formed one of the key associations to the 'second dream' of her treatment:

49

She remained two hours in front of the Sistine Madonna, rapt in silent admiration. When I asked her what had pleased her so much about the picture she could find no clear answer to make. At last she said: 'The Madonna'.[3]

Straightaway we may draw an initial conclusion about the difference between Freud's and Dora's perception of the painting. Where Dora saw the Madonna, Freud could see only a nursemaid – that is, not the mother, but a woman who takes care of a child – and was disappointed. What he had hoped to see was an image 'neither a woman nor a girl'.[4] This hope, we might say, expressed itself in his wish that his beloved might be with him.

Perhaps I am not alone in thinking that Dora's contemplation of the Madonna is linked with the only clear-cut image from her childhood that Freud's narrative yields:

Dora herself had a clear picture of a scene from her early childhood in which she was sitting on the floor in a corner sucking her left thumb and at the same time tugging with her right hand at the lobe of her brother's ear as he sat quietly beside her. Here we have an instance of the complete form of self-gratification by sucking . . .[5]

Where Dora experiences complete gratification contemplating the image of the Madonna and child, the repetition of the scene of gratification side by side with her brother, Freud finds a lack of satisfaction, that lack against which masculine sexuality characteristically defends itself by splitting the woman into two, the nursemaid and the mother, the whore and the virgin. As he put it in a letter to Fliess in 1898, 'In all analyses, one therefore hears the same story twice: once as a fantasy about the mother; the second time as a real memory of the maid.' Freud could not see what Dora saw in the Madonna: he asked her what she saw and she replied, simply, the Madonna. He passed on. He overlooked something, perhaps. We might say that he overlooked the fact that Dora always found her pleasure in another, with another, her thumb and her brother's earlobe. Freud talks of this as 'self-gratification'; perhaps this is the ideal aimed at in the masculine fantasy of splitting the woman, of doubling her, the ideal that is also constructed out of splitting – the ideal ego, or the ego *tout simple*. Whereas Dora's self-gratification necessarily includes the reference to the other. But who is this other? And can we propose, as Michèle Montrelay does,[6] that this structure of gratification is that of feminine desire in its essence?

Who is this other? That is the question Freud insists upon

throughout Dora's story. But he does so in a most surprising manner. The narrative is divided into two main sections: (i) The clinical picture; (ii) Dora's two dreams. The clinical picture offers an account of the toings and froings in the *ménage à cinq* which makes up Dora's family: Herr K., Frau K., Dora's father, Dora's mother and Dora herself. Up to page 35 of the case-history, half-way through part I, Freud paints a portrait of Dora as the victim of all the machinations and egotistical manoeuvres the others engage in to get what they want; in the second half of part I, Freud uses this account as a mirror, showing Dora how her own desires are reflected point by point in the desires and actions of others: 'Dora's reproaches against her father had a "lining" or "backing" [*doubliert*] of self-reproaches of this kind with a corresponding content in every case.'[7] Freud's preliminary remarks about the difficulties of writing this case-history gradually shade over into being an intricate account of a family system built upon secret desires and mutual duplicity. The whole household would seem a prime candidate for family therapy – provided the K's came too.[8] Freud's response, however, as Lacan pointed out,[9] was to turn the position of the passive, helpless victim that Dora presented him with into the question: 'Where are *you* in all this mess?' His insistence on the question precipitates the seemingly endless series of identifications with which Dora's story is filled out – with her father, with Herr K., with her brother, with Frau K., with the young engineer in a far-off town, with the governesses . . .

Is this what the analysis of hysteria and hence the analysis of feminine desire amounts to: unpacking the identifications through which the subject has constituted her desire as always being the desire of the other? The papers on hysteria that Freud wrote after publishing *Dora* bear out this impression: they are always adding new complexities, new modes of displacement and identification to the structure of fantasy that underlies hysterical symptoms – their characteristic of multiple identification and in particular their near-universal bisexuality. Dora's case is in no way different: identification seems to be the predominant means by which her desire is made manifest. And the sites of identification are, of course, often close to hand: in the family. The family is the sounding-board for the hysteric's desire. But it is also the spider's web in which she is caught. The family is the privileged domain of hysteria, in which she disrupts the circulation of goods and services between men,[10] but it is also the means by which the hysteric remains endogamous, incestuous, faithful. Dora silently colluded with her father's infidelities with Frau K. and was thus faithful to two members of her family circle at once. The quest for Dora's hidden desire proceeds via the indefinitely prolonged detour of discovering whose desire she has taken on board as her own. The case-history then reads entirely as a history of her identifications, with the untoward consequence that we discover what everyone else wants – and are left frustrated and perplexed, like Freud, wondering what Dora really wants.

Many of the commentaries on *Dora* have followed Freud in this respect – decoding one or other aspect of the knotted family system in which Dora was caught, following Freud as Freud followed Dora's father, and as Dora's father had followed Herr K. These studies often aim to provide a clarification of the axis of masculine–feminine desire around which Freud built his account of the case and its 'failure'. Following Lacan, some have argued that Freud's insistence on Dora's love for Herr K. was a consequence of his preconceived ideas about what was good for Dora: a man, with his phallic appurtenances. But what this overlooked, as Freud was the first to argue, was Dora's orientation towards the mysterious and beautiful feminine, the body feminine in particular. Yet the array of identifications by which Dora came to have such a homosexual desire already implies that she has marked herself as a man; her desire for Frau K. is 'hers' in so far as she identifies with her father and with Herr K. What is important for Dora's 'case' is not so much whether her desire is for a man or a woman, as discovering how the masculine and feminine components were articulated together.

In this sense, Freud's technical error was not his insistence on Dora's love for Herr K. – a line of enquiry vindicated by the discovery that Dora had mimed the bearing of Herr K.'s child. Rather, he overlooked that the 'Dora' who loved Herr K. and bore his children was Frau K.; Dora's pregnancy fantasy enacted the reparation of the K.s' broken marriage. In this light, the paper 'Hysterical phantasies and their relation to bisexuality' (1908) has all the signs of being a correction of this error, by showing that all (or nearly all) hysterical fantasies (and hence symptoms) represent a fusion of masculine and feminine components. Dora loved Herr K. and had his child in so far as she had become Frau K., a wife who made amends for 'giving nothing' to the husband; she loved Frau K. in so far as, according to an active conception of sexual love of a woman, she was identified with Herr K. Where is the 'true' Dora in all this? She is there, covered over by her multiple identifications, sustaining through these identifications the hysteric's question:

'Am I man or woman? What is man and what is woman such that I might be able to answer this question?'[11]

In counterpoint with the theme of the question man–woman, we can see the other side of Freud's 'error': his disinclination to seek out the secret source of Dora's sexual knowledge and the status of the 'adorable white body' of Frau K. (Madonna). Put simply, Freud was disinclined to broach the question of the transference, since he had already assumed that what Dora was seeking in him and in analysis was something Herr K. possessed, rather than something a woman might offer. As a number of writers have pointed out, Freud found it exceedingly difficult to accept the position of woman in the transference. He found it impossible to conceive, or was reluctant to allow, that such a transference would be possible with him. But in Dora's case it was not just a question of Freud appearing in female garb; the psychoanalytic situation would have to receive a new meaning once Frau K.'s significance had become the centre of attention. For the relation that Dora had with Frau K., and with the governess who had also sacrificed her to her desire to seduce a man (her father), was one of intimate talk about sexual secrets between two women. The most hidden of all Dora's secrets that Freud's techniques failed to uncover[12] was that the psychoanalytic conversation itself, in which Freud thought he held all the keys, had become the scene in which two 'women' talked about sex, Dora's scene of 'gynaecophilic' satisfaction. The opposition between logos (Freud's technique, explicitly analogous to gynaecology) and philia (Dora's secret), which Hertz draws out, is what Freud wishes to maintain, so that psychoanalysis retains its scientificity, and is prevented from degenerating into natter, into old wives' tales. Not only had Freud's work been called a 'scientific fairy tale' by a respected senior colleague, Freud had himself, in 1895, pointed out that his case-histories read more like short stories, lacking 'the serious stamp of science'.[13] This line of thought offers us a clue as to why Freud so implausibly chose a case such as Dora's to present to his scientific colleagues in the medical journals – a case that was so unsatisfactory from the therapeutic point of view. Dora's case was appropriate precisely because it demonstrated that the scientific interest and the therapeutic claims of psychoanalysis were separate issues: a therapeutic failure had as much to offer in scientific terms as a success. And to make it quite clear that the aim of Freud's work is primarily scientific, Freud *writes* the case-history, writing being the indisputable mark of the permanence of knowledge that the scientific ideal prescribes.[14]

The temptation of Sigmund Freud

As Melvin Scharfman has argued, Freud's commitment to science amounted to his being an unfaithful ally in Dora's eyes: 'like her father and like Herr K.', Freud also had a mistress, even if that mistress was psychoanalysis and science.[15] We might take a further step and surmise that Freud's attachment to this mistress was complicit with his refusal to see himself as embroiled in women's chat, in the caressing oral intimacies that Dora was repeating with him. Earlier in his therapeutic career, in fact earlier in the same year in which he treated Dora, he had felt obliged to give up his scientific pretensions:

I adopted the expedient of renouncing working by conscious thought, so as to grope my way further into the riddles only by blind touch. Since I started this I have been doing my work, perhaps more skilfully than before, but I do not really know what I am doing. I could not give an account of how matters really stand. In my spare time I take care to avoid thinking. I abandon myself to my phantasies, play chess, read English novels; everything serious is banned.[16]

No writing; no thought; no account. By some contemporary analytic standards, this is the ideal condition for the analyst to aspire to. But, nine months after he had written this, Dora jolted Freud into quite another analytic expedient, the inner conviction of mastery and authority: 'the case has opened smoothly to my collection of picklocks'.[17] And the scientific authority, which her walking out on him undermined, was then reasserted by the writing of her story. In this way, Freud maintained his analysis of Dora in the 'masculine' mode, fending off the scenario of endless feminine chat into which she had seduced him.

It is curious, then, given the explicit scientific pretensions of Freud's case-history of Dora, that readers have been fascinated by it as if it were literary. Steven Marcus writes of it as if it were a novella – 'a great work of literature'.[18] And it is not only Freud's readers who take it to be such – their precedent is the author, and at the most sensitive turning-point in the narrative:

I must now turn to consider a further complication to which I should certainly give no space if I were a man of letters engaged upon the creation of a mental state like this for a short story, instead of being a medical man engaged upon its dissection . . . For behind Dora's supervalent train of thought which was concerned with her father's relations with Frau K., there lay concealed a feeling of jealousy which had that lady as its *object* – a feeling, that is, which could only be based upon an affection on Dora's part for one of her own sex.[19]

Freud evokes the opposition between the creative man of letters and the dissecting doctor. Where the man of letters puts together, omitting what is superfluous, the medical man breaks down, finding a residue to which he must grant space. It is his obligation towards this residue that prevents Freud from being a man of letters.

Yet the act of *writing* Dora's story gives the impression of having been something urgent for Freud, a way, perhaps, of transforming something which Dora left behind. On the 25th of January, three and a half weeks after she said goodbye, Freud wrote to Fliess: 'I finished "Dreams and hysteria" yesterday, and the consequence is that to-day I feel short of a drug . . . it is the subtlest thing I have so far written.'[20] Five days later he added: 'the chief issue in the conflicting mental processes is the opposition between an inclination towards men and towards women'.[21]

Yet, on reading the narrative, it is by no means clear from its architecture that this conflict is the 'chief issue'. All references to it appear as after-thoughts, footnotes: the 'further complication' concerning Dora's gynaecophilia is appended to section I; further references occur mainly in footnotes towards the end of the dream-analyses. And we find Freud reflecting that this homosexual strand of Dora's mental life takes on greater significance the more time separates him from the end of the analysis.[22] We may surmise that this 'complication', the residue, was the *effect* of the end of the analysis. It was what Dora's departure did to Freud. While the analysis was in progress, Freud behaved like the man of letters, not taking the further complication into account. It was only once she had left him with the residue that he became the medical man in writing her story. What is more, he could only express any sense of her having betrayed him in a medical dialect, fifteen months after the end of the analysis, when he promised to forgive her for having deprived him of the satisfaction of affording her a radical cure of her afflictions. His denial of her betrayal of him thus duplicated Dora's own denial of having been betrayed by Frau K., though Freud thought she had every reason for thinking that she had been. In all manner of ways, Dora's idealised love of Frau K., her secret, became the hidden motor of the analysis, which could be revealed only by its ending.

It was in this way that the themes of transference and homosexuality became intertwined. The analysis consists in a rapid criss-crossing of the system of identifications which Dora mobilised as representations of her desire. And, then, at the end, the failures become apparent: in the full text of Freud's account, this failure is the overlooking of the transference. In the footnotes, the failure is the overlooking of Dora's love for Frau K. But the transference that Freud recorded himself as having failed to bring up is the transference from Herr K. to Freud – not a whisper of Frau K.

As Collins *et al.* have pointed out, Freud's insistence on the centrality of Herr K. in his discussion of the direction taken by the analysis is undercut by two key footnotes in which the spotlight shifts on to Frau K.[23] In both passages, the Madonna is the pivot around which the shift from the masculine to the feminine line takes place. Freud belatedly recognised that Dora's contemplation of the Madonna for two hours was the time she then allotted him; similarly, her seeing the Madonna alone, refusing to be accompanied, was an allusion to her decision to go on alone without him. But Freud failed to see that, in dismissing him, Dora was repeating the dismissal of her mother, a dismissal in which Freud had colluded. Freud blithely accepted Dora's view of her mother, rendering it medically validated with the term 'housewife's psychosis'.[24] What is more, his collusion extended to the point of committing a number of 'symptomatic' acts when dealing with the female side of Dora's family: on page 75 he notes without commentary that he had forgotten in what year Dora had accompanied her mother to a spa while she was recovering from a venereal disease (he who was normally so careful about chronology). More strikingly, on page 78 he writes, apropos of a letter which Dora hurriedly concealed from him, 'Something then came out which was a matter of complete indifference and no relation to the treatment. It was a letter from her grandmother, in which she begged Dora to write to her more often.' This 'matter of complete indifference' which had 'no relation to the treatment' concerned precisely the theme which belatedly appears as the 'key' to the case: communication between women. Freud instead believed that Dora was playing at secrets with him, the male doctor – thus repeating, without realising it, the demand that the grandmother made on Dora ('tell me more'), and without realising that he was occupying the position of a woman when making this demand.

Freud had concluded that Dora's revenge on him was modelled on her revenge on Herr K. and on men in general: 'she *acted out* an essential part of her recollections and phantasies instead of reproducing it in the treatment'.[25] But Freud failed to see that the treatment itself was an acting out, or, as some analysts have put it, an 'acting in' of Dora's relationship to Frau K. and, behind her, with her mother. The point in common between Dora's love of women and the psychoanalytic situation was the intimate discussion of sexual topics.

When Freud ventured to justify, in the case-history, the open and frank discussion of sexual matters, his manifest intention was to demonstrate the respectability of his practice, in contrast with the covert titillation, prurience and wilful ignorance of other doctors.[26] Freud rounds off his pre-emptive defence against charges of corrupting innocent females with a remarkable claim:

> There is never any danger of corrupting an inexperienced child. For where there is no knowledge of sexual processes even in the unconscious, no hysterical symptom will rise; and where hysteria is found there can no longer be any question of 'innocence of mind'.[27]

This *theoretical* argument – any patient with genuine hysterical symptoms has *already* been corrupted (seduced) – undercuts the arguments Freud had already used, namely that employing technical terms – '*J'appelle un chat un chat*' – is the way in which to avoid titillation and harm. We can see two lines of thought coming together in this passage: a demarcation of Freud's technique from the titillating, pleasure-seeking and pleasure-averting methods of his colleagues, and a denial of the suggestive seductiveness of his language, so that he will be able to recognise the transference as entirely his patient's responsibility, not his. He was well aware that the patients find the analytic process and situation sexually stimulating; indeed, he had already come to think that sexual feelings for the doctor were a universal part of the therapeutic process. Freud was preparing the way for a description of the attitude the analyst must adopt *vis-à-vis* the transference: he must ensure, by means of his honesty and trustworthiness, that he is not suggesting or colluding with the anticipated sexual feelings of his patients. But to maintain this honourable position, Freud had to discount the idea that there might be pleasure simply in talking (about sexual matters). Yet he did have to make it plain that talk about sex was a necessary part of the treatment. Since he had shown it was impossible to corrupt an inexperienced girl, his arguments were as much intended to safeguard *himself* against being corrupted by the talk of the patient as anything else.

Yet his rigorous stand against the corruptions of speech was to run counter to Dora's own desire – or so he was to hypothesise in retrospect. As Toril Moi has pointed out, there is an obsessive refrain in Freud's text concerned with the sources of Dora's sexual knowledge, a refrain that is a counterpoint to Freud's own concern with elaborating a theory of the effects of sexual knowledge.[28] The question of the sources of her sexual knowledge became closely allied with Dora's secret homosexual love for Frau K. – both items that escaped him. The scenario that Freud's scattered remarks on these two subjects evoke is one in which Dora's gathering of sexual information is synonymous with the ripening and bringing to fulfilment of her love for a woman. The fact that Frau K. had allowed Dora's confidences to be passed on to a third party had considerable pathogenic effect on Dora,[29] but she, acting as she thought Frau K. should have done, would never allow Freud to know this. Freud's quest for the source of Dora's sexual knowledge thus repeated the masculine violation of this feminine space of intimacy and confidences. Yet, at the same time, psychoanalysis recreated this space of intimacy and confidence; but Freud refused to recognise it, since it would necessarily implicate his technical terms and avoidance of verbal titillation in the scene of epistemological seduction that Dora's relationship with Frau K. had realised. More to the point, such a recognition would reveal that Freud was acting the part of a *woman* in the scene that Freud was unwittingly repeating.

Yet this may, oddly enough, be one of the reasons why Freud failed to detect the transference of Herr K. on to him: he failed to detect it because he was (unconsciously) *too much at ease* playing the part of a woman. It is in bearing this in mind that we should read the touching and wistful question Freud asked himself in the wake of Dora's desertion:

Might I perhaps have kept the girl under my treatment if I myself had acted a part, if I had exaggerated the importance to me of her staying on, and had shown a warm personal interest in her – a course which, even after allowing for my position as her physician would have been tantamount to providing her with a substitute for the affection she longed for? I do not know.[30]

Surely there is a curious *naïveté* in this question? Should not Freud have been asking himself not, 'should I have acted a part?', but rather, as he was to a few pages on in the Postscript, 'what part *was* I playing, unbeknownst to myself?' When Freud did get around to asking himself that question, he could only guess at the 'unknown quantity', '*das X*', in himself which reminded Dora of Herr K.[31] And this very way of phrasing it places the unknown quantity which Freud and Herr K. shared in common in the field of reality: this X undoubtedly has a phallic reference.

What Freud did not ponder was that he already had all the clues as to what the unknown quantity was that he shared with *Frau* K.: he talked of sex to Dora, although he did so employing terms which he believed he had defused of their capacity for titillation. In this light, Dora's second dream, with its latent fantasy of defloration couched in exactly those technical terms that Freud had saved from the accusation of erotic suggestibility, was a demonstration, for Freud's benefit, of the erotic possibilities of *his* language, the language of medical books and impotent doctors. Dora was indeed taking her revenge here, but in an ironic mode, showing Freud, the verbally acrobatic interpreter of dreams, how his neutral language was as easily eroticised as any other. Dora may well have already been 'corrupted' by the time she came to analysis, as her hysterical symptoms led Freud to think, but she showed how Freud's attempt to disengage himself from corruption had failed. Dora's revenge was to teach Freud a lesson: that psychoanalysis could as easily be a hothouse for the eroticisation of language as an enclave protected from it.

Hence all the 'secrets' of the case had come together, if only Freud had known where to look. The secret of the sources of Dora's sexual knowledge and the deepest layer of her erotic life were one: the scene of two women talking. Let me refer back, in Freudian fashion, to two sentences from Freud's letter to Martha about the Madonna: 'You are sure to know her, the Sistina. My thoughts as I sat there were: Oh, if only you were with me!' Admittedly, these words are now out of context, but they bear a second reading: they evoke a Freud certain that Martha 'knows' the Madonna, a thought that is linked with his desire to bring her to him. The scene is thus: the two women, Martha and the Madonna, followed by the thought of Martha at his side, watching with him this Madonna. But what happens now to the Madonna? She becomes a nursemaid, from our world.

The mother/nurse duo is a well-known feature of the Freudian lexicon: in his childhood, they appear as Nannie/Mater; in the Leonardo essay we are shown them in the Virgin and St Anne. But we only find them in Dora's story in retrospect, after the analysis had been broken off. Freud could recognise himself neither as Madonna nor as nursemaid. In the final session, he knew immediately to place Dora in the part of maidservant or governess giving a fortnight's notice, but would not draw the appropriate conclusion that whoever was playing the part of the servant – and Cixous and Gallop point out Freud's reluctance to recognise himself, rather than Dora, as the wage-earning employee being put out the door[32] – the other party must be the employer and, most probably, the mistress of the house. Once again, Freud missed his chance to place himself in the transference – once again, because he could not adopt the position of woman.

Why was this so? Surely this question has received enough cogent answers for us not to have to ask it again? Are we not sufficiently aware of Freud's patriarchal inclination and his disinclination to play the woman's part – as evidenced, for instance, in the case of female homosexuality cited by Gearhart and others, whose treatment Freud terminated as soon as he came to the conclusion that her hostility to her father was so profound that therapeutic progress could be hoped for only from analysis with a woman?[33] I can offer a further reason, beyond those personal idiosyncracies of Freud's, and beyond his embodiment of patriarchal values, a reason structural to his conception of psychoanalytic technique. It pertains to his conception of the maternal analyst. In 1931, Freud wrote to Ferenczi criticising his innovations in technique, in which the analyst made up for the patient's deprivations in childhood with expressions of affection. 'Why stop at a kiss?', he asked, and continued later in the letter:

In this warning I do not think I have said anything you do not know yourself. But since you like playing a tender mother role with others, then perhaps you may do so with yourself. And then you are to hear from the brutal fatherly side an admonition. According to my memory the tendency to sexual playing about with patients was not foreign to you in pre-analytic times, so that it is possible to bring the new technique into relation with the old misdemeanours.[34]

As Granoff has pointed out,[35] what is striking about this paternal admonition is that it treats the seduction of patients as part of the tender mother role, in which the analyst offers patients the affection they so long for (the expression Freud used of Dora). It is a desire for such seduction that Freud attributed to his hysterics, once he had rejected the theory that the patients had actually been seduced in childhood. And, at about the same time as his letter to Ferenczi, Freud was returning to the belief in the reality of seduction in childhood; but now it was the mother's nursing and ministrations which counted as the reality of seduction.

When we put these elements together, we find the following picture: Freud conceived of the maternal analyst (Ferenczi, dominated by 'the need to cure and to help'[36]) as ready to give affection and play the part of the mother in the form of seductive caresses. It was precisely this course of action that Freud declined to engage in with Dora, as we have already seen: he declined to 'act a part' and to show 'a warm personal interest in her', 'tantamount to providing her with a substitute for the affection she longed for'. Instead, Freud 'played' the paternal analyst, the scientist intent on limitation rather than extending, 'practising the humbler arts of psychology', respecting the 'limits set to the extent to which psychological influence may be used': 'I respect as one of these limits the patient's own will and understanding.'[37]

Are we then to recognise the failure of Dora's treatment – if failure it was – as yet another twist in the complicated history of the seduction theory?[38] In 1900, Freud withheld playing a part which would yield his patient the satisfaction she longed for, and in 1931 he gave this eschewed technique a name – the tender mother role – and spelled out that it was tantamount to seduction. We may surmise that, from the 1890s on, seduction was the chief danger that threatened analytic technique, just as it had been the chief danger to mental health in childhood. The echo of this avoidance of seduction can then be found in the recommendation that psychoanalysis be undergone in a state of frustration. Yet Dora found her satisfaction; she found her secret pleasure in the gaining of sexual knowledge, so much a part of her construction of an object. But Freud was not prepared to recognise it. We now know why: he would have found that he was playing the part of the seducing mother, the part he most urgently wanted to avoid playing, the part he declared he would not play on account of his ignorance of the 'unknown factors' in every case, the X in the analytic situation he had created which, for Dora, evoked the presence of Frau K.

If Dora did indeed find her satisfaction, she was also betrayed once again: Is not our discussion of her the consequence of her betrayal? Are not the discussions of *Dora*, so sympathetic to her, by so many feminist writers so many attempts to make up for the lack of a female interlocutor which Freud's refusal of that position entailed for her? Is not our discussion her betrayal repeated yet again? Freud felt obliged to betray her confidence because she had discovered the one form of satisfaction that Freud would neither analyse nor recognise: the seduction of words, of knowledge, of oral intimacy, of a mode of analysis in which Freud found himself feminised. As likely as not, for both of them, the secret lay in the picture of the Madonna – but they preferred not to find the words to say it.

4

RAPE, SEDUCTION, PSYCHOANALYSIS

Introduction

In the 1890s, Sigmund Freud proposed a theory of the aetiology of the neuroses which has come to be known as the seduction theory: the claim that neuroses were caused by the after-effects of the sexual abuse and seduction of children. Around 1981, I began to ask myself the question: why did Freud characterise this theory by the term seduction rather than rape?

In reading feminist writers on rape, I was driven to recognise that many of them regard psychoanalytic writings as being profoundly iniquitous. At a cursory glance, it seemed as if these writers assumed that *any* psychoanalytic account of rape would paint the rape victim as *wanting* to be raped, so that *any* psychoanalytic account became synonymous with *excusing* the rapist, by portraying him as a seducer rather than a rapist.

In this, the feminist writers were in part reflecting the practice of rape defence trials, in which the victim is often imputed to have tacitly consented to intercourse. Such defences often revolve around the folklore wisdom that 'No' sometimes means 'Yes'.

So I was led to consider the difference between rape and seduction. In particular, I found myself concerned with psychoanalytic writings (in which rape is never mentioned, despite Freud's early concern with sexual assault as the original trauma in the neuroses), with feminist writings on rape (which assume that psychoanalysis excuses rape and vilifies rape victims by giving a cast-iron defence case to each and every man suspected of rape) and with legal writings (in which heterogeneous views of intention, motive and sexual behaviour are woven together around the basic concept of consent). This chapter attempts to unravel the issues raised and confused by many of the writings drawn from these three heterogeneous discourses.

My argument hinges on the consequences that flow from distinguishing between rape and seduction, so important in legal practice. Yet I examine this primarily from the perspective of psychoanalysis, in which the distinction between rape and seduction is seemingly ignored, in favour of the interminable ambiguities of seduction. It is precisely this preoccupation with the ambiguous and the ambivalent that seems to be recognised by feminist writers on rape as antithetic to their certainties, which embody a hasty temptation to regard seduction as just rape under another name. In psychoanalysis, on the other hand, the tendency is the opposite: an inability to recognise rape as falling within the field of the analyst's operation and action. Both tendencies elide the distinction between rape and seduction. It is this elision that the chapter explores.

Rape and psychoanalysis

We may thank the legacy of Freudian psychology for fostering a totally inaccurate popular conception of rape . . . the serious failure of the Freudians stemmed from their rigid unwillingness to make a moral judgment.[1]

Susan Brownmiller puts her finger on the problems raised by linking rape with psychoanalysis, as she does with so many other questions relating to rape in her influential work, *Against our will*. Yet within her discussion of rape and psychoanalysis there is an interesting contradiction that this chapter will aim to explore. Brownmiller recognises the paucity of material on rape produced by Freud and the Freudians, and yet claims that their legacy fostered 'a totally inaccurate popular conception of rape'. How can both these claims be true?

Perhaps we should first enquire whether it is true that the great modern authority on sexuality said nothing about rape and rapists. *The Concordance to the Standard edition of the complete psychological works of Sigmund Freud* records only one usage of the word 'rape' – and that is an 'attempted rape'. There is certainly no case history of a rapist, nor of a rape victim, in the fifty or so cases listed in the Index of Cases. Rather, it is through the psychology of women propounded by Freudians that an influentially misleading conception of rape is said to have arisen, and in particular, for Brownmiller and others, from the work of Freud's close disciple, Helene Deutsch.[2]

Men have always raped women, but it wasn't until the advent of Sigmund Freud and his followers that the male ideology of rape began to rely on the tenet that rape was something women desired.[3]

Brownmiller reconstructs a chain of arguments stemming from Freud's work, elaborated upon brilliantly by Deutsch as her 'dictum of the hysterical, masochistic female',[4] and finding their way into the dominant Freudian school of criminology of the 1950s, which essentially *does away* with the crime of rape by proving that there are no victims. In Brownmiller's portrayal of the argument, Freudian psychology provided a scientific *carte blanche* for anyone wishing to doubt the word of a rape victim. Feminine sexuality was by nature masochistic; hence rape could not take place since it encountered female masochistic nature and was immediately accepted by it.[5] It is this argument that feeds into the four 'deadly male myths of rape', in particular the belief that 'ALL WOMEN WANT TO BE RAPED'.[6]

But, of course, there is also the other side of the coin – the rapist. How has Freudian theory presented him? Certainly, there are very few accounts of the psychoanalysis of a rapist, but there are a number of psychologically oriented studies of the rapist-in-prison (no doubt a different creature from the rapist-at-large). It is these studies that Brownmiller castigates for their moral neutrality. She quotes without comment – as if the preposterous and demeaning character of the argument were obvious for all to see – from a study of the *wives* of rapists, which aimed to show that the sexual frustration these wives induced in their husbands was one of the factors motivating rape, since they elicited from their husbands 'a displaced attempt to force a seductive but rejecting mother into submission'.[7] With a rhetorical flourish, Brownmiller abandons, with relief, the individual-oriented, clinical, psychopathological studies of rapists for the more modern sociological studies, which give us, 'above all, hard, cold statistical facts about crime'.[8]

Such treatment of the Freudian criminological literature, by no means restricted to Brownmiller, is designed to head off argument concerning her major contention that the act of rape is committed by ordinary men on ordinary women. The profile of the rapist is not to be cordoned off into the specialist field of the psychiatrist since the 'typical American perpetrator of forcible rape is little more than an aggressive, hostile youth who chooses to do violence to women'.[9] Brownmiller, and many other feminist writers since, are concerned to demonstrate that the rapist is not capable of being distinguished from ordinary men by his character structure, or his early development, or his relations with women, in the same way that the rape victim is not to be distinguished from ordinary women by her disposition to hysteria, to masochistic fantasy and to telling lies. The argument aims to render void both strands of a psychological account of the rapist, the one pertaining to him, the other pertaining to his victim. Freudian theory is seen to be the main support for both of these psychological accounts. Indeed, the implication of this argument is that *any* psychological account of the facts of rape, whether it be Freudian or any other, is potentially dangerous and misleading, since it will obscure the conclusion that:

police-blotter rapists are dreary and banal . . . Rape is a dull, blunt, ugly act committed by punk kids . . . not by charming, witty, unscrupulous, heroic, sensual rakes, or by timid souls deprived of 'normal' sexual outlet, or by *supermenschen* possessed of uncontrollable lust.[10]

These dreary punks have as their 'historic mission the perpetuation of male domination over women by force'.

There are a number of responses one could make to this line of argument. The first, and least fertile, is to defend the psychoanalytic concept of masochism from certain misunderstandings.[11] It is possible to retrieve psychoanalytic accounts from these criticisms without disputing the detrimental effects psychological and psychopathological theories have had upon discussion of rape. Brownmiller herself, like many other feminists, has complex reactions to Deutsch's 'sombre' view of sex and feminine sexuality, and to Freud's version of the feminine psyche. The feminists sense a truth which they usually repudiate in the form: this applies to what happens now, in patriarchal society. One can also show how Brownmiller misreads both Freud and Deutsch: where Brownmiller simply states that Freud put forward the 'dogma that women are masochistic by nature and crave the "lust for pain"',[12] one could easily show that she is misunderstanding Freud, whose discussion of feminine masochism is entirely based, as he, perhaps ironically, notes, on work with male patients. He found that fantasies (and sexual acts) of a feminine masochistic character are those that 'place the subject in a characteristically female situation; they signify, that is, being castrated [i.e. 'the wish to have a passive (feminine) sexual relation with the father'], or copulated with, or giving birth to a baby'.[13]

The overall details, however, are not what is at issue. Brownmiller's has been the strongest, but by no means the only, voice taking issue with any intrusion of psychoanalytic ideas into discussion of rape. There is a sense of a real threat here, even though psychoanalysis does not talk of rape. Why?

Unconscious motivation

There is one, seemingly insignificant, passage in Freud's works which deals with sexual attacks on women. It appears as a footnote in *The psychopathology of everyday life* (1901), in the chapter on 'Bungled actions'. Freud is discussing whether 'half-intentional self-injury' exists, and proposes a model in which an unconscious intention to self-injury or self-destruction may make skilful use of a threat to life in order to manifest itself. He then turns to suicide:

Even a *conscious* intention of committing suicide chooses its time, means and opportunity; and it is quite in keeping with this that an *unconscious* intention should wait for a precipitating occasion which can take over a part of the causation and, by engaging the subject's defensive forces, can liberate the intention from their pressure.

There then follows a footnote:

After all, the case is no different from that of a sexual assault upon a woman, where the man's attack cannot be repelled by her full muscular strength because a portion of her unconscious impulses meets the attack with encouragement. It is said, as we know, that a situation of this kind *paralyses* a woman's strength; all we need do is to add the reasons for this paralysis. To that extent the ingenious judgement delivered by Sancho Panza as governor of his island is psychologically unjust (*Don Quixote*, part 2, chapter 45). A woman dragged a man before the judge alleging he had robbed her of her honour by violence. In compensation Sancho gave her a full purse of money which he took from the accused; but after the woman's departure he gave him permission to pursue her and snatch the purse back again from her. The two returned struggling, the woman priding herself on the fact that the villain had not been able to take the purse from her. Thereupon Sancho declared: 'If you had defended your honour with half the determination with which you have defended this purse, the man could not have robbed you of it.'[14]

The complexity and allusiveness of the argument here should not prevent us from extracting the important point from it. Freud is proposing a model whereby a conscious desire to repel a man's assault is subverted by an unconscious impulse to meet it with encouragement: hence the well-known paralysis of women when sexually attacked.[15] But the point in quoting the story from *Don Quixote* is to show that discovering such an unconscious impulse at work in a given case of *successful* sexual assault is *not* a reason for declaring that the woman had not been raped. The presence (or, for that matter, the *absence*) of an unconscious desire for sexual relations is not relevant to the question of whether the assault was against the woman's will or not. One might add: how could the question of consent be resolved by the existence of such an unconscious desire, since, in the Freudian universe, everybody has such unconscious desires? As Freud had argued in the penultimate pages of *The interpretation of dreams*, despite declaring himself unqualified to answer the question as to the ethical significance of suppressed wishes, 'would it not be right to bear in mind Plato's dictum that the virtuous man is content to *dream* what a wicked man really *does*? . . . we shall have to conclude, no doubt, that *psychical* reality is a particular form of existence not to be confused with *material* reality'.[16] Similarity, one does not hold a woman responsible for the unconscious desire for sexual contact made manifest in the paralysis she evinces when assaulted.

It should be noted that the force of this argument does not depend upon whether or not one believes that women, or some women, or any women, have such unconscious desires. The argument applies to all cases in which unconscious desires that are different from conscious desires exist and manifest themselves on specific, stressful occasions. There is also an immediate corollary to the argument: whatever unconscious desires a subject may possess should play no role whatsoever in evaluating whether they did or did not consciously wish such and such an event to take place. Or, to put it another way, the domain of the unconscious is entirely separate from the domain of the will. And, it should be noted, from the nineteenth century onwards, the will, or consent, has been taken to be the crucial touchstone by which the existence of the act of rape has been judged.

So, the sole and unique passage in which Freud discussed the question of the adjudication of a case of sexual assault allows one to construct a clear argument as to why psychoanalysis is *irrelevant* to the class of questions raised by juridical investigations into rape. We also gain a sense of the differences between Freud and those of his followers who did enter into discussions of the motivations of rape victims: for Freud, such investigations were flawed since they did not take into account the difference between a conscious and an unconscious motive or impulse. As he put it:

the pathogenic conflict in neurotics between mental impulses is not to be confused with a normal struggle between mental impulses both of which are on the same psychological footing . . . the disputants can no more come to grips than, in the familiar simile, a polar bear and a whale. A true decision can only be reached when they both meet on common ground.[17]

The temptation of Sigmund Freud

Many of his followers, however, regarded the discovery of unconscious impulses and the demonstration of their effects in symptoms, character traits etc. as giving an imperialistic licence for according them a privilege *over and above* conscious motives. For them, there was only one 'common ground' that counted, which might just as well be a court room as a couch. For Freud, psychoanalysis is the study of where conscious and unconscious motives fail to meet: he could give an account of the paralysis of victims of assault, but this would not lead him to commit the *injustice* (the word is his) of weighing such motives in the scales of justice. However, for many of his followers, psychoanalysis vouchsafed a *disregard* of conscious motives, since they subscribed to a view of unconscious motives as being the 'real' motives behind any and every act.

This distinction aids us in considering another question that has bedevilled discussions of rape: the relevance of women's rape fantasies. Many feminists have written as if the very *existence* of rape fantasies were an embarrassment, a collective shame of women, as if admitting their existence might give hostile men, or even simple sceptics, cause for returning to one of the male myths that all women (or, more moderately, those women who have rape fantasies) want to be raped. On this point, Brownmiller astutely keeps the arguments concerning unconscious and conscious rape fantasies entirely separate. With respect to conscious rape fantasies, she has little in the way of argument besides the statement:

The rape fantasy exists in women as a man-made iceberg. It can be destroyed – by feminism.[18]

This statement seems to me only to repeat the disowning of responsibility that lies at the heart of the rape fantasy itself. It perpetuates, rather than examines, the common fantasy that sexuality is introduced into the woman from the 'outside' by an external force ('man-made'). That is, it refuses the paradox of masochism (how can pain be pleasurable?) by regarding as a ridiculous imposition the question, how can something against my will be something I desire?

The resolution of the problem for feminists anxious to keep the seemingly incriminating fact of rape fantasies at a distance seems to me to be the following: taking responsibility for one's fantasies is not the same sort of mental act as taking responsibility for one's actions. It is much more like taking responsibility for one's memories, or for the conditions of one's early childhood, than for one's projects and conscious aims. If it is objected that psychoanalysis, as I have discussed it above, does not legitimate taking a rape victim's unconscious rape fantasies into account in considerations of rape as it actually happens (indeed quite the opposite – and now I seem to be arguing that one can reduce the conceptual tension associated with rape fantasies by taking responsibility for them), the objection allows me to point out the difference between the third party (police, court, friends, family) imputing 'responsibility' for a rape to a rape victim simply because they infer that she was prey to fantasies of violation or of 'irresponsible' sexuality, and the case I am considering here, in which the subject 'recognises as his or her own' a fantasy, desire or memory. To be sure, the act of taking responsibility for one's memories affects one's projects and aims (that, after all, is precisely the goal of psychoanalytic therapy), but these projects and aims will not be faithful reproductions or blind repetitions of the past. Turning a rape fantasy to good use is no more likely to result in a project of being raped than turning a vengeful fantasy of suicide to good use will result in one's death.

Glanville Williams addressed these questions in his classic textbook, *Criminal law. The general part* (1953). In a section on unconscious motives, he recognised that the discovery of unconscious motives (and he here cites the chapter of Freud's *Psychopathology of everyday life* that the Don Quixote story comes from) presents difficult problems for legal thinking about intention. It must be said that the various arguments he employs do not sit well together. Williams is inclined to set aside unconscious motivation '(1) because it is difficult to prove satisfactorily, (2) because we have little knowledge of how far the threat of a sanction can influence the unconscious'.[19] However, he goes on to give an example of a neurotic symptom, arguing that

it is not brought about by conscious intention, it is concealed from awareness; and it is therefore regarded as involuntary . . . a man is not criminally responsible for what he does in a *dream*. This would be so even if the dream happened to coincide with a conscious desire. The *mens rea* of a dream is not a *mens rea* for which a man is punishable; it is only the waking consciousness that involves criminal culpability.[20]

The argument is very close to that advanced by Freud. However, something goes amiss when Williams comes to address the question of proving the absence of consent in rape cases, in his *Textbook of criminal law* (1978). Having recognised that 'the facts of life make consent to sexual intercourse a hazy concept', he argues, first, that

69

'Many complaints of rape are false, since the woman in fact consented.' Secondly, he raises the question of the peculiar character of female sexuality:

That some women enjoy fantasies of being raped is well authenticated, and they may welcome a masterful advance while putting up a token resistance . . . [He cites Deutsch at this point.] This possibility needs consideration where the man was well known to the woman and where it is clear that she was not intimidated. If in these circumstances the woman failed to use all means open to her to repel the man, including shouting for help, the jury may well think it unsafe to convict him. Obviously the argument has no force where the man made an express threat or used *real* violence, for these are inconsistent with a *merely pretended* rape . . . One woman faced with a rapist intruder reported that her limbs seemed to go like jelly – though in the particular case she put up a resistance. Another confessed that her abhorrence of violence was so great that she preferred to submit than to attack. There is no evidence that juries are unduly prone to take the woman's non-resistance in such circumstances either as consent or as giving the man a credible defence of belief in consent.[21]

This passage pays careful attention to considerations of unconscious interference with a woman's capacity to resist (exactly Freud's point about paralysis due to unconscious interference), but it slides from recognising the existence of rape *fantasies* to inferring from their existence a woman's conscious consent. It is beside the point whether a woman enjoyed the masterly advance or not; what is at issue is whether she consented. And in the final quoted sentence, Williams recognises that assent is not the same as the absence of dissent, and it is the absence of assent which the law regards as sufficient to lead to conviction.

The scenario evoked is one in which both man and woman are play-acting at rape. Williams is evoking a seduction masquerading as rape. Yet if the seduction misfires, if the woman does not consent, then there is no reason for attenuating the degree of her non-consent (in any case, a legally impossible procedure), simply because it started off as play. Horseplay may well always end in tears, but a seduction that ends in rape is still rape.

We thus see that Williams is sensitive to the limits of psychoanalytic arguments about the significance of unconscious states of mind (including here unconscious consent, if needs be, although there are good grounds for believing that the unconscious is beneath the age of consent, given that Freud maintained that in the unconscious there is no negation – and hence no affirmation of the sort required in law). However, Williams does not maintain this conceptual vigilance when the question of rape fantasies is at issue. There are parallel arguments in the law of assault, where consent to bodily harm is not taken to be legally viable. The analogy may be extended, since it is clear that certain forms of violence can be consented to: in boxing, for instance. But these are highly ritualised and controlled forms of assent to assault, corresponding to the play-acting account of the masterly advance and the token resistance. The question is, what are the limits of this game, and if one of the parties stops playing, can the other validly claim that the signal to end the game is a part of the game itself? As we shall see, psychoanalysis does venture on to this territory, but Freud was clear that invoking unconscious fantasies to remove responsibility from the assailant is not sanctioned by his concept of the unconscious.

The concept of conflict

One can, however, go one step further. Not only does psychoanalysis in Freud's version specifically exclude itself from weighing the impact of unconscious desire on conscious states of mind; there is also an immiscibility of the topics of rape and psychoanalysis of a more fundamental character. Put simply, I want to argue that psychoanalytic discourse and legal discourse are entirely antipathetic.

In his study of the use of the insanity defence in nineteenth-century murder trials, Roger Smith describes the conceptual confusions of doctors and lawyers alike in their attempt to integrate a psychiatric conception of mental states with a legal conception.[22] Psychiatrists often conceived of psychiatric descriptions as replacing traditional legal categories, such as *mens rea* (the legal term for the guilty state of mind). To enlightened positivistic psychiatrists, it seemed that the simple and crude, all-or-nothing categories required by law were anachronistic and inhumane.

The conflict between the two modes of discourse still exists, and has recently re-emerged in the context of notorious sexual murders, specifically the cases of the Boston Strangler and the Yorkshire Ripper. The function of court cases as public spectacle, reaffirming, or affirming with special emphasis, the guilty man as morally abhorrent, has once again become of special importance. This is also the sense in which, as we have seen, Freudians are reproached for their unwillingness to make a moral judgement. The argument always seems to be, either mad or bad. Yet, as our discussion above made clear, Freud was careful to distinguish moral judgements according to whether they were based on conscious or unconscious contents. For him, 'mad' and 'bad' work on entirely different axes. Yet it is of course true that if one looks to Freudian theory for moral support, one is sure to be disappointed, and with reason: its claim to avoid moral positions one way or the other is a jealously guarded privilege through which it offers asylum to its clients.

However, rape has become the site for a social and ethical crisis associated with the women's liberation movement. Disappointment with liberalism, with live-and-let-live attitudes to ethics, with radical politics and with the defence of liberties (especially those of the rape defendant) at all costs has included disillusionment with any institution that fails to offer an ethical or indeed spiritual lead. In this area, psychoanalysis is doubly offensive, since its very existence stems from an a-moralism, a refusal of ethical positions. (This refusal stems, as I will show later, from the discovery of the 'transference'.) What is more, the ethical crisis is often couched in terms of a struggle for the recognition of absolute and inviolable rights. For some, what is offensive is the imagined condoning of rape, by psychoanalysis or other discourses, through invoking the universal presence of rape fantasies or the naturally masochistic nature of feminine sexuality. But for others, the issue of rape symbolises any restriction of the right of women to sexual self-determination. Rape is the principal violation of and the principal challenge to this right: it is the strategic site for the battle that will determine the course of the war.

Psychoanalysis turns its back on social conflict; or, more accurately, it brackets off social conflict, conflict *between* individuals, to highlight the conflict *within* individuals. If the iconography of rape is ideally suited for an allegorical portrayal of social conflict, and of sexual conflict, psychoanalysis can find no or little use for rape as metaphor, model or theme. In the Greek ceramics that Froma Zeitlin discusses,[23] the conflict is between *demand* (on the part of the god, usually male) and *resistance*. Similarly, as Norman Bryson demonstrates, in his 'Two narratives of rape in the visual arts', rape provides a code for developing founding myths, although the 'privatisation' or internalisation of the experience of rape leads away from this function, sexualising rape and bringing it closer to a seductive, fantasy-rich representation. Psychoanalysis, however, both as theory and practice, avoids conflict between parties, replacing it with a two-fold strategy. First, the theme of intra-psychic conflict, e.g. between the ego and the id, in which the id might well 'rape' the ego (Freud's term, in an early draft, was 'overwhelm', a term that also crops up in *The sexual offender and his offenses*, by the much-criticised psychoanalytically influenced Benjamin Karpman). Secondly, any conflict that is seen to exist between analyst and patient is interpreted as a repetition of a past conflict or a present unconscious conflict.

The exclusively intra-psychic conflict model of psychoanalysis has no place for rape, because it is solely concerned with the intra-subjective. Equally important, however, is the fact that rape cannot permit any hint of intra-subjective conflict to be admitted. If there is evidence that the victim was in a state of inner conflict, not attributable to the threat of force or duress exerted by the assailant, the prima facie case for rape is considerably attenuated. If it is thought the woman sets a 'price' on her consent,[24] if it is consent that can be measured against some other good, if it is a consent that can be argued with, or around, the case may well be set aside.[25] For instance, the police marked as 'unfounded' a case in which a woman consented to various sexual acts, believing that the man had agreed to stop short of vaginal intercourse: 'I did not want to have intercourse with him as the word is out that he has something wrong with him.'[26] In this case, the fact that she experienced orgasm, both before and during intercourse, probably had some influence on the police assessment of the immutability and intransigency of her lack of consent, despite this factor's being strictly beside the point.

This latter case might well be seen to illustrate the psychoanalytic category of ambivalence: this woman both had good reasons for withholding consent and did in fact withhold her verbal consent, while having an inclination to engage in the act. It is this perception of ambivalence, of competing and conflicting motivations, that seems to deprive the category of 'without her consent' of its necessarily absolute character. Note, however, that this is not an instance of *psychoanalytic* ambivalence, since there is no recourse to the notion of an unconscious impulse. Moreover, as we have seen, such a recourse is an illegitimate application of the psychoanalytic hypothesis of the unconscious, or of ambivalence. But it is exactly this sort of case that has earned psychoanalysis a bad reputation in the rape literature: its categories are seen to encourage the perception of mitigated or less than whole-hearted lack of consent. The crucial point is that, legally speaking, the concept of consent is an all-or-nothing one. To secure a rape conviction, the only psychological (if it is properly described as psychological rather than legal) state of the victim's mind that bears examination is her state either of consent or non-consent.

Such a presupposition about mental states parallels the controversial considerations of *mens rea* in murder cases (though many other crimes involve complex consideration of *mens rea*; in particular, the notorious 1975 *Morgan* rape case, discussed by Temkin,[27] was very important within 'subjectivist' legal thinking in general). But such presuppositions are incompatible with those of psychoanalysis. To take one example: Freud noted in his *Dora* case history that the inner consistency of the life history the patient recounts is a means for differential diagnosis. Where there are inner inconsistencies, or manifest gaps, the diagnosis is probably hysteria. Where there are no such inconsistencies, the physician should look for an organic nervous disease. The assumption of psychoanalysis is that inner states of conflict manifest themselves in neurosis, and that these manifestations will always appear as faults, breaks, jumps in the life story recounted. But if there are any breaks in the narrative of a rape, if there is a gap in which the question of consent remains unsettled one way or the other, the police and/or the court are liable to regard the rape as unfounded.

A theory of rape?

It may be true that the word 'rape' does not figure in Freud's vocabulary, but he did give prominence to sexual assault as a widespread trauma in the aetiology of the neuroses, especially in his early work. In this respect he has been regarded as an early precursor – and traitor – of the recent spate of researches, conducted very much in parallel with detailed work on rape, on the sexual abuse of children.[28] If we were to follow the recent accounts of Florence Rush and Jeffrey Masson, we would regard Freud as one of the earliest discoverers of the widespread sexual abuse of children, an early pioneer of understanding the extent of the permanent damage this caused to their psyches, but also one of those responsible, through failure of nerve, cowardice and self-deception, for engineering a cover-up on behalf of the perpetrators, taken to be male, of this crime.

In the 1890s, Freud slowly works his way towards a full-blown theory of neurosis as resulting from the after effects of sexual abuse in childhood.[29] Beginning in May 1893, when he notes the absence in one specific case of memories of sexual abuse combined with things seen or heard and only half-understood,[30] by November

1895 he is actively searching for 'infantile abuse' in his patients, both male and female: excitedly, he writes to his friend Fliess that one of his 'male hysterics . . . has given me what I was waiting for'.[31] In 1896 he went into print with his theory in an article entitled 'The aetiology of hysteria'. In January 1897, he writes that the period when 'sexual abuse' in childhood brings about neuroses in later life covers the first three years of life.[32] In 1897, he hypothesises that, as children grow older, the father treats them with more circumspection, so that the 'seducers' in such instances are older brothers and sisters.

But on his return from his summer holidays in 1897, Freud confesses the great secret that had been dawning on him for some months, namely that he no longer believes in this theory: he implies that he had never had an explicit case of sexual assault in childhood that adequately accounted for the structure and character of the adult neurosis his patient presented him with. None the less, though abandoning this theory, he retains much of the language: in July 1898, he is still referring to the 'seducer' when giving his interpretation of a work of the novelist Ferdinand Meyer, *Die Richterin*, and in his own analysis, in October 1897, he refers to his childhood nurse as his 'instructress in sexual matters'.

In place of the theory that every neurosis can be traced back to the effects of infantile sexual abuse, Freud argued that the infantile scenes still had a causative function, but that it did not matter whether they were real or imagined scenes. This discovery of the importance of fantasy opened up the way to the recognition that infantile sexual fantasy includes elements that are not usually present in adult sexual activity, involving the anus and the mouth. Beyond that, Freud recognised that the great theme of childhood fantasy is the fantasised relations to the parents – what he was later to call 'the Oedipus complex'. Most historians of psychoanalysis thus regard the abandonment of what Freud had called his 'seduction theory' as opening up the possibility of the discovery of two fundamental elements of Freud's later theory: infantile sexuality and the centrality of the Oedipus complex.

Yet a number of writers, including Jeffrey Masson and Alice Miller,[33] have regretted this action of abandoning the early seduction theory. They think that the turning away from the reality of sexual abuse – which both entailed and was a consequence of this abandoning – was really a turning away from an unpalatable reality that Freud did not *want* to recognise. They, together with others who are less interested in psychoanalytic theory and more interested in determining the reality of infantile sexual abuse, claim that the extent of such abuse is enormously underestimated, as are its long-term effects. Such claims are often linked with the recent concern with rape, sometimes seen as a modern epidemic or alternatively as an age-old consequence of a patriarchal, or male-dominated, social system. What I now want to examine is this seeming contradiction: Freud is said both to have ignored rape in a quite remarkable fashion, given his extensive concern for sexuality, while others have claimed him as a precursor, albeit a cowardly one, of the present concern with the widespread damage caused by rape and infantile sexual abuse.

The seduction theory

As we have seen, Freud did not call his theory the 'rape theory', nor did he use the word 'rape'. Instead, he employed the term 'seduction'. The incidents this theory referred to were sometimes called 'abuse' (*Missbrauch*) or 'passive sexual experience'; but the most frequent term was 'seduction' (*Verführung*) or, just as frequently, the verb form, and often the term 'seducer'. Why did Freud employ this term?

It is not straining the historical or textual evidence to claim that the reason Freud employed the term 'seduction' instead of 'rape' was that the traumatic effects of the event *when remembered* arose from the events not being experienced as rape. Instead, the subject's reactions to the memory were ones that suggested his or her implication in the event: they might feel shame, guilt or tenderness. By 1895, Freud's cases had convinced him that it was always *sexual* fright that characterised the key trauma in the neuroses. The original trauma consisted in an adult performing sexual acts with a child. What distinguished Freud's theory from Charcot's and others', however, was his claim that the trauma became *effective* in causing a neurosis only by acting as a memory: the fright occurred only later, on the occasion of the second, seemingly innocuous scene. It was not the trauma that was 'traumatic' but rather the *memory* of the trauma, the trauma as memory.[34]

The idea that a distinctive process of remembering was a crucial part of the pathological process predated both the sexual thesis and the infantile thesis. This importance of remembering was bound up with the process of discovering the trauma: tracing a set of memories, conceived of as a chain or sequence, back through the past in search of an experience that would be judged appropriate to count as an original trauma. At first, this process led to events at the age of puberty. At this point Freud raised an objection to regarding these memories as being the efficaciously 'traumatic' ones:

In some cases, no doubt, we are concerned with experiences which must be regarded as severe traumas – an attempted rape, perhaps, which reveals to the immature girl at a blow all the brutality of sexual desire, or the involuntary witnessing of sexual acts between parents, which at one and the same time uncovers unsuspected ugliness and wounds childish and moral sensibilities alike, and so on. But in other cases the experiences are astonishingly trivial . . . For [one] young lady, simply hearing a riddle which suggested an obscene answer had been enough to provoke the first anxiety attack and with it to start the illness.[35]

What is more, he noted that in some cases the experiences were 'actually innocent': hence he was driven to look for the appropriate memories further back than puberty. He was quite explicit that a necessary condition of these experiences being traumatic was that they be bodily or organic in some respect; 'sexual experiences affecting the subject's own body – of *sexual intercourse* (in the wider sense)'.

However, pushing back towards the period of childhood, 'a period before the development of sexual life',[36] only confirmed the centrality of memory:

And since infantile experiences with a sexual content could after all only exert a psychical effect through their *memory-traces*, would not this view be a welcome amplification of the finding of psychoanalysis *that hysterical symptoms can only arise with the co-operation of memories?*[37]

Freud highlights this specific feature later, when he reflects that

we are not accustomed to the notion of powers emanating from a mnemic image which were absent from the real impression.[38]

In dealing with the vigorous objections he anticipated to this hypothesis, Freud recounted how venturing back into infancy had obliged him to reflect on the murky conditions of belief, lack of conviction and the grounds for verisimilitude of memories. Yet his response was already a sophisticated, some might say sophistical, one:

While they are recalling these infantile experiences to consciousness, they suffer under the most violent sensations, of which they are ashamed and which they try to conceal; and, even after they have gone through them once more in such a convincing manner, they still attempt to withhold belief from them, by emphasizing the fact that, unlike what happens in the case of other forgotten material, they have no feeling of remembering the scenes.

This latter piece of behaviour seems to provide conclusive proof. Why should patients assure me so emphatically of their unbelief, if what they want to discredit is something which – from whatever motive – they themselves have invented?[39]

Freud outlined other sources of confirmation or support for his claim as to the reality of the scene of sexual assault: the uniformity of the scenes described, the inclusion of details in the scenes whose significance the patient could not have known otherwise, the fact that the case-history suddenly acquires a clear-cut, logically structured and self-evident character once the details of the scene are placed at the centre. The one 'really unassailable' proof would be the corroboration of the reality of the event by a third party who had participated in it. He cites two such cases.

Having disposed of the twin objections that childhood seduction is either too frequent or too infrequent an event to be the cause of neurosis,[40] Freud then proceeds to give an account of the material at his disposal, asserting that 'it seems to me certain that our children are far more often exposed to sexual assaults than the few precautions taken by parents in this connection would lead us to expect'.[41] He divides his cases into three groups, according to the character of the other person providing the stimulation. The first category was assault by strangers who engaged in isolated acts of abuse. 'In these assaults, there was no question of the child's consent, and the first effect of the experience was preponderantly one of fright.'[42] The third category was seductions of children by children; he lays down the rule that this can occur only if one of them has previously been seduced by an adult, the scene being an exact repetition of the original seduction. The most important class, however, is the second, much more frequent than abuse by strangers, in which an adult looking after the child 'has initiated the child into sexual intercourse and has maintained a regular love relationship with it – a love relationship, moreover, with its mental side developed – which has often lasted for years'.[43]

It is at this point that a different tone enters Freud's paper. Until this point he might well have been thought to have been sustaining the moral tone and engaging in the moral judgement that Brownmiller found so singularly and regrettably lacking in the writings of the Freudians. Freud does say:

For the idea of these infantile sexual scenes is very repellent to the feelings of a sexually normal individual; they include all the abuses known to debauched and impotent persons, among whom the buccal cavity and the rectum are misused for sexual purposes.[44]

But, in the next sentence, he puts himself at a distance from this position of moral distaste:

For physicians, astonishment at this soon gives way to a complete understanding.

Replacing amazement and repulsion by understanding, rather than indignation, allows Freud to describe the sexual abuse as an important and complex *relationship* between the adult and the child (or between the two children):

All the singular conditions under which the ill-matched pair conduct their love-relations – on the one hand the adult, who cannot escape his share in the mutual dependence necessarily entailed by a sexual relationship, and who is yet armed with complete authority and the right to punish, and can exchange the one role for the other to the uninhibited satisfaction of his moods, and on the other hand the child, who in his helplessness is at the mercy of this arbitrary will, who is prematurely aroused to every kind of sensibility and exposed to every sort of disappointment, and whose performance of the sexual activities assigned to him is often interrupted by his imperfect control of his natural needs – all these grotesque and yet tragic incongruities reveal themselves as stamped upon the later development of the individual and of his neurosis . . .[45]

Here, Freud was specifically pointing to a class of cases in which the question of the child's consent did not arise; here, the predominant immediate effect or affect was not fright. In most of his cases of 'sexual abuse', the relationship is of the sort described above, in which (as recent commentators on child abuse have hastened to point out) the question of the child's consent is beside the point.[46] In Freud's cases, the relationship is as complex as one between adults: right from the start, before he had developed the concept of infantile sexuality, Freud was writing as if the child is as capable as an adult of complex relations involving sexual intercourse, 'with its mental side developed'.

Let us pause at this point and take stock. Freud may well have been an early discoverer of the surprising prevalence of childhood abuse, but what he focused on was the fact that it was *memories* of these events that were of significance to him as a neurologist–psychotherapist. What is more, the sexual abuses frequently, and most importantly for their later effects, included a complex relationship between child and adult. Consent is beside the point here. To be sure, Freud recognises the absolute authority which the adult exerts over the child. Yet it is the *dialectic* of authority and servitude, of power and helplessness, of mutual dependence, of expectation and disappointment, of shame and embarrassment, which characterises the relationship *and which leaves its mark on the child*.

It is clearer now why Freud called his theory of neurosis the seduction theory rather than the rape theory. In his account, it is not so much the presexual sexual shock (his phrase) or the fright induced in the child that is aetiologically significant. Rather, it is the implication of the child in a world that is foreign to it, a world which it is none the less destined, come puberty, to be obliged to make its own. 'Seduction' is etymologically a 'leading away'; Freud's theory is close to this sense – with a difference: the child is more properly being 'led towards'. What children flee from through repression is what the fleeing runners on the Greek vases described by Zeitlin in her 'Configurations of rape in Greek myth' may be fleeing from – the loss of childhood.

So Freud's theory was never a simple cause–effect model of traumatic sexual abuse followed by neurotic effects. Three features of his seduction theory already point to psychological complexity well *before* he discarded the seduction theory, well before he ceased to attach importance to the reality of the infantile scenes. First, neurosis only arises when an infantile scene gives rise to an unconscious memory that is defended against in puberty; if the memory is not unconscious, defence has no pathological effect. Secondly, he was emphasising that the coherence and inner consistency of the patient's life story (present symptoms leading back to early adolescent memories and traumata, which themselves lead back to the unconscious infantile scenes) was an important proof of the reality of the infantile scene.

With hindsight, we can see that this second argument has little force: it proves the necessity of invoking a scene in early childhood, with such and such characteristic detail, but the reality of the scene is incidental to the criteria of consistency and coherence. What Freud's argument actually proves is that the patients did not *arbitrarily* invent the scenes: the detail of the scene has a logical or associative connection with later memories and symptoms. Its reality was first and foremost psychic, and only secondarily real in the sense of 'having occurred *out there*'.

Thirdly, he was as interested in the inter-subjective dialectic of adult and child as he was in the effects on the child of a sexual experience for which he or she was unprepared. Fright might well have been an immediate effect, but for Freud the necessary condition was that the scene become unconscious, and fright was not closely connected with that process. More to the point, the interest in the dialectic of adult and child pointed somewhat imprecisely, but with far-reaching implications, towards focusing less on what the adult did to the child than on what elements in the child's complex response to the adult left traces. In Freud's account, the child is not a passive *tabula rasa* whose surface an adult violently breaches. Freud diverges from the original, Greek sense of trauma, meaning the breaching of the skin by external violence, by reconceptualising it as a trace, a mark, like a tattoo, a lasting memorial of a communication. Precisely because the memory of a complex relationship was from the beginning of his work so central, the child's desires, fears, shames and guilts are Freud's focus.

The psychological complexity of Freud's account, even before he decides to regard the distinction between reality and fantasy as not applicable to memories of early childhood, entails that the shift from reality to fantasy was not such a marked break as it has seemed to many commentators (amongst whom Freud sometimes included himself). Indeed, the formulation I have been employing – *disregarding* the distinction between fantasy and reality, which is by no means the same as taking reality to be fantasy – indicates why Freud's technique was from then on to place the utmost *trust* in what his patients told him, but *without deciding* whether the stories they recounted described a real event. The event was now bracketed off, with its reality-sign (*Realitätszeichen*) regarded as an added feature, rather like quotation marks in the written reporting of speech.

Here we see how psychoanalytic discourse differs so radically from legal discourses about rape. In practice, rape cases centre on two questions conveniently grouped by lawyers under the headings external and internal evidence. The external evidence pertains to the act itself: whether it took place, and who were the parties involved in the act. The internal evidence pertains to the reality of the state of mind, *as remembered*. Note that memory is crucial here, since implicit in the crime of rape is the notion that the victim was capable of consenting and of *maintaining* that state.[47] Moreover it is crucial that the memory pertain to a real event at the time (and not to a before or an after).

81

Freud's seduction theory, then, was never a theory of the consequences of the rape of children: it was a theory of the pathogenic effects of memories of sexual relationships in child-hood. In this sense, it was akin to those studies of the long-term effects of rape on victims which have emphasised that the victim often has the feeling of being implicated in the attack.

> She wonders if she resisted actively enough, if she used every possible avenue of escape, or if she cried out loudly enough. In these cases, the victim harbors doubts about the appropriateness of her behavior. She wonders if, perhaps, her behavior was tantamount to consent even though she refused the encounter.[48]

Freud was more concerned with the effects on the general psychic economy of guilt and doubt than whether the victim had, in effect, consented. Whether or not, in actual fact, the victim had consented was a matter for the law courts, not the psychoanalyst. Inevitably, however, we will be obliged to return to the contentious question of consent.

Freud's lack of interest in the adult 'assailant' and the general issue of assigning moral blame would necessarily seem to follow from the fact that his professional interest lay in the patient who was recounting these stories, under severe internal pressure, with help and 'pressure' from the analyst. By its very nature, Freud's contract with the patient did not lead him to an interest in the adult of those early years, the 'seducer'. The three factors mentioned above, together with the professional fact that his client (as opposed, say, to a lawyer's) was the patient reporting the facts of sexual abuse, entailed that discarding the seduction theory and shifting the emphasis to fantasy was not such a major step.

Transference and seduction

I will now turn to another sphere of Freud's work that is crucial to understanding why his seduction theory, which seemed so close to being a study of the effects of the 'rape' of children, was in fact something entirely different; the new factor is the transference. Thinking ahistorically for one moment, the problem I wish to address can be simply stated. The major feature of psychoanalytic practice as distinctively conceived of and organised by Freud is the development of the transference: a powerful emotionally charged relationship between patient and analyst. The analyst's task is to analyse the transference: to demonstrate to the patient, with the patient, how the patient's feelings towards and perception of the analyst are structured like a symptom – derived from past experience, often in the form of a repetition of a past relationship. But it should be emphasised that both parties experience the relationship as a *real* relationship: there is a good case for arguing that the burden of reality in psychoanalysis shifted on to the present relationship between patient and analyst once Freud had consigned to the limbo of 'non-proven' the question of the reality of the patient's *memories* (of past sexual abuse, seduction, etc.).

We have no right to dispute that the state of being in love which makes its appearance in the course of analytic treatment has the character of a genuine love. If it seems so lacking in normality, this is sufficiently explained by the fact that being in love in ordinary life, outside analysis, is also more similar to abnormal than to normal mental phenomena.[49]

Some sense of the *reality* of the relationship founded on the state of being in love can be gained from the following passage, in which Freud makes it clear that the analyst experiences the patient's transference-love as presenting him with a temptation – in short, it is experienced as being a seduction:

. . . when a woman sues for love, to reject and refuse it is a distressing part for a man to play; and, in spite of neurosis and resistance, an incomparable magic emanates from a woman of high principles who confesses her passion. It is not a patient's crudely sensual desires which constitute the temptation. These are more likely to repel, and it will call for all the doctor's tolerance if he is to regard them as a natural phenomenon. It is rather, perhaps, a woman's subtler and aim-inhibited wishes which bring with them the danger of making a man forget his technique and his medical task for the sake of a fine experience.[50]

Transference can be conceptualised only if the analyst withdraws from an engagement with the patient on her (or his) terms. Yet, as Octave Mannoni notes,[51] it could be 'discovered' only by the physician's accepting the relationship as exactly that – a relationship, whose components were real – and not dismissing it as an 'illusion', a 'fantasy' or a 'lie'. The analytic position is one which accepts the patient's feelings, beliefs, perceptions as genuine, but which does not *engage* with them.

The experience of the analyst is thus an exceedingly uncomfortable one: the seduction must be declined, but it must not be rejected.[52] Even if the transference takes the form of a hostile attack, or a condescending undermining of the analyst's usefulness, his kindness, or his belief in himself, the analyst will be *tempted* to step out of the position of neutrality and react to the patient's hostility with sarcasm, or a *tu quoque*, to his condescending undermining with self-justification (even if unvoiced to the patient). At every step, then, the analyst experiences temptation to react 'normally' and to step out of the analytic position. Of course, as soon as he were to react 'normally', the transference would disappear. Instead, he would be engaged in 'the pursuit of a fine experience', or a slanging-match, or a contest to see who can treat the other with a more refined and self-flattering *hauteur*.

The discovery of the position to adopt in analysis was made on the terrain of sexual advances and retreats. Freud, writing in 1895, outlined a series of obstacles centring on the erotic attachment the patient develops for the analyst.[53] The case he discussed at greatest length occurred when the physician became the object (or 'subject') of an erotic train of thought. The instance he gave was of a patient who was horrified when she realised she wished the analyst 'to take the initiative and give her a kiss'.[54] Such transference-thoughts are to be interpreted, not responded to. Yet they must not be dissipated, Freud finally came to recognise, since psychoanalysis depends upon them for its continued existence: 'the patient's need and longing should be allowed to persist in her, in order that they serve as forces impelling her to do work and to make changes'.[55]

Harnessing the force of the transference becomes the sole aim of psychoanalysis: 'We are no longer concerned with the patient's earlier illness but with a newly created and transformed neurosis which has taken the former's place'[56] – the transference *is* that neurosis. In this process, the aim of the analyst is always double: to entice or attract, and then to decline and evade, to defer and delay. He or she must avoid the charge of suggestion – of inserting foreign material into the patient's mind (and here, the patient's consent is immaterial for the charge to be seen to be serious) – while making use of the forces that make such an intrusion possible in the form of a genuine emotional tie. Whether the bond is affectionate or hostile is neither here nor there.[57] Thus seduction in psychoanalysis appears both as affection and hostility. True, the transference was discovered on the more obvious terrain of the erotic, but whatever its 'sign', plus or minus, the analyst, seemingly surprised by being the object of a seduction, now behaves as if he or she were seducing the patient on to his or her own terrain. To comprehend this sequence of seductions, a theory of seduction is needed.[58]

A theory of seduction

I have emphasised that, right from the start, Freud's descriptions of seduction recognised that an inter-subjective relationship existed between adult and child. Even though the adult's authority and will were absolute, the relationship was still one of mutual dependence; it is not a case of the blind alley of tyranny, but of something much more dialectical, like Hegel's master–slave dialectic. Even though one is truly in thrall to the other, there is a future to the relationship. This is the possibility inherent in seduction which rape excludes.[59]

For Freud, the seduction theory opened out on to the dialectic of fantasy and memory.[60] Recognising the relation as dialectical immediately forecloses the possibility of calling it rape. Yet others have gone beyond this implicit contrast between the dialectical inter-subjectivity of seduction and the brutal annihilation of the other aimed at in rape.[61] In *De la séduction*, Jean Baudrillard advances a philosophy of seduction whose main themes are as follows.[62] Seduction is a play on the appearances of things, but it does not try to dispel appearance for the sake of a reality beyond. Instead, it dwells in and on appearances, flaunting its mockery of the idea of a reality beyond appearances. Seduction is a mastery of signs, in contrast with power, which is mastery of the real. In gender terms, the masculine is certain of itself, sovereign and phallic, sure in its sexual identity, whereas the feminine dissembles and undercuts the direct sexuality of the male (Freud's phallic stage, in which both boy and girl believe there to be only one sex, only one sexual pleasure). Seduction is play, a challenge, a strategy of appearances. Seduction is ritualistic, in contrast to the naturalism of modern sexuality.[63] Baudrillard argues that 'naked' sexual desire appears at the expense of seduction. Hence, there are two primary senses of seduction: first, its opposition to naturalised sexuality and, secondly, its undermining of all discourses aimed at truth, aimed at piercing through the veil of illusion and dissemblance to appropriate the truth (identified with what is real).

Seduction, however, does not play only with truth; it is a challenge to our ideals of freedom. Our ideal of love is one that requires perfect freedom, a free choice, and yet it would not be thought of as love without the blindness of the hold of desire, the enslavement that we sense as the consequence of passion. When viewed from outside, free choice is the salient feature of love. Yet, if love were experienced as a 'free choice' from the inside, it would not have the quality of being taken over by the object that is its hallmark, making it so longed for and dreaded. Seduction is thus the mediation of freedom and slavery in the sphere of love.

Is love or seduction primary?[64] However we resolve that question, we recognise that love cannot but be refracted through the prism of seduction, and that the prism of seduction can darken and become the wedge of rape. Seduction is the art of love, and, for Baudrillard, it is more: it is what saves humans from the normalising discourse of truth and the objectifying pornography and instrumentalisation of sexuality of our epoch.[65] Yet seduction is also first cousin to rape, and it is rape whose representation we see haunting many discourses on male–female relations. Seduction, unlike rape, has a positive and a negative face, as even *The Concise Oxford Dictionary* is careful to point out:

Seduction, n. Seducing or being seduced; thing that tends to seduce; tempting or attractive quality *of* [often with merely playful or no imputation of blame].

In law, seduction was originally an action that a father or guardian brought against a man for loss of service of a servant (hence the need to demonstrate that daughters who were seduced had performed services for their parent). Breach of promise actions performed this function for the middle classes.[66] However, even the crime of seduction, where it existed, had or has this two-edged quality to it: the recently reformed state law of Nevada defines statutory seduction as 'ordinary sexual intercourse, and intercourse, cunnilingus, or fellatio committed by a person 18 years or older with a consenting person under the age of 16 years'.[67] This reform is very much in the same spirit as other states' reforms, in which statutory sexual offences depend upon the age of *both* parties involved. As Feild and Bienen note, 'feminists generally wanted to legalize consenting or nonforcible relations between teenagers while protecting children of both genders from being preyed upon sexually by adults'.[68] Similarly, in English law, there is the 'young man's defence': if a man under twenty-four believes the girl to have been over sixteen, he may be acquitted – though this defence can be offered only once.[69]

So this area of law, regarded as covering the field of seduction, continues to be couched in terms of innocence and authority (or 'supervisory power'[70]). Age and consent are juggled together, so that the law enters into territory that it recognises as being that of seduction (without necessarily calling it such). Logically, and intersubjectively, law recognises that the 'consent' of a fourteen-year-old (male or female) has a different legal status depending upon to whom his or her 'yes' is addressed.

The area of consent has provided the most anguishing experiences for the principal witness in rape trials, and the most leeway for the sexual imaginations of commentators on rape. Rape defences focus either on the question of consent or on the question of the identity of the assailant (in these cases, the fact of rape is usually not denied). If consent is the defence, the defendant is portrayed as a seducer, and the 'victim' as a woman who says 'no' and means 'yes', or says 'yes' at one time and then claims that it was really a 'no'.[71] If the rapist often masquerades as a seducer, by casting the victim's 'yes' or 'no' in doubt, what of the seducer?

Most men enjoy a young girl as they do a glass of champagne in a single, frothing moment . . . This momentary enjoyment is, if not in a physical yet in a spiritual sense, a rape, and a rape is only an imagined enjoyment; it is like a stolen kiss, a thing which requires no art.[72]

Rape is seen here, by Kierkegaard, to lie on the borderline of seduction; the seducer sets himself at a distance from it, in a twofold manner: in the distinction between physical and spiritual rape, and in his emphasis on the time of seduction. Seduction takes time, but how much time? In theory, seduction is endless. It is only spiritual rapists who take the achieving of intercourse, or orgasm, or marriage (as in the Jamesian or Balzacian parables of fortune-hunters) to be the end of seduction.

So we can see one form of defence by which the seducer puts him- or herself at a distance from rape. Rape is punctual, instantaneous, involving not only physical violence but temporal violence. Seduction is interminable, and even the spiritual rapists may imitate this interminability through their endless repetition (as in Leporello's list). Other strategies of seduction may affront the charge of rape. The seducer may turn him- or herself into the seduced by introducing into the other a passion which then overwhelms him. Kierkegaard portrays Don Giovanni as such a seducer: he embodies the 'exuberant joy of life' which communicates itself infectiously to all.

Nor are they disappointed, for he has enough for them all. Flattery, sighs, daring glances, soft handclasps, secret whispers, dangerous proximity, alluring withdrawal – and yet these are only the lesser mysteries . . . the gifts before the wedding.[73]

This account places seduction at the level of desire, not that of judgement, where questions of consent intrude. The seducer counts on introducing desire into the other; he casts himself as midwife to desire, so that a reversal of roles takes place. He is the one who can then cry rape, feel overwhelmed.

Wherever there is desire, there will be doubts as to rape – even though we have shown that the question of desire and the question of consent are entirely separate. (I have already mentioned the case of the woman who consented to sexual acts other than intercourse, experienced orgasm during the rape/intercourse but had quite clear *other* reasons for not consenting to intercourse.) Given that, we now see a further reason why psychoanalysis speaks to seduction and love rather than rape: in the Freudian universe there is no zero state of desire; there is always *some* desire (even if it manifests itself as horror).[74] Even if there is a nothing at the heart of the experience, an absence, something will be read back into it afterwards, and this is the kernel of the traumatic reaction, the kernel of what will later be repudiated. Rape victims experience this crisis when they torment themselves with asking why did they not resist more, asking themselves whether they perhaps gave a sign that was misread as consent. A rape victim might well wish to take the chance offered by psychoanalysis of thinking her way into the unthinkable – a theoretical and clinical preoccupation of the later work of Wilfred Bion. But the risk will always be that the rape will turn into seduction as she discovers that, to quote one rape victim trying to come to terms with the experience, 'it's not *that* different from ordinary sex'. The domestication of rape, like the domestication of mourning, may well lead to a healing in which the moment of non-consent is filled in, in a reassertion of omnipotence: the victim implicates herself, retrospectively, in the experience.

To be asked to do so in a court of law, however, is not only conceptually confused; it goes against the ethics of psychoanalysis, and against those, one would hope, of the court. None the less, there is one feature of the court room experience of rape victims which has a structure that may well give rise to feelings of extreme distress. To the court, the rape victim is simply a witness for the prosecution: she has to give evidence of the acts of the defendant; she is cast as a *witness* to his act. Yet she is recounting the violation of her own capacity to act as a subject.[75] In being asked to be a *witness* to this violation, she is being asked to *repeat* the experience of being deprived of this capacity. In the nature of the legal functions of 'witness' and 'complainant', she is being asked either to *repeat* the rape by alienating herself from the experience of being raped, or to *identify* with the position of the raped victim (herself).

Rape, seduction, psychoanalysis

Either way, she is 'raped' again. No wonder that the victims, when acting as witnesses or as complainants, adopt evasive action. And, as I have tried to demonstrate, any evasive action will be perceived as her having been engaged in seduction, not rape. Psychoanalysis is the mapping out for a subject of her or his evasive actions – no wonder that it is caught up in seduction.

5

'. . . A PERFECT LIKENESS OF THE PAST'

Consider your diary. For many of us, what we mean when we talk about the future is what our diaries contain. My diary contains details of meetings, conferences – it might contain *rendez-vous*, though I am not sure it is quite the place for them. Yet there is a curious ambiguity about the word 'diary', since it also refers, as in *The diary of a nobody*, to a record of events, recently past, written *without hindsight*. If it is written in a time when hindsight becomes possible, then the diary becomes a memoir, or even an auto-biography. Similarly, the ordinary conception of the diary, the sort of diary that you and I have in our pockets and bags, is that it is a record of the future *without foresight*.

My title is a perfect likeness of the last six words of Freud's *The interpretation of dreams*. Perhaps it would be as well to quote the last paragraph in its entirety.

And the value of dreams for giving us knowledge of the future? There is of course no question of that. It would be truer to say instead that they give us knowledge of the past. For dreams are derived from the past in every sense. Nevertheless the ancient belief that dreams foretell the future is not wholly devoid of truth. By picturing our wishes as fulfilled, dreams are of course leading us into the future. But this future, which the dreamer takes [*genommene*] as the present, has been moulded by his indestructible wish into a perfect likeness [*Ebenbild*] of the past.[1]

This final sentence, the final sentence of Freud's *magnum opus*, gives a very accurate sense of the relation of past, present and future in Freud's work. But the passage does have curious features. It asks a question concerning the premonitory possibilities of dreams only to dismiss them. But it then states that of course[2] dreams lead us into the future: *führt er uns allerdings in die Zukunft*. But they do so because the dreamer takes his or her present to be the future, whereas this present is, unbeknownst to the dreamer, a perfect likeness, an image of the past. In other words, dreams do create a future, but only insofar as that future is

90

like the past. A future that is not like the past is not to be found in dreams.

As James Strachey so delicately points out, it was only six days after the publication of these words that Freud wrote a brief paper entitled 'A premonitory dream fulfilled'.[3] The solution of the meaning of premonitory dreams contained in this paper came to him the very day *The interpretation of dreams* was published. So the final sentences of that book which I have quoted are themselves a premonition of something that was to happen in the future: they were a premonition of Freud's solving the problem of premonitory dreams.

The dream in question came up in the course of the analysis of one of Freud's estimable women patients. Some years previously, she had dreamt that she would meet Dr K., a friend and former family doctor of hers, in the street. The very next day following the dream she bumped into him at that very spot. This was a meeting by accident: neither of the parties had this event written in their diaries. Freud adds:

I will only add that no subsequent event proved the importance of this miraculous coincidence, which cannot therefore be accounted for by what lay in the future.[4]

Freud explained this premonitory dream by unravelling the story of her life, in which Dr K. stood for another Dr K., a barrister helping her put the affairs of her late husband in order. She had been in love with the barrister Dr K. – the first and last love of her life; this Dr K. was and remained a firm friend. Her dream, which Freud conjectures was in fact 'remembered' and constructed on the spot, on the very spot where she bumped into the other, medical Dr K. by accident, was simply a dream of a *rendez-vous*: she dreamt that the barrister Dr K. had met her by accident the way lovers do, the way he had done so many years before, in that *glücklich–unglücklich* time when she was in love.

The key term here is the kernel of her premonitory dream: *rendez-vous*, or meeting.[5] Freud shows how the 'remarkable coincidence' of this meeting, which inclines us to believe that the dream foretells the future, is in fact the realisation of a *wish* for such a remarkable coincidence, a wish for a time when this remarkable coincidence actually happened. He does not deny that remarkable coincidences occur – indeed, as we shall later see, he is much preoccupied with such remarkable coincidences – but rather that they have happened in the past under circumstances that apparently do not give cause for belief in anything supernatural, anything which pertains to piercing the veil of mystery that surrounds the future. He says,

Moreover, accidents which seem preconcerted like this are to be found in every love story.[6]

The 'accident' [*Zufall*] he is referring to is the following:

She was in her room, kneeling on the floor with her head buried in a chair and sobbing in a passionate longing for her friend and helper the barrister, when at that very moment the door opened and in he came to visit her.[7]

The phrase that does all the work here is: 'at that very moment'. Wish and event coincided, with no lapse of time between them. It is this remarkable coincidence that rules Freud's consideration of prophecy of the future. In every love story, there are moments when the normal rules which prescribe a delay or a gap between a wish and its fulfilment do not apply. In every love story, wish and reality coincide. Since wish and reality coincided once, in this *rendez-vous* which had not been prearranged, not inscribed in their diaries, the very act of remembering the *rendez-vous* was such as to induce the belief that one can foretell the future. And we can also note that this very fact of the coincidence of wish and reality is the trauma in this case. The woman censors the fact that her wish and reality coincided in a remarkable coincidence, precisely because they did so. And it is this censorship that gives rise to the projection of the remarkable coincidence from the past into the present. The present? Yes, because Freud specifies that the dream is created in the moment of meeting Dr K., the indifferent Dr K., so that the 'true' dream had been entirely forgotten, except in so far as it referred to *rendez-vous*.

Clearly, in the dreamer's dialect, *rendez-vous* was a key term, covering her unrequited longing both for her youth and for her friend Dr K. However, Freud gives us a definition of *rendez-vous* to oppose to this: 'for a *rendez-vous* consists in two people coming to the same spot at the same time'. Nothing could be more prosaic than that: it is very much in keeping with my remarks about the nature of the diary. Yet the *rendez-vous* the dreamer has in mind is strictly contradictory of this definition: the barrister, her friend, should not have been in that place. In every love affair, we might say in parodying Freud, the place and time of meeting are illicit, and that is what makes this a *lover's* meeting. And clearly the time is not the pre-arranged time of the diary, but the preordained time of lovers' destinies, the time which allows the vast deserts of future time to be conquered:

I'll love you, dear, I'll love you,
   Till China and Africa meet,
And the river jumps over the mountain
   And the salmon sing in the street.[8]

Hence Freud's explanation of premonitory dreams is that they are transposed references, echoes of the remarkable coincidences that actually do happen. The remarkable coincidence is unplanned, unwritten and surprising. Hence it becomes ripe for transposition into a future whose surprising unplannedness the precedent of the remarkable coincidence is intended to tame.

When Freud turned to the question of the relation between psychoanalysis and the occult in the 1920s, his most important example concerned an incident which turned around a man called Forsyte and the novels of Galsworthy known as the 'Forsyte Saga'. Hence my insistence at the beginning that our way of arranging the future, using our diaries, is accomplished without foresight. But Freud first pinpointed both prophetic dreams and telepathy as being worthy of consideration. However, his tone has changed; instead of the elegiac analysis that he had engaged in five days after the completion of *The interpretation of dreams*, he dismissed prophetic dreams as lacking in all plausibility. Nonetheless, the same structure of instant dismissal, followed by the return of the dismissed thought in a renewed, now plausible version, still rules his argument. Having dismissed premonitory dreams, he turns to telepathic phenomena and discovers a trustworthy source of data in 'unfilled prophecies made by professional fortune-tellers'.[9] This curious source has two advantages for Freud: firstly, the prophecies were issued long before, so that the specific time when the prophecies were meant to come to pass had long since gone by without the prophecy being fulfilled; hence Freud's analysis could switch between two events in the past – the moment of prophecy and the moment of failure of the prophecy. The structure of *Nachträglichkeit* is preserved.

Secondly, the failed fortune-teller is quite clearly a stand-in for the psychoanalyst. He is the analyst in a different garb. Reading tea-leaves, reading free associations are cognate activities. Let me illustrate with one of Freud's examples.

He tells of a twenty-seven-year-old woman's visit to a fortune-telling Professor who had set up shop in the lobby of a Paris hotel. He prophesied that by the time she was thirty-two she would have two children. This did not come to pass. Yet for Freud, analysing this woman some fifteen years later, it became clear that these facts were true of her *mother*, who had had two children by the age of thirty-two. Or rather, to be more precise, the prophecy would have been a true prophecy if the fortune-teller had been addressing this woman's *mother* at the age of twenty-seven. In psychoanalytic terms, however, and this is what is persuasive to Freud, this is a 'remarkable coincidence', since the woman's life and neurosis were ruled by her competition and identification with her mother. The fortune-teller's prophecy is true, then, in the sense that it goes to the heart of the woman's unconscious structuration of time. The fortune-teller had prophesied on the basis that she was her mother: i.e. the fortune-teller had not prophesied the future at all, but divined the past, and then reprojected it as the future, the perfect future, whereas the analyst puts it in the future perfect. What Freud's analytic work showed is that the fortune-teller had offered her a construction of her unconscious on the basis of her identification with the mother. Analysis thus *reveals* that the prophecy is good evidence of thought-transference. Freud describes it as follows:

a strong wish on the part of the questioner – the strongest unconscious wish, in fact, of her whole emotional life and the motive force of her impending neurosis – had made itself manifest to the fortune-teller by being directly transferred to him.[10]

In short, the fortune-teller is acting as a wild analyst while remaining completely unconscious of so doing.[11] Instead of analysing, he reads the future, on this occasion by studying the imprint of the woman's hand in sand.

Yet this story tells us as much about the function of the analyst as it does about the function of the fortune-teller. When the analyst addresses himself to the unconscious identification with her mother, much of the material that requires interpretation is produced precisely because the unconscious identification has *consequences* for the patient's unconscious view of the future. The neurosis, the patient's symptoms, are an incomprehensible version of the life-history of the person identified with; it is a version of the future based on the premise that the patient is someone other than he or she is. So when the analyst interprets such an identification, he is showing the way in which that identification orients the future through its construction of a past. As Lacan puts it:

The sole goal of analysis is the advent of a true speech and the realisation by the subject of his history in its relation to a future.[12]

So the analyst is not so very different from the fortune-teller, except that he is always dealing in hypotheticals. He says: 'It is *as if* you were your mother, and, on that basis, you expect to have two children by the time you are thirty-two.' Whereas the fortune-teller says: 'You *will* have two children by the time you are thirty-two.'

But this invoking of the hypothetical[13] reveals something crucial to Freud's epistemological stance. The aim of psychoanalysis is to undo such identifications. In this sense, its aim is to *un*write the future, which the neurotic lives as already written, structured by the words and deeds of those he or she has identified with, whether these be those of mother, father, Marilyn Monroe or Sigmund Freud. For Freud, such a future is a blank page, with invisible writing on it.

What does Freud oppose to the view that the future is already written? It is in so far as chance does exist in the physical, as opposed to mental world, that Freud distinguishes himself from a superstitious person.[14] Yet the analyst never takes a chance event at face value. Everything mental – that is speakable – is determined. This sense of determination, the famous determinism that Freud is rebuked for, is in truth more of a parody of nineteenth century Laplacean determinism than its extension. From the dream in *The interpretation of dreams*, we derive the simple formula that dreams foretell the future insofar as the future is a perfect likeness of the past. This model seems to be akin to the Laplacean determinism of the nineteenth century, the view that, given knowledge of initial conditions, of the present state of forces and elements in the universe, the entire history of a system can be predicted, both forward, into the future, and backwards, into the past. This determinism is broken up, we are told, by twentieth-century physics. But this Laplacean future is the future invoked by the *dream*; the real future, if such a thing can be allowed to escape the clutches of the Augustinian paradoxes, is a very different thing. One simple index of Freud's avoidance of the Laplacean denial of a difference between past and future is the fact that the question of chance and coincidence bulks so large in discussions of foretelling the future. In a sense, the future is the privileged domain of the miraculous for psychoanalysis. And yet, psychoanalysis itself essays to enter into the domain of the future by undoing the Laplacean determinations the patient constructs for him or herself.

Freud's discussion in *The psychopathology of everyday life* makes it clear that the Laplacean determinist is akin to the paranoiac in this respect. The salient feature of the paranoiac universe is that it has no place for a future, no room for manoeuvre, leaving only the option of apocalypse as marking the difference between now and what is to come: this was a problem that caused Isaac Newton considerable difficulties. In contrast, Freud says:

I believe in external (real) chance, it is true, but not in internal (psychical) accidental events. With the superstitious person it is the other way round.[15]

Although Freud does note that

the compulsion not to let chance count as chance but to interpret it is common to both of us.[16]

However this compulsion of his is intended to *erase* chance from the mind in order to restore it to its proper place: to the external world of accidents, in which there are no *rendez-vous*, planned or unplanned, in which there is no diary by which the future is arranged. The aim of analysis, basing itself on premonitions, prophecies and whatever, is to unwrite the future, to erase the future.

II
THE MOMENT OF JACQUES LACAN

Passé *le temps pour comprendre le moment de conclure*, c'est *le moment de conclure le temps pour comprendre*. Car autrement ce temps perdrait son sens.

Gone is *the time for understanding the moment to conclude*, now's *the moment to conclude the time for understanding*. Because otherwise this time will lose its meaning.

Jacques Lacan, 'Le temps logique'

A NOTE ON TRANSLATION

I had intended to pay off my debts to Jacques Lacan in the long hours of wrenching back from his texts a version of his alien meaning which would smooth the way for others like myself. I set out to translate, to render his words, violently, into another language. I did not anticipate that, rather than paying them all off, I would instead incur more debts. Translation involves the murder of the original: what once was in one language must come to be in another, *as if* it had always enjoyed this freshness, this potential yet perpetual striving for ever greater intimacy with and proximity to the moment of utterance. The translator attempts to efface all trace of the original language. One can even make theory out of this effort when it is argued, as I often have been tempted to, that it is in principle possible to translate anything from one language to another, that there is no such thing as an untranslatable word, phrase, ejaculation even. Hence my strong opposition to the tendency on the part of some translators, aided and abetted by some authors (including Lacan), to leave certain words in the original language, on the grounds that they are 'untranslatable'. In psychoanalytic works, two examples come easily to mind: Lacan's term, *jouissance* and Freud's term, *Nachträglichkeit*. The function of language may be philosophically mysterious, but the proper respect to be accorded to this mystery is only fetishised and ritualised when crystallised in the awe with which these terms are treated – as fetishes of the arbitrariness of the signifier.

One simple textual detail indicates the superficiality of this heated attention to the untranslatability of certain words. In *Seminar I*, Lacan, in commenting on Balint's discussion of 'enjoyment', notes: 'So character signifies limitation of the capacity *for love and enjoyment* [last four words in English in the original]. The dimension of enjoyment [*joie*], which is extremely extensive, goes well beyond the category of *jouissance* in a way that one should spell out. Enjoyment [*joie*] implies a subjective plenitude which

99

well deserves being expanded on.'[1] Lacan here counterposes the different semantic resonances of two words that have similar roots.[2] The translator's thought is: while both 'enjoyment' and *jouissance* have the connotation of fullness, *jouissance* also has the connotation of sharpness, the sharpness of a pleasure felt – carried over, perhaps from its being more often used than 'enjoyment' to denote directly sexual pleasure, and orgasm. None the less, it is quite clear that 'enjoyment', with its connotation of property rights, the exercise of those rights in a metaphorically sexual sense, and the state of taking pleasure, is as good an equivalent as any other word a translator plumps for usually is. The irony is, of course, that followers of Lacan and, following them, Lacan himself, have fetishised this term, flatly decreeing that it is untranslatable; English language readers have often followed suit, with the predictable consequences of opacity, posturing authority and the bliss of ignorance. Losses of particular semantic dimensions of this sort are par for the course in *any* translation, of *any* sentence; adding extra words in brackets, extra words in languages the reader is *presumed* not to be familiar with – otherwise why isn't she or he reading the original? – only lulls one into feeling that all the other words are unproblematic. To put it another way, the fetishisation of one particular term leads readers of the translation into believing that the rest of the 'translation' – the bits that are translated, rather than left hovering in no man's land between French and English – are more reliable than they actually are.

Behind such a practice of translation lies the ideal of a mathematical language, which has only one semantic dimension.[3] If the intention is, as it obviously became for Lacan, to make certain words behave in the same way that mathematical symbols behave – one cannot translate into French the c in '$E=mc^2$' one can only rebaptise it (see Kripke, *Naming and necessity*) – this is an entirely different question, bearing on the untranslatability of mathematical languages (and hence the peculiarity of calling them languages in the first place), not of natural languages. But was the intention ever to make *jouissance* into a mathematical function?

Hence, I became convinced that if it is part of a natural language, then it can be translated. Indeed, this 'theorem', if I may call it such, helps to distinguish natural from mathematical languages: it draws attention to the primary *communicative* function of language – that is, the fact that its primary aim is to make the same (communicate) *that which is different*. In contrast, mathematical languages only aim to make the same (that is, place two 'speakers' of that mathematical language in exactly the same position), thereby excluding all reference to an actual or even possible difference. In mathematics, difference emerges retrospectively, in the interpretations that new theorems give to old functions.

The aim of making Lacan's 'French' prose 'English' did not mean that he would thereby become easily understood, nor did it mean that the errors in the text that a translator necessarily stumbles on and recognises as errors would disappear. 'Editorial' work became necessary; the work of a host who wishes to introduce this new guest in the most accurate of lights. Such, however, were the differences in philosophy of translation between the writer of the original versions of Lacan's *Seminars*, Jacques-Alain Miller, and myself, that this was not possible. Nor was I permitted to include the notes to the text which attempted to indicate significant literary allusions, significant errors of fact or, most intriguingly, those most psychoanalytic of 'errors', Freudian slips, particularly those numerous occasions on which Lacan mistook one name for another. All vetoed and censored, although they have been 'silently' corrected in the English translations – whence the promise to 'correct' eventually the original French editions.

6

IN PLACE OF AN INTRODUCTION:
THE SEMINAR OF JACQUES LACAN.
BOOKS I AND II

I

On 16 June 1953, a group of analysts and analysts in training seceded from the Société Psychanalytique de Paris (SPP) following a controversy regarding two major issues. The first issue concerned the constitution and ethos of the new Institut de Psychanalyse, designed for the training of analysts, which was at last becoming a reality after several years of effort on the part of the Société. The second issue concerned complaints about the authoritarian practices and structure of the Société. Things came to a head when Jacques Lacan – then President of the Société, although a member of the anti-authoritarian faction – received a vote of no confidence and was obliged to resign. He was then invited to join the secessionists, who immediately created a new society: the Société Française de Psychanalyse (SFP). On 18 July 1953, Lacan gave the Société's inaugural lecture, entitled 'The symbolic, the imaginary and the real'. In September of the same year, the SFP held a conference in Rome at which Jacques Lacan presented his 'position paper', the 'Rapport (or Discours) de Rome', later published as 'The function and field of speech and language in psychoanalysis' in the first number of the journal the Société founded, *La Psychanalyse*. His paper became the intellectual manifesto and practical inspiration for a sizeable portion of the members of the new Société and was one of the factors which was instrumental in creating the atmosphere of euphoria, fraternal solidarity and pride in a common work that marked the Société at its inception.

In November 1953 teaching for the new Société began, in three different formats: firstly, lectures were given in the first term on 'Elements of psychoanalytic theory' by Juliette Favez-Boutonier, and in the second term on 'Principles and theories of the psycho-analytic cure' by Daniel Lagache; secondly, 'Clinical examination of patients' was led each Friday by Jacques Lacan; thirdly, there was a *séminaire de textes* each Wednesday led by Jacques Lacan. This *séminaire de textes* is what is meant when 'the *Séminaire* of Jacques Lacan' is referred to. For the year 1953–4, the theme of the *séminaire de textes* was announced as 'De la technique psychanalytique'. The transcript of this seminar was originally published in French in 1975; the text was prepared by Jacques-Alain Miller with Lacan's guidance and advice. It was also prepared as part of a bet between Miller and Lacan, who thought it impossible to prepare a satisfactory version.

Lacan had been teaching psychoanalytic theory and giving a commentary on texts within the SPP for a number of years prior to this. By the early 1950s, he had acquired a reputation there as someone known to hold a distinctive theoretical position, to have important views on technique and to have a flair for teaching. The reputation of his weekly seminar was already well established in analytic circles.[1] Indeed, his views on the teaching of analysis – the supervision of cases, the pedagogical style and content of theoretical courses – had been one of the sources of the conflict with Sacha Nacht, his one-time close friend, which marked the founding of the Institut. But Lacan had been a popular teacher well before, when in the 1930s he would lecture at the Sorbonne to packed auditoriums.[2] One can gauge the importance he attached to his teaching from a long letter he wrote to his ex-analyst, Rudolph Loewenstein, a few weeks after the secession:[3]

I see that, through this letter, I've been getting you to relive some of what has for me been a nightmare, these few months, and that in truth I've only been able to survive them by keeping going, alongside the horrible emotions evoked in me, my seminar of texts and supervision, without having once missed one, nor, I believe, without its inspiration or quality having in any way wavered. On the contrary, this year has been particularly fruitful, and I think I've made real progress in the theory and the techniques proper to obsessional neurosis. Yes, I've lived thanks to this labour, undertaken at times in a genuine state of despair.

II

Jacques Lacan was born in Paris on 13 April 1901, the son of Emilée Baudry and Alfred Lacan.[4] Educated by the Jesuits, he trained as a doctor and then as a psychiatrist. His first professional communication was given in 1926, and his doctoral thesis (1932) was on the paranoiac psychoses in their relation to the personality. His academic mentors within conventional psychiatry – to the extent he had any – were Henri Claude and Gaëtan Gatian de Clérambault. The former had been instrumental in allowing those French psychiatrists who first took an interest in Freud the freedom to try out the new ideas at a time when such 'German' 'pansexualism' met with a chauvinistic and morally outraged response from much of the medical profession. Clérambault was famous for his nosological innovation of 'mental automatism' and for his linguistic expertise and encyclopaedic knowledge of the history of clothes.

Lacan, however, was soon independent of his mentors and joined the group *L'Evolution psychiatrique*, which introduced Freudian ideas into France and was also open to the 'functionalist' approach of the English evolutionists (John Hughlings Jackson and Henry Head) as well as the phenomenological school that developed in Zurich and Germany during the 1920s and became the psychiatric avant-garde of the 1930s (Karl Jaspers, Eugen Minkowski, Ludwig Binswanger).

From early on, Lacan was a member of the surrealist circles around André Breton, writing poetry, inviting his friends to the wards of the Hôpital Sainte-Anne, where they decorated the walls and conducted experiments in automatic writing. However, having written two pieces for the surrealist magazine *Le Minotaure* in 1933 – including one on paranoia which went very much hand in glove with a companion piece by Salvador Dali – he appears to have dropped his links with these groups.

Lacan presented a first version of his mirror stage paper to the International Psycho-analytical Congress at Marienbad in 1936.[5] An article that he wrote for the *Encyclopédie française* in 1938, entitled 'La Famille', and a paper of 1936 called 'Beyond the reality principle' (included in his collection *Ecrits* of 1966) give an idea of the density of the conceptual apparatus he had already elaborated around the concept of the mirror stage: the drama of the child in front of the mirror combines the essential elements of Freud's conception of narcissism with the struggle for death of the Hegelian dialectic of master and slave – themes that are still prominent in *Seminar I*'s treatment of the mirror stage. In his articles of the 1930s, Lacan's distinctive principles were already evident: an extraordinary fidelity to Freud; an unrelenting suspicion of the intellectual modes of his times (including the 'humanistic' innovations associated with phenomenology, to which as early as 1933, in a review of Minkowski's classic work on the pathology of time, he had opposed the more rigorous and esoteric philosophy of Heidegger); and, perhaps most importantly, the new Hegelianism that he had absorbed in the lectures of Alexandre Kojève from 1933–9. Indeed, someone seeking an introduction to the philosophical world that Lacan inhabited can do no better than read 'In place of an introduction', which prefaces Alexandre Kojève's *Introduction to the reading of Hegel* (1947).

At the end of the war, Lacan made a journey to England in search of a moral climate that owed its strength to a war spent in defence and struggle rather than in capitulation and deception: his sense of freedom at being outside France was marked and communicated itself in the enthusiasm with which he encountered the psychoanalytic work with groups that Wilfred Bion and John Rickman had started.[6] To Lacan, for a brief moment, it seemed that Bion's group analysis was the way of the future for psychoanalysis. Such a convergence was perhaps facilitated by Lacan's new ideas as expressed in two papers of 1945 (which broke a self-imposed silence of seven years), one on the logic of groups and the function of time, the other on the logic of suspicion and paranoia.[7] Certainly the practical consequences of the first of these papers were to be momentous, since, following the logic of his argument concerning the nature of time's relation to action and hesitation, Lacan began to vary the length of analytic sessions. It was this variation in the time bought by the patient that was to be the grounds for the persistent and damaging criticism of his practice, starting in 1952 (when he gave a guarantee to other members of the SPP to cease his experiments with variable session lengths), and later in the early 1960s, when Lacan was held to have not conformed to a new Code of Practice introduced by the International Psycho-analytic Association (IPA), guaranteeing the patient that each session be of fixed duration. In later years, the variable length of the session remained and still remains the hallmark of the Lacanian analyst. It was the one clearcut issue out in the open that decided Lacan's 'excommunication' from the International Psycho-analytic Association in 1963.[8]

Lacan's critics in the International Psycho-analytic Association used his clinical practice as the benchmark against which his competence as a *training* analyst was measured (no one ever questioned his right to be an analyst). About his writings, they were even more circumspect, to the point of indifference, and, it should be said, quite ill-informed.

It was his weekly seminar that brought Lacan fame. By the mid 1950s, Lacan's version of psychoanalysis was, in France, becoming the one to be reckoned with, as the writings of Michel Foucault[9] and Paul Ricœur[10] demonstrate. The seminar became not simply the principal focus of students of analysis and young analysts of the SFP, but the centre of gravity for diverse intellectuals – Louis Althusser, Philippe Sollers, Julia Kristeva amongst many others. By 1963, when Lacan was forced by the crisis in the SFP concerning his status to close his seminar at Sainte-Anne, only to reopen it two months later at the Ecole Normale, over five hundred people were attending. By the mid 1970s, now ensconced at the Faculté de Droit, the weekly showing was well over a thousand. The regular visit to Lacan's seminar became an essential part of the *vie mondaine* of Paris.

Lacan's teaching, however, always moved ahead of his followers, not only to outstrip the hounds of Diana, as he portrayed them,[11] but also because of the dialectical instability of his own thought. Lacan was a didact first, theorist second. If he was on occasion allusive in person, in the immediacy of the weekly session when he was responding off the cuff, then he was doubly so in his writings. These writings were nearly all derived from seminar sessions, guest lectures or conferences, but were then refined on paper to a fever pitch of compression, manifold reference and syntactical complexity and obliquity. Lacan was a master of conversation – something he claimed was the essential accomplishment of the analyst. And, like a good conversationalist, he never retraced his steps solely in order to repeat himself, as a teacher may feel obliged to do, but only in order to be able to see more clearly where he was going. The transcribed Lacan of the seminars is that much closer to the magician of the word Freud found himself cast as,[12] and less obviously the cabbalist and alchemist Lacanian *writings* sometimes make him out to be.

Lacan often refers to the lectures that Freud proposed should be given in any future institute for training analysts: courses in the history of literature, in philology, the history of religion and of mythology.[13] Lacan set Freud's explicitly anti-medical conception of analytic training against the predominant Nachtian emphases of his own time, captured in the phrase with which Lacan heads his Rapport de Rome: 'human neuro-biology', the conception which underpinned the new French Institut of 1953 and provoked the split in the SPP. Lacan's seminars, together with the influence he had on the overall training programme of the SFP, were intended to put this Freudian conception of training into practice. Hence, in the year in which *Seminar II* took place (1954–55), guest speakers who included the most illustrious French philosophers, anthropologists and linguists were brought in from outside to speak to the general theme, 'Psychoanalysis and the human sciences'. Within Lacan's own seminar, he was determined to keep psychoanalysis open to new influences and conceptual challenges, whether they came from the exact sciences, from philosophy or from the distinctive cultural heritage of the writings of poets, moralists or mystics. This is what makes Lacan unique as an analyst: he was the first analyst since Freud to mobilise the whole of his culture's resources in the edification of his analytic house.

Anyone familiar with Lacan is aware of the rapidity with which he changed his theories. The seminars of the 1970s read very differently from those of the 1960s and are even more estranged from the language of those of the 1950s. Yet each seminar is built out of a set of themes that Lacan would return to, year in and year out. And the basic framework of the seminar remained the same. Firstly, there were the Freudian texts or concepts that were the proper object of the group's interest – though these were invariably approached from an unexpected angle (thus in *Seminar I*, questions of technique are discussed as part of a lengthy commentary upon the theory of narcissism; in *Seminar II*, the question of the ego is addressed by reading Freud's *Project* and *Beyond the pleasure principle*). Secondly, we find the level of articulation already attained by Lacan's own theoretical elaborations as measured primarily by the extent to which students and disciples had engaged with his teaching (thus in *Seminar I*, Lacan takes the mirror stage for granted only so he can criticise its overuse by those students particularly enamoured of his teachings; in *Seminar II*, the dialectic of ego and other is sufficiently well established for him to introduce the new dialectic of subject and *O*ther). Finally, Lacan continually returned to a relatively constant set of cultural and conceptual triangulation points or ever-fruitful problems: the Cartesian subject and method of doubt; the importance of truth, lies and deception for the analyst; the baleful influence of the analytic ideal of a 'strong ego'; the relation of psychoanalysis to the philosophical tradition, whether classical (both Ancient and eighteenth-century), moralist (La Rochefoucauld, Baltasar Gracián and Friedrich Nietzsche) or logical (Russell, Wittgenstein, Tarski); and a whole range of other stable points of reference. And, of course, every seminar includes a demonstration, in front of our ears, as it were, of the power of language: a reflection on the analyst's speech, on the ambiguities and glittering brilliance of the symbol, and the logic of conversation.

The 'Rapport de Rome' was the first of Lacan's writings to bring speech and language to the centre of the psychoanalyst's concerns; its extraordinary prose was itself a celebration of that reorientation.[14] Two epigrams, or formulae, offer a clear sense of Lacan's project: 'the unconscious is structured like a language'; 'the unconscious is the discourse of the other'. We can distinguish a number of different levels in this project. Firstly, speech is the working material of psychoanalysis: speech is what allows a conceptualisation of the processes discovered by Freud in the dream, in slips of the tongue and in jokes. By 1955, Lacan, following Jakobson, was arguing that Freud's condensation and displacement are alternative names for the processes of metaphor and metonymy at work in language.

Secondly, Freud's discovery that symptoms are symbolic ('mnemic symbols'), *representing* repressed thoughts and memories, indicates that symptoms (and, by inference, the unconscious) are structured linguistically. The key to the unravelling of their meaning is found, as all analysts agree, in the process of transference, during which the patient's discourse slowly translates the symptoms, phobias and patterns of behaviour and character traits into speech offered to and implicating the analyst. The analyst is thus cast as the witness to the patient's revelation or as the other conjured into existence by the mediation of speech. What the analyst says in response, in so far as it is an unexpected or lucky find which has an *effect* on, takes hold in, the analysand (elicits laughter, or tears, gets the cold shoulder or a soft word), is what is unconscious: the unconscious is the discourse of the other.

Employing a theory of language derived in part from Hegel[15] and Heidegger, but equally from the structuralism of Ferdinand de Saussure, Roman Jakobson and Claude Lévi-Strauss, Lacan emphasised the *structure* of linguistic elements which determines the material offered by patients in analysis. Interpretation and analysis are to be viewed as working synchronically on the linguistic elements unique to each patient – in other words, on the linguistic elements which are lost, distorted and transformed in constructing both symptoms, on the one hand, and the patient's subjectivity as speaker on the other.

However, Lacan put into question the parallelism of the two systems of signifier and signified which, according to Saussure, make up language. Instead, he stressed the priority of the signifier in determining meaning (a play on words may make the construction of a symptom possible; e.g. the Ratman's hatred of an

American is expressed in compulsive behaviour aimed at losing weight through the equation: *Dick* (the man's name)=*dick* (German for fat)). Despite highlighting the *formal* systemic features of language, he emphasised these less than the *dynamic* relation between the subject and his speech. Starting from his theory of the mirror stage, with its accompanying concept of the imaginary, he distinguished the *ego* (an imaginary constructed unity) from the *subject*, which has complex relations with the ego, the other (the ego's imaginary counterpart) and the Other – the *principle* of otherness that any act of speech presupposes. This last, or 'big Other', is the locus of the linguistic code, the guarantor of meaning, the third party in any dual relationship – whether it be analysis or love. The subject's speech is vouched for by this Other, even if the speech is primarily intended as a lie to the other. Yet it is distorted and transformed in having to pass via the fantasy structure, in which the ego and its (fantasy-) relations to its objects predominate. The relation of the subject to the Other is thus the mainline of the unconscious, for which analysis aims to clear the way. It should be noted, though, that the concept of the Other is absent, at least explicitly, from *Seminar I* and is introduced only in *Seminar II*.

The development of these theories went hand in hand with Lacan's famous 'return to Freud'. All analysts read, discuss and cite Freud, but Lacan gave this practice of reading an entirely new character.[16] Whereas many analysts, especially those trained in Britain and America, cite Freud as if he were a scientific authority who had produced 'findings' upon which one could build another level of theory, or another level of collated fact, Lacan acted on the conviction that psychoanalysis can only be reinvented each time the analyst and the analysand enter into their contract by repeating, going over once again, the inaugural *acts* recorded in Freud's writings. Reading Freud is subject to the theory of the analytic relation that is psychoanalysis; it is not akin to reading *Nature*. Instead of reading Freud in the fashion of the scientist, Lacan demonstrated how the *psychoanalyst* should read Freud: as the literary critic would read Shakespeare or the philosopher Plato. A sentence cannot be taken out of its context; it relies on that context for its meaning. A paper cannot be read without ascertaining the more general conceptual problem, or practical difficulty, to which it is an answer. And he is always raising the question: what psychoanalytic effect is at work in this text? Hence, at every step, Lacan's own theories were entwined with readings of Freud, demonstrating how Lacan was both offering something new to problems already to be found in Freud and was retracing the path that Freud had trod before him. So, the mirror stage is linked closely to Freud's concept of narcissism and to the notion that both the ego and love are fundamentally narcissistic in character. Or, to take another example of this entwining, he highlighted the concept of *Nachträg-lichkeit* (deferred action), the retrospective causality proper to the unconscious, a formal consequence of the battery of signifiers that make it up. Similarly, Freud's account of the origin of society and law in *Totem and taboo* is read as a myth that highlights the essential function of the father in the constitution of the human subject. In contrast to other recent psychoanalytic theories, which stress the pre-eminence of the mother–child relationship (pre-Oedipal, pre-genital), Lacan affirms the centrality for the subject's history of the triadic Oedipus complex, in which the function of the father is both essential and mythical: essential, since the father is the representative of the law, in the last instance the (senseless) law of language, and supplies the third term or mediating function that allows the child to find a place in the symbolic order (language) and escape from the blind alley of fascination with the image (other) of the mirror stage, experienced in fantasy as fascination with the mother; mythical, because the father's function is strictly metapho-rical – he functions neither as real father (flesh and blood) nor as imaginary father (though the latter figures in fantasy as an ideal and punitive agency) but as the Name of the Father, with his name assigning the child a place in the social world and allowing the child to become a sexed being through the phallic function (i.e. sign of sexual difference) to which the Name of the Father refers.

Lacan's account of the entry of the child into the Symbolic by courtesy of the father's mythical function is thus a revised version of Freud's Oedipus complex. The Oedipus complex represents the way in which infants become sexed (through their various responses to being deprived of the phallus) and become human (in escaping from the mother of the mirror stage, whose own incom-pleteness renders the child's sense of wanting insupportable, into the Symbolic, in which lack is symbolisable through the generation of desire). With the triad of concepts appropriate to each sector (need/Real, demand/Imaginary, desire/Symbolic), elaborated in the *Seminars* of the late 1950s, Lacan continues his criticism of those versions of psychoanalytic theory which equate Freud's concept of drives with biologically determined need, arguing instead that the true realm of psychoanalytic action is the world of desire, which is created by language transforming need into desire in answer to the unsatisfiable demands of the (m)other[17] for love. Desire, like the Freudian drive, is never fulfilled, always there, continually displaced and transformed. Yet Lacan is as opposed to those who repudiate Freud's drive-theory in the name of 'object relations' (Marjorie Brierley, Ronald Fairbairn and the 'British school') as he is to those who identify drive and need. In fact, Lacan argued that the object relations theorists often repudiated what *they* called the drive theory precisely because they blindly *assumed* that it equated drive and need. Lacan's readings of Freud were correctives to this crude, pre-interpretative assumption. Much of the argument for this double critique is to be found in *Seminar I* and *Seminar II*, where he teases apart papers by these and other analytic theorists to see how their theories and practices lead to impasses.

Lacan's later theories, from the mid 1960s on, concentrated on the relations between the signifier, the subject, the Other and the '*objet petit a*' (a concept linked, on the one hand, with the other of the mirror stage and, on the other hand, with the privileged objects of Freudian drives: the breast, faeces, urine, penis – to which Lacan added the voice and the gaze). His concern was to specify the formal characteristics of psychoanalytic discourse – an extension of his emphasis on speech as the uniquely efficacious medium of psychoanalysis. The linguistic aspect of his teaching ventured more and more into a formal mathematical idiom, including an attempt to define the properties of the various 'spaces' postulated by psychoanalytic theory (e.g. outside/inside; conscious/unconscious): but not only the space of the unconscious, distinct from and yet continuous with consciousness (and thus well represented by a Möbius strip), but also the Borromean knot, in which the signifying chains of demands and desires are linked together by the subject. The close alliance with mathematics (topology and number theory) and philosophy (epistemology and logic) furthered his attack on 'psychologism'.

Lacan's thought in this phase became ever more liable to being parroted and parodied, as many of the writings of his followers demonstrated. And in step with the proliferation of Lacanian discourses, both within and outside of the Ecole Freudienne de Paris (which he founded in 1964, when the SFP tore itself apart in its attempt to accommodate both Lacan and the IPA), he proposed a theory of four discourses, a theory which ventured to show how such parodies and parrotings arise; the discourses of the hysteric, mirrored by the discourse of the analyst, and the discourse of the

Master, rendered innocuous and ridiculous in the *discours universitaire*, academic discourse. By the end, in the late 1970s and early 1980s, there was no knowing which discourse Jacques Lacan himself was speaking: as he sometimes said, in his seminars he was doing the analysing, and his audience were his analysts. Nineteen months after he peremptorily dissolved the Ecole Freudienne in a letter to *Le Monde* (of all places) which opened with the words, 'I, Jacques Lacan, alone as I have always been . . . ', he died, on 9 September 1981.

III

Some comments on Lacan's relation to English-language analysis are called for. It is still common for discussions of Lacan to mention him only to dismiss him as a crank and a charlatan. Given that premise and conviction, the only thing that needs to be said about him is that he is impossible to read (and therefore must be a charlatan) and is of importance only because he is dangerous, owing to the fawning followers who disseminate his foolish theories and distort the general public's understanding of what psychoanalysis really is. The fact that he is French, the fact that he writes difficult prose in a highly idiosyncratic manner, is taken to be yet more self-evidently conclusive proof of his insignificance.

Criticism of this calibre would not normally need to be rebutted. It is more properly material for the historian and sociologist of chauvinism and philistinism. What is more, it seems clear that the two volumes of Lacan's seminars now published in translation by Cambridge University Press are rebuttals in themselves. Yet something should be said of the relation between Lacan and his school – and the analysts he has influenced – and the context, both analytic and non-analytic, of those who work in the English language.

'In France, we are all Lacanians, just as we are all Freudians.' So said Joyce MacDougall, an English-speaking analyst resident in France, by way of introduction at a recent international psychoanalytic symposium. Such a view is not a declaration of adherence to a faith; it is a recognition of the fact that any analyst working in the French language, in the French cultural context, with its own individual history, cannot but be Lacanian. Even the French language is Lacanian: open up the standard French dictionary, *Petit Robert*, equivalent of the *Shorter Oxford English Dictionary*, and turn to the entry *Symbolique*. Under the masculine noun form, you will find: 'Specialt. *Psychan.* "L'ordre des phénomènes auxquels la psychanalyse a à faire en tant qu'ils sont structurés comme un langage" (LACAN)' ['Specialist. *Psychoanal.* "The order of phenomena with which psychoanalysis deals in so far as they are structured like a language" (LACAN)']. You will also find other references to Lacan, who, it should be noted, figures here strictly as a *linguistic* authority. Far be it for a *psychoanalyst* of all people to fight against the acceptations of the language.

More importantly, while many, perhaps most, analysts do not belong to schools openly espousing the theories of Lacan, and while many analysts who have had long years of training along Lacanian lines would put as great a distance between themselves and the self-declared Lacanians as the most insular of American analysts, yet all these analysts would and do, given suitably auspicious circumstances, still recognise themselves as Lacanians.

Such a capacity for splitting and denial is not new in psychoanalysis. One has only to think of the behaviour of many British analysts in the process of coming to terms with the Melanie Klein/Anna Freud split in the British Society since the 1940s – there, both sides are 'Freudians'. Yet *at the same time* the doctrinal dispute appears to the participants to be absolute, to be created by unbridgeable gaps. Unlike the situation with respect to Lacan, at no point were Melanie Klein or Anna Freud obliged to leave the International Psycho-analytic Association – though rumour, standing in place of an adequate historical account, has it that at one point it came close to that. These, though, may have been specific, unique historical circumstances in which a well entrenched group, who had formed the backbone of a national society and given it its distinctive cast, were challenged by an outside group coming to live under the same roof – except that this outside group had the unique quality of bringing with it the name of its leader's father. Under these circumstances, it would have been next to impossible to exclude one or other of the groups from the IPA. Not so with other disagreements and clashes, less well known. Who now attaches much importance to the disputes of the American psychoanalytic Societies associated with the names of Sandor Radó and Jules Massermann?

The original split in the French society, that of 1953, was not, by all accounts, much to do with the personality or the person of Lacan, although some of his views on the character of psychoanalytic training institutions played a significant part in the conflict. Yet in 1961–4, the issue became more and more pared down to one insoluble problem: the question of Lacan's person. Finally, the ultimatum came: the French analysts in the SFP would be allowed to join the IPA if they agreed to remove Lacan's name from the list of training analysts. Proposition 13, as it came to be known, required the SFP to strike off Lacan's and Françoise Dolto's names from the list of training analysts. It was delivered, seemingly as an afterthought, to the negotiators at the steps of the plane they were boarding, returning from Edinburgh to Paris to report on the success of the negotiations. And it stuck in the throats of many of the French analysts. Strike off the name of the analyst who had analysed many of them, supervised more, and whose seminar was the linch-pin of their analytic education? Some did indeed don the proffered cloak of Cassius. Out went Lacan, excommunicated, as he called it, out with him went the possibility of the SFP surviving, and there was born the first psychoanalytic institution centred on the figure of Lacan: the Ecole Freudienne de Paris (EFP).

For those who want to understand the Lacan phenomenon that then took hold of a sizeable portion of the French intelligentsia, there are two works already in print in English: Sherry Turkle's ambitiously sociological *Psychoanalytic politics* and the subtly sympathetic, because based on long years of acquaintance with the Lacan phenomenon, *The life and legends of Jacques Lacan*, by Cathérine Clément. In the early 1950s, everything seemed a storm in a tea-cup: in 1952, the number of students attending Lacan's seminars was twenty-five, and he was proud that the number did not diminish as the year progressed; the number of analysts permitted to participate in the crucial votes leading to the 1953 schism was less than twenty. Thirty years later, when Lacan died, nine pages of a French daily were devoted to the event. Across these different epochs, Lacan taught his seminar. He also helped found one psychoanalytic society which could neither survive with him, nor without him, and founded another, which he, single-handedly and single-mindedly, proceeded to dissolve nineteen months before he died. But his influence on psychoanalytic affairs outside France was, according to the official IPA, virtually zero. Yet there is now growing up, in Britain, America, Australia and elsewhere in the English-speaking world, not to speak of the far more rapid effects he has had in Italy, Spain and South America, a psychoanalytic culture which is dominated by Lacanian ideas and catchphrases, but a culture which is not shared by those whom the IPA qualify to call themselves psychoanalysts. Lacan was obliged to set up his shop 'outside'. That obligation and its consequences is one the international psychoanalytic movement has yet to come to terms with.

In place of an introduction

If there is one means by which psychoanalysts can come to understand Lacan, it is surely through the transcripts of the teaching he offered to analysts undergoing training each year from 1953 onwards. These seminars are continually preoccupied with questions of technique, of methods, and with demonstrating how theoretical disputes impinge directly and daily on the analytic session. To those who are not analysts, these seminars may offer something comparable to Freud's *Introductory lectures*, something more accessible, more inviting, more seductive, even, than his other writings, and yet very much the genuine article: the psychoanalyst in conversation, where he or she is, or should be, at home.

IV

Book I. Freud's papers on technique. 1953–1954

Lacan ran his seminars as a major part of the training programme of the Société Française de Psychanalyse. They had as their general title 'Seminar and commentary on Freud's texts'. *Seminar I* deals with Freud's writings on technique. However, it is not concerned only with those of Freud's writings known to readers of the *Standard Edition* under that title (namely the group of papers gathered together in volume XII, under the general title, 'Papers on technique', including four grouped together as 'Recommendations on the technique of psychoanalysis'), but ranges widely over Freud's work, particularly those papers belonging to the important transition period introduced by the concept of narcissism. *Seminar II* has as its topic the ego in Freud's theory and psychoanalytic technique. *Seminar III*, which develops the theory of the ego, the imaginary and the symbolic, and discusses at great length the Schreber case and psychoanalytic theories of psychosis, is also being translated into English. In 1986, another seminar from the 1950s was published in French: *Livre VII. L'Ethique de la Psychanalyse. 1959–1960*, which considers the ethic of psychoanalysis, of the analyst, starting from a meditation on Aristotle's *Nicomachean ethics*, Sophocles' *Antigone* and the Marquis de Sade.

It is important to emphasise that these seminars were intended for analysts in training. Hence two perennial foci of concern: technical questions (what does the analyst do, what should the analyst do, what have analysts done – 'what do we do when we do analysis?'[18]) and the addressing of contemporary psychoanalytic theory, both as regards its theoretical coherence and its consequences for questions of technique. In the 1950s, the contemporary psychoanalysts Lacan addresses are primarily those of the British school – he took the British far more seriously (and approached them more sympathetically) than he did the Americans. In *Seminar I*, there are lengthy discussions of the work of Anna Freud, Michael Balint, Melanie Klein. Similarly, in *Seminar II* the theme of object relations brooks large, and the work of Ronald Fairbairn is examined closely. Indeed, throughout his work Lacan tended to oppose European to American analysis, his most acerbic comments being reserved for the refugee analysts who had emigrated to America and forgotten the true meaning of Freud's discovery as they struggled to 'adapt' psychoanalysis to ways alien to the traditions of European culture.

In the 'Rapport de Rome' of September 1953, Lacan had set out three questions which contemporary psychoanalysis found itself faced with:[19]

a. the function of the imaginary, in particular the question of fantasy and its symbolic status (this question was framed very much with Klein in mind);

b. libidinal object relations (with the 'object relations' theorists in mind);

c. counter-transference and the question of the training of the analyst (Lacan had in mind a series of papers by Paula Heimann, Annie Reich, Margaret Little – the last of which was to be discussed in some detail in *Seminar I* – which had been published in the *International Journal of Psycho-analysis* in 1950, and, together with Winnicott's seminal paper of 1947, 'Hate in the countertransference', had placed this question on all analysts' agendas).

Not surprisingly, Lacan's seminar in the year that followed the 'Rapport de Rome' persistently addressed these questions, and in a variety of forms.

To understand fully the manner in which Lacan conceived of his seminar, one must recognise the highly idiosyncratic cognitive map that his work sketches out for the listener and reader. At the heart of his conception there is, of course, speech. And from his recognition that speech is the unique medium of psychoanalysis and the vehicle of all its effects, whether beneficent or maleficent, stems his interest in language. Yet language is never just one concept: it is conceived of in a number of different modes. In *Seminar I*, Lacan is developing many of the points touched on in the 'Rapport de Rome': speech as the exchange constitutive of human society (the password), truth as emergent in the dimension of lies and deception, the omnipresent ambiguity of analytic speech, whereby it allows something new to become conscious. But this is a Lacan who is not yet concerned to integrate psychoanalytic theory with Saussurean linguistics. The characteristic discussions of the function and the supremacy of the signifier are not to be found here; when the term *signifiant* crops up, as it occasionally does, there are good grounds for translating it as 'signifying' rather than 'signifier'. It is not until late 1955 or 1956 that Lacan begins to employ the terms in a straightforwardly Saussurean manner. The first reference in his *Ecrits* to Saussure occurs in 'The Freudian thing', written in late 1955 and 1956 – and the section devoted to the signifier and signified in that paper is one of the sections that was most heavily rewritten between its appearance in 1956 and its republication in the *Ecrits*.[20] Indeed, one could well argue that Lacan's use of Saussure in this period was simply to indicate that Freud was a linguist *avant la lettre*, since he had stated, in his books on dreams, slips and jokes, the laws of language to which the dream and the symptom were subject, albeit using non-linguistic designations. And the *rapprochement* between Freud's dream theory and the terms 'metaphor' and 'metonymy' was probably introduced in 1956, with Lacan's reading of Jakobson's brief discussion, published that year, of Freud's dream mechanisms.[21]

Similarly, it is only in the course of *Seminar II* that Lacan develops the distinction between the 'other' and the 'Other', so important a theme in all of his later work, and which distinguishes his work from the phenomenological tradition of post-war France best represented by Sartre and Merleau-Ponty. It is clear, though, that the conceptual distinction this covers had been adumbrated in the 'Rapport de Rome' and was bound up with his emphasis on language, itself closely linked to his attention to the medium within which psychoanalysis takes place. In retrospect one can see that the notion of speech and language spelled out there was crying out for this distinction to be made.

Lacan's thinking about language was always closely tied to reflections on the subject and its relations to the object or 'other' – the recipient. Earlier, in 1945, in the paper on temporality entitled 'Le temps logique et l'assertion de certitude anticipée', Lacan had drawn sharp distinctions between three concepts of the subject in order to set out three stages of the dialectic of the subject. Firstly, there is the logical subject, which does not require the existence of others to make its judgement: the noetic subject, the 'one' of 'one knows that . . . ' (or, more frequently in English, the 'it' of 'it is known that . . . '), 'who might just as well be God, a table or a wash-basin'.[22] Secondly, there are the anonymous subjects of inter-subjective relations, of relations between equals, undefined except in so far as they are reciprocal with one another, subjects equivalent to the other in general, in a relation of pure reciprocity in which self-recognition is possible only through a recognition of the property in question in the other (the '*on*', or 'one'). Thirdly, the individuated *je*, uniquely specified by the action in which the 'I' emerges through a process of isolation, of separation or of 'decanting' off from the others.

At that time, Lacan drew an explicit parallel between the dialectic of the logical subject as outlined here and the production of the psychological subject from the indetermination experienced between the self and the other of the mirror stage. At this stage, Lacan explained the move beyond the mirror stage's confusion of self and other in terms of the emergence of jealousy. He also claimed that the argument of his paper furnished the essential logical form (rather than existential form) of the psychological subject.

In his later works, Lacan would probably not have drawn such a sharp distinction between the psychological and the logical subject. Certainly we can say that he was not particularly interested in the psychological subject, despite the fact that he often described the mirror stage in psychological terms as a phase in the development of the psychological subject. One gains some sense of his scepticism as to the value of the study of the psychological subject by considering his statements about the psychology of the ego, so important a part of the revisionist theory of psychoanalysis he attacked in the work of the American ego-psychologists and of Anna Freud's group. In *Seminar I*, he describes the ego of psychology as having the function of synthesis, whereas the ego of psychoanalysis always has a dynamic function: 'The ego makes itself manifest [in analysis] as a defence, as a refusal.'[23] Indeed, the general trend of *Seminar I* is away from the developmental account of the mirror stage – which, it should be remembered, had originally been put forward by Lacan in 1936, his major paper on the topic appearing in 1949 – towards studying the stage as an 'exemplary function': exemplary of the subject's relations in so far as the mirror-image is the *Urbild* of the ego.[24] Having been interpreted as proposing the mirror stage as a stage in development much like any of the other psychoanalytic stages or phases, Lacan's argument in this seminar is as much a critique or such uses as it is an extension of them. In criticising the uses of the development stage model of childhood, which he attributes to Ferenczi as much as to Freud (and Abraham's name should surely be included alongside Ferenczi's), he remarks:

Perhaps it would be better, in fact, not to refer here to falsely evolutionary notions. This probably isn't the place for the fertile idea of evolution. It is a question, rather, of elucidating structural mechanisms, which are at work in our analytic experience, which is centred on adults. Retroactively, one may clarify what happens in childhood, in a hypothetical and more or less verifiable manner . . . [W]hat Freud always insisted upon was . . . the preservation, at every level, of what may be considered as different stages.[25]

In fact a large section of this seminar must be considered as a reappraisal of 'what use, simultaneously limited and various, should be made of the mirror stage'.[26] One of those uses is to demonstrate that the realities of the oral, anal, genital 'stages' are 'those of the images of the human body, and of the hominisation of the world, its perception in terms of images linked to the structuration of the body'.[27]

The mirror stage was only one part of a sustained and sophisticated attempt to give an account of the subject's relations to others, to which the 'Logical time' paper was another, equally important though very different contribution. In that 1945 paper, we can see the sophistication of the conception of the subject in relation to 'others': to the 'other' as the addressee or interlocutor of a scientific statement; to the other as 'inter-subjectively equivalent' to the subject ('qui doivent "*l'un l'autre se*" reconnaître');[28] and to the other as that which the 'I' separates itself off from. The complexity of this account presages the emergence of the concept of the Other in Lacan's thought. But what triggers this emergence is not the development of the theory of the mirror stage, but rather Lacan's sustained reflection on language. Here we must examine the set of linguistic concerns from which the concept of the Other emerges.

A central preoccupation of Freudian psychoanalysis is deception. The intersection between philosophy and psychoanalysis so natural to Lacan, and so foreign to other psychoanalytic schools, is of great importance here, as witnessed by the crucial position occupied by the phenomenology of bad faith, of self-deception, in Sartre's critique of psychoanalysis in *Being and nothingness* and in many English-language discussions stemming from this.[29] Other psychoanalysts accept that the themes of self-deception, of honesty and lies, are a normal and inevitable part of their practice, but they do not accord them great importance on the theoretical level.[30] In Lacan's work, the preoccupation with the theoretical significance of deception is there from the start in connection with two themes: firstly, the extent of self-deception in the theoretical work of psychoanalysts, particularly in the theory of the ego. This theoretical self-deception strikes at the heart of the psychoanalytic discovery, namely that the ego is not master in its own house. But it goes beyond that, since Lacan depicts contemporary psychoanalysts as being deceived by the illusions constitutive of the function of the ego in a very specific fashion: it is not so much the egos of the patient that they are so deceived by as their own. These analysts present the ego of the analyst as a model for the patient, as what the patient can identify with in reforming his or her own subjective structure, whereas for Lacan the position of the analyst may be that of death (of the dummy – in French, *le mort* – in bridge), of the dead master in the dialectic of master and slave, or of mediator, even diplomat, in the art of conversation the parties engage in, or simply of witness to the truth – but certainly not in a position that approximates to that of the ideal, or that of the super-ego.

Lacan thus discovers a primary manifestation of the self-deception of the ego in the development of psychoanalytic theory: the self-deception of theorists, intimately tied to the importance accorded to identification in analytic *practice*, which is what the return to Freud is intended to counter. But this form of deception is linked to an older theme: the illusions fostered by the image – the (Platonic) mistrust of appearances (including here that special variety of illusion generated by lenses and mirrors, which could so plausibly legitimate Galileo's opponents in their refusal to look through his telescope, knowing that such an instrument could only generate illusion). Interwoven with the optical model, however, we find a sustained discussion of animal ethology based on the work of Tinbergen and Lorenz. Their work is drawn upon to emphasise the essential function of the image in cycles of behaviour, particularly of sexual behaviour. The key terms here are 'lure' and 'captation'.[31]

The reliance on animal ethology may seem surprising in view of Lacan's critique of naturalism. Indeed, some take Lacan to be monolithically anti-biological. However, he never suggested that one neglect or avoid biology, that one treat it phobically, just because he believed, as he firmly did, that those attempting to found psychoanalysis on a biological basis were mistaken. There is, none the less, a very sharp contrast between him and those who, like John Bowlby, in the 1950s used the recent work of the ethologists to dispense with the supposedly mythical and outmoded bio-hydraulics of Freud's theory of instincts. Bowlby dispensed with instincts, supplanting them with concepts of attachment, imprinting, naturalistic conceptions of loss and separation; and there is a curious irony here, since it is quite possible, given what Lorenz and others wrote about the original Freudian impulsion of their work, that Bowlby was borrowing back from ethology concepts that had originally been straightforwardly psychoanalytic before being 'naturalised', believing these concepts to be more firmly based on (because derived from) objective observation of animal behaviour. In contrast, Lacan showed little interest in such concepts. What animal behaviour indicated to him was the universal function of the *image* in sexual behaviour – the universal function of deception and displacement. Animals and man have a common propensity to become ensnared by an image: indeed, sexual life is uniquely characterised by the centripetal force of the image. Here, he is taking up a classical Freudian theme: the 'abnormality' and 'insanity' (to use Freud's terms) of sexual love, in which deception is the rule, indeed the *sine qua non*, rather than the exception.

. . . in the animal world, the entire cycle of sexual behaviour is dominated by the imaginary . . . The possibility of displacement, the illusory, imaginary dimension, is essential to everything pertaining to the order of sexual behaviour.[32]

Lacan had already implicitly alluded to the paradoxes and illusions of the optical image in his mirror stage paper.[33] In *Seminar I*, he extends his discussion, linking his work up with the analogy that Freud drew between the production of psychic phenomena and the workings of a microscope or telescope. In a subtle progression of argument, he shifts from the image as found in ethological research – a caricature, a sketch of a figure – and the reflection of the image in a mirror, in a lake, to an optical schema, the schema of the inverted bouquet of flowers which makes use of a spherical and a plane mirror. All this is an apparatus, like the telescope Freud took as a model of the psyche, for showing how images are produced and what their properties are: real and virtual images. The mirror stage could be taken to refer to a real event, the child looking at its image. The optical schema, like Freud's telescope, could not be taken as a representation of a real structure or even of a *tableau* of characters looking at one another. The image is now entirely within the boundaries of optics, and its use for thinking about psycho-analysis can only be that of a model, not that of an abbreviated description.

Clearly the shift from the mirror stage to the optical schema takes one away from a chronological account to a logical or structural account. Lacan goes so far as to say that the most important thing about the mirror stage is its sudden disappearance in the moment when the symbolic takes over the functions that up until then had been served by the recognition of desire in the other. Lacan is clearly aware of the implications of the logical, rather than developmental, argument and asserts that this is necessary:

This anteriority [of the recognition of desire first and foremost in the other] is not chronological, but logical, and here we are only performing a deduction. It is no less fundamental for all that, since it allows us to distinguish the planes of the symbolic, of the imaginary and of the real.[34]

It is the linking of this optical schema with the discussion of Freud's paper on narcissism that adds stringency and force to the argument. Naturally, Lacan had looked to Freud's discussion of narcissism for support for his theory of the mirror stage: Narcissus looking in the pool, oblivious to the voice of Echo, is a mythic representation that approximates closely to Lacan's account of the formation of the ego. Yet Freud's argument left it unclear how tightly he wished to link the concept of narcissism to an optical model. Lacan introduces the optical model in order to extend Freud's discussion of ego ideal and ideal ego – concepts that he distinguishes in the paper on narcissism only to leave to one side as he went on to develop the theory of the ego and the super-ego in the 1920s.[35] Lacan picks up the conceptual pieces Freud had introduced and articulates them with the optical schema and his theory of the imaginary in order to show how the optical model can give an account of the 'hinge' between the imaginary and the symbolic. Again, this procedure parallels Freud, whose work on narcissism leads to the super-ego, the embodiment of the law and of morality – very much the same terrain as that covered by Lacan's symbolic. But within the theory of narcissism, the theme of the image as illusion returns in full force in the theory of love (narcissistic and anaclitic) and of its crucial position as *Verliebtheit* in the papers on technique and transference. With the introduction of love, Lacan is ready to move on to another major theme of the seminar: a discussion of the work of Michael and Alice Balint in *Primary love and psycho-analytic technique*.

In place of an introduction

Lacan's discussion of Balint sets a tone both sympathetic and critical. A great admirer of Balint's work with patients (to the point where he will demonstrate later in the seminar the utility of his own conceptions – of the pact of speech, and his claim that the domain of analysis is that of the lie and the mistake – with one of Balint's clinical episodes), Lacan dissects Balint's theory in order to demonstrate how a deviation in technique goes hand in hand with a stalemate in theory. Balint is 'entangled in a dual relationship, and denying it'[36] (a phrase introduced into the seminar by Wladimir Granoff, which Lacan appropriates). His critique of analysis as modelled on the dual relationship (the imaginary) covers both Klein and Balint. With Klein, he observes how it is she, the analyst, who sponsors the symbolic reorganisation by giving the child words which will form the nucleus of the Oedipus complex, while failing to theorise this move. With Balint, Lacan enters into a long discussion of the necessity of viewing analysis as 'inter-subjective' (a term which he was on other occasions, for instance, as we have seen in the 'Logical time' paper, to criticise as imprecise and misleading): 'In so far as we remain within the register of analysis, we will be obliged to admit an original inter-subjectivity.'[37] As if as a counterweight to Balint, Lacan discusses the dialectic of the gaze, of seeing the other seeing me, as proposed by Sartre in *Being and nothingness*. The theme of the gaze, of the subject as 'eye', is clearly important in the mirror model developed from the concept of the mirror stage, and was to be developed at further length in *Seminar XI*. For Lacan, the gaze indicates how the 'concrete topology of the body',[38] which determines the forms of the imaginary, includes a dimension of imaginary space which is not confined to the body surface or its 'apertures': it includes a reference to the presence of the other within this imaginary space. A conception of psychoanalysis centred on the self, on the ego or on 'selfish love' (Balint), can only deny the essential reference to the other.

Although Lacan's approach to Freud's papers on technique is an oblique one (he never considers going through the collection 'Papers on technique' one by one), there is one theme that emerges out of their consideration that is of considerable importance as a thread running through the seminar: the phenomenon of love. Naturally, the key reference is to the transference and there are a considerable number of discussions of the phenomenon of *Verliebtheit* (infatuation, or the state of being in love) and to the position of the analyst in relation to it. Nowhere is it clearer that an adequate answer to the question 'What is the analyst doing?', is crucial to questions of technique. On the one hand, there is the theme of fascination, of the gaze, of the theory of the parade and of the mirror. On the other, there is the theory of the pact, the symbolic bond and the characterisation of love as governed by the laws of the gift (which in later seminars will lead Lacan to define love as the gift of what one does not have). All of which leads Lacan to conclude that the transference, despite its being conventionally viewed as 'illusory', actually takes place on the symbolic level.[39] And in the penultimate session, he ties the Lévi-Straussian and Maussian theme of the pact, of reciprocity and the gift, together with the theory of speech and the relation between the subject and the other, so as to propose that a crucial dimension of the transference, beyond the love and the hate that are assumed to be ready to spring into action in the analytic transference, is the passion of ignorance.

Lacan's later developments of this line of thought are clear: the concept of the 'subject presumed to know', and the struggle of the subject with the issues of mastery and knowledge implicit in the demand the analysand brings to the analyst. Yet it is important to see that this idea is connected on the one hand with the theory of transference as a *passion*, and on the other hand with the topics of truth, lies and deception, to which some of the most brilliant episodes in the seminar are devoted. If ignorance and honesty, as some have claimed, constitute the fundamental attitudes of the analyst, Lacan wished so to reorient analytic theory as to make of these not psychological attributes of the analyst, but principles around which to build a technique and a theory of the subject's relation to the analyst, to the other and to the Other.

Each of these themes returns in later seminars, being continually reworked in different terminology, so that it is often only after a considerable labour that one realises that one has been here before, that this is a recognisable analytic (and Lacanian) landscape. This form of the spiral or the gyration of concepts is the distinctive manner by which Lacan reproduces the movement of analytic sessions which curve back on themselves, repeat themselves in uncanny ways, go backwards and forwards, in zigzags, in the knight's move to which Freud likened the movement of the discourse,[40] or in the see-saw that Lacan discusses in *Seminar 1*. This is the process of working-through: neither repetition nor progress, but certainly necessary movement. Lacan's genius was to repeat his theoretical arguments and his commentaries on practice, or his interpretations of Freud's works, in very different contexts, so that the 'same' idea (the idea of mirroring, or the concept of the symbolic pact) would appear anew, silhouetted against a different background. 'The word is not the thing, but a flash in whose light we perceive the thing' (Diderot). With Lacan, what is seen through the flash of the word is a landscape that shifts abruptly at times, very little at others, and yet the overall effect is one of continual change. Lacan's theories changed drastically as time passed, as each seminar prompted him to develop and reflect. There is no Lacanian theory, but there was a unique and distinctive teaching. Much of that is embodied in the seminars, of which the *Seminar on Freud's papers on technique*, from 1953 to 1954, is the first of which we have a relatively complete record.

V

Book II. The ego in Freud's theory and in the technique of psychoanalysis. 1954–1955

You can be Lacanians; as for me, I'm a Freudian.

Jacques Lacan[41]

The topic for the second year of Lacan's training seminar for the SFP was announced as 'The ego in Freud's theory and in the technique of psychoanalysis'. Certain sessions of the seminar provided Lacan with the basis for publications produced later in the 1950s, in particular the famous 'Seminar on *The purloined letter*', which appeared in the journal of the SFP, *La Psychanalyse 2* 1956. Lacan chose this as the opening text in his *Ecrits*, published in 1966.

From these seminars in the early 1950s on, Lacan's work centred on his teaching. Any writing he did was essentially a distillation and extraction of material that had been produced for, and gone over in, his weekly seminar – sometimes reworked a number of times and in a variety of forms. In the early 1950s, the weekly seminar was almost the only point of access to Lacan's thought; now, several years after his death, the published transcripts of these seminars serve as the preferred means of access to that thought. The notorious difficulty of Lacan's 'writings', as he called them when collecting some of them for publication in 1966, is very much attenuated in these records of his didactic practice. The fact that he returned again and again in his seminars to certain themes, described briefly above, allows the reader to view the question, the concept at issue, from a number of different vantage-points.

Here, I intend to give the potential reader of *Seminar II* a guide to a text which has more the form of a baroque mosaic than a linear sequence. Lacan refers to his seminar as a 'panoramic table', and I hope to do no more than establish an inventory of themes, indicating to the reader a number of places where he or she might stand in order to gain a view of at least some of the main landmarks. Amongst these main themes, there are three that stand out: the machine, the Other and – providing the overall unity for the year's seminar – repetition.

In *Seminar II*, one finds the same mixture of textual commentary, of digression, and of unexpected analogy and reference that characterised the first seminar. If anything, the degree of lively controversy and questioning of Lacan's discourse by participants in the seminar is sharper there than in *Seminar I*, and the seminar displays the same unpredictable mixture of literary reference, philosophical argument, of analytic case-history and conceptual dissection. Here, however, the overall slant is different.

Whereas in *Seminar I* Lacan was primarily concerned with developing and correcting notions that had been set out in his earlier works, particularly in the 'Rapport de Rome' (published as 'The function and field of speech and language in psychoanalysis' in 1953) and his papers on the mirror stage, in *Seminar II* there is a distinctive new theme: the theory of the machine, of communication and of cybernetics. The climax of the year's seminar was the lecture Lacan contributed to a parallel series on 'Psychoanalysis and the human sciences', which he had organised under the auspices of the SFP; his lecture was entitled 'Psychoanalysis and cybernetics, or on the nature of language'. In fact, the course of the year's seminars was fundamentally affected by this series, which ran in parallel with his seminar. Both the theme of the machine and cybernetics and that of the human sciences (entwined in Lacan's presentations) give a slant to his teaching that leads it away from being the commentary on the Freudian texts which it was advertised as (not that he had ever restricted himself to straightforward commentary) and towards being a broad meditation on the epistemology of psychoanalysis and an examination of the true novelty of Freud's work. Often enough, the seminars opened with references to the lectures that had taken place the night before and to the discussions to which they had given rise – particularly to the lectures given by Benveniste, Hyppolite, Koyré, Lévi-Strauss and Merleau-Ponty. In consequence, the reader of *Seminar II* becomes aware that the extant transcripts record only part of a sequence of discussions that were going on in the SFP as the year went on.

In place of an introduction

What may surprise the reader of *Seminar II* is the direction from which Lacan approaches his chosen topic, the ego in psychoanalytic theory and technique. There are virtually no references to the Freudian text which has become canonical for similar discussions in Britain and America: Freud's *The ego and the id*. Nor, even more surprisingly, does Lacan discuss Freud's paper on narcissism, and his own complement to this paper, the 'mirror stage'. Lacan assumes that the members of the seminar are familiar with the work that had been accomplished the year before, in *Seminar I*, where the topic of the ego had been discussed at length in connection with the theory of the imaginary and with questions of technique arising from identification and the dyadic relation. There, Lacan had elaborated upon the mirror-stage theory of the ego's formation, supplementing it with his 'schema of the inverted bouquet', which he then employed as a model for the analytic process. In *Seminar II*, Lacan is moving on from the introduction of narcissism – which was contemporaneous with Freud's writings on technique, and is read by Lacan as the great watershed in the development of Freud's thought – to the second topography of the 1920s. Lacan takes it for granted that the ego of this second topographical model (*Group psychology and the analysis of the ego* (1921), *The ego and the id* (1923)) marks a shift in Freud's theory, a shift made possible by the concept of narcissism; but for him the key to examining this shift lies in the first of Freud's three major works of the early 1920s – *Beyond the pleasure principle* (1920).

In order to understand *Beyond the pleasure principle*, the most difficult and recalcitrant of all Freud's larger works, Lacan engages in a considerable amount of reflection on and clarification of the epistemological foundations of psychoanalysis. In general, Lacan's project in commenting on Freud's text was not so much to give them one reading among others as to attempt to 'express the conditions thanks to which what Freud says is possible'.[42] There are numerous occasions when Lacan sums up an argument by saying, in effect: 'If Freud's discovery doesn't mean that, then it doesn't mean anything.' Engaging in such a project, such a method of reading, requires even more ground-clearing preparatory work than usual when dealing with *Beyond the pleasure principle*. As a piece of avowed speculation, it lends itself to, indeed requires, speculative interpretation.[43] Hence the larger part such methodological, historical and philosophical discussions play in this seminar: the early passages on the place of Freud's discovery in the history of the ego from Socrates to today, in which Lacan places Freud in close relation with the 'moralist' tradition, from La Rochefoucauld and Pascal to Nietzsche; the claim that Freud's shift in the 1920s, and particularly in *Beyond the pleasure principle*, amounts to an attempt to save psychoanalysis from its absorption back into academic psychology, as well as from neutralisation by the very patients who had first been cured by it, and who, through its very existence, had become immunised against it. This latter was, and was to remain, a perennial theme in Lacan's work:[44] the claim concerning the 'general lessening of therapeutic effectiveness'[45] after the First World War (and continuing after the Second World War). It forms one of the bases for his call for the necessity of reworking the foundations of psychoanalysis, through a return to Freud. But the return to Freud must repeat Freud's strategy, i.e. re-invent psychoanalysis just at the moment it becomes familiar and loses its alien character: the patients who can offer psychoanalytic interpretations of themselves display 'the most annoying trick one can pull on an oracle's priest',[46] so the priests must keep one step ahead of the supplicants.[47]

Key passages in *Seminar II* are devoted to discussions of the epistemological position of psychoanalysis in relation to the exact sciences, culminating in the proposal, in the lecture on 'Psychoanalysis and cybernetics', that psychoanalysis belongs with the 'conjectural sciences': those disciplines concerned with the 'signification of chance'.[48] It is not entirely clear how Lacan came to choose the term 'conjectural'.[49] 'Conjecture' is here opposed to 'exact', in the way 'probable' is opposed to 'certain', but also in the way 'opinion' is opposed to 'knowledge'.[50] What is clear, though, is the context in which Lacan advances this claim: as a claim, or hope, on behalf of psychoanalysis, that psychoanalysis should not lose itself in a hopeless quest for the respectability of the exact sciences – a respectability which they retain only because of the blindness which leads epistemology to overlook man's crucial relation to the symbol, which defines the limitations and the possibilities of both 'exact' and 'human' sciences.

This is by no means the first occasion on which Lacan introduces the notion of the conjectural sciences.[51] However, the background furnished by the lengthy discussions of the machine, of the real (the question Lacan addresses in *Seminar II*: 'Why don't the planets speak?'[52]), of cybernetics, of chance and the nature of mathematics gives a much stronger sense of the limits and nature of the conjectural sciences to which psychoanalysis belongs. (Others, coming later, might well have taken this privileged epistemological field to be that occupied, for a brief and glorious period, by structuralism.)

Perhaps the starting-point for Lacan's discussion of questions pertaining both to the relation of psychoanalysis to the history of philosophy and of thought in general, and to questions of vital importance to analytic theory and technique is the simple thesis: humans are more like machines than they are like animals.[53] The statement brings together two somewhat controversial, but very familiar, premises and constructs something entirely new and daring out of their conjuncture.

Firstly, there is the fruit of seventeenth- and eighteenth-century materialism (Descartes's *L'Homme* to La Mettrie's *L'Homme machine*): animals are machines in the crude sense that they are made up and function in the same way as bits of clockwork and hydraulic engines. Then there is the fruit of nineteenth-century naturalism (Darwin): humans are animals, in so far as their bodies perform the same functions, in accordance with the same laws, as animals, and, most importantly, share a common history with animals. To many twentieth-century minds, it has always seemed to follow that, *therefore*, humans are *both* animals *and* machines. It does follow. Lacan's thesis is at once perfectly compatible with the two claims and yet immediately presents one with a task, usually avoided by the somnolent complacency, or the anxious panic, with which one accepts or confronts the naturalisation and mechanisation of humans: the task is the specification of the exact kinships and analogies implicit in these claims. Taken within the context of mid-century psychoanalysis, to which it seemed inconceivable that anything but biology could play mother and nursemaid to the fledgling psychoanalysis, its consequences are revolutionary: instead of mother biology always promising (or is it threatening?) to absorb (or is it repudiate?) her natural offspring, psychoanalysis, the fledgling finds itself in a field all of its own, but one in which its near neighbours at least speak in its own language, namely the language of the symbol.

In *Seminar I*, Lacan employed detailed arguments and considerations concerning animal behaviour to explain his theory of the imaginary, without running the risk of being taken for a biological reductionist, a charge he so often levelled at his psychoanalytical peers. In *Seminar II*, it is the turn of the other bugbear of Freud's metapsychology, its mechanistic orientation, to receive unexpected development. To many, Lacan, with his emphasis on speech and language, imbued with the philosophy of Hegel and Heidegger, would be expected to line up on the side of the humanistic, anti-biological, anti-mechanistic defenders of the autonomy of psychoanalysis. Instead, he is virulently anti-humanistic (in much the same way that Michel Foucault was later, in the closing chapter of *The order of things*, to welcome the spectre of the 'death of man'). And he repudiated any defence of the autonomy of psychoanalysis which denied the claims of other disciplines to relevance to its theory or practice. Such a defence (akin to the 'ostrich policy' he describes as evidenced in Poe's *The purloined letter*[54]), he perceived, was often allied to a complacent neglect of biological and physical thought.

Lacan's views on the epistemological status of psychoanalysis accorded it an altogether grander status: a dynamic relation of equals between psychoanalysis and the other, the exact, sciences. For Lacan, Freud's was a Copernican revolution not only in the sense that it changed *man*'s position in the 'universe', by displacing man's centre away from himself, but also in that it fundamentally affected the meaning of *physics* (and hence of the very notion of a universe). Physics is as much a product of man's relation to the symbol as is psychoanalysis, save that in physics the symbol in question is mathematical, 'a little letter written on the blackboard'. In physics, moreover, the subject is obliged to adopt a specific position *vis-à-vis* the symbol: the position of the impersonal, intersubjective subject, completely interchangeable with any other subject. Psychoanalysis, on the other hand, revealed the asymmetrical relation of the corporeal and mortal subject to the symbol: it is the action of the individual subject that reveals and constitutes his or her unique relation to the symbol. To give an example, one which Lacan later made very much his own: each of us has a relation to a pure symbol, the family name, surname, or name of the father, which carries within it a relationship to our birth and our future progeny (and thus our own deaths). The name of the father here distills an essential dimension of all language: the rock-like permanence that language aims at imposing upon a chaotic, ephemeral world, and the freedom that the ephemerality and inconsequentiality of speech grants to the animal that refuses the constant pressure of reality and instead indulges in creating an alternative, possible world not subject to the biological laws of life and death.

The symbol itself, the unit of natural languages, has altogether different properties from the formal languages of mathematics, as the existence of dreams (and Freud's method of deciphering them) showed. Yet Lacan wished to indicate how the subject of psycho-analysis was caught between these two functions of the symbol: between natural symbols (caught in the imaginary) and the laws of the symbolic.

The first symbols, natural symbols, stem from a certain number of prevailing images – the images of the human body, the image of a certain number of obvious objects like the sun, the moon, and some others. And that is what gives human language its weight, its resources, and its emotional vibration. Is this imaginary homogeneous with the symbolic? No. And it would be a perversion of the meaning of psychoanalysis to reduce it to an emphasis on these imaginary themes . . . [55]

In contrast, the symbolic is the formal, systemic – what Lacan calls the 'combinatorial' – aspect of language, which is no less primitive than natural symbols, and, more importantly, constitutive of the very existence of the symbol:

Meaning is the fact that the human being isn't master of this primordial, primitive language. He has been thrown into it . . . Here man isn't master in his own house. There is something into which he integrates himself, which through its combinations already governs . . . Man is engaged with all his being in the procession of numbers, in a primitive symbolisation which is distinct from imaginary representations. It is in the middle of that that something of man has to gain recognition. [56]

In consequence, the new discovery about the subject that Freud's discovery represents for Lacan inevitably requires a revision of the concept of the 'subject of science' (the subject seemingly presupposed by the existence of science as a system of knowledge), since science, as much as psychoanalysis, depends upon the symbol for its effects.

Each time that Lacan discusses the conjectural sciences he makes a sortie into the history and philosophy of science:

. . . it is impossible not to make a general theory of the symbol the axis of a new classification of the sciences where the sciences of man will once more take up their central position as sciences of subjectivity. [57]

He juxtaposes the possibility of the conjectural sciences with the exact sciences which, beginning with Newton, rendered Nature mute and measurable, in accordance with the law of the symbol – that is, in accordance with mathematical laws: Lacan ceaselessly reminds his audience that the purest symbol available is the little letter on the blackboard, the $\int$, the π and the ∞. The experimental sciences rely on mathematics to introduce the measurable into the real. Yet any string of little letters, or, more straightforwardly and teasingly to the mathematically innocent, of little numbers, such as 000100011101, requires an order and a sequence to be imposed on them, so that they take on meaning. That is, they are perceived as conforming to a rule – they necessitate an interpretation. Lacan is here, self-consciously, echoing the critiques levelled at the then-new probability theory during the eighteenth century by mathematical purists such as d'Alembert. It is the fact that rules are required to generate mathematical truths, and hence are required to interpret the measurable world, that also shows Lacan how to assimilate the Freudian concept of repetition – upon which the very idea of transference is finally based – to an effect of the combinatory of signifiers which make up the unconscious.

Hence, for Lacan, Freud's project at a scientific psychology is the first psychoanalytic attempt to render rule-governed the phenomena of consciousness. But this is not accomplished by a purported reduction to matter and motion, which is the nineteenth-century dream of a world-machine, a world steam-engine, but through returning to an older conception of the machine, that of Pascal and the probabilists of the eighteenth century, a conception which is also, all of a sudden, both in 1954 and today, in fashion in the cybernetic and mathematical conception of a machine as nothing more than a finite system of instructions to perform simple operations on strings of symbols which constitute the 'input'.

Lacan's conception of repetition in psychoanalysis thus renders it far more akin to information theory and to what is now called 'artificial intelligence' than to a quasi-biological property of the animate. The groundwork for a reorientation of the history of science that this interpretation of repetition and its relations to the post-Freudian sciences entails has been accomplished by professional historians only within the last ten years, through work on the history of probability theory and of thermodynamics – for instance, in the epoch-making work of Ian Hacking, *The emergence of probability*, and the revolutionary re-interpretations of eighteenth-century psychology and mathematics of Daston, of statistics of Porter and others.

With such an outlook on the cartography of the sciences, Lacan could not but be sensitive to the broad-based movement in the history of ideas associated with the theory of information and the science of cybernetics (as Wiener, in his book of that name, published in 1948, called it). However, any use of the new concepts of message, communication, information, system would have to retain the masterful sensitivity to linguistic nuance and the contours of conversation that Freud's case-histories and dream-analyses demonstrated, which were such a feature of Lacan's own style and which Wiener had duly noted, in his *The human use of human beings* (1950), as crucial to the fledgling cybernetics. What made Lacan's analysis in *Seminar II* of the Edgar Allan Poe story, *The purloined letter*, so successful was that he crafted his discussion of chance, number and the sign so as to make possible an entirely new approach to the concept of repetition upon which *Beyond the pleasure principle* is based. Repetition is not just an empirical fact, something that the psychoanalyst has discovered through noticing that neurotics repeat their forgotten traumas, that they repeat (in the transference) their forgotten relations to their parents; repetition is also a formal interpretative principle, akin to a Kantian category appropriate to psychoanalysis. When something the patient does or says is not understood, it is a guiding principle that this is because the act or speech is a repetition of something yet to be discovered. As Freud put it, in a sentence whose inherent paradoxicality and profundity I have often insisted upon: 'Above all, the patient will *begin* his treatment with a repetition . . . '[58] Since the analyst *necessarily* takes up the position of not-understanding (the patient comes, asking to be understood, thus creating the state of not-understanding which analytic work requires in order to be possible), what is always being sought is the unknown scene which is being repeated, or the rule in accordance with which the act or speech has taken on the character of a repetition for the subject. A patient enters the analyst's den wearing a walkman – what is being repeated here?

At the same time as he proposed this new conception of repetition as the category upon which analytic understanding is founded, through discussing Poe's story, Lacan offered a literary reading of that short text that is still exemplary and revolutionary in its implications for literary criticism, whether psychoanalytic or not.[59] Lacan approached these questions by the seemingly inauspicious avenue of 'the machine'.

Lacan's use of the term 'machine' would have been much clearer if he had made use of, or had available to him, the term 'Turing machine', which is pretty much what he was talking about for much of *Seminar II*. Dennett has defined the Turing machine as 'nothing more than a finite system of instructions to perform simple operations on strings of symbols which constitute the "input"'.[60] Yet certain of Lacan's meditations would not be so stimulating if he had restricted the term 'machine' to this, the now-standard definition. Lacan links two machines together, gets them into conversation, in order to demonstrate how the concept of the imaginary, of man's essential bond with the image, is to be grafted on to a world of machines-in-conversation. He also wishes to point out historical difficulties in the development of thought about machines, from Descartes to Hegel and then to Freud. He thus wavers between discussing machines in relation to energy (as is also the case in cybernetics and works dealing with entropy and its relation to information theory) and machines in their relation to 'thought' (as is the case with the classic papers on Turing machines by Turing, Lucas, Church and others): the machine that Gödel's methods of proof and Turing's extensions of them made possible.[61]

Lacan was arguing what the proponents of artificial intelligence now propose: that the abstract theory of the machine, founded on the concept of information, and not on the concept of 'mechanics' in the eighteenth-century sense, nor on the concept of 'unified organism' of nineteenth-century science, supplies a non-reductionistic and powerful model of the distinctively human. It does so because its mathematics and its models deal solely with the laws of the symbol. Lacan was to return in his later work to the Gödelian side of this field of enquiry, in his discussion of number theory and its relation to the concept of identification.[62] The cybernetic side was, however, left more in abeyance in his later seminars.

Mapping out the consequences of his novel approach to the machine and of its philosophical accompaniments led Lacan to address the 'biologies' of Freud's *Beyond the pleasure principle* and libido theory.[63] He concludes that neither is a true biology, that they both constitute a non-biological 'biology'. Indeed, his conclusion, in the closing sentences of the year's seminar, is that 'the death instinct is only the mask of the symbolic order . . . The symbolic order is simultaneously non-being and insisting to be, that is what Freud had in mind when he talks about the death instinct as being what is most fundamental . . . '[64] The sequence of argument links Freud's concept of repetition with the theory of the machine, by giving a novel interpretation of nineteenth- and twentieth-century energetics and its progeny, information theory. Such an interpretation has become less idiosyncratic since Prigogine and Stengers' global re-interpretation of the concepts of physics as centred around thermodynamics and the description of non-reversible systems.[65] But to understand how Freud misconstrued phenomena manifested by the subject in analysis (in particular those of repetition, more globally those grouped under a concept of 'the circuit of discourse' that Lacan introduces into the seminar) into a seemingly biological mould, Lacan turns back to the model upon which *Beyond the pleasure principle* was based: the metapsychology of the *Project* and of chapter 7 of *The interpretation of dreams*.

With the *Project*, Lacan once again discovers the machine, the machine that, in Freud's own words, 'almost ran by itself'. Lacan makes it quite clear that, for him, the machine is not alien to the human sciences, as 'humanistic' thinkers have supposed. 'The machine embodies the most radical symbolic activity of man.'[66] It is cybernetics that furnishes Lacan with the materials to flesh out this thesis. Giving what we might call an information theory reading of Freud's *Project*, he indicates how the so-called psychological version of this model to be found in *The interpretation of dreams* is an attempt to take a further step forward by introducing the dimension of temporality (from whence all its own inner contradictions arise). Lacan then turns to his (cybernetically oriented) claim: Freud's dream-theory is less about the psychology of the dream than it is about the message of the dream (and the 'dreamer'); what Freud is interested in is the message *as such*, in the message as part of 'interrupted, but insistent, discourse'.[67]

A perennial theme of this and other seminars is the argument that what passes for a one-body 'psychology' – on occasion in Freud and in those psychoanalysts who conceive of themselves as constructing a psychology – is in fact more akin to a description of the analytic process, the relation between analyst and analysand. Thus, Lacan shows how Freud's concept of censorship does not refer to an internal psychological event, or process, but rather is related to, while distinct from, the concept of resistance in dream-interpretation and analytic practice, and is more akin to the 'law of discourse' and to the specific 'law' that one cannot understand the whole of the law. Similarly, resistance is argued not to be an internal psychological state, to be 'attributed', as if this were a question of responsibility (no matter how excusable), to the patient (or, even more implausibly, to the symptom), but is the correlate of the pressure and the work of the analyst. ('There is only one resistance, the resistance of the analyst.'[68]) When Lacan comes to deal with Fairbairn's anti-drive theory, an object-relations version of psychoanalysis, the concept of the 'internal object' or the 'internalised object' goes hand in hand with a technique in which the analyst's ego is the only measure for the patient's imaginary world; what is more, the notion of the 'observing ego' is simply another name for the analyst 'observing' the patient.[69] Each of these criticisms is an attack on a psychoanalytic psychology, conjoined with the enactment of the injunction to tie psychoanalytic theory more closely to the practice of analysis. 'Similarly, when it comes to our patients, please give more attention to the text than to the psychology of the author – the entire orientation of my teaching is that.'[70]

To illustrate one version of this injunction, Lacan turns to Freud's dream theory, in order to show how Freud is concerned less with the psychology of dreams (despite writing a final chapter in *The interpretation of dreams* entitled 'The psychology of the dream-processes') than with their meaning and the methods for their interpretation. That is, Freud is more concerned with textual singularities than he is with mental processes. Here, Lacan engages in one of his seeming digressions – one of those unexpected *tours de force* for which he has become famous: a reconsideration of the dream of Irma's injection, demonstrating that the question Freud asked himself was: 'What is the meaning of dreams?', to which his dream answered: 'Meaning'. Yet this answer takes on its full significance only once it is articulated within the theory of the subject's relation to the symbolic – which is the dimension in which Lacan situates this term 'meaning'. Much of the rest of *Seminar II* is devoted to the exploration of the symbolic and of the introduction of the term that was to be central to so much of Lacan's later work: the Other.

Having demonstrated that the practice of analysis requires a recognition that intersubjective relations are there 'at the beginning', Lacan, following Freud, goes 'beyond'. The route he takes to this beyond is the path of the symbolic: as so often in this seminar, via the machine. Through a consideration of the game of even and odd – which Lacan identifies as mirroring the most primitive of modern machines, the machine that works in binary notation, namely the digital computer, the game itself giving a foretaste of the analysis of Poe's story, since it is taken from that story – Lacan clarifies the notion of the discourse of the unconscious and the relations of the symbol and the real. The weight of the symbolic is here accentuated: the subject is seen to stand in a passive relation to those amongst the chain of discourses which require his response (for instance, Freud's family romances, which were such an important ingredient of his conception of the Oedipus complex[71]). From

there, Lacan shifts tack, moving on to the analysis of *The purloined letter*, truly a lucky find for him, as it integrates the repetitions of scenes so familiar to the analyst with the mathematical
precision of a sequence determined by a structure (the rules by
which the sequence is produced), from which something unexpected arises.[72] The movement of the letter in Poe's tale provides an
allegory of the analytic process, whilst it also demonstrates that it
is the structure in which the letter is placed which determines the
effects of meaning and the possibility of understanding for the
participants in the transmission of the letter. The letter is the unit
of the machine of language, the action of the participants is the
speech of this letter, this machine, whilst the letter is truly what
speaks, or bespeaks, *them*. And it is at this point, via the question
of the relation of speech to language and of play and games (*le
jeu*), that Lacan introduces the Other and, with it, the schema L
(or Z-shaped schema), with which he goes on to describe the
vicissitudes of the process of analysis in terms of his concepts of the
ego and the other, of the subject and the Other, and the imaginary, the symbolic and the real.

The importance of the concept of the Other in Lacan's thought
cannot be over-emphasised; nor can the essential polyvalence of
the concept. Hence the background to the concept of the Other is
too vast a topic to be discussed at sufficient length here. Some brief
pointers will have to suffice.

The dimension of deception and lying, already of great significance in *Seminar I* and a recurrent and characteristic theme of
Lacan's, here guarantees the necessity of the concept of the Other.
The fact that the subject can lie obliges us to think that there is a
beyond of intersubjectivity.[73] Lacan often juxtaposes the experience of deception and lies, so familiar in everyday life, and doubly
so in the psychoanalyst's everyday life, with its significance in the
history of philosophy and science. Once again, he turns to a
discussion of Descartes's demon (who might trick him into
believing what is not true) and the necessarily truth-saying God
that Descartes invokes in order to ground the universe of science,
and of Einstein's reprise, with its reference to the God of the
scientist, who is not malicious. Wiener had also traversed the same
territory, interpreting Einstein as assuming that God does not
bluff in his poker game with the physicist – Lacan had avidly
absorbed his and other cyberneticians' work.[74] But it is as much
the lie of the patient as it is the trick that God may play on the
analyst that gives Lacan's meditations on deception their force. In

Seminar III, Lacan put the reason for introducing the Other as follows:

And why with a capital A [for *Autre*]? For a no doubt mad reason, in the same way it is madness every time we are obliged to bring in signs supplementary to those given by language. Here the mad reason is the following. *You are my wife* – after all, what do you know about it? *You are my master* – in reality, are you so sure of that? What creates the founding value of those words is that what is aimed at in the message, as well as what is manifest in the pretence, is that the other is there *qua* absolute Other. Absolute, that is to say he is recognised, but is not known. In the same way, what constitutes pretence is that, in the end, you don't know whether it's a pretence or not. Essentially it is this unknown element in the alterity of the other which characterises the speech relation on the level on which it is spoken to the other.[75]

As I have noted above, one must not forget the influence of Claude Shannon, of John von Neumann and Oskar Morgenstern's *The theory of games*, and of Norbert Wiener's work on Lacan's thinking in *Seminar II*, and hence on the generation of the concept of the Other. However, if the concept of the 'other' or 'Other' found its immediate post-war echo in Sartre's re-addressing of the Kantian problem of the 'other' in *Being and nothingness* (and also of the related Kantian question of the relation between transcendental and empirical egos), the detailed framework for Lacan's concept owes more to his interpretations of Hegel's *Phenomenology*, together with the Lévi-Straussian and Maussian context of language, exchange and structure. From Hegel, and particularly from the dialectic of the 'beautiful soul', Lacan takes as given the necessarily intersubjective character of all human cognitive, affective and moral states. Here is the source for Lacan's claim that the fundamental desire seeking expression in analysis is the desire for recognition. And any desire for recognition immediately invokes a conception of what that other's desire could be that would lead it to recognise the subject. Hence Lacan's gnomic formula that 'desire is the desire of the other'. From Mauss and Lévi-Strauss, he takes the assumption that exchange relations, of women, of words, of Mauss's 'gifts' – with the mirroring obligation they bring with them – are primary in human social relations. And beyond these ingredients, there are Lacan's meditations on specific turns of speech, specific ways of addressing the other, which imply an Other beyond the other: in particular, when I lie to the other, invoking the Other as the repository of the truth I conceal. And also, when I address an other in speech which aims at a pact or a contract – Lacan's favourite examples being 'You are my wife', 'You are my master.'[76] And, apart from these cultural references, Lacan's meditations on the limits and consequences of his *own* version of the 'other' (with a small 'o') of the mirror stage and on the relation of the imaginary to the symbolic are obviously of great importance. Lacan's great advantage over Sartre, Merleau-Ponty and his other peers is that he is obliged to confront a specific question concerning a specific practice: 'What sort of "other" is the psychoanalyst?', 'What sort of theory of "otherness" is required to account for the existence of psychoanalytic discourse and direct the analyst's action?'

It is the neglect of intersubjectivity, manifest in the neglect of the dimension of speech and language, that Lacan criticises in Fairbairn, as he had done with respect to Balint the year before. What is at issue in analysis is not need, as many British analysts argued, conceiving of need as modelled on peremptory physiological states, but desire: the desire for recognition. Hence the subject is not faced with just an object; all analytic experience indicates that it is the relation to another subject that 'places' the relation to the object. Object relations are always triadic (others might say Oedipal), in much the same way as Freud describes all jokes as involving three persons: the teller, the hearer ('the joke's third person'),[77] and the absent second person, the 'object' of the joke.[78]

It is this schema that Lacan employs to analyse the comedy *Amphitryon*: 'in the end, it is always a matter of me, you and the other'.[79] In both Molière's and Plautus' plays, the ego appears as the comic figure most capable of arousing intimations of the uncanny and of arousing the desire to annihilate the other: the double. Yet Lacan's analysis intertwines the miserable fate of the ego and its double (the dimension of the imaginary) with a disquisition on the structure of marriage and its ideals: the woman, the husband and the god (that of the symbolic). And here the seminar draws to a close, with its summarising lecture on cybernetics, and a final tour of the schema L, with which Lacan sums up the articulation of theory and practice. His promise for the following year is the exploration of the structure of paranoia and of Schreber's system. He kept that promise, in *Seminar III*, on *Les Psychoses*. Yet there is a sense in which the disquisitions on the machine of *Seminar II* might well have been developed more fully, a retracing of his steps that Lacan never got round to, whether or not he ever contemplated it.

Certainly the intellectual climate of 1954 was to be – indeed, was being, at that moment – radically transformed in one way which

Lacan did not suspect: the revolution in biology associated with the deciphering of the genetic code. How would the realignment of biology and psychoanalysis have seemed to him, given that biology itself was incorporating the symbol and its coding into a new combinatory, made up of four letters? Certainly the biology utilised by those analysts whom Lacan criticised was from that moment on displaced, so that, in replacing biology with linguistics, and adaptive function with significatory insistence in *Seminar II*, Lacan was perhaps engaged in an unnecessary pre-emptive strike, given the conceptual necessities (and the scientific Dunkirk or Trojan horse) that would be forced upon the human sciences once biology had become molecular, and had thus become the brightest, newest and best-funded sub-department of the sciences of codes, of reading and writing, and the transmission of messages. I even fancy that Lacan's ebullient pessimism and irony might well have been touched by the recognition that, in the age of AIDS, the sexual destinies – as well as the lives and deaths – of men and women are now inextricably bound up with an obscure entity that goes by the name of reverse transcriptase.

7

WHAT THE PSYCHOANALYST DOES WITH WORDS: AUSTIN, LACAN AND THE SPEECH ACTS OF PSYCHOANALYSIS

I shall show that there is no speech without a reply, even if it is met only by silence, provided that it has an auditor: this is the heart of its function in analysis.
Jacques Lacan[1]

Why is language most efficacious when it says one thing through saying another?
Jacques Lacan[2]

Prefatory remark

The argument of this long chapter can be put quite straight-forwardly. I begin by pointing out the virtuosity with which the analyst deals with syntactically peculiar communications. These tempt one to locate certain fundamental features of the analytic interpretation in a mode of grammatical analysis. However, such a view proves to be less fruitful than focusing on the surprisingly convergent ideas of Austin and Lacan on the nature of speech acts: performatives and founding speech. These not only help one understand the *action* to be expected from speech in general, and the transformation of the patient that is projected from that action, but also give a more satisfactory idea of the transference interpretation. The analyst acts so as to *undo*, or to *neutralise*, the unconscious effects of the speech acts the patient, despite him- or herself, employs, whilst opening the way for full speech: speech which transforms the speaker in the very act of saying.

I

We are all familiar with the Wittgensteinian view that philosophy arises from the abuse of language; philosophical problems arise when language goes on holiday.[3] We rid philosophy of itself by replacing the philosophical question in a context of use of language which resolves the problem, makes it disappear, just by re-establishing that use – what Wittgenstein calls its place in the language-game. This activity has obvious, and no longer novel, similarities with psychoanalysis: 'The philosopher's treatment of a question is like the treatment of an illness.'[4]

We are also more familiar than we used to be with the idea that the psychoanalyst is a specialist in linguistic matters, both theoretical and practical. I would even go so far as to claim that Wittgensteinian philosophical questions concerning language are an everyday, if uncelebrated, part of the analyst's, or at least of Freud's, practice. Take an example from the analysis of the Ratman. From a very young age he was under the delusion that his parents knew his thoughts.

. . . at that time [age six] I used to have the morbid idea that my parents knew my thoughts; I explained this to myself by supposing that I had spoken them out loud, without having heard myself do it.[5]

He started the sixth session of his analysis by reminding Freud that he had had this persistent belief that his parents knew his thoughts, and then continued with a story from his twelfth year, when he had been in love with a little girl, who had not shown him as much affection as he desired.

And thereupon the idea had come to him that she would be kind to him if some misfortune were to befall him; and as an instance of such a misfortune his father's death had forced itself upon his mind. He had at once rejected the idea with energy. And even now he could not admit the possibility that what had arisen in this way could have been a 'wish'; it had clearly been no more than a 'train of thought'.

– By way of objection I asked him why, if it had not been a wish, he had repudiated it.

– Merely, he replied, on account of the content of the idea, the notion that his father might die.

– I remarked that he was treating the phrase as though it were one that involved lèse-majesté: it was well known, of course, that it was equally punishable to say 'The Emperor is an ass' or to disguise the forbidden words by saying 'If any one says, etc. . . . then he will have me to reckon with.' I added that I could easily insert the idea which he had so energetically repudiated into a context which would exclude the possibility of any such repudiation: for instance, 'If my father dies, I shall kill myself upon his grave.'

– He was shaken, but did not abandon his objection. I therefore broke off the argument . . .[6]

142

There are many points of interest in this passage. For the moment, I wish simply to point out that Freud is trying to persuade his patient that his 'thought' must have been a wish, since he reacted to it as if it were a wish. The means of persuasion were to demonstrate that the phrase, 'My father is dead' does not behave like the phrase, 'I wish my father dead.' The Freud we come upon here would have been perfectly at home hammering out the various uses of the phrase, 'I apologise', as we find it in the Oxford ordinary language philosopher Austin, or even pondering on the various available responses to 'How're you doing' that the post-ethnomethodologist Harvey Sacks recently investigated.[7]

Yet Freud's aim was evidently not simply the sorting out of the grammatical and philosophical confusions of his patient for its own sake,[8] as if he were the turn-of-the-century Viennese equivalent of the English language columnist of a Sunday newspaper.[9] He is attempting to find out why the phrase, 'If my father dies . . .' had been repudiated with such energy, and what connection it had to the patient's persistent fear that his parents knew his thoughts. The discovery that the Ratman treats this thought *as if* it were a wish is only the first stage to discovering what catastrophe the Ratman thinks would befall him if he were to wish such a thing.

Freud ascertained that, in true obsessional style, the Ratman introduced the conditional sentence: 'She will be kind to me if father dies', and then repudiated the whole sentence. Freud's responses were all focused on offering sentences whose various structures contained the phrase, 'my father dies'. What Freud intervened to provoke was the introduction of the wish, and a clarification of its relation to, maybe even its assumption by, the first person: 'I wish that my father were dead, so that she would be kind to me.' He wants to know where the first person is to be found hidden in this sentence, and how it is related to the second and third persons. The original preconscious thought had been: 'I wish she were kind to me.' The energetic repudiation was a clue which pointed Freud in the direction of the element which apparently gave rise to that repudiation: /My father dead/. To open up the structure of the resistances, 'to set the conflict going in the field of conscious mental activity',[10] he indicated a variety of other sentence structures open to the speaker which had all been foreclosed by the repudiation:

1 If /my father dies/, she will be kind to me.
2 If anyone says /my father is dead/, they will have me to contend with.
3 If /my father dies/, I will commit suicide.

By making explicit the discursive rules governing the structure of *lèse-majesté*, Freud has indicated how the obsessional can absorb the 'you' of the punitive superego firstly into the impersonal form of 'If anyone . . .', 'If . . .', and then into his self, so that the references to the 'I' and the 'me' can cover all the functions usually taken up by the punitive 'you' of conscience.[11] Freud's manipulations of the various possible constructions to be derived from such a repudiation make it clear that he was searching for a way into the closed, ghost-filled world[12] of the obsessional patient, by trying to make it possible for him to avow a statement in which the functions of the 'I', the 'you' and the impersonal forms had become more explicitly articulated; the sentence Freud had in mind was 'I wish that my father were dead.'[13]

The Ratman thinks that he speaks without hearing himself do so. One might say that the Ratman's relation to the other who listens is disturbed. Already, at age six, the Ratman's 'I' is alienated in his act of speaking in such a way as to foreclose the possibility of his saying anything substantial to the other – does he not already know his thoughts?[14] A first crude description of this state of affairs would be: once the 'real' other is no longer there, the speaker installs an imaginary other in his place, an other who, in contrast to the real other, is skewered by the patient's words, but is also an imaginary parent figure who already has heard everything: a universal and effective superego. Such an interpretation of analysis was offered by Foucault, possibly following Lacan,[15] in his little-read book, *Mental illness and psychology*: mental illness arises from a regression into the imaginary from the real of dialogue.

The reality of the analytic dialogue can only be assessed once one has introduced the concept of transference. In the transference, it appears as if the second person, the 'you', truly enters the explicit discourse of the session. Then the analysis of the patient's 'I's and 'he's will take on an added dimension. This is true and important. But before we come to discuss the transference, it is already clear that 'pronoun' analysis would appear to be another of the analyst's tools. Such a view would make of the analyst not only someone who fills in the gaps left by censorship so as to make a coherent narrative, not only someone who infers the explicit from the implicit clues the patient leaves for him or her, but also someone whose attention will be centred on the pronouns, the 'I's and the 'thou's the patient uses.[16] I will eventually conclude that this view is inadequate; but for the moment I wish to pursue the idea somewhat further.

What the psychoanalyst does with words

As the passage quoted at the beginning of this chapter indicates, the act of speech in analysis implies a reply, as long as the analyst fulfils the function of auditor, and it is one of the main functions of the analyst to clarify from whom the reply is expected. The analyst must not only pay attention to the subject (and object) of the statement – the 'I' of 'I fear that something terrible will happen to my father and my fiancée'; he or she must pay attention to the 'I' that utters this sentence, to the subject of the utterance.[17] The function of the analyst, we might say, is not only to listen (as if he or she were 'listening *in*'), but also to *hear* – where hearing (as opposed to listening) implicates the hearer in the utterance of the speaker. The analyst places him- or herself in the speaker's firing-line, as it were, and assumes he or she is the 'you' that is implied every time the subject of the utterance sallies forth, whether as the speaker or as the speaker who is covered over by the proliferation of 'I's (or 'you's) in the statement.

But the analyst is also addressed as the other on the level of the statement – he or she is *called* things, is named as a charlatan, a crook, a tyrant, a pricktease, and every other figure in the personal armoury of the patient's imagination. One of the major features of the analyst's interventions will be to clarify, by beaming back to the patient, the exact character of the 'you' who is being addressed, and via geometrical projection, as it were, or even projective identification, the correlative 'I' posturing in front of it – noting how the charlatan always finds his ingenuous sucker, the sadist his masochist and the tyrant his slaves.

What this amounts to may be no more than the familiar analytic technique of uncovering the ego's identifications.[18] Yet paying attention to the pronoun usage of patients may have its own advantages. We might say that it was no accident if Freud engaged in such a virtuoso analysis of the linguistic acrobatics implied by *lèse majesté* – the rules of censorship of this monarchical mode of repression apply most directly to any indirect form of speech. We could plot the rise of the psychological novel, that genre which celebrates and interrogates the individuated subject, by mapping onto an axis of such forms: the epistolary novel, the rules governing the representation of dialogue and so forth. By introducing the notion of *lèse majesté*, Freud was invoking a certain relation between speaking subjects. The absolutist monarch requires that all his subjects be subject to his desire. If one of them were allowed to quote another as having said 'The Emperor is an ass', a differentiating grade of subject would have been created, which would have had repercussions at the level of the absolute object; it would have created the possibility of another collectivity alongside the domain of the Sovereign, whereby he would be obliged, by a rule of demarcation of one subject from another, to acknowledge the possibility of their talking together. This grade – and I purposely employ the term Freud used in *Group psychology and the analysis of the ego* – is the superego, the agency which introduces the possibility of indirect speech: the conscience, which addresses us in the intimate second person, and from thence gives rise to the impersonal narrative function.[19] In other words, banning indirect speech amounts to an attempt at banning certain imaginary relations between subjects, and requires that all speech be addressed to the monarch. A similar structure holds for certain conceptions of one's relation to God: without the law on blasphemy, God would not know whether he was being spoken to.

However, the psychoanalyst adopts the mirror image of the absolute monarch's position, in that he is posited by the fundamental rule as someone to whom one can say anything. That is, the analyst does not, to start with, recognise the distinction between direct and indirect speech; if the subject says: 'She then said, "The key to understanding you is the fact that you dance well" ', the analyst may well ignore the quotation marks, and take this statement as one that the 'subject' himself has said – as indeed, in that very moment, he has. The analyst hears everything as if it were addressed *directly* to him, just as the monarch does. Such a recognition or codification of the analytic rule of thumb gives us a clearer understanding of the laws of the unconscious as Freud stated them: there are no hypotheticals[20] or tenses[21] in the unconscious, there is no negation,[22] no citation. The 'if's, 'but's and 'as if's of ordinary discourse are placed on a different axis from that of syntactic organisation; as Freud reflected in somewhat sanguine fashion, in a phrase that reveals both that he was not so alienated from philosophy as he sometimes made out and that he was acutely aware of the complex object to which his account of the unconscious had to do justice: 'even the phenomenology of obsessional thinking has not yet had sufficient attention paid to it'.[23] On the one hand, then, the analyst ignores negation, treats as inaudible the (invisible) quotation marks of indirect speech; but on the other hand, as we saw, the analyst may well attempt to *restore* to the patient's speech these quotation marks or the hypotheticals that get dropped in the dream-work. To hear the unconscious, the analyst ignores syntax; to interpret it, he restores it. The analyst's interventions always have these two sides: on the one hand seductively open to getting embroiled in the fantasised figure of the arbitrary punitive monarch of language, who punishes whatever is said, however it is couched. This axis of fantasy is the imaginary relation of the 'I' to the father. On the other hand, each intervention is intended to open up the possibility of a revelation in which what is said to the 'I' – either by his unconscious or out of the mouth of the analyst – is taken from the locus of the Other, from the resources of language.

II

In *Language and the origins of psychoanalysis*, I coined the phrase the 'propositional' or 'grammatical' mode of analysis to describe the preoccupation with grammar, with formalistic transformations of propositions, as found in Freud's paper on the Schreber case and other texts of Freud's. In the Schreber case, Freud shows how the core proposition of Schreber's psychosis is a distorted transformation of the sentence, 'I love him.'[24] This method is eminently textual, and we do find Freud quite often talking of the text of a neurosis, employing bookish metaphors. Indeed, one of the most striking of these occasions is when, in the Dora case-history, he likened the transference to a new edition of an old text.[25]

The procedure I have discussed so far, in which the analyst's work is described as a form of pronoun analysis coupled with syntactic analysis, or a to-ing and fro-ing between syntactic reduction and syntactic elaboration, could well be thought of as an extension of this method, a deepening of the analysis I offered there. Yet, there is something misleading about these models of the analytic process. There is also something similarly misleading about some of the ways in which Lacan's work has been read and interpreted. Jacques Lacan became famous for his emphasis on the importance of language for psychoanalysis. Amongst his gnomic formulae we tend to get stuck on ones such as: 'The unconscious is structured like a language' or 'The unconscious is the discourse of the other.' If we then go more deeply into Lacanian theory, we encounter the complexities of the theory of the signifier. A number of explanatory texts have made us more or less familiar with his linguistic reading of a variety of other psychoanalytical concepts, such as his notion that repression is metaphor, that desire is metonymy.[26] At times Lacan argued that he was returning to Freud, supplying him with an explicit and formalised version of linguistics – the structural linguistics of Saussure and Jakobson – in order to render to Freud what was truly Freud's. Hence – the logic of the signifier, its relation to the signified, the theory of meaning – symbolic and the real. All these aspects of Lacan's theory have received some attention, have gained some notoriety because of the extraordinary difficulty of Lacan's writing and of his theory.[27] They have also given the impression – an impression compounded by the larger hearing Lacan has gained in the English-speaking world in non-analytic circles than in analytic or therapeutic ones – that Lacan was primarily a theorist and that his writings have at most indirect consequences for the actual practice of psychoanalysis. This chapter is intended to show the opposite – that Lacan's central concern is not with psychoanalytic theory as a complex system, whether of egos or signifiers, but is rather about how to be an analyst.

Then why, I may well be asked, are Lacan's writings so remote from most psychoanalytical writing, in which patients are either parcelled out into egos and ids, into unconsciouses and consciouses in classical psychoanalytic theory (or into the various selves of later ones), or are the subjects of clinical case-histories, narratives of lives and of treatments?

The answer lies in Lacan's recognition that the working material of analysis is speech and that the function of the analyst is to listen and to intervene. In teaching analysts, as Lacan did from the late 1940s in his weekly seminars, one must teach *how* to listen and *how* to intervene: how to say the right thing at the right moment. The various models of the psychoanalytic encounter will all attempt to give some idea of how to do this. And it is clear that what is thought to be the referent for the intervention and to whom the intervention is spoken will be among the crucial factors in the analyst's finding out how to intervene.

What my formalist reading of Freud and the overly theoretical readings of Lacan draw attention away from is the speech of the psychoanalytic session. Lacan, unlike faithful Saussureans, was as much concerned with speech (*parole*) as with language (*langue*).[28] I will now argue that Lacan's notion of speech, as found in the seminal 'Rapport de Rome' – whose title is: 'The function and field of speech and language [*langage*] in psychoanalysis' – and in many of his seminars, has strong affinities not only with Heidegger, a fact noted by others,[29] but with the conception of speech acts put forward by J. L. Austin at about the same time.[30]

In his 'Rapport de Rome', Lacan took as the necessary starting-point for the analyst's reflection on the speech of the session the following:

> Even if it communicates nothing, the discourse represents the existence of communication; even if it denies the evidence, it affirms that speech constitutes truth; even if it is destined to deceive, the discourse speculates on faith in testimony.[31]

Lacan then organised much of his discussion of the function of speech in analysis around what he called three paradoxes of the relation of speech to language.[32] The first of these is when the subject's speech has 'given up trying to get itself recognised' – psychosis, which Lacan calls an objectification of the subject in a language without dialectic.[33]

The second paradox of the relation of speech and language is the privileged domain of psychoanalytic practice, the study of neurosis, in which 'speech is driven out of the concrete discourse that orders the subject's consciousness, but finds its support in the natural functions of the subject or in images'. Lacan emphasises, however, that, in contrast to psychosis, this is 'speech functioning to the full, for it includes the discourse of the other in the secret of its cipher'. Thirdly, the subject may lose his meaning in the objectifications of discourse. 'Here is the most profound alienation of the subject in our scientific civilisation.'

What these three characterisations of disturbances in the relation of speech to language have in common is the notion of a disturbance of the discourse of the other. Lacan's notion of the unconscious is just that: the unconscious is the discourse of the other.[34] But here it also has the immediately visible sense – something goes wrong when conversing with the other. These concerns – the communicative function of speech, certain blindly restrictive conceptions of language, the misfirings and infelicities of discourse – are also those of speech act theory, as initiated by Austin's *How to do things with words*.

Austin's work is firstly a critique of the reification of discourse found in many theories of language influenced by logical positivism and the early Wittgenstein, which presuppose that language is primarily descriptive, or constative. In this sense, his argument speaks to the third of Lacan's disturbances of speech and language: the alienation of the subject in science. Austin intends putting a limit on the hegemonic tendencies of positivistic claims to demarcate all statements into true and false ones. Instead of conceiving of utterances as statements to be tested for their truth or falsity,

Austin pointed out that most utterances have nothing to do with truth or falsity.[35] Sometimes his arguments have a critical function: like the therapeutic function Wittgenstein accorded philosophy, they are meant to cure us of bad linguistic habits. And they do so with a characteristic wit.[36]

Of course philosophers have been wont to talk as though you or I or anybody could just go round stating anything about anything and that would be perfectly in order, only there's just a little question: is it true or false? But besides the little question, is it true or false, there is surely the question: *is* it in order? Can you go round just making statements about anything? Suppose for example you say to me 'I'm feeling pretty mouldy this morning.' Well, I say to you 'You're not'; and you say 'What the devil do you mean, I'm not?' I say 'Oh nothing – I'm just stating you're not, is it true or false?' And you say 'Wait a bit about whether it's true or false, the question is what did you mean by making statements about somebody else's feelings? I told you I'm feeling pretty mouldy. You're just not in a position to say, to state that I'm not.' This brings out that you can't just make statements about other people's feelings (though you can make guesses if you like) . . .[37]

But Austin also advanced a positive theory of how speech works. Instead of statements being divided into true and false ones, he argued that most utterances are acts, they perform – hence he called these utterances 'performatives'. The sorts of examples he chose to illustrate how speech acts are instructive: the words, 'I do', uttered in the marriage ceremony, words which constitute the act of getting married; the word 'Done!', which is the conclusion of a wager accepted; the words, 'I name this ship Mister Stalin' – which is the naming of the ship, and not the description of the ship. The most striking and exemplary act soon became the promise – promising is not a statement about the world, and the utterance of a promise is quite clearly the act of promising itself.[38]

So such utterance cannot be translated or transcribed into a form that looks like a description – to do what they do, no other words will do under these circumstances. One cannot say: 'I state that I do', or 'I believe that I am correct in calling this ship Mister Stalin.' These utterances are no longer the same as the speech act they are meant to transcribe; they do not amount to the act of marrying or naming – they are now instances of the speech act misfiring.

Speaking very roughly, Austin's twin targets in this theory were, firstly, the positivist idea of language as consisting in poor approximations to scientific statements and, secondly, the notion that utterances are a re-presentation of inner, psychic states. Lacan shared this double critique: indeed, he assimilated them to each other in his criticism of the notion of inner psychic states to be found in the scientistic ego-psychology of post-war America, which reified the dialectical movement that the psychoanalytic dialogue set in motion. Hence, when Austin criticises the view that the words 'I do' in the marriage ceremony are a report on an inner state of mind, and that this can either be a true or a false report, he recognises that this view is implicitly maintained by positivist moralists, who cannot accept language as its own guarantee. Austin points out, impishly, as ever, how such an amoralistic, spiritualist view would allow someone marrying to squirm out of the charge of bigamy by saying: 'My inner spiritual state was not the whole-hearted affirmation that my utterance of the words might have led you to believe.' Allied as Austin so often was with legal thinking at this point, he spelt out why such a defence is inadequate: in such circumstances as a marriage ceremony, indeed in all speech acts, our word is our bond.[39] As such, it eclipses all speculation about inner states.

Austin's broadly legalistic philosophy, in which our word is our bond, in which social life requires some kind of expectation that we will tell if not at least the whole truth, then something akin to it, in tune with Wittgensteinian behaviourism (the meaning of a word is its use), thus converges with a contractual notion of intersubjectivity, and with a quasi-religious view of the pre-eminence of the word – themes we find repeated and reworked in Lacan's conception of psychoanalytic discourse. Lacan speaks of the symbolic law embodied in language, of the primordial act of witnessing, of the primary social function of the password. None of these functions is to be found in structuralist accounts of language, which purport to analyse the laws of *langue* (often enough as if it were *langage*): Austin and Lacan both share in the recognition that the individual utterances of language, *parole*, are not just instances, as Saussure led some to believe, but are the heart of the study of language. What is also striking is that neither Lacan nor Austin chose the path that the post-Chomskean sociolinguists,[40] or the ethnomethodologists, followed: both Austin and Lacan refused to take a functionalist account of 'communication' as the basic, Kantian-like category for the analysis of utterances.[41] Lacan, psychoanalyst, cannot for one moment suppose that language succeeds in communicating, as any functionalist account will assume:[42] the very existence of psychoanalysis is a permanent testimony to the failure of communication. And Austin's insistently witty commentary never lets us forget that speech acts misfire, are null and void, professed, hollow, purported, empty – misunderstanding is the rule as much as it is the exception, and the task is as much to investigate the rule of misunderstanding as it is to explain it away. When a person who is already married goes through the form of marriage ceremony, we say, according to Austin, that the ceremony is void or without effect.

This does not mean, of course, to say that we won't have done anything: lots of things will have been done – we shall most interestingly have committed the act of bigamy – but we shall *not* have done the purported act, viz. marrying. Because despite the name, you do not when bigamous marry twice. (In short, the algebra of marriage is BOOLEAN.)[43]

And it is quite clear that these misfirings, misapplications, misexecutions, misinvocations, these misunderstanding are first cousins to that other group of linguistic phenomena isolated and permanently re-baptised by Freud: mistakes, misnomers, mislayings, misprints, misreadings – Freudian slips.

Austin's attention to the unsuccessful performative, the natural outgrowth of his view that these utterances are acts, and thus, like all conventional acts, liable to failure, prevents him from adopting the specious conception of speech as always succeeding. Like all distinction-levellers, such a functionalist interpretation of discourse would be self-defeating, since the very notion of success is destroyed if there is no failure. Freud, Lacan, Austin each give voice to acute – sometimes tragic, sometimes comic – appreciation of the ubiquitousness of failure.[44] But another very common conception of language that is immediately exposed as impoverished is the notion that speaker and hearer are in a symmetrical position. If speaking is acting, instead of an utterance being the voicing of a statement about the world which then becomes implanted or transferred into the mind of the other, then only one party can commit that act – whatever part the other has to play, he or she is not the agent. Indeed, certain speech acts will undercut the supposed freedom of the listener in the very act of their utterance: Austin erects a category of perlocutionary speech acts, whose salient feature is that they transform the other through the fact of their utterance.[45] Austin's twin critique, of science and of the mythology of inner mental states, is again well served by this conclusion. One of the epistemological foundations of scientific institutions and method is the complete and mutual substitutability of any given subject of knowledge; the ideal and rigorous demand for repeatable experiments, the notion of a democratic community of scientists, is part of the apparatus fulfilling this epistemological condition. Austin's account of speech acts reveals just how foreign such a notion of the subject is to the ordinary use of speech. Interpretations of the psychoanalytic situation that cling to this scientific ideal of symmetry require one to hold that such inner mental states are somehow imitated, in some ghostly fashion or other, in the mind of the hearer of the utterance. This is exactly the ideal of psychoanalysis as a communication from ego to ego, or from unconscious to unconscious – the ideal that Lacan attacked.[46] Lacan's approach to this question was to concentrate on certain classes of speech act in which pronouns behave in a rather odd way.[47]

The special behaviour of pronouns which Lacan emphasised was something he called 'founding speech' – archetypally a form of naming of the other that is also a transformation of the subject.[48] Founding speech transforms both parties in the act of saying.

The form in which language is expressed itself defines subjectivity . . . [I]t refers itself to the discourse of the other. As such it is enveloped in the highest function of speech, in as much as speech commits its author by investing the person to whom it is addressed with a new reality, as for example, when by a 'You are my wife', a subject marks himself with the seal of wedlock. This is in fact the essential form from which all human speech derives rather than the form at which it arrives.[49]

Muller and Richardson make the following enlightening comment on this passage from Lacan's 'Rapport de Rome':

What is *la forme*, *la forme essentielle* which is at stake here? Judging by Lacan's examples, it would seem to be the second-person singular and as such indicating the opening of a domain inclusive of the other in so radical a fashion that to address another in any way (not just with the solemnity of vows) is to invest him with a new reality, a new role, minimally the role of respondent.[50]

The other is transformed; but the crucial aspect of founding speech for Lacan is that the *subject* is also transformed. Such propositions necessarily imply another proposition, predicated on 'I': 'I am your husband.' Now these utterances are certainly speech acts in Austin's sense, even though they do not include performative verbs; indeed, they go beyond those acts that he studied most closely, in *necessarily* implicating both subject and other in the act.[51]

It is true that no one in his or her right mind would think that asking whether I am telling the truth when I say 'I love you' is a demand on me to offer the same kind of confirmation as when I am questioned about my saying 'These stones will be green until the year 2000.' Such a recognition underlines Lacan's description of the antinomy between speech and language:

As language becomes more functional, it becomes improper for speech, and in becoming too particular to us, it loses its function as language.[52]

Psychoanalysis aims at the transformation of the subject. It aims at 'full speech' – at times equated in Lacan's texts with founding speech:

Full speech is speech which aims at, which forms, the truth such as it becomes established in the recognition of one person by another. Full speech is speech which performs [*qui fait acte*]. One of the subjects finds himself, afterwards, other than he was before. That is why this dimension cannot be evaded in the analytic experience.[53]

Analysis aims at such a transformation, yet it is prey to a one-sided portrayal as a sort of game, a form of play, a trial run, or an illusory *mimesis* of reality.[54] Yet, paradoxically, its means are those of the inauthentic and the irresponsible:

the analytic method, if it aims at attaining full speech, starts off on a path leading in the diametrically opposed direction, in so far as it instructs the subject to delineate a speech as devoid as possible of any assumption of responsibility and that it even frees him from any expectation of authenticity. It calls on him to say everything that comes into his head. It is through these very means that it facilitates, that is the least one can say, his return on to the path which, in speech, is below the level of recognition and concerns the third party, the object.[55]

Speech can either be directed towards a third party, towards the object, or it can make explicit the dimension within which the speaker and the auditor have achieved, or are in the process of achieving, or failing to achieve, the mutual recognition that is the a priori condition of speech itself. The act of naming is exemplary of the implicit condition which is realised in the very act of speech. 'I name this ship *The Good Ship Psychoanalysis*' implies that this is what *you* name it as well – if it is not what *you* call it, then I have not really named it. But I do not have to ask your permission to name it that; what I do is anticipate your agreement.[56]

Schematically, we can say that the pivot around which these two functions of speech turn is the 'you': as addressee, as mirror of the 'I', and as staging-post towards the third party, the third term, the object of speech – that of which one speaks.[57] It is the double movement of speech that Lacan focuses on here:

The symbolic function presents itself as a double movement within the subject: man makes an object of his action, but only in order to restore to this action in due time its place as foundation.[58]

The creation of the object, or the attention accorded it, preoccupies the speaking subject, to the exclusion, for the main part, of the founding act through which the speaker and the auditor are transformed.

One might think, from the examples that Lacan chose, that in founding speech we are dealing with sets of binary terms, defined as such by the dictionary: master–disciple, husband–wife. But Lacan offers another example in *Seminar III* which indicates that, although such examples yield the most striking instances of the transformation of the subject in the naming of the other, such effects are not confined to such pairs, and that the effects of uttering such a founding sentence are extremely subtle. He suggests the following two utterances:

1 'Tu es celui qui me suivras.'
2 'Tu es celui qui me suivra.'

The first depends upon a construction we do not possess in English (it is rare and baroque in French): the verb in the clause agrees, not with the impersonal, 'third-person' demonstrative, but with the second-person singular subject of the main clause. To characterise the second utterance, Lacan employs a term Austin had employed: constative. This second utterance takes note of, purports to describe, a future state of affairs: this 'tu' *will* follow me. It is almost as if the first person were making a promise on behalf of the second, thus pre-empting the second person's doing so. This taking note of a state of affairs which is a mask for the commandeering of the other's action easily allows the sense of the statement to slide into one of persecution: that person is following me. The fact that the verb has a third-person ending means that the distance between the 'tu' who is and the (third) person who follows is elided; this elision requires the 'I' implied by the sentence to adopt a corresponding posture.

The first sentence, with 'suivras', the second-person ending of the verb, indicates the faith that the speaker has in the 'tu' who will follow, whereas in the second sentence, the speaker betrays certitude rather than confidence. One might say that in the first sentence the 'I' of the speaker is implicated in a special plea, a demand, on the other, the 'tu'. This is even clearer in the other example that Lacan gives: 'Tu es la femme qui ne m'abandonnera(s) pas', 'You are the woman who will not abandon me.' When the verb, 'abandonnera', has a third-person ending, the assertion 'you are the woman who will not abandon me' borders on threatening behaviour. With the second-person singular verb ending, the desire of the speaker, that he should not be abandoned, is voiced, precisely because it accords greater freedom to the other.

Lacan calls this function of language 'invocation', 'with all the religious connotations of the term'. He adds:

Invocation is not an inert formula. It is how I bring into existence [*je fais passer*] in the other faith which is mine.[59]

In Austinian terms, this is a perlocutionary faith. But Lacan is touching here on the dimension of convention, of the contract, the pact of language. There is nothing beyond speech which grounds it; but none the less it is as if it were grounded on a pact. Every act of speech brings with it the possibility of the pact's being broken, of the other intending to mislead me, even through telling the truth. Austin is entirely clear about the contractual underpinning of speech acts; Searle implies it when he refers to institutional theories of communication and the necessity of the concept of rule for analysing speech acts.[60] The promise is exemplary in this respect, for Searle, Austin and Lacan:

The unconscious is that discourse of the Other in which the subject receives, in the inverted form appropriate to the promise, his own forgotten message.[61]

Why inverted? If we take the promise to be a social organisation of the present around a predication as to the future,[62] it is the inversion of the relations of future and present that becomes striking. Take a famous and literally foundational promise: 'I promise to pay the bearer on demand the sum of . . .' If anyone ever arrived at a position where he or she felt obliged to make this demand, we know the promise would not be worth, as the saying goes, the paper it is written on. This promise as to the future is a pure speech act, and guarantees only (financial) reality, the pure exchange relation, in so far as the demand (in general, or for the delivery of what the promise promised) is deflected elsewhere, in a never-ending circuit that is sustained by and sustains this promise. Such a promise, which we would do well to regard as exemplary of promises, those most exemplary of all speech acts, indicates how the act of speech is its own guarantee. It is only the fantasy of a miser, the root of both metaphysical and social realism,[63] which could imagine that the capacity of a bank to 'fulfil' such a promise would be impaired by making all the gold in its vaults radioactive. Here, indeed, confidence is at a premium, because the certainty is that the promise could never be delivered.[64]

Lacan found another, perhaps simpler way of putting it:

You know those messages that the subject sends out in a form which structures them, grammaticalises them, as coming from the other, in an inverted form. When a subject says to another *you are my master* or *you are my wife*, it means precisely the opposite. It passes via the Other and via the ego, and then gets to the subject, who it all of a sudden enthrones in the perilous and problematic position of spouse or disciple.[65]

Confidence, the pact, the social contract, the institution of marriage, 'institutional facts'[66] – these lead Lacan to invoke my faith as speaker, in the relation I have to this Other who is 'only the guarantor of the Good Faith necessarily invoked, even by the Deceiver, as soon as what is at issue is no longer the paths [*passes*] of struggle or of desire, but the pact of speech'.[67] It is also surely no coincidence that Sartre's critique of psychoanalysis, with which Lacan was extremely familiar, was directed at the inadequacy of the psychoanalytic explanation of bad faith – admittedly as conditioned by his mechanistic reading of psychoanalysis.[68] Here again, the practice of psychoanalysis involves a curious reversal; as I have already pointed out, the subject in analysis is asked to forgo all intention to be sincere, forgo all striving for authenticity.

In analysis one lets go of all the moorings of the speaking relationship, one eschews courtesy, respect, and dutifulness towards the other. *Free association*, this term is a very poor one for defining what is involved – we try to cut off the moorings of the conversation with the other. From then on, the subject finds himself relatively mobile in relation to this universe of language in which we engage him.[69]

The fundamental rule invites, although it does not require, the subject to behave irresponsibly. Yet within this 'free speech', cut free of its moorings, it turns out that, perhaps predictably, the subject loses its bearings. And it is just then that the subject's bearings, its *points de capitons*, come clear: in the authentic speech that it inadvertently offers to and requires of the analyst. If the obsessional seems to believe that language was discovered in order to prevent him from knowing anything, even his own desire, the hysteric finds in speech the unique means for testing the gullibility, indeed the nerve, of the other, of determining whether he can find anyone who can give him an answer that testifies to the existence of good faith.[70]

What are the most appropriate terms to employ at this juncture? Searle plumps for the term 'commitment';[71] Lacan often employs the verb *engager*. We are dealing with an area implying social bonds, links, the very cement of the social, the institutional – the Symbolic. Lacan demonstrates this very neatly in connection with a woman patient of Balint's, who cannot get going in analysis because she, quite rightly, realises that speaking responsibly will be painful. One day, she chatters away in analysis even more than usual, until the analyst discovers what she is evading: admitting that she has a letter, a character reference, in her purse, which says that she is a trustworthy person. That is what she cannot avow. From then on, the analysis gets going. Lacan comments:

So as not to be committed, located in the world of adults, where one is always more or less reduced to slavery, she chatters away so as to say nothing and fill the sessions with hot air. We can stop for a moment, and ponder on the fact that the child also has speech. It is not empty. It is as full of meaning as the speech of the adult. It is so full of meaning that adults spend their time marvelling at it – *See how clever he is, the sweet little thing! Did you hear what he said the other day?* . . . The wonderful speech of the child may perhaps be transcendental speech, the revelation of heaven, the oracle of the little god, but it is clear that it doesn't commit him to anything . . . In the transference situation . . . what is at issue is the value of speech, no longer this time in so far as it creates the fundamental ambiguity, but in so far as it is a function of the symbolic, of the pact which links the subjects together in one action.[72]

This network of 'speeches' ramifies in Lacan's text, until the entire history of the subject can be seen as a genealogy of commitments, of pacts, into which the subject enters, in large part without quite knowing how:

Each subject doesn't simply have to take cognisance of the world, as if it all happened on the level of noetics, he has to find his way about in it. If psychoanalysis means anything, it is that he is already engaged in something which has a relation to language without being identical to it, and that he has to find his way about in it – the universal discourse . . . I have often underlined that already before his birth, the subject is already located not only as sender, but as an atom of concrete discourse. He is in the chorus line of this discourse, he himself is, if you prefer, a message.[73]

Nor can the analyst maintain such an Olympian position in the cut and thrust of the session. The murmur of the universal discourse – and of the subject's insertion into it, the sense in which he is the bearer of his forebears' messages, the consequence of 'all the fornications of our parents, grandparents, and the other scandalous stories which give psychoanalysis its piquancy'[74] – all this is like the breaking of the sea which has to be heard through the incessant traffic along the coastal highways which makes up the discourse, and the day-to-day life, of the speaking analytic subject. The analyst will be obliged to pick up the echo of a life ruined by a broken pledge of marriage through the insouciance with which the subject, whenever he has the opportunity to do so, arrives late. Freud, of course, knew how to hear such murmurs. Even in the *Studies on hysteria*, we can read, admittedly between the lines, but with no great effort, how Miss Lucy R., the governess who had fallen in love with her widower employer, had constructed her neurosis out of the doubly intolerable position that her keeping, and her breaking, of a promise had placed her in, behind which we can hear the murmur of an arduous identification with her mother:

– 'Was there something particular, apart from their fondness for you, which attached you to the children?'
– 'Yes. Their mother was a distant relation of my mother's, and I had promised her on her death-bed that I would devote myself with all my power to the children, that I would not leave them and that I would take their mother's place with them. In giving notice I had broken this promise.'[75]

Lacan's category of 'founding speech' goes one stage further, though in the same direction, as Austin's description of speech acts in general: founding speech is an invocation in which the *I* and the *you* are simultaneously modulated. We can get a sense of the extent to which this is a step beyond Austin by considering one of Austin's examples: the ceremony of marriage. Everything he says about the marriage, the possibility of bigamy, the ceremonial circumstances that guarantee that the marriage takes place – all this is enlightening, amusing and profound. Yet he assimilates one of the most striking features of marriage to the unexamined notion of convention: the fact that you need two people, both saying 'I do', for the marriage to come off, or, as he says, to be consummated.

However, this idea of convention, conceived of as if all it takes to come off is for every individual subject to place him- or herself in the same position *vis-à-vis* the rule governing it and then follow the rule, conceals a peculiar interdependency, whereby the two parties are not *just* each following the same rule. After all, they are getting married to each other, as well as joining the institution of marriage. Imagine one of the two people saying 'I do', upon which, at the last moment, the other party flees from the altar. What status does the first 'I do' have in retrospect? It obviously receives its ratification as a solemn pledge from the other 'I do' – and not from an inner state of true-heartedness or intentionality. In other words, this initial 'I do' contains within it something like a condition that 'You do as well.' Of course, one couldn't say so – since saying so would change the nature of the speech act. Just imagine if the first respondent said, 'I do on condition that you do.' Some queer looks would be exchanged, and some deep feelings hurt.[76]

The imaginary instance shows how Austin's homing in on marriage, on betting, on naming, lends itself to Lacan's point: namely, the intimate interconnection of the 'I' and the 'you' in founding speech.

III

The next step I want to take is a simple one, and the most momentous one, and it will bring us back to Freud.[77] It is that 'transference' is the name given to this striking use of pronouns, this transformation of the speaker and the auditor, in the analytic situation. What is crucial is that the analyst reacts to this emergence of founding speech, these transforming pronouns, in an equally striking way. To Lacan, the shift from founding speech to transference was straightforward. He implies that psychoanalysts all along have been (and quite probably are) hypersensitive to the dimension of founding speech, in which the speaker and the auditor's relation is transformed, because that is what the transference is.

In its essence, the efficacious transference which we're considering is quite simply that speech act. Each time a man speaks to another in an authentic and full manner, there is, in the true sense, transference, symbolic transference – something takes place which changes the nature of the two being present.[78]

One handy, though crude, definition of transference is: any reference by the analysand to the person of the analyst, or to the present situation in which the dialogue is taking place.[79] Let us take a simple example:[80] the first mention in Freud's writings of something he called the transference.

What the psychoanalyst does with words

In one of my patients the origin of a particular hysterical symptom lay in a wish which she had had many years earlier and had at once relegated to the unconscious, that the man she was talking to at the time might boldly take the initiative and give her a kiss. On one occasion, at the end of a session, a similar wish came up in her about me. She was horrified at it, spent a sleepless night, and at the next session, though she did not refuse to be treated, was quite useless for work. After I had discovered the obstacle and removed it, the work proceeded further; and lo and behold the wish that had so much frightened the patient made its appearance as the next of her pathogenic recollections and the one which was demanded by the immediate logical context.[81]

There is something ever so slightly coy about this passage. Freud passes over in silence the exact means by which he removed the obstacle, and we are then treated to the rhetorical splendours of 'lo and behold' – though I should say that this is a gratuitous addition of the English translation, albeit one which is not out of keeping with the original tone: Strachey probably added it to emphasise Freud's feeling of relief once the obstacle had been surmounted. What was this obstacle?

The patient had the thought: 'Why doesn't he take the initiative and give me a kiss?' There is already something peculiar about this thought: is the wish that someone else take the initiative itself taking the initiative, while disowning the responsibility? In other words, is it not already the splitting of the performative down the middle, so that the other appears as a wilful automaton, acting in Austin's sense, but in fact acting *out* the wishes of the other? Let me leave that question to one side: the paradox is inherent in the very logic of seduction itself – seduction is either a performance that two people put on together or it is not seduction, it is rape (see chapter 4). It is just – or even more – like marriage, you cannot do it alone.

But let us return to the obstacle and the patient's wish for a kiss. Note how it is the 'he' of her wish which Freud causes to vacillate, taking his cue from the linguistic fact that it is the act of speaking that gives this shifter its reference. So, she wishes that 'he' will give her a kiss, and it is this wish that torments her sleepless night. How did Freud overcome the obstacle? Clearly, in some unspecified way, he engineered her into avowing that she wished a kiss from him; he managed to get her to utter some such sentence as: 'I want you to kiss me.' More likely than not, Freud, being Freud, then gave her one of his little lectures on psychology (as he had done with the Ratman, in the sessions discussed at the beginning of this chapter); but the upshot of this lecture must have been

161

something like this. It is not 'me' you want to kiss – something has gone wrong with the pronoun you are employing here. What has gone wrong stems from something you are not aware of, something which is unconscious – something that the 'I' of your sentence does not want to acknowledge.[82]

Something complicated has happened, something has gone 'wrong' (because, after all, who is to say to whom it really refers?) with the pronouns, 'I' and 'you' – that is what the transference interpretation amounts to. Behind the seemingly determinate 'you' is an indeterminate 'he', whose specification in the discourse as 'you' and its clarification as the analyst's 'not-me' then allows the scene of the memory to emerge: the 'he' becomes this other man, with his name, proper name, description and so forth. Freud puts all this clearly and succinctly, when he summarises the nature of the obstacle as follows:

It lay in inducing the patient to produce information where apparently personal relations were concerned and where the third person coincided with the figure of the physician.[83]

This third person here starts off its analytic life as a grammatical third person. And the act of sorting out the 'I's, 'you's and 'he's is a grammatical analysis. Yet it is also the sorting out of the speech acts involved. Freud not only disentangles the pronouns that have become displaced and transferred; he restores the dimension of 'wish' to the patient's disturbing image of the man kissing her. It is this process of restoration that indicates that interpretation includes the dimension of force associated with speech acts.[84] When reflecting on the 'phenomenology of obsessional thinking' necessary for the understanding of the treatment of obsessional neurotics, Freud wrote:

. . . it would be more correct to speak of 'obsessive thinking' [rather than obsessional ideas], and to make it clear that obsessional structures can correspond to every sort of psychical act. They can be classed as wishes, temptations, impulses, reflections, doubts, commands, or prohibitions. Patients endeavour in general to tone down such distinctions and to regard what remains of these psychical acts after they have been deprived of their affective index simply as 'obsessional ideas'. Our present patient gave an example of this type of behaviour in one of his first sessions, when he attempted to reduce a wish to the level of a mere 'train of thought'.[85]

One can say that putting it this way allows one to recognise the dimension of affect, of energy, what Freud in this passage calls the *Affektindex*,[86] in the relations between the two parties. This is because the category of speech covers the same domain as that of affect: of wishing, fearing, promising, taking pleasure, of distrusting, and so forth.[87]

I want now to turn to another passage from Freud's account of his sessions with the Ratman, so as to bring all these themes together. The passage comes from the patient's second session. He was attempting to describe the experience which had led him to seek help from Freud. While on manoeuvres during his military service, he had come into contact with a Captain who was obviously fond of cruelty, and who told him a story about an especially horrible punishment used in the East:

Here the patient broke off, got up from the sofa, and begged me to spare him the recital of the details. I assured him that I myself had no taste for cruelty, and certainly had no desire to torment him, but that naturally I could not grant him something which was beyond my power. He might just as well ask me to give him the moon. The overcoming of resistances was a law of the treatment, and on no consideration could it be dispensed with . . . I went on to say that I would do all I could, nevertheless, to guess the full meaning of any hints he gave me. Was he perhaps thinking of impalement? – 'No, not that . . .'[88]

Having told his story, with what Freud took to be a feeling of 'horror at pleasure of his own of which he himself was unaware', the patient went on to describe the confused and complicated story of a debt that he had had to pay off, which he had so embedded in a network of prohibitions and compulsions that he had ended up in a terribly confused state. As he told the story of his confusion, he became more and more confused. Freud commented:

I will only add that at the end of the second session the patient behaved as though he were dazed and bewildered. He repeatedly addressed me as 'Captain', probably because at the beginning of the hour I had told him that I myself was not fond of cruelty like Captain N., and that I had no intention of tormenting him unnecessarily.[89]

In this second session, then, we find an example of the transference that is quite visible and quite close to the 'pronoun' formulation that I put forward in the first section of this chapter: the Ratman addressed Freud as the Captain (i.e. he said something that is equivalent to saying: 'You are the Captain') at the end of the session, thus indicating a systematic confusion of the third person with the analyst (the 'second' person). But the actual point in the conversation that I want to pick up on is at the beginning of the first long passage I quoted: the patient 'begged me to spare him the recital of the details'. The patient begged. This verb, 'to beg' is precisely one of Austin's performative verbs. It is also the first occasion in the treatment when the patient addressed Freud directly – that is, employed the second person. Perhaps his actual words were: 'Please excuse me from giving all the details' – something between a request and an imperative. He might even have said: 'You will *have* to excuse me from giving you details.' The German phrase Freud uses is 'er bittet mich, ihm die Schilderung der Details zu erlassen'. If I am correct in proposing that the management of the transference consists precisely in the distinctive analytic response to being addressed in the second person and, more importantly, in the distinctive reponse to the performative in which this second person is implicated, what follows, then, can only be described as a transference-interpretation: Freud makes it clear that he has *no* taste for cruelty, *no* desire to torment him, but that he is *impotent* in the face of the law of the treatment. What this amounts to is a splitting in the 'you' that the Ratman had addressed: on the one hand, there is the kind, considerate Freud, on the other the implacable, inflexible, anonymous servant of the psychoanalytic contract. And the contract is one to which the Ratman has pledged himself – 'pledge' again being one of the strong performatives, like 'promise'.[90]

Let me spell out one of the points I am making here. This account of the rat torture is one of the best-known and most frequently discussed passages in Freud's case-histories. The rat torture gave the patient his psychoanalytic nickname, and there is no doubting the sheer power of the patient's fantasy, if George Orwell's redeployment of it in the climactic scene in *1984* is anything to go by. But analysts have found Freud's *activity* rather perplexing, if not downright misguided, even wild. How, they ask, could Freud be so interventionist at such a crucial moment of the analysis; how could he walk so blithely into a ready-made fantasised scene, in which he will inevitably be an active party in collaborating with the patient's sado-masochistic scenario, in which Freud will become the torturer by obliging the patient to tell the story, and the patient will become the torturer by inflicting on Freud what the cruel Captain had previously inflicted on him? I am arguing that Freud knew very well what he was doing; he was not responding to the seductions of a narrated sexual fantasy, but to the revelation of the unconscious, to what Lacan calls 'the enactment of the reality of the unconscious': the transference. Freud responded to the performative verb and the second-person singular pronoun that accompanied it. He knew that that is how the analyst acts, and in particular that that is how the analyst gets an analysis going: by inducing the transference neurosis, by inducing the reorganisation of the universal discourse of the patient around the figure of the analyst. Of course, he did not know what that discourse would consist in. And, indeed, he rather wittily pointed out to the patient how ignorant he was of the exact contents of this discourse: 'Was he perhaps thinking of impalement? – "No, not that . . . the criminal was tied up . . ." Into his anus, I helped him out.'[91] Well, Freud might have been ignorant, but he knew the word for the orifice the rats would bore their way into.

Freud knew that in saying he had no taste for cruelty, that he was impotent to undo the pledge the Ratman had made, he would play havoc with the 'you' aimed at in the patient's discourse. The Ratman started the session begging Freud, as if the analyst were someone outside the session who could make it stop, who had power over time and the obligations of speech: he ended up calling him the cruel Captain.[92]

Let me just clear up one possible misconception. One might argue (as Freud was inclined to) that the Ratman identified the analyst and the Captain because Freud had used the words 'cruel', 'torment'. On this account, just setting these signifiers in motion would encourage the patient into the identification, even though Freud had prefaced each word with a negative particle: *no* taste for cruelty, *no* desire to torment. This alternative Freudian explanation would simply run: the unconscious knows nothing of negation, so the Ratman hears Freud as saying: I am cruel, I want to torment you, just like the cruel Captain. Hence the identification.

Such an account seems plausible; one important consequence would be to view Freud's intervention as a mistake, as being too interventionist.[93] However, it is misleading, since it overlooks the fact that what Freud said was very much a direct response to the original transferential moment of the analytic dialogue – the moment when the patient *begged* Freud. Not only that: it also fails to reflect that the *excessive* response Freud gave his patient had a rationale. 'I cannot do anything, I am impotent, I am not what you think I am, but I will do everything I can to help, given the meagre means at my disposal' – this 'part'[94] that Freud plays is an indication that Freud saw his opening and made his move. The opening was the moment when the patient addressed him *directly*, using the second person. In effect, the Ratman was saying: 'yesterday you bound me to say everything – now I want you to unbind me from

165

this pledge to say everything to you'. Freud's reply thus amounted to saying: 'the capacity of the other to hear everything, which is the condition of psychoanalytic treatment, cannot be repudiated by my unbinding you. I am impotent alongside of this function of the universal ear which we have created with your bond. Think what you will of this universal ear, but I can assure you that I myself have no taste for cruelty; things have come to the point where I am deaf to your cries – you must say what you have to say to this other' – and, quite obviously, this other is what Lacan calls the Other. The Ratman responded in his own way, by addressing this big Other as Captain.

Let me recapitulate: I have traced out a string of speech acts, with which the psychoanalytic process is set in motion: first, the pledge; second, the begging; third, the disclaimer. Each of these modulates the relation between the 'I' and the 'you' of direct speech – these *are* the utterances in which the 'I' and 'you' appear. It would be a mistake, one psychoanalytic writers often make, to describe the transference, or the transference-fantasy, as a report on the patient's inner world made to a neutral observer.[95] This is the constative conception of language that both Lacan and Austin reveal to be limited to the language-game created by modern science (if indeed it can be found even there, which is highly doubtful). The psychoanalytic conversation has other laws, other rules.[96]

What I hope to have shown is that the easy management of distorted speech acts, of founding speech gone on holiday, is what the psychoanalyst is doing in the management of the transference. At the beginning, we saw how fluently Freud argued his way round the different speech functions of wishing and thinking. In this other example from the Ratman's history, we saw the full awareness he possessed of the momentous implications of his disclaiming response to the direct appeal for help that the Ratman made upon him. Later in the Ratman's analysis, there occurred another incident relating to the initial pledge, the initial performative the Ratman gave Freud; indeed, this incident could well have been the moment when the knot of the patient's neurosis, his story, could finally be untied, as Lacan points out in 'Le mythe individuel du névrosé'.[97] This incident was the transference fantasy that Freud was kind and patient with him only because he wanted him to marry his daughter. The patient's entire family history, his family romance, was bound up in this fantasy. The solution to the understanding of this history, this romance, came through interpretation of a dream, in which he saw Freud's daughter with two patches of dung instead of eyes. The meaning of the dream? He was marrying Freud's daughter not for her *beaux yeux*, for love, but for money.[98] Money? Well, that is the other side of the psychoanalytic contract. Freud was getting rich on all those florins, those rats, that the patient was giving him: on hearing how much Freud's fee per session was, the patient had 'said to himself': 'So many florins, so many rats'.[99] The dream thus repeats in a densely symptomatic form the patient's wish to be released from the obligation to follow the rules of the treatment: if he marries the daughter, he will undo the pledge he made at the first meeting with Freud, by regaining all that money, as if he were undoing his own words. For the Ratman, his truth, his founding speech, would be to say to Freud: 'You are a man who would give up the thing he loves most, his daughter, to save yourself from me torturing you with my rats.' And he would 'hear' this inverted message, this 'interpretation', in the discourse of the Other, in what Freud might have said, perhaps did say, to him: 'You are a man who would give up the thing he loves most, his fiancée (and thus the very possibility of having daughters[100]), simply to get back the money you've paid me.' Whence we are tempted to ask: are we to moor all those other distorted speech acts on to the acts of payment, of pledging and agreement, with which the treatment begins?[101] Are the 'I' and the 'you' of the analytic contract the primal elements, the founding pronouns of psychoanalysis?

Somewhere I've said that the analyst has to pay to hold onto his function. He pays with words – his interpretations. He pays with his person, in that, in the transference, he is quite literally dispossessed of it. The entire evolution of contemporary analysis is the misunderstanding of this, but, whatever one thinks and however panicky is the recourse to the Counter-Transference,[102] one really does have to take that path. He is not the only one with the person apropos of whom he has made a certain commitment.[103]

8

DEAD ON TIME: LACAN'S THEORY OF TEMPORALITY

Why is the primal scene so traumatic? Jacques Lacan[1]

You must wait for the right moment at which you can communicate your interpretation to the patient with some prospect of success.
'How can one always tell the right moment?'
That is a question of tact . . . Sigmund Freud[2]

I think that it is the earliest possible moment that is the right moment for an interpretation. But I am economical in my interpretations, and if I am not sure what to interpret I have no hesitation in playing for time.
D. W. Winnicott[3]

The timelessness of the unconscious is no doubt determined only in opposition to a common concept of time, a traditional concept, the metaphysical concept: the time of mechanics or the time of consciousness.
Jacques Derrida[4]

That the unconscious knows no time has become one of Freud's metapsychological dicta whose interpretation is most subject to misunderstanding. After all, how could something that exists not be subject to the ravages of time? One presumes that the unconscious came into existence at a given point in time. That it disappears at a given point in time. Lacan put the philosophical critique succinctly as follows:

If indestructible desire escapes from time, to what register does it belong in the order of things? For what is a thing, if not that which endures, in an identical state, for a certain time? Is not this the place to distinguish in addition to duration, the substance of things, another mode of time – a logical time? You know that I have already touched on this theme in one of my essays.[5]

This chapter will be an attempt to clarify the function of time in psychoanalysis: it will be primarily addressed to the enigmatic remarks and aphorisms that Jacques Lacan devoted to the question. Parallel to this exploration is the argument that Lacan's distinctive psychoanalytic theories cannot be fully appreciated without an understanding of his theories of time. Most of the studies devoted to Lacan's work pass over this aspect with a few brief remarks. Yet the practice of variable-length analytic sessions, the *séances scandées* as the French analysts call them, was the key issue over which Lacan was obliged to leave the International Psycho-analytic Association. It is my contention that this practice was not entirely whimsical nor solely dependent upon the grand experiment in and with psychoanalytic technique that Lacan's bombastically imaginative character lent itself to. However, even Lacanian analysts, far more imbued with the teachings and concepts of Lacan than I, admit that the theory of time was never sufficiently elaborated.[6] I undertook this study in search of such an elaboration, and, whilst it may still be true that such a theory never existed in the form in which it *should* have done, the materials presented here will amount in effect to a theory that not only deserves attention but is one of Lacan's most original contributions to the reading of Freud he called his theory. But where are we to start in this reading?

I

The sessions lasted between fifteen and thirty minutes and often seemed long to me. Only once, at the beginning, did he forget that I was in the library and, when I ended up knocking on the door of his study, he was very vexed and almost yelled at me for not having made my presence felt before. I ended up organizing my own *rendez-vous* so as not to have to wait any longer . . .[7]

This is not the normal way analysts and their patients arrange their meetings.[8] Hofstein seems to have been a particularly forceful analysand, deciding to arrange his *rendez-vous* on his terms, rather than Lacan's. Indeed, he goes on in this account of his analysis with Lacan to give another example of successful self-assertion:

I found out that it was the time when he was publishing his *Ecrits*. Everyone started talking about him and I heard things about his practice that didn't correspond to my experience with him. One day I told him a particularly nasty story that was going the rounds. 'That is just not true', he said. I decided that it was, and said so. When I refused to back down on certain points, he didn't insist. It was the analyst who was present and not the 'I' of Lacan. And one could oblige him to keep himself to his position of analyst when he left it. That is something I learnt with him. Like a technique.[9]

'One could oblige him to keep to his position . . .' When it was a question of time, one had to oblige him to meet at one's own convenient moment. But how do you do this? How do you fix a *rendez-vous* unilaterally?[10]

Such questions would inevitably be created by Lacan's unusual practice of having variable times for his sessions. The most obvious and striking consequence, in the various accounts rumour gave of that practice, was the importance of the waiting room. Analysands waiting in groups, expecting (or not as the case may have been) to be called in. When compared with conventional waiting – when one unexpectedly finds oneself early for an appointment, and thus deduces that the experience of waiting is in some sense superfluous, unnecessary, self-induced, when measured besides the objective time of the *rendez-vous*, or when one waits for the other, who is late, but only according to the clock – the Lacanian period of waiting deprives the clock of its senselessly objective tyranny. The question becomes: what is the objective time by which I can measure my waiting? The puzzle of logical time gives an answer, as we shall see later in this chapter. But we can see straightaway that the problems are very much those concerned with the relation to the other – all the others in the same position, waiting, and the other upon whose word they are waiting. Arranging meetings for the other, waiting for the man, pre-empting the other, extending to finding a technique for keeping the other in his proper position.

There is quite a lot to be said for the view that Lacan developed his practice of sessions of variable duration as a specific 'active technique'. 'Active technique' refers here to the cluster of practices discussed by Rank and Ferenczi in their classic work, a work which had a mixed reception at the time and has inspired controversy ever since. More specifically, Lacan's activity of closing the session when he thought fit, rather than when the clock informed him that he should, in accordance with a prior agreement between patient and analyst,[11] may well have been directed at a specific sort of patient: the obsessional. However, Lacan encountered these obsessionals on two fronts: his patients and his analyst colleagues. As he said of the latter:

A technique is being handed on in a cheerless manner, reticent to the point of opacity, a manner that seems terrified of any attempt to let in the fresh air of criticism. It has in fact assumed the air of a formalism pushed to such ceremonial lengths that one might well wonder whether it does not bear the same similarity to obsessional neurosis that Freud so convincingly defined in the observance, if not in the genesis, of religious rites.[12]

Lacan was well aware of the phenomenology of obsessional neurosis that led to its being a parody both of the reality-principle and of the processes of thinking: the delay, the doubt, the hesitation, the procrastination, the ability to make nothing happen either very quickly or very slowly. Lacan picked up this theme from Freud's work and made it the centre of the obsessional world of non-time. Lacan interleaved a Hegelian theory of the master–slave dialectic with Freud's theory of the punitive father, ever ready to punish the obsessional's desires, so as to produce the picture of the obsessional forever waiting for the death of the master, the father,[13] and working while he waits. Ideally, from the obsessional's point of view, he will work so as to produce nothing – to fill up the time of waiting with acts that are not acts, *ungeschehenmachen*, as Freud puts it, making unhappened, undoing what has been done:[14] 'it is as though neither action had taken place, whereas, in reality, both have'.[15] Undoing is firstly precautionary: to prevent the occurrence or *re*occurrence of an event – in this sense, it is rational. The 'irrational' element lies in the 'making it not to have happened' – in tampering with the past: 'the neurotic person will try to make the past itself non-existent [*aufzuheben*]'.[16] The obsessional thus waits because he has entered time that is non-existent, predicated on the non-happening of an event that did happen: he has entered an impossible world, and, just as any number becomes infinite when divided by zero, any time becomes empty, becomes pure duration, when it is deprived of anything that has actually happened. This time of pure duration is the time of the pure object: the object defined by nothing more than its duration.

The obsessional is thus alienated from time, and Lacan juxtaposes this with the alienation to be found in Hegel and Marx: not only is this

handiwork taken from him by another – which is the constituting relation of all labour – but the subject's recognition of his own essence in his handiwork, in which the labour finds its justification, also eludes him, for he himself '*is* not in it'. He *is* in the anticipated moment of the master's death, from which moment he will begin to live, but in the meantime [*en attendant quoi*] he identifies himself with the master as dead, and as a result of this he is himself already dead.[17]

The *waiting* of the obsessional has an essential dialectical relation to this *moment* of death. In analysis, the labour the obsessional engages in is first and foremost the labour of free association, which he experiences (in contrast with the hysteric) as a forced labour. Dutifully – 'he makes an effort to deceive the master by the demonstration of the good intentions manifested in his labour'[18] – seductively – 'the subject's "working-through" is in fact employed for the seduction of the analyst'[19] – yet, in Lacan's view, extremely vulnerably:

How, then, can we doubt the effect of any disdain shown by the master towards the product of such labour? The subject's resistance may even become completely disconcerted by it.[20]

It is this recognition of – which other analysts might well mistake for a sympathy with – the plight of the obsessional which prompted Lacan to give such technical weight to his 'short' sessions.

I would not have so much to say about it if I had not been convinced that, in experimenting with what have been called my short sessions, at a stage in my experience that is now concluded, I was able to bring to light in a certain male subject phantasies of anal pregnancy, as well as the dream of its resolution by Caesarean section, in a delaying of the end of the session where I would otherwise have had to go on listening to his speculations on the art of Dostoevsky.[21]

Lacan's criticism of other analysts, colluding 'disdainfully' with their patient's obsessional symptoms, is thus matched by his awareness of the significance of time, of endings, of punctuation for the obsessional and his labour.[22] Yet the technique is a curious one: we picture the analyst, weary of hearing speculations on Dostoevsky, *deliberately prolonging* the session, fully in the expectation of hearing *more* of these sterile speculations. Instead he is gratified by the fantasies of anal pregnancy that emerged in the 'delay [*délai*]' of the end. The analyst deliberately *prolongs* the waiting, and, paradoxically, thereby cuts it short. He does not show the disdain that the clock-analysts have for their patients' products – though the disdain is undoubtedly present, in the implicit assessment of the speculations on Dostoevsky. Instead, he seems to say to the patient in the act of delaying: 'What you are saying is so significant – because it is so unimportant and sterile – that we must hear more of it, far more than you, reckoning by the clock, thought we would have to hear.' The significance of this moment of irony in the dialectical progress, when the analyst 'begins to approach the question of the intentions of the *ego* in our subjects',[23] is that it arrives at significance by rubbing in the insignificance. It is the opposite of being breathless to hear, read, see the final instalment of the detective thriller you have become engrossed in, week by week. It is the opposite of the punctuation mark that is required by the genre of the 'whodunnit?' – in which the question mark is far more telling than the who-, the dunn- or the it-. Here, the analyst shows the subject that the 'and then?' of narrative time is mirrored by the 'oh, nothing' of obsessional time, and can be parodied to everyone's advantage and satisfaction.

This understanding of the technique of variable-length sessions was often to be subsumed under the simple term I have already used: punctuation. Seemingly almost as an afterthought, Lacan could note that in using this technique, 'we do no more than to confer on the subject's speech its dialectical punctuation'.[24] But this is only one sense in which he used the term punctuation; we could call it the structural sense, concerned with the structure of the discourse, the organisation of the narrative, of the subject's recounted history. There are at least three other meanings of this 'punctuation', and probably more. One, closely related to the structural sense, is that of 'underlining', or 'emphasis'; a non-verbal means of emphasis, one which is not *too* emphatic:

Every analyst accords great importance to anything which, in the course of a session, suddenly throws some light on the beginning of the session. Sometimes one may choose to share it with the patient; but if I don't want to draw his attention too obviously to it, I will limit myself to ending the session at that point, considering that the tying up of the signification is worth a punctuation. All the more so since it is more often than not something to do with the transference.[25]

This notion of punctuation meshes with the view of the analyst as scribe, as commentator, writing in the margin of the patient's text. However, it immediately raises a question. Why not use other means of emphasis, means that are already given within the framework that accepts that analysis is a practice of speech? Indeed, there is no doubt that analysts have converted the grunt into a delicate and nuanced instrument of communication.[26]

A further sense of punctuation, beyond structuration and emphasis, is that of 'time between': the pause for breath, the stopping and starting, hesitation and hastening, the precipitousness and dwelling upon – an entire phenomenology of time, of its vacillation and thickening, its pulsation and its quiescence, that has the utmost significance *within* the act of speaking. With this dimension of the term, we broach the semantic field into which

Lacan's paper of logical time made its way, and which I will discuss in detail in the next section of this chapter. But in raising the question of the internal spacing of speech, we are also in recognisably Derridean territory: why should we not employ the Derridean terms of spacing, of *différance*, to describe this function of the analyst's temporal intervention?[27]

The final sense of 'punctuation' that I want to spell out is also close to the field of reflection to which we will turn when we examine Lacan's paper on logical time. When the analyst intervenes by punctuating the patient's discourse (whether by closing the session or by any other means), he or she is inflecting the time of analysis in concert with the patient's experience of temporality, or, better, his or her being-in-time; whether he or she will it or not, whether he or she is aware of it or not, this is a major form of intervention. It will, inevitably, introduce haste, precipitate a conclusion – or perhaps prolong the waiting, sharpen the sense of hesitation. Lacan developed this *inevitability* of such temporal punctuation and its relation to logical time as follows:

It is, therefore, a beneficent punctuation which gives to the subject's discourse its meaning. This is why the adjournment of a session – which according to present-day technique is simply a chronometric break and, as such, a matter of indifference to the thread of the discourse – plays the part of a metric beat [*une scansion*] which has the full value of an intervention by the analyst for hastening the concluding moments. This fact should lead us to free this act of termination from its routine usage and to employ it for the purposes of the technique in every useful way possible.[28]

Such was the form of justification of the practice; we will explore the theoretical underpinnings and ramifications in the next section of this chapter.

However, for now, let us return to the obsessional, who provides the analyst with the acutely immediate experience of doubts as to the reality of time, and hence provokes in him or her dilemmas concerning the temporal practices appropriate to such an experience. In the 'waiting for death' of the obsessional, there are two components: the waiting and the death. Yet these two themes may not be separable: the waiting may not be simply postponing; the very concept of time hollowed out by waiting may prepare the way for, or make possible, the idea of death. Freud insisted, against considerable 'empirical' evidence,[29] that the unconscious knows nothing of death: 'death is an abstract concept with a negative content for which no unconscious correlate can be found'.[30] The axiom goes hand in hand with another – that the unconscious knows no time, is timeless. Freud preserved a continuous tension between the fact of death as the end, total finality, and the denial of death, its leavening, its symbolisation by other things. In *The interpretation of dreams*, he argued that children make no distinction between 'dead' and 'gone'.[31] In 'Thoughts for the times on war and death', he posited the resolution of the contradiction between the recognition of death as the termination of life and the denial of death and its reduction to nothing, in the experience of pain over the death of a loved and hated person, and in the consequent generation of the idea of the soul and an after-life: a preservation and continuation of life *into* death.[32] It is then the reverse movement, the preservation and continuation of death into life, that, at about the same point in Freud's writings, opens up a new and fundamental direction of his thought: the idea of the 'introjection' of the absent loved one as the foundation of the ego – the theory put forward in 'Mourning and melancholia' and then, in more detail, in *The ego and the id*.[33] Yet there is no death in Freud's unconscious, only the ego's fear of the super-ego, given content by the avatars of the castration complex, or 'the anxiety due to separation from the protecting mother',[34] itself only possible, retrospectively, owing to the fear of castration.[35] If the ego of the 'analytic catechism'[36] is seducing the super-ego through its forced labour in analysis, it is only because it fears the super-ego, fears the threat of anxiety that the super-ego's turning away promotes: it works, and its working is secretly a postponement, a waiting that propitiates the master, the very possibility of death.

Here Lacan is revising, refuting, as well as extending Freud's treatment of death. For Freud, in 1923, death has no unconscious correlative because it is an 'abstract concept with a negative content'. For Lacan, this 'abstract concept with a negative content' is the symbol: the category that defines the limit of the Freudian field. In this connection, Lacan can legitimately point to Freud's remarkably subtle meditation on 'Negation' of a couple of years later. True: the unconscious knows no time, knows no death, knows no negation. All these are linked together for Freud. Instead of death, we find the representation of separation and the fear of loss; instead of negation, we find repression and expulsion.[37] For Lacan, however, Freud's arguments here need to be supplemented or transformed. Lacan introduces a meditation on the relation between symbol and thing: 'the name is the time of the object'.[38] The fundamental feature of the object for Lacan, its duration in time, is given it in the pact of naming, in which two subjects create a symbolic world. Linked with this is the claim that the symbol 'manifests itself first of all as the murder of the thing, and this death constitutes in the subject the eternalization of his desire'.[39] In raising the thing to another level, its thinginess is lost forever: it becomes a thing-in-relation-to-other-things – that is, a part of the symbolic order.

The very possibility of absence is given by the existence of the symbolic. There are no holes in reality – there is no 'real' absence. Absence is made possible in the symbolisation of presence[40] – presence includes as its very condition the limit beyond which is its absence. Death is the name for this primordial absence.

So when we wish to attain in the subject what was before the serial articulations of speech, and what is primordial to the birth of symbols, we find it in death, from which his existence takes on all the meaning it has.[41]

What for Freud, then, is abstract, pure negativity and therefore unrepresentable (in the unconscious), becomes for Lacan the privileged motor of all representations, of all meaning. Insofar as death is installed in me, in my beginnings,[42] in so far as I am a speaking being, conjuring the death of things through the birth of language, in so far as I have an *ego*, an effect of an identification with a fundamentally always-already dead other, in so far as I am a human who recognises the existence of an after-life (in Freud's dialect), of a symbolic order (in Lacan's), then I am alive. In Lacan's account of the obsessional as slave, if he clings to life, he forgoes the essence of life, the certainty of death as its horizon; instead he *lives* this waiting for death as his life. As we will see, Lacan reorganised the traditional dialectical categories of temporality (those of life/death and past/future) around waiting/haste, placing the accent on the *act* that puts an end to the objective time of waiting, in the same way as when, in 'The theme of the three caskets', Freud charted the replacement of repression by choice, he pinpointed Lear's tragedy as the refusal to choose death, the only choice left an old man.

Practical familiarity with the time-world of the obsessional does not necessarily require a change in technical practices. It may require a particular form of analytic *impatience* – the obvious example is the impatience to which Sándor Ferenczi's therapeutic zeal gave rise. Even he, famous for his active techniques, was quick to point out, when attacked, that his intention had solely been to 'enable the patient, by means of certain artifices, to comply more successfully with the rule of free association and thereby to assist or *hasten* the exploring of the unconscious material'.[43] That the analyst's impatience is at stake here may be gauged from Ferenczi's description of the only situation in which active techniques could be justified: 'the *stagnation* of the analysis' was 'the only justification for and the only motive of the modification'.[44] Was Ferenczi's impatience the same as Lacan's perception of the flexibility required of the analyst by the obsessional? There were certainly many points in common. Ferenczi explored the respective 'activities' of both analyst and patient:

Analysis demands no *activities* from the patient except *punctual* appearance at the hours of treatment; except for this no influence is exercised on the general mode of life . . .[45]

While the fundamental rule may require the patient to be passive, with the important exception of his punctuality, no analyst is ever passive: the opposition between active and passive techniques is a false one, since every analyst is active in so far as he or she interprets.[46] However, Ferenczi's active techniques were designed to act *across* the masked gratifications that patients seize from analysis, whereas Lacan's were designed to break the collusion between obsessional ceremony, analyst and the delaying strategies of the obsessional patient. One picture of the normal obsessional session we find in Lacan consists in doubt, hesitation, silence – nothing happening.[47] Another portrays a subject whose strategic grasp of the discourse is so complete, so successful, that nothing *untoward* will ever happen.[48] For Ferenczi, the patient has found a perfectly equilibrated substitutive satisfaction, which the analyst must break into, as if from outside. For Lacan, the stability is to be found in the intersubjective relation established by the patient with the analyst:

. . . since he knows that he is mortal, he also knows that the master can die. From this moment on he is able to accept his labouring for the master and his renunciation of pleasure in the meantime; and, in the uncertainty of the moment when the master will die, he waits.

Such is the intersubjective reason, as much for the doubt as for the procrastination that are character traits of the obsessional subject.[49]

The contrast is between Ferenczi's active technique, focused on the patient whose world has become *too* impregnable, for whom the world of others seems to have lost all its importance and leverage, and Lacan's technique, predicated on the recognition that the analyst, through his very correctness and orthodoxy, colludes – is active through his very passivity – with the obsessional, faithfully shadowing the patient's pacing out of the master's path to the tomb. The key term, one that is characteristic of Lacan's work of the late 1940s and early 1950s, is 'intersubjective'. It appears in the above-quoted passage, where it functions to render Freud's account of the phenomenology of obsessional doubt and hesitation an intersubjective one.[50] But what Lacan really pinned his hopes on was a new scientific basis for psychoanalysis: a science of the intersubjective.

Psychoanalysis will provide scientific bases for its theory or for its technique only by formalizing in an adequate fashion the essential dimensions of its experience which, together with the historical theory of the symbol, are: intersubjective logic and the temporality of the subject.[51]

These two concepts, 'intersubjective logic and the temporality of the subject', had a privileged status for Lacan. They refer directly to two articles he had written in 1945 – breaking the silence he had imposed upon himself during the war. So, the reference both looks back, to work he had already done, and, in so doing, offers a promise, the promise embodied in these two papers. To understand the concept of time, of intersubjectivity, of psychoanalysis as a science, and hence to understand how time became so crucial to both Lacan's practice and his theory, we must consider these two papers in some detail.

II

> But at my back I always hear
> Time's wingèd chariot hurrying near,
> And yonder all before us lie
> Deserts of vast eternity.
>
> Andrew Marvell, 'To His Coy Mistress'

A prison governor brings three inmates before him and says to them:
'For reasons which I need not disclose to you now, gentlemen, I must free one of you. To decide which, I leave your lot to be determined by a test which, if you are willing, you will undergo.

'There are three of you here. Here are five discs which differ only in their colour: three are white, and two are black. Without letting you know which of them I have chosen, I am going to fasten one of these discs between each of your shoulders, that is to say, out of the bearer's direct vision; all possibility of his being able to catch sight of it indirectly is also excluded by the absence here of any means of looking at himself.

'Thereafter you will be free to consider at your leisure your companions and their respective discs, without being allowed, of course, to communicate to each other the fruits of your inspection – which, in any case, considerations of your own self-interest alone would prevent you from doing. For the first who can deduce his own colour shall profit from the measure of liberty of which we dispose.

'Moreover, his conclusion must be grounded upon logical and not simply probabilistic reasons. To this end, it is agreed that, as soon as one of you is ready to formulate such a conclusion, he will cross the threshold of this door, so that he will be judged individually by his answer.'

This proposal having been accepted, each of our three subjects is arrayed with a white disc, without using the blacks, of which there were, it should be remembered, only two.

How can the subjects solve the problem?

The perfect solution runs as follows:

After they have pondered *a certain time*, the three subjects together make a *few steps* towards the door, arriving there abreast. Each of them then separately provides a similar answer, as follows:

'I am a white, here is how I know it. Given that my companions were whites, I thought that, if I were a black, each of them would have been able to make the following inference: "If I were also a black, the other, immediately realizing from this that he is a white, would have left straight way; therefore I am not a black." And the two others would have left together, convinced of being whites. If they stayed put, it is because I am a white like them. Thereupon, I made for the door, to make my conclusion known.'

Hence all three exited simultaneously, armed with the same reasons for deciding.[52]

The crucial element for Lacan's discussion of this sophism is the 'certain time', the period of hesitation which is required for the problem to be solved. A, the first subject, can deduce that he is white only if he sees B and C uncertain as to what *they* are: the only sign of uncertainty he can be given is their immobility. Yet, once A realises that their immobility signifies that he himself is white, he must make haste, since not only does he wish to be the first to reach the door, but he will also necessarily recognise that his own waiting signifies for them the fact that he does not see a black disc. What is more, if he waits too long, the others will start before he does, and the basis of his argument for being white will disappear beneath, as it were, his hesitant feet. Hence, the value of the temporal feature to the logic of the problem is verified in the act by which each demonstrates that he has brought the period of waiting, the temporal feature, to an end.[53]

It is important to make clear the structure of the problem that Lacan extracts, a structure which will serve him later in his work as *the* model for all the relations between the subject, a set of signifiers and temporality. There are three evidential moments necessary for the solution of the problem.

1   Firstly, there is the instant of seeing: by logical exclusion, if one *saw* two blacks, one would *know* that one is a white. This evidential moment is given with the structure of the problem; it is an instantaneous moment, one whose logical time is zero. Thus the appropriate form for the deduction is the impersonal logical 'One knows that . . .'

2   Secondly, the subject builds upon this logical intuition the next step of the argument, the next logical moment. The argument is: 'If I were a black, then the two whites that I see would not hesitate to conclude that they were whites.' The key term here is 'hesitate'. It is in so far as they hesitate that the subject realises that they would *not* hesitate if they saw a black on his back. For each of them, there is a time of meditation observed in the other, such that each traverses a time of understanding which is directly articulated upon the time of meditation of the other. If subject A were black, then he would be able to see the thoughts of the others unrolling in their time of meditation: 'If I were a black, the others would have left without waiting a moment. If he stays and meditates, it must be because I am a white.' The time of waiting thus has an objective meaning. But how to measure the time of meditation?

The time for understanding can be reduced to the instant of looking, but this look can include in its instant all the time necessary for understanding. Thus, the objectivity of this time vacillates with its limit. Its meaning only resides in the form engendered by it of subjects who are undefined except by their reciprocity, and whose action is suspended by a mutual causality in a time which disappears even in the return of the intuition which objectified it. It is in this modulation of time that is opened up, with the second phase of the logical movement, a path that leads to the next step.[54]

3   The third and final step. Each says to himself: 'I hasten to assert myself to be white, so that the whites, who I have been considering, do not pre-empt me in recognising themselves for what they are.' Here, following the time for understanding linking reciprocally undetermined subjects, we find a moment of self-assertion, of judgement. Following the time for understanding is a reflection upon being *already late*: 'If I am a white, then I must hurry if they are not to get there ahead of me.' The moment of being *already (too) late* presents itself logically as an urgency in the moment of

concluding. From hesitating, a pulsation leads immediately to being too late. This precipitation is not simply a contingent effect of the dramatic situation; the subject must make haste, because if he does not, and the two others beat him to it, then he will no longer be sure that he is not black. Indeed, he will probably conclude that he is black, since his argument for not being black depends upon the inertia of the other two subjects. Hence, the need for precipitation, the need to make haste is not one that arises from the contingent conditions of the problem: rather it is inherent in the logical form, just as the fact of hesitation is the only means by which the subject can find the solution to the problem. This assertive and personal quality of the judgement acted out in the haste with which the subject takes to the door is the argument that Lacan gives for characterising this logical moment as 'subjective assertion', in which the logical subject is the same as the personal subject, the 'I'. This personal form of the subject, in contrast to the impersonal subject of the instant of looking, or the intersubjective subject of the time of understanding, is isolated in the temporal pulsation whereby the time for understanding is transformed into the moment for concluding.

I will not here go into the further interest that this sophism engenders when we consider the doubt that seizes each of the subjects, as they see the other subjects also running for the door – the doubt takes the form: 'Have I chosen the right moment to conclude that I am white?' Rather, we can pass on to note that the certainty of being white is engendered in the act itself, rather than prior to the act. And the possibility of truth, of being right, is founded upon the precipitation that induces certainty, while error would be based upon an inertia of the subject, unwilling to seize the moment to conclude. (If he waits too long – how long would that be? – he will see the two others go on before him and conclude that he is black.)

The next consequence that Lacan draws is that this logical form that includes within it a temporal reference is that appropriate to the relation between the first person, the 'I', and the intersubjective subject of reciprocity (the ego as defined in Freud's *Group psychology and the analysis of the ego* as the agency whose separation off from the ego ideal is promoted by the formation of the group through identification);[55] the first person is engendered in a relation to the common measure of the reciprocal subject, that is, to its time for understanding.[56] Thus, in this collective logic, which Lacan counterposes to classical logic, the truth is dependent on the other as temporalised, and there is no way that the subject can arrive at his own truth except in the company of, and via the truths of, the other.

So, in so far as we are all neurotic, in so far as we are all a little inhuman, a little beyond the pale or beneath the mark, Lacan will apply this collective logic to any argument concerning so-called human nature:[57]

1 First step: A human being knows what a human being is not.
2 Second step: Human beings recognise each other as human beings.
3 Third step: I affirm myself to be human, for fear of being convinced by them that I am not human.

It is on this note that Lacan ends his short paper – a note which points towards a theory of the collective, or group: a collective logic. What examples of this logic does he adduce? He mentions two: a game of bridge and diplomacy. It is immediately clear where the game of bridge gives rise to this group logic: in the moment when I am finessed.[58] Diplomacy, the art of being sent abroad in order to tell lies for one's country, conforms very closely to the situation in which Lacan's three prisoners find themselves: the various diplomats spend long periods of time trying to gauge what the others are thinking, in order to arrive, in haste, at a conclusion that no one intended but upon which they all agree. The agreement is the moment when all participants simultaneously arrive at the door, proclaiming themselves to be white, white as the driven snow.

However, Lacan's references were also more formal than this: he had in mind not only the eccentric temporality of negotiation but also the contemporary advances in the theory of games, upon which so much diplomatic thinking has been based since the Second World War, which took as a model the game of poker and the logic of the bluff.[59] More grandly, Lacan had formulated the idea of a group logic – a continuation of Freud's project to be found in *Group psychology and the analysis of the ego*.[60] Whereas Freud's analysis had centred on highly organised institutions (the Church and the army) and loosely organised large groups, showing them to have a common structure, the ego's relation to the ego-ideal, Lacan's group logic focused on 'groups' whose constitution was specified by highly specific rules – the rules of the game.[61] Whereas Freud was mainly preoccupied with the process of identification in the group, the process by which the group is constituted through identification, Lacan showed how the subject marks itself as different in the process of identification. Where Freud and many of his contemporaries were fascinated by the herd-like characteristics of groups, the effacement of difference, Lacan wished to demonstrate how difference emerged out of the rules that specified the constitution of the group.[62] He explored these ideas further in another paper published in the *Cahiers d'Art* at the end of the war: 'The number thirteen and the logical form of suspicion'.[63]

Like the paper on logical time, this paper presents a problem which it then solves. The interest of both papers lies solely in the peculiarity of the solution. Here, Lacan gives some idea of the general framework within which to view these essays into the rigorous analyses of human behaviour as absolutely determined by the rules of the game. This analysis constitutes one of the initial formal analyses of a 'logic of suspicion':

It is one part of our attempts to generate ways of conceiving of logical forms which govern the relations of the individual to the collectivity, before the class is constituted, in other words before the individual is specified.[64]

There are twelve objects, seemingly all alike, but one of them is 'bad' – it differs in weight from the other eleven, though it is not known whether it is heavier or lighter. Using a simple balance, the problem is: find out, in three weighings, which is the odd piece out. The solution is as follows: divide the twelve pieces into three groups of four, A, B, and C. Weigh A against B; if they are equal in weight, then the bad piece must be in C. Take two of the four pieces in C, C_1 and C_2, weigh them against each other; if they are equal in weight, then the bad piece is one of the other two. Weigh one of these, C_3, against C_1; if they are equal in weight, then C_4 is the bad piece; if they are not, then C_3 is. If C_1 and C_2 are not equal in weight, a similar procedure will decide which one of them is the odd piece out.

If A and B are not equal, a different method must be used, since all eight of the pieces remain under suspicion, it not being known whether the odd piece is lighter or heavier than the others. Lacan says that we now have a problem with eight pieces, rather than four, but with 'divided suspicion'. He continues:

here we are coming close to a dialectic that is essential to the relations of the individual to the collective [*collection*], in so far as they include the ambiguity of the too much or the too little.

The principle for solving the problem now is one of rotation:

replace three of the pieces in the heavy group of four pieces with three taken from C, which, in this case, since A and B are not equal, is known to be made up of four 'good' pieces; this group is weighed against the three pieces displaced from the heavy group together with one from the light group. The three from the light group are set aside with the one piece which is known to be good. If the result of this weighing is equilibrium, then the bad piece is known to be in the three from the original light group, and, since it is now known that the bad piece is lighter, rather than heavier, than all the others, one weighing can decide which of the three it is. If the result of the weighing is not equilibrium, then there are two possibilities: if the side which was originally heavier is still heavier, then the bad piece must be either the one left in the heavy side, or the one left in the light side: which it is can be decided by using one of the pieces known to be good. If the side which is heavier changes on rotating the three pieces, the bad piece must be amongst the three which changed sides, and will be known to be heavier. One weighing will decide which of the three it is.

Lacan then demonstrates that one can decide the question with only three weighings even when there are thirteen, rather than twelve, pieces. One divides the thirteen pieces into one group of five and two groups of four. One weighs the two groups of four against each other; if they are not equal, then the bad piece will be found in one of them, and the above procedure will decide which it is. If they are equal, then the bad piece is to be found in the group of five. For the second weighing one takes a good piece, α, from the eight pieces known to be good, and places it in one of the pans with β, one of the group of five, weighing these two against γ and δ, also taken from the group of five. If the two groups are equal in weight, then the bad piece must be one of the two pieces not in the pans; a weighing with a piece known to be good will decide which. If the pan with α and β is heavier than that with γ and δ, then *either β or δ* is the bad piece. To decide which, place π, known to be a good piece, in the first pan with α, shift β to take the place of γ, and remove γ. If α and π is still heavier than δ and β, then the bad piece must be δ, *which is the only one that has not moved*. Lacan calls this position, the position occupied by δ, the 'par-trois-et-un', the through-three-and-one position. If the two pans are now equal in weight, then the bad piece must be γ, which is the piece that was expelled. If the first pan is now lighter than the second, the bad piece must be β, since that is the one piece that changed sides.

'This through-three-and-one position is the original form of the

184

logic of suspicion.' The general case of the problem is given by using the 'tripartite rotation' and the 'through-three-and-one position': 'The through-three-and-one position is singled out in one of the groups, the disjunction of which is created by the *tri* [tripartition].' With three weighings one can solve the problem for 13 pieces, with four weighings for 40 (1+1+3+9+26), with five weighings for 121 (1+1+3+9+27+80); with n weighings, one can solve it for $1+3+3^2+3^3 \ldots +3^{n-1}$. Lacan remarks how powerful the tripartition exerted by the balance is, after the second weighing. But he also remarks that the number 13 here is determined completely by the structure of the operations which resolve the problem, and in particular it is determined by the 'through-three-and-one'. This is not the determination of a coincidence, but rather:

It stems from the fact that thirteen, representing the collectivity determined by three weighings, is required by the through-three-and-one position to have, for its development, three proofs: a first one to supply an individual purified of suspicion, the second which divides the suspicion amongst the individuals that it includes, a third which discriminates one from the other after the treble rotation.

Lacan thus draws his conclusion from the problem, a conclusion that deals with the concepts of difference and suspicion:

This reference of the individual to each and every one of the others is the fundamental requirement of the logic of the collectivity.[65]

His final remark is to note that this return to logic will rediscover a base that is as solid as a rock and no less implacable, when it enters into motion.

The paper on logical time had drawn towards its conclusion on a similar note:

But it is sufficient to generate by recurrence the demonstration of the sophism to see that it can logically be applied to an unlimited number of subjects, given that the 'negative' attribute can only intervene if there is a number of them equal to the number of subjects minus one.[1] But the temporal objectification is more difficult to conceive of the more the collectivity increases its size, seeming to present an obstacle to a *collective logic* with which one might complete classical logic.[66]

In 1966, Lacan added a note to this passage: Cf. the condition of this minus one is the attribute with respect to the psychoanalytic function of the One-in-addition in the subject of psychoanalysis, p. 480 of this collection ['Situation de la psychanalyse et formation du psychanalyste en 1956'].

Indeed a very similar aspiration was included in the final sentence:

A movement which yields the logical form of each and every assimilation of
the 'human', precisely in so far as it purports to be assimilative of
barbarism, which nonetheless holds in reserve the essential determination
of the '*I*'.

The phrasing is the same; the recourse to a formal and logical
demonstration is the same. We can thus regard the paper on the
logic of groups as a precursor and parallel effort towards giving a
formal ground for some essential findings for what Lacan was later
to call 'the conjectural sciences'. Yet, even here, where the
formalistic, some would say scientistic, strain of Lacan's work,
which came to dominate his last seminars, in the late 1970s, is so
prominent, there is a current from clinical practice. And it is a
current that, as so often in Lacan's thinking about technique, came
from England.

After the end of the war, Lacan spent some time in England. He
made contact with psychoanalytic colleagues there, and eventually
wrote an article entitled 'La psychiatrie anglaise et la guerre',
published in 1947.[67] He opens by recording that 'the war left me
with a vigorous sense of the atmosphere of unreality within which
the collectivity of the French had lived it, from top to bottom.' In
contrast, 'the victory of England has a moral source': 'the intrepid
character of her people rests upon a truthful relation to the real'.

Turning to the manner in which psychiatrists had organised
recruitment in the army, he noted how they had concentrated on
the elimination of 'dullards' who could not be forced into the model
of identification that Freud's *Group psychology* represents – what
makes this mode of identification impossible is the fact that they
bring with them an 'inadequacy [*déficit*]'. We immediately see the
implications and the applications of the notion of 'too much' and
'too little' that Lacan had formalised in his paper on the number 13,
or of the identificatory disc that each prisoner bears on his back.

Lacan praised both the manner in which English psychiatry was
becoming informed by psychoanalysis and the way in which group
psychology and techniques of mathematisation were being employed.[68] But his most effusive praise was reserved for Wilfred Bion and
John Rickman, with their study of the internal dynamics of groups
at a military hospital:

In their work, I rediscovered the feeling of the miracle that accompanied
the first of Freud's steps: finding in the very fact of the way ahead being
blocked the vital force of intervention.[69]

Bion had been given 400 people to re-educate; the number of hours of work available would have been 'arithmetically insufficient to resolve the basic problem raised by each of these cases, if one took them singly. It was this very difficulty that led Bion to cross the Rubicon of technical innovation.' The structure of the group and its aim was determined by the very conception of a group in war, which is defined by the existence of an enemy and that of a leader. Every failure to recognise the communal danger is treated, as always in psychoanalysis, as a resistance. Bion deliberately constructed a group without a leader, so that the only means he had at his disposal was 'to hold the group through the significance of his speech [*verbe*]', so as to force the group to take account of the difficulties of its own existence, and to render it more and more transparent to itself,

the ideal of such an organisation stemming, for the doctor, from its perfect lisibility, so that he can at any moment gauge towards which exit each 'case' that has been entrusted to him is making his way: return to his unit [*unité*],[70] to civil life or subsisting in neurosis.

Having described the fashion in which these groups operated and the techniques that Bion developed, Lacan reaffirmed the necessity of psychiatry's close relations with society, with the ambiguously named 'Child Guidance' movement, exhorting his colleagues to shoulder the professional burdens that will inevitably be theirs: the qualification of the psychiatrist for this task resides in his 'sensitivity to the depths of man's world'.

This remarkable, seemingly uncharacteristic text of Lacan's certainly indicates the enthusiasm, even idealisation, inspired in him by English psychiatry and the moral fortitude of the English war. Yet it also indicates the clinical backdrop to his two papers on the relation between the individual and the collectivity: 'Logical time' and 'The number thirteen'. Both these papers are preoccupied with the mark of difference: the disc on the back, the 'too much' or 'too little'; both are concerned to demonstrate how the individual marks itself off from the collective, but only in specifying and recognising the links it has with others. These two papers are the primary sources for what Lacan called his 'subjective logic': not the logic that a subject obeys, which is objective logic, nor the logic that a subject employs, which is subjectivised logic, but the logic which the concept of a subject, in relation to other subjects, and in relation to an individuating propensity, inherent in the rules of the game, requires. In the one paper, it is the logic of time: the logical requirement for the dialectic of hesitation and haste, for waiting and concluding; in the other, it is the logic governing the use one makes of the others in determining which one is in deficit, the logic through which suspicion finally and permanently falls on the element that has not moved, that has not been displaced amidst the general tripartition.

There are a number of continuations of this line of thought in Lacan's later work. One might point to his espousal of Lévi-Straussian structuralism. The structure of language there takes on the function accorded to the rules of the sophism; the end result is still the individuation of the subject, its ability to utter full speech.

Man speaks, then, but it is because the symbol has made him man. Even if in fact overabundant gifts welcome the stranger who has introduced himself to the group, the life of the natural groups that constitute the community is subjected to the rules of matrimonial alliance governing the exchange of women, and to the exchange of gifts determined by the marriage . . . The marriage tie is governed by an order of preference whose law concerning the kinship names is, like language, imperative for the group in its forms, but unconscious in its structure. In this structure . . . the startled theoretician finds the whole of the logic of combinations . . . And this would suggest that it is perhaps only our unconsciousness of their permanence that allows us to believe in the freedom of choice in the so-called complex structures of marriage ties under whose law we live. If statistics have already allowed us to glimpse that this freedom is not exercised in a random manner, it is because a subjective logic orients this freedom in its effects.[71]

Getting married, then, may well have the same form as the decision to conclude 'I am white' in the paper on logical time: not primarily because it shares the same temporal structure of hesitation tipping over into haste – which, after all, Lacan wishes to propose as the fundamental temporal structure of all actions which make true a claim of the excluding form, 'I am . . .' – but because there is a system, both 'unconscious' and 'imperative', of rules, whose effect is to induce hesitation, haste and certainty in arriving at one's uniquely specified solution as the necessary accompaniments of a decision. At this point, however, we veer over into the contrast between full, founding speech, and the logic of the laws of language,[72] a trail we cannot follow here, except to note how Lacan's contrasting of speech and language has a temporal dimension: if language, always already there, appears timeless, the embodiment of the death of things,[73] it is speech which introduces a human temporality, the temporality of action in time, of action in haste, to pre-empt the grim reaper. Archetypally, marriage is such an action, in which founding speech, 'You are my wife' ('I am your husband'), is a Pascalian wager, the best bet under the circumstances, the circumstances of mortality in which speaking, human subjects find themselves.

There is a . . . dimension of time which [machines] are undeniably not party to, which I'm trying to get you to picture via this element [in the logical time sophism] which is neither belatedness, nor being in advance, but haste, the relation to time peculiar to the human being, this relation to the chariot of time, which is there, at our backs. That is where speech is to be found, and where language, which has all the time in the world, is not. That is why, furthermore, one gets nowhere with language.[74]

If Freud's family romances correspond to the structures underpinning the marriage ties, the decision to marry, the emblem of freedom conferred by the term 'complex', is assimilated to the freedom of each white disc bearer as he races to the door, to declare what he knows only through discerning what the others have done. The sophism becomes the model for all decisions, whether it is the Ratman's, as he tries to decide between marrying for money (as his father did) or love (as his mother implied his father should have done – in which case he would not exist and the decision would no longer be his[75]), or the prisoner's, trying to decide if he is white or black.

But the sophism, or the subjective logic, or the later theory of the four discourses,[76] had another application: as an allegory of the psychoanalytic process.[77] To the instant of seeing corresponds everything that is given in the analytic situation, together with everything that comes to the subject therein: the analyst, the couch, the waiting room, the dreams, the interpretations. The labour performed, the time of analysis, the time of labour, of working through, the time which is neither *endlich* nor *unendlich*, whose time is governed by this impossible 'either/or', reveals itself to be resolvable in the moment for concluding: the end of analysis. The true reason for deciding only becomes apparent once the decision has been taken, just as, in Freud's descriptions of the analytic process, recollection only follows conviction, rather than vice versa.[78]

That waiting has a logical function, has a logical relation to a decision whereby one arrives at the truth when it is a question of deciding in relation to others, to one's fellow human beings, may also help explain, or at least give insight into, Lacan's sang-froid when confronted by the numbers of analysands sitting waiting outside his consulting room – the direct consequence of his variable-length sessions. If, as Lacan's sophism indicates, waiting is a necessary logical moment in the arriving at a correct decision, which is itself manifested as an act, then it is not so surprising that the analysis that one engages in *chez* Dr Lacan will be conducted as much in the waiting room as on the couch. Nor, in this connection, should we overlook the analysis offered by the other problem of the bad piece: the paranoid reactions – that were so characteristic of this waiting to be called, waiting for it to start (and finish), in the stories told of such analyses – would be exactly the properties of the group that the operations of *triage* and the 'through-three-and-one position' would cause to surface. Waiting for the man, wondering which way to go – intrinsic to the Lacanian practice and mirroring with an unlikely verisimilitude his most esoteric theoretical *jeux d'esprit*.

Will this allegory of analysis have the same structure as that other, more famous allegory, the 'Seminar on *The purloined letter*', in which analysis is modelled on the passage of the letter through the three positions marked out by the inter-relations of the gaze?

Thus three moments, structuring three glances, borne by three subjects, incarnated each time by different characters.
The first is a glance that sees nothing . . .
The second, a glance which sees that the first sees nothing and deludes itself as to the secrecy of what it hides . . .
The third sees that the first two glances leave what should be hidden exposed to whomever would seize it . . .
Given the intersubjective modulus of the action which is repeated, it remains to recognise in it a *compulsion to repeat* in the sense that interests us in Freud's text.[79]

This reference to the intersubjective modulus indicates that the search for an intersubjective logic is now being continued in a different mode from that of the paper on 'Logical time': one which links subjects together, requiring them to *repeat*, rather than to *act in a determinate haste*. That other great dimension of analytic temporality, the theme of repetition, is cutting across the irreversible tripartite structure of the logical time sophism. The link between these two different allegories is clearer in the spoken version of the 'Seminar on *The purloined letter*', in Seminar II,[80] where Lacan examines the game of odd or even that Poe's Dupin had recounted in 'The murders in the Rue Morgue'.[81] Lacan's analysis of the intersubjectivity required to play the game invokes the language of the three moments (*temps*) introduced in 'Logical time' in order to portray the sequence of identifications with the thought of the other by which one attempts to forestall their bluff and double-bluff:

there may be a second period [*temps*], in which a less partial subjectivity is manifested. The subject is in fact capable of making himself other, and to end up thinking that the other, being himself an other, thinks like him, and that he has to place himself in the position of a third party, to get out of being this other who is his pure reflection . . .[82]

But this attempt to replicate the success of the logic which allows the prisoner to conclude that he is white fails when there are just the two players, playing odd or even. In this instance, it leads to an ineffable, because entirely imaginary, identification with the other,[83] whereas the path to follow in this instance, 'the one which can be made logical',[84] leads to a consideration of what it would mean to play a game of chance with a machine, a computer – where identification is impossible, whence 'everything pertaining to the order of the psychological profile is completely eliminated'.[85] With the machine of the 'Seminar on *The purloined letter*', what emerges is not the hesitation and haste of an imaginary identification that is adequately mediated by the symbolic (as in 'Logical time'), but the function of repetition, as generated by the pure logic of the symbol – by the machine. This inexorable logic is the necessary pre-requisite, according to Lacan, for an understanding of Freud's notion of a death drive.[86] The machine opens up the dialectic of chance and over-determination, and then of the emergence of something new out of the repeated application of a rule. Or, as Lacan put it:

Hence from the initial composition with itself of the primordial symbol . . . a structure, remaining just as transparent in relation to its initial givens, brings out the essential relation between memory and law.[87]

Indeed, with the rule-governed procedures that Lacan posits, operating on a sequence of 'little letters', he engenders a form of memory that is retroactive[88]: in order to get out a particular sequence, a later term will affect an earlier.

But now we seem to be dealing with a different mode of psychoanalytic time. Whereas the sophism of logical time led to the categories of hesitation and haste, categories which seemed alien to the conceptual armoury of the Freudian analyst, if not to his or her descriptions of symptoms,[89] the 'sophism' developed from Poe's story of the game of odd or even led to a reappraisal of temporal categories which are universally admitted to be fundamental to Freud's thought: repetition, memory, history. Yet Lacan's reappraisal was not simply a quasi-philosophical, or formalist, reflection upon these concepts; his 'return to Freud' was at its most potent here, in the rediscovery he made of a fundamental Freudian concept, a concept which is the axis of all of Freud's thinking about the time of neurosis, the time of childhood, the time of causality in human affairs – and this fundamental concept had been well-nigh ignored, glossed over, glossed, often enough, by translators, into something else: I am referring to *Nachträglich-keit*.[90]

So, to continue my discussion of Lacan's concept of time, I propose we now need to consider the history of this concept, and the use that Lacan was to make of it, always remembering that the sophism on logical time had given Lacan a certain amount of fixed intellectual capital in this area of psychoanalytic theory and practice, capital which he was never to allow to be foreclosed.

III

Ontically, then, the unconscious is the evasive – but we are beginning to circumscribe it in a structure, a temporal structure, which, it can be said, has never yet been articulated as such.

Jacques Lacan[91]

3 August, 1938 The ultimate ground of all intellectual inhibitions of work seems to be the inhibition of masturbation in childhood. But perhaps it goes deeper; perhaps it is not its inhibition by external influences but its unsatisfying nature in itself. There is always something lacking for complete discharge and satisfaction – *en attendant quelque chose qui ne venait point* ['Always waiting for something which never came'] – and this missing part, the reaction of orgasm, manifests itself in equivalents in other spheres, in *absences*, outbreaks of laughing, weeping, and perhaps other ways. – Once again infantile sexuality has fixed a model in this.

Sigmund Freud[92]

'*Absence*': this was a term that *fin-de-siècle* neurologists used to describe both a pathological phenomenon and a putative cause of other pathological phenomena. The *absence* could be observed, as a minor form of the loss of consciousness found in epileptic-like states.[93] Freud equated *absence* with Breuer's concept of the 'hypnoid state', which, in the Theoretical Chapter of *Studies on hysteria*, was the main aetiological factor in the genesis of hysteria. Freud thus had to discard the causal role of *absence* so as to introduce his distinctive concept of defence-mechanisms. The concept of 'hypnoid state' conformed to Freud's descriptive unconscious, yet was granted powers by Breuer in the construction of the dynamic, repressed unconscious that Freud ceded only to defence. Breuer, and many others following him,[94] were so impressed by the *fact* of the loss of consciousness, by the *possibility* of an *alternative* consciousness to which this gave rise, that they saw no need to look further for the foundations of pathological mental structures. Freud was less impressed; he required some other force, exerting a positive pressure, for an absence to be 'fertilised' and begin to proliferate a true symptomatic form.

Yet, as the citation from 1938 indicates, Freud did confer one important function upon the *absence*, once he had, to his own satisfaction, found its correct psycho-physiological location: as the moment of orgasm or, equally, and surprisingly, the moment of the absence of orgasm. Take an important passage in his paper on hysterical attacks of 1908:

The loss of consciousness, the '*absence*', in a hysterical attack is derived from the fleeting but unmistakeable lapse of consciousness which is observable at the climax of every intense sexual satisfaction, including auto-erotic ones[95] . . . The mechanism of these *absences* is comparatively simple. All the subject's attention is concentrated to begin with on the course of the process of satisfaction; with the occurrence of the satisfaction, the whole of this cathexis of attention is suddenly removed, so that there ensues a momentary void in her consciousness. This gap in consciousness, which might be termed a *physiological* one, is then widened in the service of repression, till it can swallow up everything that the repressing agency rejects.[96]

One could, schematically, hypothesise that Freud had made the absence associated with orgasm the model for the hypnoid state, indeed, the model for hypnosis in general – remembering the concatenation of childlike trust in authority,[97] the close relations between hypnosis and love,[98] that Freud was to sculpt out of his experience of hypnosis and of its close relation psychoanalysis.[99] We see that dispensing with the concept of hypnoid state was not so easy. There were other reasons why this was so.

First amongst these was the close connection between the concept of trauma and the concept of hypnoid state. The metapsychological lines of development in Freud's work are clear here: the excess of stimuli (the trauma) and the protection of the inside from this excess, such that the perfectly transparent exterior of the psychic apparatus is the remnant and the product of the effect of traumata, such that consciousness itself is the effect of trauma, an effect that then allows the possibility of a triumph over these self-same effects.[100]

But we do not feel satisfied with the answer that consciousness is both the product of trauma and the guarantee against its triumph. We feel, perhaps, that this answer, while important, is too meta-psychological an answer: it does not seem quite to cover the importance of the notion of trauma, which, it would seem, is first and foremost a clinical conception, one that – perhaps less now than then[101] – presents itself unexpectedly, and always *urgently*, in the consulting room. We feel that we must approach the problem more textually and historically. However, such a history will demonstrate to us how inextricably tied up with theoretical concerns the designation of an experience as traumatic always was.

Traumatic neuroses came to the attention of the medical profession in the mid to late nineteenth century as a result, we are told by Ellenberger and others,[102] of the rise of industrial manufacturing and the importance of claims pertaining to industrial accidents for the insurance companies. These were the 'pension hysterias' of which Abraham wrote in 1907.[103] As one might have expected, given early railways and industry, the English physicians were preoccupied with these questions first, coining the terms 'railway spine', 'railway brain' and others to cover the clinical pictures that seemed to be a direct result of accidents suffered on the railways and in the factories. But it was Charcot and, following him, Breuer and Freud who made the most of these clinical pictures. Thus Charcot argued that these neuroses, which seemed to follow from accidents, displayed the same symptoms as hysteria and neurasthenia, thus qualifying them as classical neuroses. In doing so, he opened the way for a number of scientific arguments: light could be thrown on the character of the traumatic neuroses by the analogy with the older and much-examined hysterias; and, similarly, the clear-cut causal factors displayed in the traumatic neuroses could throw light on the vexed question of the aetiology of hysteria.

However, what was clear from the examination of those patients afflicted with railway spine or other symptoms was the fact that the physical injury suffered did not have any direct relation to these traumatic symptoms: a man, thrown from a small railway shunt by a collision with a train, developed symptoms of fatigue, vertigo, faintness, none of them directly related to the physical injuries suffered in the collision. What was also clear from Charcot's account was that the symptoms did not follow on temporally from the injury; there was almost always a delay in the emergence of the symptoms – so that in the case cited above, the railway worker was eager to get back to work having spent a few days in bed recovering from the accident, and it was only on so doing that the symptoms of fatigue and anxiety crystallised as the emblems of his traumatised condition.[104]

Thus Charcot built up the picture of traumatic hysteria which, clear as it was, and influential as it became for the later theory of the neuroses, had certain peculiar features. Firstly, a trauma could be objectively characterised: it was an 'accidental' event, whose main characteristic was the danger it threatened to the physical integrity of the human organism. Through being used to characterise a neurosis, the notion of trauma, borrowed from the Greek term for 'wound', and itself long incorporated into medical terminology, subtly changed its meaning, while retaining the connotation of a sudden violence. It became the term applied to an *external* event, whose effects upon the subject were largely unknown; precisely because they were obscure, the emphasis shifted from these effects – the 'wound', the breaking of the 'skin' – to the *excessive* character of the event which caused the effects. Thus the term trauma came to be attached to an excessive event, whose effects were obvious but indefinite, whose effects corresponded more to the excessive character of the event than to its intrinsic nature. Thus the railway man we have encountered above was travelling in a railway shunt when it was struck full on the side by a train and crushed into a thousand pieces – 'littéralement broyé'. The railway worker could not say very much about what happened after ('Il ne saurait trop dire ce qui s'est passé en ce moment-là . . .');[105] he was found, unconscious, in the debris of the railway shunt.

All of us can, sympathetically, vouchsafe the characterisation of this event as a trauma: its excess *speaks for itself* – the transformation of a guard's van into a 'thousand pieces' of 'debris' bears witness *all by itself* to the shock impressed upon a human organism caught up in this accident. Yet it was Charcot who introduced the idea that we can call this a trauma only when there are no 'visible' effects on the organism. Our conception of trauma is thus one that combines the overwhelmingly obvious with the mysteriously *ineffective*. What has direct and visible effects – the *actual* crushing of the arm, the *organic* brain lesion leading to loss of speech – would automatically be excluded from the set of symptoms belonging to traumatic neurosis.

Thus, from the start, the concept of trauma only attained its importance once it had been emptied of much of its content, once it had become the story of a near miss, or a misfire, rather than a bull's-eye. Naturally one side of this 'emptying' aspect was of great importance for the development of psychological explanations of neurosis: the negative findings of pathologists when they searched for organic lesions of the nervous system corresponding to the symptoms of the patients. The importance of this denial of the existence of localisable and specific organic lesions was intimately tied up with the development of the notion of a trauma; yet the specific relation of the concept of trauma to this physical absence of cause was not always the same. It was not until Freud had developed psychoanalytic theory that he might come to regard this *absence* as the reason for the *efficacy* of the trauma.

On the one hand, then, the trauma was clearly characterised by the external force associated with it, such force shifting the emphasis away from the subject's reactions to this force. On the other hand, the efficacy of this event, its traumatic character, was specifically predicated upon the *lack* of physical effects. When Charcot employed hypnosis to demonstrate the analogy between traumatic hysteria and 'classical' hysteria, the concept of trauma began to undergo some change. In so far as a hypnotic suggestion could be shown to be equivalent to the trauma, Charcot, and following him Freud, shifted the emphasis onto the ideational aspect of the trauma: how the external accident is represented by the subject to himself. With this move began a long and complex sliding in the reference of the concept, from which the concept of trauma has emerged as an indispensable but extremely ill-defined notion.

The next step in the development of the concept of the trauma is a well-known one. Charcot having shown that traumatic hysterias were symptomatologically similar, for all intents and purposes, to 'classical' hysterias, it seemed natural to look for the traumatic experiences underlying these latter. Breuer's case of Anna O., combined with Freud's desire to generate a therapy based on Charcot's theory of the neuroses, led them to develop such a theory, in the *Studies on hysteria*: hysterics suffer from reminiscences, and these reminiscences are (of) traumata. The therapy associated with this theory required the transformation, via the cathartic talking cure, of these traumata into *normal* memories. But we already have a crucial ambiguity embedded in this theory: are these events that are remembered so insistently by the symptoms traumatic because they were originally of the order of external energy that the railway accidents embodied; or did the traumata become such as a result of the process of remembering? Was it the memory *of* the trauma that was traumatic or was it the memory itself, the act of remembering, that was traumatic – memory *as* trauma? Freud's answer, developing over a number of years in the 1890s, was: it was both. There was something specific and proper to the traumatic events themselves that entailed the possibility of their being remembered in such a way as to lead to neurotic symptoms, *and* the processes of remembering and not-remembering were themselves pathological causes.[106]

The first line of argument seemed to rise out of his complicated and ever more protracted therapeutic endeavours: once a remembered event had been shown to be linked to a given symptom it was necessary to go beyond this event, to further events, seemingly less traumatic, or less directly connected with the first appearance of the symptoms, in order to dissolve the system of symptoms (what might even, at this early date, have been called the 'neurotic disposition'). And these events were always earlier, reaching back into childhood. Two questions seemed to hang in the air as these events took their place in the more and more remote past: Firstly, what could one call a trauma for a child aged three or four? Secondly, what could one make of the specific neurotic processes of remembering in the remote past? If neurosis stemmed in part from a peculiar process of remembering, what was one to make of memories stemming from that period of one's life when memory was commonly accepted to be at best unreliable and at worst pitted with holes?

From this movement towards the remote remembered past emerged the seduction theory – the legitimate, perhaps inevitable, transformation of the attempted assimilation of all neuroses to the model of traumatic hysteria. The story is familiar. Instead of the impersonal power of railway trains, looming up unexpectedly, threatening the frail flesh of the subject, the shadowy figures of the parents, embodying their even shadier intentions, fixes the question of the investigator. And it is the sexual intentions of the parent – as filtered and translated into the equivocal memory of the child – that embody the excessive, ill-defined traumatic force.

Most strikingly, that most distinctive of Freudian concepts, *Nachträglichkeit* – the deferred action specific to neurotic causality – was borrowed from the clinical evidence of the traumatic neuroses. In Charcot, we find different formulations of an idea of delayed action – but the clinical evidence almost always includes a phrase such as 'almost immediately', 'after a short delay'.[107]

> The immediate consequences [of the accident] were a severe pain . . . and a swelling of the fist and the fingers . . . which disappeared after four days. But when *after this period of time*, the worker wanted to make use of the hand, he realized that the hand only dangled and that he couldn't move the fingers . . .[108]

Freud was to transfer this conception across to his hysterics, making his reference to Charcot explicit:

> Another peculiarity of Katherina's case, which, incidentally, has long been familiar to us, is seen in the circumstance that the conversion, the production of the hysterical phenomena, did not occur immediately after the trauma but after an interval of incubation. Charcot liked to describe this interval as the 'period of psychical working-out' [*élaboration*].[109]

However, in this early work of Freud's, this *delayed* action characteristic of neurotic effects might be concealed beneath his conception of summation of causes:

> In the case of common hysteria it not infrequently happens that, instead of a single, major trauma, we find a number of partial traumata forming a *group* of provoking causes. These have only been able to exercise a traumatic effect by *summation* and they belong together in so far as they are in part components of a single story of suffering.[110]

Such a conception of coherence and summation, while not directly contradicting the temporal separation of cause and effect, in effect *concealed* it,[111] since it bound each element into a 'single story', a continuity whose underlying character could cancel out the temporal gaps in this narrative.[112] Yet even in these early accounts of the summation of traumatic causes, Freud was moving towards a phenomenology of symptoms and their causative traumata in which the 'first' trauma had a distinctive status:

> There is, however, in principle no difference between the symptom appearing in [a] temporary way after its first provoking cause and its being latent from the first. Indeed, in the great majority of instances we find that the first trauma has left no symptom behind, while a later trauma of the same kind produces a symptom, and yet that the latter could not have come into existence without the co-operation of the earlier provoking cause; nor can it be cleared up without taking all the provoking causes into account.[113]

Yet these early arguments still vacillated, sometimes recognising that the first trauma operated as necessary cause precisely because it acted as a memory rather than a 'fresh impression', sometimes conceding that 'fresh symptoms' and 'recollected ones' may have an equal share in conversion. However, the seduction theory did narrow the conditions as to what could function as a causal trauma down to *sexual* events in early childhood. It was to be this newly narrowed specification of what could count as a trauma adequate to cause a neurosis that would, as we will see soon, prompt Freud into making the theory of deferred action explicit and rigorous.

But the development of this theory was to mean that it was Freud who then suffered something of a shock: the demise of his seduction theory. We do not need to rehearse here all the reasons for this collapse; we will note only the features relevant to our genealogy of the concept of trauma, which now looked decidedly different from railway accidents and brushes with death: if the adult's *intentions* were no longer in question, then what could be traumatic in the fantasies spun around the figures of adults?

In the extensive revision of his theory that this setback necessitated, Freud managed to retain a surprising number of the elements integral to the seduction theory. Here we will mention two of these elements. Firstly, the starting-point of a neurosis could still be referred to as an event or set of events. However, these events were now as much 'internal' as external; their accidentality no longer stemmed from external chance, entirely situated in the external world, but rather from some complex relation *between* the real world and the internal world. On this point, the development of Freud's theory that it was a *way* of remembering that was traumatising, rather than *what* was remembered, obviously led the way. Secondly, the aim of analytic technique did not change at all: the search was still for an event, a memory that had the appearance of being *the* cause of the symptomatic structures at issue.

What is equally important is the fact that Freud retained the logic of deferred action that he had slowly built into the seduction theory, having borrowed it from the concept of trauma he had developed. The manner in which he did this is rather singular. As I have emphasised, the concept of trauma involved the notion of a delay between cause and symptomatic effect; in the seduction theory, as put forward in 1895, this delay now became a causal delay: the fact of the difference in temporal moments became the reason why a pathological structure was created. We have shifted from the concept of *delayed* action to that of *deferred* action.

The *locus classicus* for this account is the brief clinical vignette to be found in the overwhelmingly theoretical *Project for a scientific psychology*, written in the summer and autumn of 1895. The fact that this is the only clinical material to be found in the *Project* should alert us to the theoretical (and personal)[114] importance of the point it is introduced to make; and that point is precisely how the temporality proper to the trauma becomes the means by which pathological defence comes about, instead of the normal defences against pain that Freud had already modelled. Freud's was a general theory of the psyche, dealing with normal defence, thought, memory; however, no matter that this was a description of normal processes, if it could not explain the appearance of pathological forms, it would be entirely useless. The case of Emma showed how such pathology could come about.

The case of Emma involved not two, but three 'events': the recounting of her story in analysis (which Freud calls 'the present time', a symptom involving a 'compulsion of not being able to go into shops *alone*'); 'a memory from the time when she was twelve years old (shortly after puberty)' (Scene I); and a 'second memory' of a scene at age eight, recovered after 'further investigation' (Scene II). In Scene I, she went into a shop to buy something,

saw the two shop-assistants (one of whom she can remember) laughing together, and ran away in some kind of *affect of fright*. In connection with this, she was led to recall that the two of them were laughing at her clothes and that one of them had pleased her sexually.[115]

Scene II explains this incomprehensible scene:

On two occasions when she was a child of eight she had gone into a small shop to buy some sweets, and the shopkeeper had grabbed at her genitals through her clothes. In spite of the first experience she had gone there a second time; after the second time she stopped away. She now reproached herself for having gone there the second time, as though she had wanted in that way to provoke the assault.[116]

Emma herself pointed the way to the association between the two scenes: the *laughing* of the shop-assistants reminded her of the leer of the shopkeeper.

The course of events can now be reconstructed as follows. In the shop the two assistants were *laughing*; this laughing aroused (unconsciously) the memory of the shopkeeper . . . Together with the shopkeeper she remembered his grabbing through her clothes; but since then she had reached puberty. The memory aroused what it was certainly not able to at the time, a *sexual release*, which was transformed into anxiety. With this anxiety, she was afraid that the shop-assistants might repeat the assault, and she ran away.[117]

What is peculiar, what is pathological about this process is not the fact of unconscious ideas, but rather that the *wrong* idea enters her consciousness – misleading her. Instead of the memory of the assault entering consciousness, she becomes aware of her *clothes* and of a *sexual release*, which she attaches to one of the shop-assistants.

If we ask ourselves what may be the cause of this interpolated pathological process, only one presents itself – the *sexual release* . . . [I]t is highly noteworthy that [this sexual release] was not linked to the assault when it was experienced. Here we have the case of a memory arousing an affect which it did not arouse as an experience, because in the meantime the change in puberty had made possible a different understanding of what was remembered.

Now this case is typical of repression in hysteria. We invariably find that a memory is repressed which has only become a trauma by *deferred action*. The cause of this state of things is the retardation of puberty as compared with the rest of the individual's development.[118]

The key to this form of explanation is put in either one of two ways: either 'a memory arouses an affect which it did not give rise to as an experience', or 'every . . . individual has memory-traces which can only be understood with the emergence of sexual feelings of his own'.[119] In early 1896, Freud put this argument in a theoretically concise form:

An inverted relation of this sort [in which the memory has 'a far stronger excitatory effect than the experience did at the time it happened'] between real experience and memory seems to contain the psychological pre-condition for the occurrence of a repression. Sexual life affords – through the retardation of pubertal maturity as compared with the psychical functions – the only possibility that occurs for this inversion of relative effectiveness. *The traumata of childhood operate in a deferred fashion as though they were fresh experiences; but they do so unconsciously.*[120]

What is remarkable in this theory – although this is so true of Freud's work in general that we should not find it surprising – is how faithful it is to the original Charcotian inspiration of the traumatic theory of the neuroses. There is still a *traumatic event*, to which the entire structure of the neuroses is still subject. Yet the super-structure is radically changed: not only is the field of causative events now restricted to sexual ones, but the means by which such an event can become a cause is bounded by a theory of memory, of 'retranscription', of a 'failure of translation', as Freud put it in his letters to Wilhelm Fliess.

But is it true to say, as James Strachey does, that this 'whole idea had the ground cut from under it by the discovery a year or two later of infantile sexuality and the recognition of the persistence of unconscious instinctual impulses'?[121]

In *The language of psycho-analysis*, Laplanche and Pontalis emphatically disagree, stating that the 'most effective rebuttal of this charge is furnished by Freud's account of the 'Wolfman' case, where this same process of deferred action is evoked time and time again'. They also state that: 'The credit for drawing attention to the importance of this term must go to Jacques Lacan.'[122] Unsurprisingly, this accreditation also reflects Lacan's own view of things:

When I said, at the beginning of these talks – *I do not seek, I find*, I meant that, in Freud's field, one has only to bend down and pick up what is to be found. The real implication of the *nachträglich*, for example, has been ignored, though it was there all the time and had only to be picked up.[123]

It is indeed true that, in his 'Rapport de Rome' of 1953, Lacan had pinpointed the *Wolfman* as the text of Freud's mature years that most conspicuously demonstrated Freud's continuing use of the concept of *Nachträglichkeit*:

Freud demands a total objectification of proof so long as it is a question of dating the primal scene, but he no more than presupposes all the resubjectifications of the event that seem to him to be necessary to explain its effects at each turning-point where the subject restructures himself – that is, as many restructurings of the event as take place, as he puts it, *nachträglich*, at a later date [*après coup*].[124]

Yet, in this text, having 'found' this term of Freud's, Lacan immediately turned to *assimilating* it to his own theory of time – to the time associated with the logical time sophism we have discussed above:

That is to say, he [Freud] annuls the *times of understanding* in favour of the *moments of concluding* which precipitate the meditation of the subject towards deciding the meaning to attach to the original event.[125]

This, perhaps, is the closest Lacan ever came to seeking a justification of his technique of 'precipitating' the subject towards concluding his time for understanding by citing *Freud's* practice as an analyst. It is not so much the time-limit that Freud set on the Wolfman's analysis, it is rather the manner in which Freud sets to one side the interval *between* the observation of the primal scene and the dream at age four, in order to find the structure that articulates these together. Analytic understanding, then, will be a repetition (with a difference) of the moment of concluding in which the Wolfman had, as a four-year-old child, come to understand the significance for him of the primal scene, and had defended himself against this understanding through the creation of his infantile neurosis.[126] Analysis must repeat this attempt at precipitating understanding, and Lacan may well have thought that the precipitating cause for the Wolfman, his dissatisfaction with his Christmas (birthday) presents,[127] was a suitable metaphor for the narcissistic frustration upon which analysis feeds, and which Lacan's practice of variable length sessions was to heighten.

Putting side these speculations, what is clear is that Lacan associated his *trouvaille* of *Nachträglichkeit* in the Freudian texts with the intersubjective time which he prided himself on having proved to be 'extremely favourable to the dialectical analysis through which we guide [our students] in the process of a psychoanalysis'.[128] Yet it is surprising how little use Lacan ever explicitly made of this *trouvaille*; there are very few references to *Nachträglichkeit* in the *Ecrits* or in the *Seminars*. But we should not get the impression that Lacan simply left it to others (notably Laplanche and Pontalis)[129] to fill in the significance of the Freudian concept, nor that he regarded it simply as support for his argument that the time of psychoanalysis was the time inhabited by the three prisoners of his logical sophism. One clue as to its wider significance can be seen in the following passage:

By the same token, you see that, contrary to Balint's perspective, and much more in conformity with our experience, we must start off with a radical intersubjectivity, with the subject's total acceptance by the other subject. It is by starting with the experience of the adult that we must grapple retrospectively, *nachträglich*, with the supposedly original experiences, in ranging the various degradations in tiers, without ever leaving the domain of intersubjectivity. In so far as we remain within the register of analysis, we will be obliged to admit an original intersubjectivity.[130]

Psychoanalysis starts with, and always works within, an original intersubjectivity; it then works *backwards*, to earlier states, whose reality and significance is only conferred on them retrospectively. Psychoanalysis works backwards – this is a simple summary of the significance Lacan draws from the concept of *Nachträglichkeit*, and it is on this simple fundamental principle that an entire critique of the developmentalism so apparent in much psychoanalytic thought can then be constructed:

Let us be clear that we do not engage in retracing a succession of stages of development but rather in grasping how positions which are already taken up are retrospectively reorganised.[131]

Indeed, Lacan taught that, far from being an exemplary instance of developmental thinking, psychoanalysis was distinctive in eschewing developmentalism:

. . . the very originality of psycho-analysis lies in the fact that it does not centre psychological ontogenesis on supposed *stages* – which have literally no discoverable foundation in development observable in biological terms.[132]

The distinctive and tragic finding of psychoanalysis is that 'development is entirely animated by accident, by the obstacle of the *tuché*'.[133] In replying to his colleague, Françoise Dolto's insistence on the necessity of developmental thinking in analysis, Lacan took up what he at least, after his discovery of the axis of *Nachträglichkeit*, now took to be the orthodox Freudian position (to be seen, for instance, in the manner in which Freud mounted his critique of Rank's heretical developmental notion of the birth trauma, in *Inhibitions, symptoms and anxiety*):

The fear of castration is like a thread that perforates all the stages of development. It orientates the relations that are anterior to its actual appearance – weaning, toilet training, etc. It crystallizes each of these moments in a dialectic that has as its centre a bad encounter. If the stages are consistent, it is in accordance with their possible registration in terms of bad encounters.[134]

So: the notion of retroactivity, of the *après coup*, gives Lacan an important weapon in his dispute with his contemporary analysts about the character of psychoanalytic explanations; Freud's seeming developmentalism[135] can be shown to be entirely over-shadowed by a distinctive mode of explanation: one invoking the notion of *moments*, or even of *knots*,[136] corresponding to 'registrations', 'transcriptions', and the structuration of these moments in a retroactive 'reading', from later back to earlier.[137] I have tried to indicate how the development of the concept of trauma, from Charcot's delayed action, his incubatory conception of functional causality, to the solid place that deferred action occupied in Freud's thought, forms the basis for Lacan's later re-integration of Freud's concept into his presentation of the temporality of psychoanalysis. At least two features of developmentalism are taken by Lacan to be inimical to psychoanalytic explanations. Firstly, there is the notion of continuous change over time, of process. There is no way of rendering process intelligible without recourse to a false teleology, from whence the normativity of those psychoanalytic theories that cast themselves as developmental. Secondly, there is the notion that these changes can be known *in advance*, that they are preordained (and hence once again we open up into a normative version of psychoanalysis).

Psychoanalysis is concerned with *accidents*:[138] its field of operation, according to Freud, is 'the accidental that is included in the regularity of destiny',[139] the workings of 'accidental fate',[140] of 'δαίμων καὶ τύχη (fate and chance) and not one *or* the other'.[141] If developmentalism is equated with the study of a constitution, even if it be a psychic one, then Lacan's anti-developmentalism is simply reiterating the pragmatic policing operation through which Freud defined the limits of analytic knowledge:

If in our analytical work we concentrate more on the accidental influences than on the constitutional factors, we do so . . . because on the basis of our experience we know something about the former, while about the latter we know as little as – non-analysts.[142]

Let us summarise. There is no doubt that Lacan found in Freud's concept of *Nachträglichkeit* a legitimation for many of his fundamental views on the nature of psychoanalytic causality,[143] on the proper limits of psychoanalytic work (from adult to child, not vice versa). Yet I do want to repeat how unexpectedly sparse are the actual commentaries on this concept in Lacan's work. The exposition I have given undoubtedly secured a foundation for Lacan; but what did he build upon it? And what are the relations between Freud's conceptual innovations concerning the time of symptom-formation, and the idea of logical time to which Lacan accorded such importance?

I will venture two answers to this question. The first concerns the historicity of analysis; the second the discussion of chance and luck in Lacan's *Seminar XI*. Freud's *Nachträglichkeit* renders the status of the past peculiarly fluid. Evidence of this can be found in the often-quoted extreme position Freud adopted in 1899, in his paper on 'Screen memories', as to the reality of memory; at the end of this paper Freud seems to move towards a position in which *all* memories are screen memories, screens which it makes no sense to look behind in search of the 'original, primal' trace:[144]

It may indeed be questioned whether we have any memories at all *from* our childhood: memories *relating to* our childhood may be all that we possess.[145]

This recognition gives the widest latitude to a view of psycho-analysis as being not only an attempt at forgetting the past,[146] but also a manoeuvring, if not a manipulation, of the past. Yet *Nachträglichkeit* is not only about the past and its fluidity, its fading, as a later metaphor of Lacan's would help grasp it; since its internal conceptual structure involves the articulation of two *moments* with a time of delay (of incubation? of waiting?), letting the 'first' event slip free of its moorings entails that the 'second' will as well (and vice versa). And what if the 'second' event has not yet happened – what if the 'second' event is supposedly a future event? This is the scene evoked in a well-known passage in the 'Rapport de Rome':

It is not a question of reality in psychoanalytic anamnesis, but of truth, because it is the effect of full speech to reorder past contingencies in giving them the meaning of necessities to come, such that the little bit of freedom through which the subject makes them present constitutes them.[147]

Such an articulation of 'history' with the future is then clearly specified as the goal of analysis:

Analysis can have for its goal only the advent of a true speech and the realization by the subject of its history in its relation to a future.[148]

The reorganisation of the past *and* the future go hand in hand; their articulation will come to depend upon the transferential function, whereby the past dissolves in the present, so that the future becomes (once again) an *open question*, instead of being specified by the fixity of the past (Scene II, the primal event, the 'first' event in the double articulation of *Nachträglichkeit*).[149]

Yet this reordering of the past, the present and the future also raises further questions for the theory both of the psychoanalytic process and the production of symptoms. These questions are again ones that Lacan's commentaries on Freud's texts reveal to be the most fruitful *and* plausible readings of the path Freud followed: the relation of the trauma and the concept of repetition.[150] We have already followed the elaboration of Freud's concept of the trauma some way. Turning to Lacan's discussion in *Seminar XI*, we will discover further pieces of the jigsaw puzzle that we are putting together in exploring the theme of time: the concepts of chance, luck and causality.

IV

When in disgrace with fortune and men's eyes
I all alone beweep my outcast state,
And trouble deaf heaven with my bootless cries,
And look upon myself, and curse my fate . . .

William Shakespeare, Sonnet 29

There is nothing more stupid than human destiny; all it means is that we always get cheated. Jacques Lacan[151]

Was it just bad luck that the Wolfman, at age one and a half, happened to wake up from his afternoon nap and catch sight of his parents engaged in sexual intercourse? By orienting psychoanalytic thinking around luck, chance, destiny and fate once again,[152] Lacan requires us to make sense of this outrageous question. Firstly, we may ask, is it the same sort of question as asking whether it was just bad luck that Oedipus killed the old man he met at the crossroads? We know that *something like* this meeting was written, was foretold by the Delphic oracle. We could answer the question as to the Wolfman's 'luck' with a similar reply: we could attribute to the oracle of his constitution – his excessive anal-sadism, or whatever – the status of the *already written*.

We can also interpolate the corrective remark that the Wolfman's sight of his parents copulating is not an *event* until it is linked to something that comes after.[153] It is the articulation of at least two 'events' together that makes the sight of his parents copulating traumatic; and once these two events are articulated together, we have a structure, in the final analysis a network – of signifiers, of traits, a character – the Wolfman.[154] We can say that the Wolfman, in so far as he is a subject, is the network of signifiers that constitute his unique relation to the real. To take an obviously dramatic example, one that catches so many commentators' imaginations precisely because it is so *arbitrary*, and thus demonstrates this point in an absolutely transparent fashion:

The most extraordinary case [of the 'accidental circumstances' contributing to the 'choice of a fetish [*zufällige Umstände zur Auswahl des Fetisch*]'] seemed to me to be one in which a young man had exalted a certain sort of 'shine on the nose' into a fetishistic precondition. The surprising explanation of this was that the patient had been brought up in an English nursery but had later come to Germany, where he forgot his mother-tongue almost completely. The fetish, which originated from his earliest childhood, had to be understood in English, not German. The '*Glanz auf der Nase*' – was really a '*glance* [*Blick*] at the nose'.[155]

The young man, the young Englishman only became such, only retrieved his *Muttersprache* and his sexual being, when the network of English signifiers was activated by the shine/*Glanz*, whereby he could return back to looking. The fetishistic condition, the door that opens up onto the field of the sexual, *his* field of the sexual, is that network of signifiers that resonates around the term '*Glanz auf der Nase*'.

Such 'accidents [*Zufallen*]' are the stock-in-trade of the analyst. Far from being extraordinary, one might think that this instance is exemplary, in the sense of functioning as a Kuhnian exemplar: it reveals with great clarity how the arbitrariness of the signifier through which each natural language is constituted is precisely the sort of accident the analyst and the patient seek and find. This domain of causality is a distinctive one; that is why we do not expect a sensible answer to the question: Was it just bad luck that the Wolfman, at age one and a half, happened to wake up from his afternoon nap and catch sight of his parents engaged in sexual intercourse? We immediately know that psychoanalytic explanations do not have the form: the traumatic experience of seeing one's parents copulating at age one and a half is the cause of an infantile neurosis at age 4. The concept of *Nachträglichkeit* might seem to be an attempt to retain at least the *form* of such a causal explanation: the idea that an earlier event causes the later event. But even then it includes the paradoxical claim that the earlier event can be the later event's cause only once the latter has happened. At no point could one generate a conditional of the form: if X, then Y, since the possibility of isolating and describing X is entirely dependent upon the prior isolation, description and *occurrence* of Y.

To make some advance beyond this negative recognition, Lacan turned to Aristotle's treatment of causality, in chapters 4 and 5 of Book II of the *Physics*, 'the most elaborate [theory] that has ever been proposed of the function of cause'.[156] The terms he picked up from Aristotle's chapters are not ones often found in modern literature on causality:[157] *tuché* and *automaton*. Aristotle's English translator in the Loeb edition recognises the problems of translation these terms give rise to, and, in chapter 6, leaves them in their original Greek, while suggesting that English readers may be helped on occasion by regarding *tuché* as best rendered by 'luck' or 'fortune', *automaton* by 'accident' or 'chance result'.[158] In his own inimitable fashion, Lacan proposed a much bolder solution: he renders *tuché* as 'encounter with the real'[159] and *automaton* by the 'network of signifiers',[160] or 'return, the coming-back, the insist-ence of the signs'.[161]

Aristotle regards *tuché* as being a sub-class of the term *automaton*. Only beings who can do well or ill, 'in the sense either of "faring" or of "acting" so, can be described by the term *tuché*'; hence:

when *any* causal agency incidentally produces a significant result outside its aim, we attribute it to *automaton* [chance result]; and in the special cases where such a result springs from deliberate action (though not aimed at it) on the part of a being capable of choice, we may say that it comes by *tuché*.[162]

The force and the importance that Aristotle attaches to these categories stem from two separate questions. The first concerns the nature of causality in general:

For some question the existence [of fortune, luck or accident], declaring that nothing happens casually, but that everything we speak of in that way has really a definite cause. For instance, if a man comes to market and there chances on someone he has been wishing to meet but was not expecting to meet there, the reason of his meeting him was that he wanted to go marketing; and so too in all other cases when we allege chance as the cause, there is always some other cause to be found, and it is never really *tuché*.[163]

Aristotle's target then becomes those philosophers, notably the atomists, who declare that nothing that happens in people's lives comes about by chance, but who are prepared to attribute the origins of the universe, of the ordered cosmos to 'chance [*automaton*] happenings'.

In addition to the inherently paradoxical nature of such an assertion, we may note that it is exactly in the movements of the heavenly bodies that we never observe what we call casual or accidental variations . . . Some, moreover, hold that fortune is a genuine cause of things, but one that has something divine and mysterious about it, that makes it inscrutable to the human intelligence.[164]

The second question concerns 'the power of luck or fortune to influence the goodness and praiseworthiness of a human life'.[165] Certain philosophers believe that good living *means* having a fortunate life – luck or fortune is '*the* single decisive factor in achieving a certain sort of life'. Others maintain that 'luck has no power at all to influence the goodness of a human life'. In the *Eudemian ethics*, Aristotle navigates a way between these two extremes. There, his discussion of luck, chance, fortune is part of an ethical, rather than a cosmological or metaphysical inquiry. Recognising the kinship of psychoanalysis with these Aristotelian arguments will also remind us that we cannot set aside the fact that psychoanalysis is both epistemological and ethical in its very conception of the trauma and its consequences. Nor did Lacan.

There are two obvious senses in which psychoanalysis speaks to these two questions. Firstly, like Aristotle, it is concerned with seemingly causeless happenings and the question of the involvement of human intentions and purposes in these happenings. The familiar principle of psychic determination would quite happily, and quite legitimately, in my view, be assimilated to the Aristotelian model of definite causality, supplemented by the 'incidental causative forces'[166] we call luck; Aristotle recognises that we may ascribe these forces only to purpose-serving actions, which he defines as ones whose result *would have been* recognised as a purpose and *would have* determined the action, had it been anticipated'.[167] These hypotheticals indicate that the field we are concerned with in such actions is the one in which intentionality has to be *ascribed by negotiation* and fundamentally *negotiated in retrospect*. This is precisely the aim of the analyst, converting non-meaningful events into meaningful actions.[168]

The second area is also the one we recognised in analysis: within the domain of the 'accident', of *automaton*, the focus is always on intentionality, on choice, and 'since choice implies intention, it follows that luck and intention are concerned with the same field of objects'.[169] The boldest way to put the psychoanalytic approach to this field of luck and intention would be to say: analysis seeks those intentions which *would have been* determinate of the good fortune, or misfortune, of the subject, *had they been recognised as such*. The clearest example of this procedure is the following reflection of Freud's, in a context which for him and the destiny of his work is of the utmost significance – the discussion of repetition which immediately precedes his 'speculation' concerning a beyond of the pleasure principle:

What psychoanalysis reveals in the transference phenomena of neurotics can also be found further in the lives of people who are not neurotic. The impression they give is of being pursued by a malignant fate, possessed by a demonic power ['*verfolgenden Schicksals, eines dämonischen Zuges in ihrem Erleben*']; but psychoanalysis has always taken the view that their fate is for the most part arranged by themselves [*selbstbereit*] and determined by early infantile influences . . . thus we have come across people all of whose human relationships have the same outcome: such as the benefactor who is abandoned in anger after a time by each of his *protégés*, however much they may otherwise differ from one another, and who thus seems doomed to taste all the bitterness of ingratitude; or the man whose friendships all end in betrayal by his friend; or the man who time after time in the course of his life raises someone else into a position of great private or public authority and then, after a certain interval, himself upsets that authority and replaces him by a new one; or, again, the lover each of whose love affairs with a woman passes through the same phases and reaches the same conclusion. This 'eternal return of the same' causes us only a little astonishment when it relates to *active* behaviour . . . Much more striking are those cases where the subject appears to have a *passive* experience, over which he has no influence, but in which he meets with a repetition of the same fatality [*Schicksals*]. There is the case, for instance, of the woman who married three successive husbands each of whom fell ill soon afterwards and had to be nursed by her on their death-beds.[170]

How are we to discuss this remarkable passage? Should we supplement Lady Bracknell's remark and say that to lose one close relative is a misfortune, to lose two seems remarkably like carelessness, and to lose three indicates there is a demon at work? Her words certainly capture the sense in which Freud is 'struck [*stärker*]' by passive experiences which only 'appear [*scheint*]' to be passive; losing one's husband turns out to be much more like losing an object – for instance a handbag – than one normally supposes it to be.

Yet the inference that Freud is led to, that there is something beyond the pleasure principle, has a curious structure. It is as if he is led, following the examination of his experience, to conclude that non-neurotic people also have intentions that they are not aware of, but that the cumulative effect of the repetition of these intentions is equivalent to their being in the grip of demonic powers, driving them to a pre-ordained fate. In the letter concerning constitution from which I quoted above, Freud conceived of the field of operation of psychoanalysis as 'the accidental that is included in the regularity of destiny', as the workings of 'accidental fate', of 'δαίμων καὶ τύχη (fate, the demonic and chance) and not one *or* the other'. Now, in this consideration of non-neurotic lives, the demonic has come to the fore, with the accidental *seemingly* set to one side. The demonic has all the force of necessity. Yet, following Aristotle *and* Freud, we can conclude that the demonic here is *part* of the field of the accidental; it is not a question of one *or* the other.

So, where, then, is the accidental, in this model of blind repetition? We immediately answer that the accidental is to be found only in the *original* accident, the original moment of disappointment which all these later failures are arranged so as to repeat, the original ingratitude that the ingrates are conscripted to resurrect. We come back to the original question: are all these failed marriages, these bitterly terminated friendships to be attributed to the 'bad luck' of the original experience, trivial as it then was?

I have been following the line of thought which Lacan's references set out for us. We can now rejoin the few pages of text, in *The four fundamental concepts of psychoanalysis*, which take the argument further.

We have translated [*tuché*] as *the encounter with the real*. The real is beyond the *automaton*, the return, the coming-back, the insistence of the signs, by which we see ourselves governed by the pleasure principle. The real is that which always lies behind the *automaton*, and it is quite obvious, throughout Freud's research, that it is this that is the object of his concern.[171]

Yet this seeking-the-real cannot be embarked upon directly; if it is, if the search for the real becomes the anxious desire of the analyst, as it did with Freud and the Wolfman, the consequences may be dire – for the Wolfman, Lacan surmises it may well have 'conditioned the belated accident of his psychosis'.[172] This real, this *terminus ad quem* of the repetitions which the analyst may see concertina back into a punctual moment, is always veiled. But the empirical realities of analysis at least let something be affirmed concerning this real:

What is repeated, in fact, is always something that occurs – the expression tells us quite a lot about its relation to the *tuché* – as if by chance . . . The function of the *tuché*, of the real as encounter – the encounter in so far as it may be missed, in so far as it is essentially the missed encounter – first presented itself in the history of psycho-analysis in a form that was in itself already enough to arouse our attention, that of the trauma . . . Is it not remarkable that, at the origin of the analytic experience, the real should have presented itself in the form of that which is *unassimilable* to it – in the form of the trauma, determining all that follows, and imposing on it an apparently accidental origin?[173]

Here, in this passage, we have Lacan's meditation in parallel to Freud's explorations in *Beyond the pleasure principle*. Yet does it take us any farther than Freud's equally enigmatic remarks? Within the field of psychoanalysis, of the 'unconscious purposiveness of Nature' as we find it in Aristotle,[174] of *automaton*, of 'δαίμων καὶ τύχη’ as we find it in Freud – within this field, we are in search of an event that, incidentally, acts as a misfortune (or good fortune – but do the fortunate ones ever land up on the couch?) *after the event.* Both Freud and Lacan are pointing to the fact that psychoanalysis deals in events that go beyond the causality of the sciences, Aristotelian, molecular-biological[175] or otherwise: beyond chance and necessity, there is luck and accident. Lacan is tracking between the psychoanalytic concepts of the real and repetition; Freud’s accidental fate, or fate and chance, are being contrasted with biological constitution (conceived as some kind of determining template, laying down the unfolding of biological experience), and they *lead* Freud to his beyond of the pleasure principle so tied to the principle of repetition that, as Derrida demonstrates, all Freud can do is *repeat* the gesture of going beyond.[176]

The fundamental concept of psychoanalysis that Lacan is investigating in the passages we have been looking at is repetition. Analysts, he insists, are blinded by the very specific sphere in which they daily confront repetition: the transference. They are too ready to identify transference and repetition, too ready to view *themselves* as the final term in the series of repetitions whose first term is the trauma. Yet, he continues, the transference is no more present than any other sign – ‘Yet is not the transference given to us as effigy and as relation to absence?’[177] To emphasise the transference at the expense of remembering, on the grounds that memory never makes present, whereas transference is, by definition, in the present, will mislead, since the true meeting point of the trauma and the transference is in the notion of a missed encounter:

For what we have in the discovery of psycho-analysis is an encounter, an essential encounter – a *rendez-vous* to which we are always called with a real that eludes us.[178]

Here, perhaps, we find an echo of what Lacan brought with him to psychoanalysis from the start: his surrealist heritage. Is not the essential encounter, the *rendez-vous* with the real, an image whose lineage goes back to the umbrella and sewing machine on a dissecting table so beloved of the surrealists – beloved because its automatic, seemingly random character offers us a means of access to the ecstatically beautiful?[179]

Lacan eschews the reading of psychoanalytic experience which would recommend the transference as a corrective emotional experience, an encounter in which the originally missed encounter could be made good, in which the appointment could be kept.

After all – we may note in parentheses – Lacan had already founded his practice, his practice of variable-length sessions, on the idea that the *rendez-vous* cannot be modelled on the well-organised diary (as in the obsessional practices of orthodox analysts, or even the symbolically maternal availability of the Winnicottian analyst, who is there, who survives, who is *reliable*).[180] The real could never be located in the analyst, in the analyst functioning, on analogy with the dream, as day-residue. To assert this with the maximum of rhetorical force, Lacan indeed turned to the dream: in search of the real, in the experience that is conventionally taken to give the limit that defines the real, and also so as to combat a tendency which he saw in psychoanalysis to treat the 'subjective experience' of the subject as if it were entirely a dream, the idea that *life is a dream*.

V

After the first death, there is no other.

Dylan Thomas, 'A refusal to mourn the
death, by fire, of a child in London'

I, too, have seen with my own eyes, opened by maternal divination, the child, traumatized by the fact that I was going away despite the appeal, precociously adumbrated in its voice, and henceforth more renewed for months at a time – long after, having picked up this child, I have seen it let its head fall on my shoulder and drop off to sleep, sleep alone being capable of giving it access to the living signifier that I had become since the date of the trauma. Jacques Lacan[181]

There is no need to justify the reproduction here of the enigmatic and oft-quoted passage which opens the final chapter of *The interpretation of dreams*:

Among the dreams which have been reported to me by other people, there is one which has special claims upon our attention at this point. It was told to me by a woman patient who had herself heard it in a lecture on dreams: its actual source is still unknown to me. Its content made an impression on the lady, however, and she proceeded to 're-dream' it, that is, to repeat some of its elements in a dream of her own, so that, by taking it over in this way, she might express her agreement with it on one particular point.

The preliminaries to this model dream were as follows. A father had been watching beside his child's sick-bed for days and nights on end. After the child had died, he went into the next room to lie down, but left the door open so that he could see from his bedroom into the room in which his child's body was laid out, with tall candles standing round it. An old man had been engaged to keep watch over it, and sat beside the body murmuring prayers. After a few hours' sleep, the father had a dream that *his child is standing beside his bed, catches him by the arm and whispers to him reproachfully: 'Father, don't you see I'm burning?'* He woke up, noticed a bright glare of light from the next room, hurried into it and found that the old watchman had dropped off to sleep and that the wrappings and one of the arms of his beloved child's dead body had been burned by a lighted candle that had fallen on them.[182]

Freud's comments on this 'moving dream' are decidedly enigmatic. Straight off, he admits that we have here 'come upon a dream which raises no problem of interpretation and the meaning of which is obvious, but which, as we see, nevertheless retains the essential characteristics that differentiate dreams so strikingly from waking life and consequently call for explanation'.[183] This dream does not resist interpretation; its *opacity* is not due to a lack of *understanding*.

Lacan's commentary on this dream has also become well known, not least because he goes in search of the source of the enigmatic power of the dream – an enigma which Freud had, it is true, made available, but which he, for once, mysteriously, seemed determined to leave intact. Freud hints that the source of the dream's power lies in its *prolongation* of the life of the child, after it[184] has died:

If the father had woken up first and then made the inference that led him to go into the next room, he would, as it were, have shortened his child's life by that moment of time [*Moment*].[185]

The wish of the father that the child be still alive is, it would seem, *realised*, fulfilled, by dreaming the dream – the child is alive for one moment longer by being represented as speaking these awful, oracular words, besides the father's bed. The wish triumphs over the 'reality' of the child's death; the dream succeeds, for one moment.

Slightly perversely, Lacan sees this dream as presenting Freud's thesis that the dream is a realisation of a desire with some difficulties. Instead, he asserts, 'what we see emerging here, almost for the first time, in the *Traumdeutung*, is a function of the dream of an apparently secondary kind – in this case, the dream satisfies only the need to prolong sleep'.[186] This is indeed true: what Freud argues is that this particular dream fulfils two functions at the same time: it prolongs sleep and it prolongs the life of the child. *In sleep, the child is alive.* Or is it rather perhaps: *In the dream, the child is alive?*

Yet Lacan is not as sure as Freud is that the dream is a prolongation. Should we assume that the child is alive in the dream – even though it speaks?[187] Its words, after all, are like a living hell for the father; they are words that are so oracular that we sense that only a dead person could have spoken them; they are words like the hypnotised M. Valdemar's cry of 'I am dead'[188] – these words are a living hell for anyone who, like us, allows his or her ears to be burnt by them.

Father, can't you see I'm burning? This sentence is itself a firebrand – of itself it brings fire where it falls – and one cannot see what is burning, for the flames blind us to the fact that the fire bears on the *Unterlegt*, on the *Untertragen* [the lining, what lies under, what is held under], on the real.[189]

Like Freud, Lacan goes out of his way to emphasise that these words – 'Father, can't you see I'm burning' – are 'forever separated from the dead child';[190] he also goes out of his way to surmise that what wakes the father is not the 'accident' in reality, the sleeping watchman and the 'glare of light that shone through the open door into the sleeping man's eyes',[191] but the reality *in* the dream:

If the function of the dream is to prolong sleep, if the dream, after all, may come so near to the reality that causes it, can we not say that it might correspond, reply [il pourrait être répondu] to this reality without emerging from sleep? – after all, there is such a thing as somnambulistic activity. The question that arises, and which indeed all of Freud's earlier hints now allow us to ask, is – *What is it that wakes the sleeper* [Qu'est-ce qui réveille]? Is it not, *in* the dream, another reality? – the reality that Freud describes thus – *Dass das Kind an seinem Bette steht*, that the child is standing beside his bed, *ihn am Arme fasst*, catches him by the arm, and whispers to him reproachfully, *und ihm vorwurfsvoll zuraunt: Vater, siehst du denn nicht*, Father, can't you see, *dass ich verbrenne?*, I'm burning?[192]

It is this question, the question – What is the reality of the dream? – towards which Lacan senses this dream propels us. Certainly we would be led astray if we were to think that the reality of the dream is the crack of light falling on the sleeping man's face. We are also led astray if we think the reality of the dream is some memory of an occasion when the child spoke the words, 'Father can't you see . . . ?', as Freud's remarks incline us to believe.[193] Nor is the reality of the dream the overwhelming desire that the child be still alive – the prolongation of the child's life for one moment more. Lacan searches beyond these possible candidates for the reality of this terrible dream, seeking the missed encounter, the missed reality. In this dream, the missed reality is the cause of the child's death. Not the physical cause, but something like the cosmic cause, the meaning of the child's death – its *tuché*.

Is not the dream essentially, one might say, an act of homage to the missed reality – the reality that can no longer produce itself except by repeating itself endlessly, in an endlessly never attained awakening? What encounter can there be henceforth with that forever inert being – even when devoured by the flames – if not the encounter that occurs precisely at the moment when, by accident, as if by chance, the flames come to meet him? Where is the reality in this accident? – if not that it repeats something, something which is in the end more fatal, *by means of* reality, a reality in which the person who was appointed to watch over the body is still asleep, even when the father re-emerges after being awoken.[194]

Lacan is developing, playing with, even, the dialectic of dream and reality. Reality is what wakes us from the dream. But the dream, the Freudian dream – not the philosopher's dream, the dream which is a world of illusion – includes the reality which awakes the man. The reality is not everyday reality, but the real which is named by, but never found in, the trauma. And what is the trauma here? It is something indescribably awful, burning, a flame that can never be extinguished:

Is the reality that determines the awakening the slight noise against which the empire of the dream and of desire is maintained? Is it not rather something else? Is it not that which is expressed in the depths of the anxiety of this dream – namely, the most intimate aspects of the relation between the father and the son, which emerges, not so much in that death as in the fact that it is beyond, in the sense of destiny?[195]

Yet again, the real appears in the guise of destiny, just as we asked the question: is it the Wolfman's misfortune – his 'accidental fate' – to awake to the copulation of his parents one hot summer afternoon?

Between what occurs as if by chance, when everybody is asleep – the candle that overturns and the sheets that catch fire, the meaningless event, the accident, the piece of bad luck – and the element of poignancy, however veiled, in the words *Father, can't you see I'm burning?* – there is the same relation to what we come upon in repetition. It is what, for us, is represented in the term neurosis of destiny or neurosis of failure. What is missed is not adaptation, but *tuché*, the encounter . . . The enclosed aspect of the relation between the accident, which is repeated, and the veiled meaning, which is the true reality and leads us towards the drive, confirms for us that the demystification of that artefact of the treatment known as the transference does not consist in reducing it to what is called the actuality of the situation . . . [I]t is necessary to ground this repetition first of all in the very split that occurs in the subject in relation to the encounter. This split constitutes the characteristic dimension of analytic discovery and experience; it enables us to apprehend the real, in its dialectical effects, as originally unwelcome.[196]

What Lacan is working towards, what I have been edging us towards, is the mutual articulation of two dimensions of temporality proper to psychoanalysis: on the one hand, the temporality of repetition, with its close relation to transference, to the real, and to the very idea of a trauma; on the other, the temporality of logical time, of the instant of seeing, the time for understanding and the moment of concluding. What perhaps unites these, in the end, is the act. After all, the transference is the enactment of the reality of the unconscious, the act is what forces repetition upon the analyst – and it is also the means by which a beyond of repetition may be reached. Lacan's logical time sophism requires the subject to precipitate his certainty in the act, and it is this dimension that rules the practice of variable-length sessions, annulling the time for understanding in favour of the moments for concluding. Of course, what is enacted is a repetition. Yet that is the only way forward in analysis, forward into the transference neurosis, forward towards the real which is always avoided.

There may well be other temporal modalities with which analysis is articulated. Who would be surprised to encounter the Hippocratic rhythms of illness, crisis and recovery,[197] or the seasonal rhythms of growth, maturity, decay and sterility? Yet Lacan chose to organise his considerations of temporality around the punctuality – in all of its senses – that Freud's analytic theory and practice had introduced: the idea of a traumatic moment, a missed encounter, as the horizon of work of analyst and analysand, a moment which is crystallised only retrospectively, and which takes on the significance of both fatality (destiny) and accidentality in the rhythm of repetition, of iteration. The rhythm of logical time, of an instant opening onto a period of waiting, of hesitation, of delay, closed by haste and certainty, matched the Freudian schema. And it also made possible a practical innovation, risking breaking the deadlock of one system of rituals being fused into another, a deadlock that condemns the two parties to the entirely predictable daily missed encounter, the 'deserts of vast eternity' of interminable analysis. And, with his practical innovation, Lacan forcibly reminded analysts that interpretation is an *act*, that beginning and ending the session is the act of punctuating the subject's discourse, that everything that both analyst and subject do and say has an analytic significance. In the end, they might do worse than both arrive at the door with the same reasons for concluding.

III
THE DESTINY OF
PSYCHOANALYSIS

An event can take place which isn't real. My usual distinction between reality and external reality is perhaps not quite adequate at this point. It gestures towards the event which no idea of 'reality' can help us think. But so what, I'll say to you, if what is announced in the announcement indeed bears the index 'external reality'? Well then, treat it as an index, it can signify, telephone, telesignal another event which takes place before the other, without the other, in accordance with another time, another space, etc. That's the *a*, *b*, *c* of my psychoanalysis. When I speak of reality, it's so as to send them to sleep, otherwise you won't understand any of my rhetoric. I've never given up hypnosis, I've simply transferred one mode of induction to another: one might say that I've become a writer and have poured all my powers and hypnagogic desires into the writing, into the rhetoric, into the staging and into the composition of texts. What do you want me to say to you, sleep with me, that's all that interests them, the rest doesn't matter. So the telepathic announcement has come true even if it hasn't come to pass in external reality, that's the hypothesis I'm allowing to be read at the very moment I foreclose it on the surface of my text.

Derrida, 'Télépathie'

. . . how can an autobiographical writing, in the abyss of self-analysis which is non-terminated, give birth to a world-wide institution?

Derrida, 'Spéculer – sur "Freud" '

9

WHO IS IN ANALYSIS WITH WHOM? FREUD, LACAN, DERRIDA

People like hearing stories about psychoanalysis. There is no doubt about that. Yet there are certain rules governing the practice of analysis which appear to ensure confidentiality, secrecy and the veritable absence of stories. If the analyst functions as a blind alley for discourse, an impasse, beyond which words cannot pass – which does not make him or her into a mirror, but which tempts one into thinking that one's words are destined to be returned to the sender, from out of the dustbins rattling around at the end of the blind alley – if the analyst's armchair is where the buck stops getting passed on, then the stories can come from only one side of the room, from the side of the couch. Yet, one would have thought that any analyst would be able to tell you that such stories about analysis are stories about one particular analyst, someone's analyst; so they are items which have escaped from the net of the transference, the most easily identifiable bits of acting out. One could call them the transference in action. In action outside analysis. Everything said outside analysis – outside analysis? where is that? – is the trans-ference gone astray, gone on holiday, taking a break, off limits, on the record. And that is how analysis inhabits society at large, as opposed to the supposed perfect interiority of its proper, its analytic habitus. In society, in public discourse, analysis exists only as wild transference.

But what of the analytical societies, those discursive spaces intermediate between analysis and its outside? Can discourse about analysis within these societies neutralize the savage effects of the transference, creating a third kind of analytic discourse, beyond the two categories of 'acted out transference', and, as the Americans will have it, 'acted in transference'? How are we to distinguish what a recent paper in the *International Review of Psycho-analysis* took as its object, the gossiping psychoanalyst, from the theorising analyst, communicating scientific papers in which it is claimed the theory of psychoanalysis is advanced and promulgated? As Stanley Olinick, the author of 'The gossiping analyst', points out, analysts gossip to analysts, and not to non-analysts – they gossip only when an analytic ear is listening, only to members of their own societies. Such conditions of gossipy discourse thus duplicate those conditions meant to ensure the scientificity of communications offered, on more formal occasions, to those societies, to those same colleagues. As early as 1910, Jung wrote a paper showing how rumour could do the job of psychoanalytic interpretation as well as an analyst could, when he was asked to give an opinion on sexual rumours that a class of pubescent girls had generated on hearing the dream of one of their classmates. Having recounted all the girls' various versions of the 'dream', Jung concluded:

So far as the interpretation of the dream is concerned, there is nothing for me to add; the children themselves have done all that is necessary, leaving practically nothing over for psychoanalytic interpretation. *The rumour has analysed and interpreted the dream.*[1]

If rumour and gossip can *replace* analysis, can perform the same function as analysis, how are we to maintain a sharp distinction between the two?

Let me put the question I am addressing a little more generally: what are the limits of analysis? Are we to understand the word 'limits' in a strictly mathematical sense? Will we be obliged to engage in an activity which may well border on the rigorously psychotic, by establishing a calculus of analysis, finding the equation that will define the limit to which analysis tends? Or should we approach it from the other side, defining the non-analytic, either on the model of an outside and an inside, or of an essence and its accidents? To take a slightly more specific, though teasing set of questions: what is the relationship between the 'analytic' and the 'Freudian', how does the relation to Freud's texts, to the name 'Freud', and to their appointed legatees, pertain to the 'analytic'?

To help approach this question, let me turn to the text of a discussion, published in Derrida's *La Carte postale*, which took place between Derrida and the Confrontation group of analysts in Paris.[2] Most charmingly and disarmingly, Derrida politely raised the question as to what his analyst-listeners were doing listening to someone who, by his own avowal, was neither analyst nor analysand.[3] Is it perhaps, he asked, because the limits of the analytic are now being put into question, in particular, by the practice of doing another stretch in analysis? This practice was recommended by

Who is in analysis with whom?

Freud for analysts – it was his riposte to the logic of interminability and one of the earlier complications of the temporal limit by which analysis is distinguished from the non-analytic. But it has come to be increasingly indulged in by so-called patients, the analysands. *Faire une tranche de plus* – that is how the French put it: cut another slice off the analytic loaf, do another stretch of time within the strict confines of analysis. Derrida points out that many of the analysands who engage in a supplementary *tranche* go to analysts with different allegiances – they go to analysts who, according to their own orthodoxies, are not analysts. And, Derrida implies, that is the inner logic of the *tranche* – the recourse to the non-analytic as the necessary supplement to analysis, thus instituting a *faux-bond*, letting something (the analytic?) down, and creating the *tranche-fert*, an amalgam of *tranche* and *transfert*, which we might translate as transit-erence, trans-iterence. If analyst A from group A does a stretch with analyst B from group B, it is clear, Derrida argues, that the analyst is *tranchefering* (transiterating) on to the non-analytic. The practice of the *tranche*, the witness to the incompleteness of analysis, thus puts into question the ordered, rule-governed relations of analysis with its exterior. And this frequent practice also brings into question the very concept of transference, and the accompanying and crucial notion of the analytic situation, the free space of analysis. This homogeneous space now becomes divisible and fractured, in the crucial sense in which the divisibility of the letter, the signifier and the phallus, in Derrida's critique of Lacan's 'Seminar on *The purloined letter*', is the ruination of the Lacanian system.[4] Analysis now becomes the site of a dissemination of its effects and its forms – to the point where the question, 'What is the non-analytic?', becomes impossible to answer, save in terms of the now subverted concept of the analytic.[5]

These issues are not entirely foreign to analysts. It has not been impossible for them at least to indicate their subversive character, and sometimes to turn them to good use. In Serge Leclaire's book, *Démasquer le réel*, what the contemporary psychoanalyst experiences as the unresolvable difficulties of his practice are discussed as they are manifested in three different phenomena. Firstly, the difficulties analysts experience in leaving behind them the safe refuge of analytic silence: when they manage to do so, they find themselves indoctrinating their analysands, rather than analysing them, or they find themselves offering interpretations which are only makeshifts, designed to entice and seduce the patient into getting to the point. Secondly, Leclaire continues, there is the practice of introducing a third party – a practice quite clearly akin to those marriages in which a third party is necessary to sustain the marital process, whether that third party be a child or any other applicant filling the role allotted him or her by the logic of the *ménage à trois*. In this instance, the third party is another analyst, and the analysand is handed on to a second analyst, in order to achieve the termination of the 'first' analysis. Such a description, while akin to Derrida's discussion of the *tranche de plus*, the *tranchefert*, transiterence, helps to deconstruct the notion of the *tranche*. Is this second analysis, whose aim is *expressly* the termination of 'analysis' (as if analysis were one thing, timeless and indivisible), a second stretch *in* analysis, a repetition, or is it just time on parole? Talking time, whose only aim is to find a way of terminating the talk. Is this 'second' analysis simply the limit of the 'first'? Both Derrida's discussion of the *tranche* and Leclaire's discussion of this second analysis designed to end all analysis indicate a crisis of self-confidence, which we might well rephrase in more abstract terms as being a crisis in the definition both of the analytic object and of the limits of analysis.

There is much that could be said about the 'third party' of any analysis: it forms the intersection of theory and gossip in a quite clear-cut manner. At the level of theory, the 'third party' is the (absent) third term of the Oedipal scenario that the analysand's discourse precipitates around the figure of the analyst. Later in this chapter, I will discuss at greater length the sense in which the construction of the psychoanalytic situation itself was consequent upon finding a conceptual locus for this 'third party'; indeed, psychoanalysis has as one of its primary aims the mastering of the wild effects introduced into human relationships by this Oedipal 'third party'. But the 'gossipy' history of psychoanalysis is as much a witness to the force of these third parties as to the power of psychoanalysis to control their disruptive effects. Precisely because psychoanalysis attempts to offer a theory of this third party, its continual disruption by it has added interest and poignancy. To take one example, which could be repeatedly supplemented: the life history of Ernest Jones. In Brome's recent biography – appropriately entitled *Ernest Jones. Freud's alter ego* – four of the central episodes of Jones' life are structured around the third-party phenomenon of analysis. To take one of these, when his long-standing sexual companion, Loe Kann, goes into analysis with Freud, at a point of crisis in her relationship with Jones, the triangle

Who is in analysis with whom?

Freud–Loe–Jones quickly develops all the marks of tension and imbalance that one might expect. Loe passes the letters she receives from Jones, on holiday in Italy, to Freud, who takes 'great pleasure' in reading them; Freud and Jones exchange letters about the satisfactory progress of Loe's treatment ('I want to thank you very deeply for the details about my wife, which were just the kind I wanted to know'). Jones writes to Freud that Loe complains in her letters bitterly about the latter, how Freud does not trust her, and twists everything she says. Freud assures Jones that Loe is improving greatly, although she does not want to write to Jones, and, having forced herself to, sends the letter to the wrong address. While in analysis with Ferenczi – another triangle (Freud–Ferenczi–Jones) that has a significant history – Jones has an affair with Loe's nurse Lina, which comes as a tremendous shock to Loe, while Lina then produces pelvic pains dramatically akin to Loe's symptoms – the nicest case of transference, Freud said, he had ever seen. Meanwhile, Loe breaks with Jones and Freud sets himself to writing the letter that Loe could not, telling Jones of her break with him, and how 'supremely difficult' it was to play the analyst between two such close friends. To round off the story, Loe next proceeds to fall in love with another man, named Jones – whom Ernest was always to refer to as Jones the Second. Freud journeyed to Budapest, the site of Jones' analysis, to attend the marriage of Loe and Jones the Second, deputising, one might say, for Jones the First.

A second Jones triangle carries us even deeper into the knotty question of third-party analysis: Jones' stormy analysis of Joan Rivière during the First World War, which he admitted was his 'worst failure'. She eventually went to Freud for her second *tranche*. Jones, based in London, finds Freud reproving him for being unreliable, Jones reading this as an effect of what Freud is hearing from Rivière, amounting to an accusation of amorous infidelity and 'inconsequent behaviour'; everything seemed to hinge around whether Jones had returned Rivière's declarations of love. Freud tried to take neither Jones' nor Rivière's side – instead he was critical of both, repeating to each the criticisms that each had addressed to the other.

These two stories from Jones' life and work prompt the question: were these 'analyses' constituted by the antecedent relations between analysts, so that Loe Kann's and Joan Rivière's analyses with Freud cannot be isolated from their relations to Jones without obscuring the essential object of analysis – the relation between

225

colleagues (as in analyst A going to analyst B from group B . . .)? Similar issues are raised by the third of Leclaire's contemporary difficulties, which furthermore offers us some insight into what the analyst's response to the problem of the third party might be.

Leclaire broaches his topic by noting the almost insuperable reticence analysts experience in talking to each other about analysis, except in formal papers, in controlled supervision, or in the privacy of the familial space constructed by hetero- or homosexual analyst couples. In parallel with this reticence, and in relation to it, he observes the increasing importance, for those in analysis, of what is happening elsewhere, on other couches – to the point where 'there are now analyses in which the networks of allegiance of the couches frequented by friends and lovers substitute for kinship relations'.[6]

Who, indeed, is in analysis with whom? The question emerges spontaneously, out of the space of analysis, assuming such a space exists, as the most urgent question that analysts hear from their analysands, and, in so far as it is urgent, and maybe insofar as it is also their question, they cannot answer it directly. In the Jones–Loe–Freud scenario, who was in analysis with whom? Yet Leclaire's argument has more force than just the mere repeating of the question in public. He is quite clear that this is not another version of the Oedipal question; it is not a disguised enquiry into the mysterious goings on in the parental bed. The primal scene of analysis is no longer the parents' bed, it is now the other couch. The need to pass an analysand on to a third party, on to a second analyst, indicates that the first analyst has become implicated in the Oedipal scenario of the analysand, most probably because he or she has failed to recognise that the analytic scenario now has ascendancy over the family. My opening sentence, 'People like hearing stories about psychoanalysis', has more truth in it than I realised when I sought out its wit.

Let me return to Derrida's talk to the analysts in Paris, and retell *his* story about analysis. It runs as follows. Someone in America said to him: 'I know that a certain analyst has been in analysis with you for more than ten years.' As is well known, known to the woman who told Derrida this, and well known to Derrida, he is neither analyst nor analysand – he comes from the 'so-called outside of analysis'.[7] His reply to her? 'Prove it.' She supplied him with all sorts of 'evidence', clues pointing in that direction, but she brushed these aside, saying: 'But that doesn't matter, you prove that it isn't true.' For important reasons, reasons, he implies, to do with the concept of the non-analyst, with the limits of analysis, Derrida could not prove it. Careful as one must be, so careful in matters of discretion, of confidentiality, of the law of the other's secret, Derrida was encouraged to enter into the discourse of gossip, where naming names is so crucial a part; he was encouraged to disclose the *name* of his rumoured analysand. Careful to call it a hypothesis, he acceded: 'What is his name? It's most unfortunate, I often forget this name – ah, that's it, Loewenstein.'

Who is in analysis with whom? Whose name is this? A well-known American analyst's, now dead. One of the New York troika of the 1950s: Hartmann, Kris and Loewenstein. Known to his intimates as Loew. But Derrida spoke this name to a mixture of analysts from the four French societies, each prizing its purity, independence, and each nursing a secret history. This proper name signifies, in this context, one thing: the premier training analyst of pre-war Paris, Lacan's analyst. With this name, this proper name, this unleashing of gossip, we sense the emergence, in an ironic and clownish mode, of a new question: are not all these supplementary *tranches* attempts to cut through the silent question of each analyst's relation to Lacan? When Derrida postulates analyst A circulating into group B, in search of his second or third *tranche*, isn't it clear that he may well be attempting to cut the Gordian knot, the Borromenean knot, perhaps, which ties him to Lacan? For each of these groups has a specific historical relation to Lacan: group A, which Lacan left in 1953 and which has attempted to pretend that he has not had an analytic existence since that date; group B, formed in 1964, by those who found they could no longer both live with Lacan and achieve the recognition they desired from *other* analysts, analysts from *outside*; group C, which left Lacan in 1968, finding his new theories of the training of analysts unacceptably authoritarian and arbitrary, offering no defence against the arbitrary exercise of his will, with no third party to mediate it; and the group of Lacanian faithful, the Ecole Freudienne, which flourished from 1964 to 1980 and is now defunct, on account of the 'arbitrary' act of dissolution by which Lacan asserted that he was determined to remain alone, as he had always been, and was quite clearly determined to die alone.

The fact of Derrida, the self-avowed non-analyst, telling a collection of analysts who had overcome considerable barriers so as to become his audience, who prided themselves on being motley, the fact that he told them a rumour going around that he was the analyst of Lacan's analyst strikes at a psychoanalytical nerve which goes well beyond the rhetorical point to be had, say, by entitling a paper – I saw this the other day in a library – 'Hume's debt to Kant'. Analytical societies have as a primary function the defusing of the potentially explosive effects of the transference mobilised in each training analysis. Analytic power in such societies consists in establishing lineages, in endowing with authority and untouchability the line of descent from one analyst to his or her pupils. Derrida's rumour, his gossip, duplicates an actual historical choice forced upon some French analysts in 1963, when they were asked to exclude from their society the analyst who trained them – that is, Lacan. In Jung's terms, quoted above, his rumour is the equivalent of an interpretation of that repressed history. Similarly, when one analyst crosses the barriers separating one group from another, to do time with an analyst with a different filiation, he or she is attempting to undo the effects of this historical knot in the systems of filiation.

The question of filiation has been raised most urgently in the French psychoanalytic world, particularly by Lacan, Granoff and Roustang;[8] it is usually the relation to Freud that is to the fore – a relation which any perusal of French analytic literature reveals to be the most central concern of French analysts. While 'Anglo-Saxon' literature has an entirely different relation to Freud's texts, often enough making use of the fact that it is still obligatory to *start* with Freud in order to show what advance *beyond* Freud is being proposed, the question of filiation does emerge, albeit in a less theoretically prominent position. A short illustration may help. Harry Guntrip, a well-known British analyst of the post-war period, who died in 1975, was in analysis first with W.R.D. Fairbairn, a founder of the object-relations school, and a major critic of Freud's libido and instinct theory. However, Guntrip's account of his analysis with Fairbairn betrays a certain regret that it was conducted on strictly classical Freudian lines – 'orthodox in practice'.[9] In 1956, Fairbairn replied to a question from Guntrip about the Oedipus complex by saying: 'The Oedipus complex is central for therapy but not for theory.'[10] Guntrip replied: 'I said that I felt Oedipal analysis kept me marking time on the same spot . . . But my Oedipal analysis with Fairbairn was not a waste of time . . . ' Guntrip 'gave up' Fairbairn gradually, partly because he had resolved to seek analysis with Winnicott.

Fairbairn first introduced me to Winnicott in 1954 by asking him to send me a copy of a paper [of his] . . . He sent it and, rather to my surprise, a letter saying: 'I do invite you to look into the matter of your relation to Freud, so that you may have your own relation and not Fairbairn's. He spoils his good work by wanting to knock down Freud' . . . I felt that Winnicott had left Freud as far behind in therapy as Fairbairn had done in theory.[11]

Guntrip's analysis with Winnicott was a great success – Winnicott became the mother who valued him. Furthermore, in contrast with Fairbairn's consistently Oedipal interpretations, Winnicott twice (twice?) remarked: 'You show no signs of ever having had an Oedipus complex.' But Guntrip's article goes on to say:

It hardly seems worth mentioning that the only point at which I felt I disagreed with Winnicott was when he talked occasionally about 'getting at your primitive sadism, the baby's ruthlessness and cruelty, your aggression', in a way that suggested . . . Freud's and Klein's 'instinct theory', the id, innate aggression. For I knew he rejected the 'death instinct' and had moved far beyond Freud when I went to him . . . By 1967 he wrote, and gave me a copy of his paper in which he said: 'I see that I am in the territory of Fairbairn: "object-seeking" as opposed to "satisfaction-seeking".' I felt then that Winnicott and Fairbairn had joined forces to neutralize my earliest traumatic years.[12]

One might conclude that Guntrip's relations to both analysts were articulated around a 'moving far beyond' Freud: the residue of disagreement with both was where he recognised Freud 'in' them – Oedipal interpretations, innate aggression. And the cure arose from a combined figure of filiation neutralising the dire effects of Freud, equivalent to 'my earliest traumatic years'. It was to undo the effect of too-Freudian an analysis that Guntrip went to Winnicott, who had, from the start, directed him towards the question of his relation to Freud. Thus the circulation amongst peers is the horizontal projection (as in geometry) of a vertical line of descent. The 'horizontal' supplement, the *tranche de plus*, is the realisation of the 'vertical' supplement along the axis of filiation, the axis which, for every analyst, abuts onto the edge of the analytic, onto Freud.[13]

Freud's legacy – *legs de Freud*.
The title of this chapter is a deliberately hijacked quotation. No doubt you have recognized it. The expression '*legs de Freud*' is most often encountered in the writings of Jacques Lacan and of Wladimir Granoff. Naturally I leave it to the reader to be the judge of what's going on in this hijacking.[14]

We might add: Lacan's 'return to Freud' *produced* the question of Freud's legacy. How? Firstly, because of the insistence of his return to Freud, which in no way can be considered as a simple textual manœuvre, but has had as its effect the recentring of attention on the question: what is the nature of the analytic act being repeated each time someone goes to visit the analyst, this analytic act which Freud was the 'first' to enact? Secondly, Lacan's work has initiated a new phase in the history of psychoanalysis, a phase in which what is interrogated is the notion of analysis itself. If the second generation of analysts of the 1920s and 1930s were concerned primarily with the modalities of libidinal expression, and with genitality as a *telos*, whether normative or purportedly subversive, as in Reich, and if the American school took as its ideal the adaptive character, Lacan's advance was to focus on the reflexivity of analysis (analysis as its own precondition), and the recreation of the Freudian discovery (return to Freud and/or return of Freud? the debt that cannot be paid off and/or the inexhaustible legacy?) in *each* analysis. Lacan recentred analysis around the didactic or training analysis. 'The aim of my teaching has been and still is the training of analysts.'[15] The *telos* of Lacan's teaching is – the analyst. Where other analysts took the symptom as the starting-point, the symptom of the patient, Lacan took the symptom of the trainee analyst as the point of entry into both theory and interpretation. And what is his or her symptom? The desire to be an analyst. This starting-point is closely intertwined with the reference to Freud, the first analyst:

The function, and by the same token, its consequence, the prestige, if I can put it like that, of Freud are on the horizon of every position of the analyst. They constitute the drama of the social, the communal organization of psychoanalysts.[16]

Lacan's theory was thus inexorably impelled towards becoming a theory of the process by which the candidate passes across the space of analysis, from being analysand to being analyst. The structure of the Ecole Freudienne was built around such a hope for a theory, a hope which few would deny was dashed; but few would deny that the failure of this attempt was most instructive. Derrida's concern with the 'origin' of philosophy may well run parallel with this strand – on the frontispiece of *La Carte postale*, we see the figure of Socrates, seated at a desk writing, with Plato looking over his shoulder. Certainly Derrida's philosophical writing is also preoccupied with the location of Freud – from his discovery of the scene of writing (1965) to the subtitle of *La Carte postale* – 'from Socrates to Freud and beyond'. Yet another index of Derrida and Lacan jostling, moving in parallel, in their conceptual development – a point to which I will return.

The central concept of Lacan's theory of the *passe* is that the analyst authorises himself. In truth, there can be no other source of authorisation, since objective assessment of the potential analyst is by definition impossible, and the analytic contract is not one that lends itself to the supplying of testimonials. No higher authority can take on the issuing of certificates of proficiency in analysis, just as a spouse is in no position to issue a certificate of proficiency in marriage, and just as turning to the divorced partners of such a spouse for such a certificate would present insuperable problems of interpretation. But the example of marriage does afford us another possible function for the third party – the witness, who may even be asked to witness those marriages that are made in heaven. So Lacan introduced the system of the *passeurs*, two neophytes nearing the end of their own analyses, who were asked to listen to the story that the *passant*, the person presenting him- or herself at the *passe*, tells of his or her analysis. The *passeurs* listen to the summing up, the 'theorisation', the story of the analysis, and then pass it on to the jury, whose main task, according to Lacan, is to elaborate, on the basis of the numerous stories they hear from the *passeurs*, a theory of the passage from couch to armchair. Within the Lacanian reorientation, that is the analytic act *par excellence*. It is also the theoretical blindspot and central preoccupation of all versions of psychoanalysis which recognise the transference as the key concept of their activity.

To discover why this system of the *passe* turned out to be an impasse, let me refer back to Leclaire's remarks about the primal scene of analysis having become analysis itself – what is happening on other couches and armchairs. Primal fantasies are about analysis; they are couched in terms of analytic theory. To put this another way, following Granoff in his remarkable book, *Filiations*, the Oedipus complex has become an open secret, everyone's open secret, and it would be more appropriate if it were renamed the Freud complex. The reference to the writings of Freud is what now constitutes the corpus from which fantasy is mined. Yet this reference to Freud may be either of two things: it may be the response to the market in Freudiana, to the French – and now British – thirst for *les charmes discrets de la freudoisie*, as an anonymous author cited by Granoff puts it. Or it may be part of the necessity imposed on any analytic enquiry that is prepared to risk discovering that psychoanalysis is simply the rationalisation of

Freud's neurosis, so as to arrive at a more satisfactory formulation, namely that psychoanalysis is the discourse built out of the lexicon of Freud's unconscious.

We can be more specific. Every analysis repeats the founding act of psychoanalysis, not only in that repression is always fresh and new, always able to surprise (indeed without surprise there would be no index of repression, save for the incomprehensible residues of a postulated 'before'), but in so far as the analyst must take up a position with respect to Freud, just as Freud took up a position with respect to the person aimed at in the transference – a position of distance, of conflict often, and, to be sure, a distance defined by theory, which we could easily show to be the distance, the *différance*, the deferral implicit in any writing. I can illustrate this with a story from Freud's consulting-room.

Accompanied by a woman friend, a lady came to see Freud, telling him of another doctor she had seen, who had advised her that her anxiety attacks would cease only if she could do one of three things: bring herself to find another husband – she was recently divorced; take a lover; or find sexual satisfaction in herself. This other doctor claimed that his advice had the full authority of psychoanalysis behind it, a statement she could verify by getting Freud to confirm it. Freud notes: 'I will not dwell on the awkward predicament in which I was placed by this visit.'[17] Freud uses this story to describe the first and most famous deviation from psychoanalysis – he calls the conduct of the doctor 'wild' psychoanalysis. No trained analyst would ever venture such opinions to a patient without extensive analytic work of preparation. Like any other practice, psychoanalysis must be learned from those already proficient in its exercise. Remember that at that time Freud had not clearly conceived of analysis as being the necessary and perhaps sole condition of apprenticeship in analysis. But his remarks point quite unambiguously in that direction. I quote:

Like other medical techniques, it is to be learnt from those who are already proficient in it. It is a matter of some significance, therefore, in forming a judgement on the incident which I took as a starting-point for these remarks, that I am not acquainted with the physician who is said to have given the lady such advice and have never heard his name.[18]

'I am not acquainted with the physician . . . and have never heard his name.' What does this phrase signify? That the physician had not introduced himself to Freud, had not sought him out in person. He had taken Freud's name in vain – not only because he had used it idly, without due respect, not only because he had taken it to be an empty vessel, but also because his own high regard for himself, his vanity, led him to overlook placing his *own* name in a substantive relation to Freud's – he had failed to introduce himself. We should not underestimate the vital importance of acts of introduction – projects for marriage have misfired because a suitor has failed to introduce himself to a grandmother, and this sense of 'misfire' is close to that applied by Austin to performatives which fail to perform. This strong sense of introduction is also akin to the exchange of names, of passwords, upon which Lacan places so much weight. Here, in Freud's story, the physician was a wild analyst not simply because he had failed to establish a relation to his *patient's* unconscious. Indeed, this failure manifests itself in the failure that is entirely bound up with that 'primal' reference to the third party, the invocation of the name of Freud. This reference to the analytic as outside thus constituted his own non-relation to *Freud's* unconscious, to psychoanalysis itself. Indeed, I am not sure that this scene warrants our ascribing an unconscious to the lady as yet – it is manifestly Freud's unconscious which is at issue. And, specifically, the effects in the unconscious of the swapping of proper names, which we call introduction. It is not for nothing that Freud's second book on the unconscious opens with the topic of the forgetting of names.

My discussion here moves in parallel with the subtle remarks of Derrida, in 'Spéculer – sur "Freud" '. He cites a letter in which Freud vigorously denies Havelock Ellis' charge – it is Freud who senses it as a charge – that he is an artist rather than a scientist. 'This is all wrong. I am sure that in a few decades my name will be wiped away and our results will last.'[19] Freud's name thus becomes, in Derrida's words, 'the insurance deposit on his science' – that with which he pays for his science.[20] Yet what is mapped out in his rebuttal of Ellis is the equation of the name and his science, just as the wild analyst's name is unknown to Freud so that, by the law of commutativity proper to introduction, he does not know Freud (Freud's science). The science of Freud's own name.

Derrida's 'Spéculer – sur "Freud" ' is concerned with *Beyond the pleasure principle* – it is a reading of that work. The theme is repetition – the 'repetition-compulsion', the compulsion to repeat, its referent, its manifestation in the text, as Freud restarts again and again, as he repeats what he is narrating (the *fort/da* of the grandson is repeated, *is* its repetition, by the grandfather), as his repetition enacts the detour that the pleasure principle takes in passing via the reality principle to return (back) to its point of departure. Derrida makes Freud repeat what Freud has already made manifest else-

where: 'Vor allem beginnt er die Kur mit einer solchen Wiederholung.'[21] Wherever Freud writes of psychoanalysis, a repetition is
enacted, which is the autobiographical work of writing called
psychoanalysis. Let me quote Derrida:

The autobiography of writing simultaneously raises and sets aside [*pose et
dépose*], in the same movement, the psychoanalytical movement . . . I
wager that this double *fort/da* cooperates, that this cooperation cooperates
in instigating the psychoanalytical cause, in setting in motion the psychoanalytical 'movement', in even being it, in even *being* it [*à l'être même*], in
its very being, in other words in the unique structure of its tradition, I
would even say in the very name of this 'science', of this 'movement', of
this 'theoretical-practice' which has a relation to its history like no other
. . . If, in the unlikely event of this cooperation, the unanalysed residue of
an unconscious remains, if this residue, out of its otherness labours and
constructs the autobiography of this testamentary writing, then I bet that it
will be blindly transmitted by the whole of the return to Freud movement.[22]

And two paragraphs later:

If one wanted to simplify the question, it would become for example, how
can an autobiographical writing, in the abyss of self-analysis which is
non-terminated, give birth to a world-wide institution? Whose birth? what
birth? And how does the interruption or the limit of the self-analysis,
cooperating in the casting into the abyss rather than hindering it, reproduce its mark in the institutional movement, the possibility of this
remarking then not ceasing to produce little ones, multiplying the progeny
of its splits, conflicts, divisions, alliances, marriages and confirmations?

Derrida's interrogation of psychoanalysis is remarkable in its
consistency and its persistence: it insists and repeats, inscribing
the same question. But note: it asks the same question of the
'Seminar on *The purloined letter*', of the Freud of *Beyond the
pleasure principle*, and of the analysts of the four Parisian groups
who crossed the battle lines to meet together under the banner
Confrontation. The point is this: psychoanalysis cannot regard
itself as exempt from the critique Derrida directs at philosophy,
despite Freud's refusal of the philosophical heritage. To be sure,
Derrida recognises the novelty of Freud's substituting his own
name for this heritage, thereby originating an autobiographical
writing. But this writing is no more the inhabitant of an homogeneous space of analysis than Rousseau's state of nature can
eschew its necessary supplements.[23] Whether it be the critique of
the theory of the signifier in Lacan – the letter that *may* not arrive

at its destination – or the practice of the *tranche* – the analyst in analysis with the non-analyst – these all disrupt the ideal free circulation that analysis posits for itself – free association, free contracts (no supplementary benefit), freedom in speech. The non-analytic comes to inhabit the analytic space. And no more clearly than in the founding acts of analysis, in which the non-analysed portion of Freud's unconscious – which is both this autobiographical writing (founding text) and its limitation (the Freud principle and its beyond) – this unanalysed portion is what is manifest as both what structures institutions of analysis and what offers them the means for their reproduction.

How does this happen? Let us return to Lacan's central question, as raised by the existence of *an* analysand in analysis: the desire to be an analyst. Freud became an analyst, the analyst, when his desire crossed (as in starcrossed) that of his patient: she remained silent until his demand for speech became so pressing that she confessed that she was thinking of him, Freud, kissing her. Very schematically, at this moment, Breuer had fled, off to a *second* honeymoon, repeating so as to forget, forgetting so as to repeat, preferring to remain a GP and not have to address this question. In his place, Breuer's place, Freud said: 'This question, this letter is not addressed to me, it is addressed to another.' So he readdressed it. He doubled up his position in the circuit of the signifier, by calling this moment the transference. The kiss is a repetition of some other scene. This scene of repetition *becomes* the analytic scene, by never being itself, by always being the promise (the bud or the echo) of some other scene. However, although he re-addressed the letter, he did not dissuade the patient from believing that the letter would arrive at its destination – the promise of analysis is that such letters will. It is in this sense that we should read the Derridean critique of Lacan – repeated in the following form in 'Spéculer – sur "Freud" ': 'there would be neither postal service nor analytic movement if the place of the letter were not divisible and if a letter always reached its destination'.[24] This notion applies very straightforwardly to Freud's position when he missed this kiss. On receipt of the letter, this SWALK, he retained its literality, but passed on the demand implicit in all speech. The writing of this incident stems from this division in the place of the letter. He passed on the demand in the form of psychoanalysis, of psychoanalytic writing – from whence the inexhaustible seductive power of this writing. But the fact that Freud retained the part of the letter pertaining to its literality might lead one to believe that he thereby affirmed the existence of the analyst as the place of the letter. And this conception of the position of the analyst is not very distant from the Lacanian conception of the analyst's position as the subject presumed to know.[25] According to this conception, it would be quite fair to describe the desire to be an analyst as the desire to be *le facteur de la vérité*. As Derrida and any analyst (any?) would agree, the analyst not only passes the letter on, he also adds his mark, the postmark, the mark of *après coup*.

This postal effect which constitutes transference and hence the psychoanalytic situation is also repeated in the innumerable accounts – including this one – of the history of psychoanalysis. Freud established a history of psychoanalysis as it began – in taking over Breuer's place. To establish the position of analyst, he made Breuer the founder of psychoanalysis, the first analyst – but Breuer knew nothing of psychoanalysis. Freud coined the very term just when his feelings towards Breuer changed to marked hostility, in the spring of 1896 – by 1897 he could say: 'How fortunate that I no longer see Breuer. He would have surely advised me to emigrate.'[26] Such was the expected attitude of the founder of psychoanalysis. But the position marked out for Breuer would never change – he was always claimed as the founder, because the logic of Freud's autobiographical writings meant that he *had* to be the founder. Here we rediscover the third party that figured in Jones' analyses, inscribed at the origins; as my later discussion will make clear, it is no accident that Freud 'discovered' psychoanalysis and the transference by 'supervising' Breuer – by receiving what his patient Anna O. said as the discourse of (Breuer's) other.

Let me attempt a concise alternative formulation. Freud's desire to be an analyst (rather than a GP, like Breuer) consisted in the act of relaying, whether this be relaying the letter on its way, or relaying those tracks of the signifier which had been torn up. The concept of transference specified the doubling up that is implicit in this act. Yet the doubling up encountered by Freud's legatees, the analysts, requires a different decision. Implicit in the demands voiced by the analysand is a reference to psychoanalysis itself, and to Freud. The dilemma facing the analyst is then: is this demand directed to me *qua* analyst, or is it also to be relayed, is it to be relayed to the other, to the other analyst, who, given this scenario, will always be called Freud? (In passing, the idea that the demand is directed to me *qua* me is the counter-transference, which I will discuss later.) In so far as he or she is not Freud, the demand to be analysed engenders the psychoanalytical aporia: is this demand addressed to me *qua* analyst, or to me *qua* stand-in for Freud? Hence a vacillation between Freud-the-analyst and 'Freud'; what will remain unanalysed in the situation is – Freud's name. Hence Freud's name comes to be composed of a multitude of elements; firstly, the unanalysed residue of the first analysis; secondly, that element by means of which each analyst repeats the founding act of psychoanalysis, namely the method by means of which it is ensured that the letter continues on its way; thirdly, what each analyst experiences as a common predicament: am I the analyst, when the demand to be analysed is directed, quite legitimately, it seems to me, to Freud? Within the recent literature of the British and American schools, this problem has been dealt with under the rubric 'countertransference'. I will tell another story so as to give some sense of the significance of this rubric for my topic.

The year 1950 is the turning-point for the examination of this question. A spate of papers concerned themselves with the countertransference. One of the earliest and most influential was by a young analyst recently qualified, named Margaret Little.[27] Her paper began with a case vignette. A young man in analysis, whose profession, while not being analysis itself, was closely related to it, was to give a radio broadcast, with a topic he knew to be of interest to his analyst. Three days before he gave it, his mother died. Despite being very upset, he refused to cancel the broadcast and delivered it, acquitting himself admirably. Arriving the next day at the session in a state of acute confusion and anxiety, the patient was given the following interpretation: 'You are confused and anxious because you are afraid that I will retaliate against you on account of the jealousy you impute to me as a consequence of your success on the radio.' The young man, brought up short, accepted the interpretation, which brought him immediate relief from anxiety. Yet, so Little writes, this interpretation was misplaced – not wrong, but misplaced, stemming from the fact that the analyst 'had actually been jealous of him'. The *real* cause of his confusion was the impossibility of mourning for his mother, which the radio broadcast had not aided, and which the analyst's 'countertransferential' intervention had not addressed. So, the true course – the true course? – of his analysis was delayed by two years, until he had worked around once again to a position in which he could mourn his mother.

Lacan commented on this paper, in his seminar of 1953.[28] He criticised the aspect of the interpretation which seemed authorised by the new conception of countertransference: the notion that the feelings of the analyst can be mobilised to good effect by speaking of them from ego to ego, in a relation of equals, of symmetry between analyst and analysand.[29] What such ego-to-ego discourse elides is the crucial third term, the symbolic point of reference. In passing, Lacan makes the point that the analyst had not paid sufficient attention to the special character of a radio broadcast:

> Indeed, a radio-talk is produced in accordance with a very specific modality of speech, since it is addressed to a mass of invisible listeners by an invisible speaker. It may be said that, in the imagination of the speaker, it isn't necessarily addressed to those who listen to it, but equally to everyone, the living and the dead.[30]

Amongst these dead, the first in line is the patient's mother.

Let me supplement Lacan's remark by pointing out that this structure – of speech addressed both to the living and the dead – is not specific to a radio braodcast. It is the structure of speech in general, specifically the structure of writing that Derrida has elaborated upon, and the Kojèveian-Hegelian account that Lacan also gives of it. This, however, is not to deny that there are special characteristics proper to radio broadcasts, or to speaking to answering machines, or to finding oneself addressing an empty room when one thought that there was someone there listening. Each of these different circumstances will facilitate the accentuation of one or another fantasy, movement or writing. But I will cut short these remarks to get to the real point.

The real point comes clear when we take into account a statement Margaret Little made in an interview published some thirty years or so after the event.

> The story in my first countertransference paper is a disguised account of my analyst, Ella Freeman Sharpe, persuading me to read my Wanderer paper for full membership of the British Psychoanalytic Society a week after my father's death.[31]

What are we to make of this 'disguise'? Instead of a male patient and a male analyst, as in the original scene, there are two women; instead of a radio broadcast, a paper given to analysts (living and dead?), signifying her qualifying as an analyst. And, it should be added, the original paper on countertransference, which opened with a disguised account of how she became an analyst, in accordance with her analyst's wish, but against her own, was not published until a few years after her analyst's death. What I want to consider is the notion that it is not an accident that this, one of the first papers on countertransference, has as its starting-point a disguised account of how the author became an analyst: in anger against the forcefulness with which her analyst brushed aside the death of her father. The analyst's 'here and now' interpretation focused solely on the question: How are you to become an analyst? The message, one might surmise, was as follows: What is the death of your father when the question of your desire to be an analyst (and your filiation to Freud) is at issue?

The way in which Little treated this case, her exemplar of countertransference, requires a little more discussion. Firstly, it is *her analyst's* countertransference – *her analyst's* exclusive preoccupation with the nature of the analytic. What is countertransferential is the analyst acting as if the patient already occupied the doubled-up position of analyst: the analyst takes the patient to be *an* analyst, perhaps, even, *her* analyst; and the patient, in her turn, treats her analyst as a patient – making theoretical capital of this move with the concept of countertransference. Just as in Freud's initial transferential act, where it is the analyst who is doubled up, by the postman's gesture, 'Pass it on', so in the countertransferential act, the patient is doubled up, into an ego that is alienated by the forceful truth of the interpretation which is beside the point, and alongside it, the ghostly figure of the would-be analyst, the analyst projected by the interpretation as desiring to be the analyst. Furthermore, this is not an isolated example in the literature on countertransference; most of this work centres on the question, 'What is an analyst?', because the material from which the work is drawn comes from supervision of analysts-in-training, so that the question of the 'second' analyst (whose transference?) is constitutive of the studies in question. What Racker calls the *névrose à deux*[32] – the system of transference and countertransference – is quite naturally the object of those who, like Racker and Lacan, are concerned with the training of analysts. As Lacan remarked, describing the specific effects of supervising someone else's analysis, it is there that one sees most clearly the validity of his dictum that the unconscious is the discourse of the other, since the supervising analyst can see, as clear as daylight, what the supervised analyst is blind to in the patient's discourse.[33] That, I might add, is the scenario portrayed in the 'Seminar on *The purloined letter*' – the scenario of structural blindness and insight: that is, the Oedipal triangle, as Derrida calls it. The blindness of that position, passing it on, is what is analysed as countertransference.

What my discussion shows is that the conceptual system of

transference–countertransference is built around the questions: What is an analyst? What is his or her desire? How can one analyse someone else's analysis, i.e. how can psychoanalysis be transmissible (the other question to which the Lacanian system of the *passe* addressed itself)? What Derrida focuses on in the name of Freud, what Granoff calls the 'filiation to Freud', what Lacan calls the 'desire of Freud' – these are what constitute psychoanalysis. Again let me quote:

> That fact that, in order to cure the hysteric of all her symptoms, the best way is to satisfy her hysteric's desire – which is for her to posit her desire in relation to us as an unsatisfied desire – leaves entirely to one side the specific question of *why* she can sustain her desire only as an unsatisfied desire. So hysteria places us, I would say, on the track of some kind of original sin in analysis. There has to be one. The truth is perhaps simply one thing, namely, the desire of Freud himself, the fact that something, in Freud, was never analysed.[34]

This formulation of Lacan's is admirable – remember the reaction, the moment of origin of the transference, when Freud said, 'Not me!' This passing it on brings the position of the analyst into being, and along with it makes it possible for the hysteric's unsatisfied desire to become evident. But the unanalysed bit of this desire is also constitutive of analysis; it is what is transmissable, what perpetuates analysis in the name of Freud. That becomes clearer from Derrida's work, and not only from his work: one new orthodoxy is that what was unanalysed in Freud was precisely his relation to the mother, to the woman. It is worth while remarking that Freud's discovery of analysis and the transference was accomplished in collaboration with women. Freud's original demand for speech from his hysterics, combined with his refusal to be satisfied with any answers, thus emerges clearly as the question he admitted not being able to answer after forty years of psychoanalytic research, at the end of his (analytic) life: 'What does woman want?'[35] Certainly an essential component of Freud's desire was the desire to analyse women. Whether or not one follows Foucault on the congruence between the hysterisation of the woman's body and the theory of hysteria in psychoanalysis,[36] it should be clear that psychoanalysis is constituted around the desire to analyse women. Maybe this necessarily implies the not-understanding of women. But the not-understanding of women cannot be placed 'outside' analysis, as if it were something one could add on to analysis, or say of analysis, without finding it already at the heart of analysis.

So it is possible that this not-understanding of women, so much held against Freud, is another facet of the 'non-analytic' whose profile I have been trying to describe as constitutive of psycho-analysis. Freud's original (unconscious) demand was for knowledge of this want of woman. His genius was to sustain this demand in the face of her desire (for a kiss . . .) and her demand for love and hate. But this sustaining had two effects. The first was the invention of the scene of analysis as always being elsewhere, as her demand always being addressed to a third party, so that the analyst must double for that other. *That scene of the other scene is analysis.* The second effect burdened the future of psychoanalysis with a neces-sary relation to Freud, whose name here covers everything that is non-analysed, maybe even not-analysable. In order to be sure that this scene is the analytic scene, and not the other scene (the primal scene, the scene of 'true love' or hate), the analyst must ensure that it is a repetition – as we have seen, Freud states that '*Vor allem*, he begins the cure with a repetition.' The guarantee of this repetition, that this repetition *is* a repetition, is the legacy of Freud, the name of Freud. Lacan proposed to offer a theory of this transmission of the legacy. Instead, it appears, he only repeated, in more concen-trated form, the resurgence of the figure of the wild analyst – but, now, no longer as the outside of analysis, but as its centre – Lacan himself.

And Derrida? Let us take as preliminary indices of his relation to analysis two passages concerning his relation to Lacan:

these reservations [concerning Lacan's work] were important enough for me not to look for a point of reference in the form of a guarantee in a discourse that is so different, in crucial phases, in its style of eloquence, in its locution, its aims, its presuppositions, from the text that I was putting forward.[37]

On the other hand, having recognised that his 'own criticisms of Lacan were so different from the ones then current, and that the critical effects of Lacan's discourse were necessary within the field in which they worked', he went on to say:

I judged that the best contribution or theoretical 'explanation' consisted in pursuing my work, according to its own paths and exigencies, whether or not this work should, according to certain axes, abut on to that of Lacan, and even, which I in no way exclude, more so than any other work today.[38]

'A discourse that is so different . . . ' – 'yet one which might abut more so than any other today'. A discourse that is so different that it might abut more than any other – such is also the tension inherent in the concept of *différance*. The phenomena grouped under this concept are also those raised by the very existence of analysis, and particularly of Lacan's development of its theory: the (other) scene, the scene of writing, and the problem of the transmissability of analysis, the topology of its inside and outside, of the legacy of the origin, in the deferred action of its effects. What I have shown is how the history of psychoanalysis is permeated with these problems, whether they emerge as the third party (the *ménage-à-trois*, gossip), the wild analyst (Freud's name and the transmissability of analysis) or the transference–countertransference system (the other scene, the mechanism of the relay). Whether they are theorised in the dialect of Lacan or Derrida, these are the aporia of analysis. Lacan's return to Freud seems only to have made the question of the legacy all the more unmanageable, and to oblige each of the faithful to recognise his or her own 'wildness', just as Lacan sported his incontestable wildness. Derrida does not succeed in avoiding these aporia. Not only can his 'readings' of Freud or Lacan be shown to repeat the same blindnesses he analyses as being the source of their effects,[39] but his exteriority to analysis is inevitably subject to the very erosion of that concept he highlights. Rumour may well have it that he was Lacan's analyst's analyst. The theory of analysis may well be able to make much of this rumour, despite – because of – the fact that we will not be sure who is in analysis with whom. As Freud wrote, in a letter written just after the death of his daughter Sophie, the mother of the little boy who played 'fort/da': 'La séance continue.'[40]

10

PSYCHOANALYSIS: GOSSIP, TELEPATHY AND/OR SCIENCE?

It is always fruitful to remind oneself that psychoanalytic practice is a matter of two people talking to one another, within the rules laid down in order to define that practice. Psychoanalytic theory offers a general view of any such encounter, and it also offers quite specific and detailed accounts of the unexpected things that happen in such encounters. However, it is not the only theory of such conversations available. In that fact lies both its suspicion of adjacent, competing accounts and the possibilities for a future infusion of psychoanalytic thought by models and perceptions from elsewhere. But the psychoanalytic discourse is distinctive in so far as it requires that it be as amenable to psychoanalytic interpretation as any other. Notoriously, this leads analysts into subjecting theories and clinical accounts to a variety of reductive manœuvres, from discerning Oedipal conflicts in theoretical dissension to tracing large-scale psychic damage inflicted on patients back to slight variations and nuances in an analyst's interpretative style or method of time-keeping. What does seem clear is that if there were ever a human subject whose life and work were living proof of the applicability of psychoanalytic theory, then Sigmund Freud was that subject. And, by extension, if there were ever a cultural ambience, an atmosphere and an institution that were appropriate objects for psychoanalytic study, then the world of psychoanalysis is that culture.

The technique of speech known as psychoanalysis requires one to examine the frame of discourse as much as the so-called meaning. What aim does this discourse have, over and beyond what it says? Is it my role here to give us something to gossip about over dinner? Am I speaking so as to elicit all those stories of telepathy, the occult that everyone has experienced, or at least heard of through the grapevine, so that we can all collectively analyse these stories, only to realise that, as Derrida so aptly puts it, the question of telepathy is not one of knowledge or non-knowledge. In his article 'Télé-pathie', he intimates this on two levels: firstly by writing in the first

243

person – a first person which is recognisably that of Freud's, so that we are tempted into asking how Derrida has come to be in a position to be able to write 'Freud's' 'I' for him: by divination, by psychoanalysis, or by telepathy? And then, amongst the things he writes, we find the following:

There's no knowing (and on this point I'm in a strong position because here there's no question of 'knowledge'. Everything in our conception of knowledge is so constructed that telepathy is impossible, unthinkable, unknowable. If there is such a thing, our relation to Telepathy won't belong to the family of 'knowledge' or of 'non-knowledge' but to another genre). So I will do everything I can so that you can neither believe nor disbelieve that I myself believe or don't: but you will never know precisely if I'm doing it on purpose. The question of *on purpose* will lose all meaning for you . . . [1]

If the question of telepathy leads us to an epistemological impasse such that it is best to leave the question of belief or knowledge entirely to one side, so also does the question of gossip, but this time in both the epistemic and the moral spheres. Knowledge had by gossip only barely maintains its claim on that word, sketching out the no-man's-land of fiction which equally constitutes the social knowledge by which we live. In addition, gossip appears as such only when there is a transgression of rules of discourse. Talking about someone who is not present is the rule, not the exception, in conversation: but that is not necessarily gossip. It becomes gossip only once the talk implicitly or explicitly addresses moral questions concerning the absent person or moral questions raised by his or her actions. And of course to think of gossip as a form of moral discourse makes as much sense as to speak of telepathy as a form of knowledge.

To give you a sense of the sort of approach I have been using in my studies of psychoanalysis, some semi-autobiographical remarks may be of some help. For some years I have been engaged in what I am obliged to call a psychoanalysis of psychoanalysis. If there is one cultural artefact that can be exhaustively subjected to the discipline of analysis, then that artefact is analysis itself. The procedures I have adopted are both historical and conceptual-analytic, and both these procedures turn around the questions: What are the limits of the analytic object? What defines the border territory between the analytic and the non-analytic, or the extra-analytic? How did the social practice we call psychoanalysis come into being, and what are the effects of its existence on the ensemble of other discursive practices?

These themes are explored in chapters 3 and 9. Chapter 3, on *Dora*, drew its inspiration from listening to the twelfth aria ('Venite . . . inginocchiateri . . . ') from *The Marriage of Figaro* – the scene where Suzanna and the Countess are dressing Cherubino as a woman, this Cherubino, who, in listening and looking, we cannot forget is a woman singing a man's part.[2] Half-way through this aria, just when Suzanna makes an aside to the Countess about how handsome Cherubino is, there is a bridge passage of counterpoint between violins, voice and cellos: a sublime procession of chattering violins, with cellos gliding gently up and down, with keys descending, then ascending, redescending and reascending, all evoking the hint of a *perpetuum mobile*. Mozart is saying: this could go on for ever, this delicate game, so delightful and touching, so gleeful and gay! It is clear that this music is depicting Cherubino walking up and down, as Suzanna appraises the cut of (her)/his/her dress. But, at the same time, the music depicts the secret talk of women in the boudoir. As Suzanna says in her aside:

> Isn't he handsome,
> What roguish glances,
> What airs, what graces!
> If women fall in love with him,
> They have good reason why.

For me, this scene came to depict the delights of feminine gossip. Now these delights are ones that men are prone to feeling excluded from, indeed even paranoid about. For instance, take the following passage from P.D. James, *A taste for death*:

Now, above the tinkle of kettle lid and crockery, he [Adam Dalgliesh] could hear their voices, conversational, almost ordinary. From the few phrases he could catch, they seemed to be discussing the merits of a make of electric kettle which both possessed. Suddenly he felt that he shouldn't be there, that he was redundant as a detective and as a man. They would both get on better without his male, destructive presence. Even the room seemed inimical to him, and he could almost persuade himself that the low broken sibilants of female voices were in conspiracy.[3]

It was the perception of the fascinations of feminine gossip, when combined with the male horror of exclusion from its mysteries, that underpinned my account of the case of Dora: in their conversations, Freud refused to take up the position of woman in his sessions with the young hysterical girl, precisely because it would have meant that his precious psychoanalysis might turn out to be just a version of gossip, of women chattering amongst themselves, the seemingly inconsequential chat of Dora with Frau K., or of Dora with her grandmother.[4] If I and others have been speculating that Freud refused to acknowledge the feminine transference in his analyses – which seems plausible, given some of the other things that went on in, say, his 'The psychogenesis of a case of female homosexuality' – then we are still obliged to ask what exactly in his masculine identification he was not prepared to give up. To say 'he was not prepared to give up his phallus, his penis', would overlook the fact that for Freud, his phallus was so transparently identified with his power as talker and writer, as word-magician. The symbolic castration that Freud feared might well have been the deprivation of the word as identified with the penetrating observation (the interpretation that uncovered the secret hiding-place of the repressed), an observation that could then be secured in the form of the written. The art of feminine gossip, especially as seen from the outside, might well have seemed to him to leave no room for these masculine powers of conversational magic.

This view of Dora takes psychoanalysis itself to be akin to gossip. In chapter 9, this eminently gossipy question is asked of psycho-analysis itself, on the assumption that it is something to be gossiped *about*. I adopt the masculine position of being 'outside', and, in order to find out what the cultural effects of this strange form of discourse were, I give up the temptation to 'look inside'. Instead, to understand it, I use, without making it explicit, a very crude model, in part derived from Lacan and Derrida, which this chapter will make more explicit.[5]

Psychoanalytic practice is a specific form of discourse between two people, defined by rules of asymmetry: the patient agrees to obey the fundamental rule, namely to tell the analyst everything that enters his or her mind, while the analyst abstains from such free discourse. Instead, he or she offers interpretations of what the patient has said. Certain rules govern the relation of this discursive dyad to the outside world: the analyst gives the patient an implicit or explicit assurance that anything said will be treated with absolute confidentiality.[6] The patient, however, does not offer such an assurance, but is implicitly or explicitly encouraged to refrain from discussing the analysis much with people 'outside'.[7] As a cultural artefact, the investigation of this discursive dyad should, I con-clude, concern itself as much with the semi-permeable membrane that is as a consequence of these rules placed *around* the two people talking as it does with the *content* of the talk.

So, we have a model of two people talking, according to certain rules, with a boundary limit operating as the third term. Psychoanalysts themselves, following Klein, Winnicott and Bion, have referred to this limit, this membrane as the container, and the themes of the inside and outside brook large in Kleinian theories of projection and introjection, as they do in Lacanian theories of the topology of analytic space.

How are we to investigate the functioning of this semi-permeable membrane? The first thing to be said concerns the fact that the very existence of the membrane gives gossip and psychoanalysis something in common: they are both conversations taking place in the *absence of the real*. Gossip always takes place in the absence of the parties being gossiped about, although naming them is crucial to the activity. Similarly, the rules of analysis require that all participating parties be absent, *including those addressed in the second person*. What I mean by this strange formulation is that even the analyst is absent when addressed in the transferential mode of the second person, the 'you'. The analyst achieves this through the technique of transference interpretation: sentences containing 'you' are treated as if they were passing him by, as if he were passing them on. In Lacan and Derrida's formulation, he acts as a postman, relaying or redirecting all the messages that come to him.[8] He tries to act like the lost-and-found department of the Post Office, ascertaining on demand to whom these communications are addressed. In this way, a declaration of love or the heaping of abuse *must* be interpreted as being about someone who is not there. One consequence of this peculiar stance of the analyst is that the patient finds it possible to gossip about him- or herself – something that in everyday life is impossible. It is this gossiping about oneself that people in analysis often find so repulsive and fascinating about their own activity; it also means that they find it difficult to recognise the charge of self-centred, narcissistic preoccupation that those 'outside' often level at those 'inside' analysis.

The consequent professional absenteeism of the analyst allows one to see the similar structure of gossip and the joke as analysed by Freud: both concern three parties, where one is necessarily absent, and the pleasure of the talk conducted under these circumstances has as its condition this absence of the third party.[9] Besides this similarity, there is an interesting opposition between jokes and gossip. In Freud's theory of jokes, a dirty joke is told by one man to what Freud calls the third person (also a man), in the absence of the woman, the second person, who is the original target of the seduction aimed at in the joke. In contrast, gossip is traditionally a feminine art – or vice, as the moral opprobrium directed at women's chat for centuries testifies – and, as we saw in the passage from P.D. James, it is the absent man, the man as rendered structurally absent, who is the fundamental precondition of gossip. Hence Freud's fright at catching himself gossiping with Dora . . . [10]

Gossip and joking thus seem to have complementary – inverted and homologous – gender structures. In addition, they both inhabit a sharply contoured space of the forbidden and the enticing. The discursivity of gossip in particular also helps to *define* the margins of the licit, whereas the punctuality of joking *celebrates* the existence of the cut-off.

Joking, however, is explicitly fictional. Jokes are first and foremost *stories*, whether about Englishmen, Scotsmen and Irishmen who are more fictional, and therefore 'made more real', than any existing national types, or about supposedly real characters, such as Gorbachev or Reagan. Any supposedly true stories that are also jokes immediately lose their quality of verisimilitude, of plausibility, and instead become true, *irrespective* of their verisimilitude and plausibility. However, one can see a common root of gossip and jokes in children's stories and jokes about adults: they often have the character of being crude fantasies which eventually climax in an imagined scene, at that moment provoking great hilarity.

Whilst the gossip of adults differs from joking in its avowed relation to the real, it shares with psychoanalysis what I will call the *fiction of the real*, alongside the already mentioned requirement of the absence of the real: in order to be a successful gossip, or a non-resisting patient in analysis, you must be seen to name names, you must tell stories earmarked as *true*, about real, live people. The patient who refuses to reveal his parents' names is a figment of the imagination, the analyst's nightmare. None the less, we have been forcibly reminded recently by the scurrilous, and by no means previously unnoticed, stories about the early history of Freud's relations with his patients that the real of analysis is an ever-receding one. Masson finds this outrageous and morally blameworthy. For the psychoanalyst, on the other hand, what defines the rules of the discourse is that there is no moment when the analyst decides: 'This actually happened.' None the less, the fiction of the real is not touched by this technical procedure. [11]

If the semi-permeable membrane which constitutes analysis allows one to draw analogies between analysis and gossip, an eminently psychoanalytic way of further investigating the membrane's properties is to ask: what happens when the membrane is broken, and the high levels of osmotically concentrated contents leak out? For the moment, let us consider the two participants in the analytic conversation as separate parties: it is clear that it is either the analyst or the patient who can do the leaking. The analyst's communications with the outside world fall into two categories: firstly, the so-called 'scientific communication' – the case-history of the patient. Secondly, the analyst may gossip about the patient. Stanley Olinick has devoted a paper to considering what he calls the gossiping psychoanalyst, employing the following definition:

By 'gossip' I refer to an indiscreet type of loose talk, with or without the use of names or other identifications. This entails impromptu, casual case vignettes that are brought up during social encounters with colleagues and others. They are not intended as scientific exchanges, but as social talk.[12]

So one of the questions implied by my title emerges: under what conditions does talk about an analysis qualify as a scientific communication, rather than as gossip?

Analysts have taken this question very seriously, as is demonstrated by a paper on the significance of the sex of the analyst for the course of the analysis by the aptly named Ethel Person. Person illustrates part of her argument by referring to two male analysts who had slept with their patients. The re-analysis of these analysts prompted Person to point out two factors. One was the self-destructive urge these seductions manifested: the male analysts knew they would be 'found out', when their female patients/lovers talked (gossiped?) to their next analysts: however, they expected that this would not become '*public* knowledge', but would be confined to the world of rumour. In the course of their re-analyses it also became clear that the seduction of their patients had been, for both of them, a repetition of what each of them had felt to be a betrayal, indeed a 'rape', to use their word, by their own analysts, who had used material from their analyses in scientific communications without asking their permission.[13] Notice how the original sin[14] of analysis here gets transmitted, transferred from analytic cell to analytic cell, with rumour and scientific communication doubling up as the means by which the piercing of the membrane operates.[15]

If we consider the patient as the source of leakage through the semi-permeable membrane, we also find two categories: firstly, those analytic communications that have been displaced from *within* the analysis, which should have been spoken to the analyst, not to someone outside: what analysts call acting out (here the act in question is the act of communicating, and hence acutely uncomfortable for the analyst, who is devoted to the purification of communication of its aspect of action). Secondly, there is the category of gossip in the ordinary sense of the word – gossip about the analysis, gossip about the analyst, the sort of self-revealing chat that analysands sharing a psychoanalytic culture indulge in. This sort of gossip is very common, and it is clear that it is the uncanny kinship with analysis, as well as the sense of potential analytic relevance and analytic power that this gossip engenders that often makes it even more interesting and dangerous than ordinary gossip about work, friends, children and so forth. Putting this another way, we all feel that gossip is dangerous, that it is illicit and exciting, but for analysts and analysands, that dangerous pleasure is compounded by the awareness that gossip is remarkably akin to analysis, both in its powers of revelation of the truth and in its revelation of the power of the truth.

It is not clear that the first category of analysand's gossip, 'acting out', and the second, 'ordinary gossip', can be kept apart. Purist analysts – and on this point any analyst worth his or her salt is a purist – would regard *all* communication about the analysis to a third party as being misplaced communications *to* the analyst. Or rather, to be more precise – and this is the source of the value of the salt I just mentioned – the rules of interpretation that analysts are following lead them to regard such gossip as misplaced communications: it is their *job* to regard gossip as misplaced communication, meaning roughly that this is what the patient is paying them to do, namely to *analyse* the gossip about analysis, as they would anything else. However, it seems to me that if one can identify and distinguish *analysts'* gossip about the analysis, it seems unduly mean and absolutist to argue that *analysands'* gossip about the analysis does not count as such. And, of course, to the outsider, to anyone other than the gossip's analyst, it simply *is* gossip. And this outsider might be tempted to ask the question: what are the consequences of retaining the symmetry of assimilation, so that where the analyst assimilates gossip to acting out, the theorist of gossip assimilates acting out to gossip?

So far I have separated three categories of leaked communication: scientific communications, acting out, and gossip. But there is also another means by which the membrane might allow unregulated passage across it: the case of telepathy. One of my arguments in this chapter is that telepathy came to have such an important part in Freud's psychoanalytic theorising precisely because once the psychoanalytic situation has been conceptualised as a semipermeable discursive membrane, telepathy becomes a threat to that situation. The aim of the rules of analytic discourse is to regulate the flow across the membrane; telepathy represents a direct threat to this attempt at discursive regulation.

The form of telepathy that would be most obviously significant would be one in which a thought from 'outside' enters into the analytic dyad rather than emanates *from* it. In the former case, telepathy and gossip work in opposite directions. Rather than placing the accent on the direction of passage across the membrane, it is plausible that what is at issue here is the membrane and its permeability. To illustrate this, let me quote at length from Freud's lecture on 'Dreams and occultism', not only to give you a sense of the generalisability of the 'membrane' model I am using, but also to indicate Freud's surprising thinking on this subject.

If there is such a thing as telepathy as a real process, we may suspect that, in spite of its being so hard to demonstrate, it is quite a common phenomenon. It would tally with our expectations if we were able to point to it particularly in the mental life of children. Here we are reminded of the frequent anxiety felt by children over the idea that their parents know all their thoughts without having to be told them – an exact counterpart and perhaps the source of the belief of adults in the omniscience of God. A short time ago Dorothy Burlingham, a trustworthy witness, in a paper on child analysis and the mother, published some observations which, if they can be confirmed, would be bound to put an end to the remaining doubts on the reality of thought-transference. She made use of the situation, no longer a rare one, in which a mother and child are simultaneously in analysis, and reported some remarkable events such as the following. One day the mother spoke during her analytic session of a gold coin that had played a particular part in one of the scenes of her childhood. Immediately afterwards, after she had returned home, her little boy, about ten years old, came to her room and brought her a gold coin which he asked her to keep for him. She asked him in astonishment where he had got it from. He had been given it on his birthday; but his birthday had been several months earlier and there was no reason why the child should have remembered the gold coin precisely then. The mother reported the occurrence to the child's analyst and asked her to find out from the child the reason for his action [is this gossip or scientific communication? – J.F.]. But the child's analysis threw no light on the matter; the action had forced its way that day into the child's life like a foreign body. A few weeks later the mother was sitting at her writing-desk to write down, as she had been told to do, an account of the experience, when in came the boy and asked for the gold coin back, as he wanted to take it with him to show in his analytic session. Once again the child's analysis could discover no explanation of his wish.[16]

The telepathic question par excellence, one which immediately reveals its kinship to psychoanalysis, is: 'Whose thoughts are these, inhabiting my inner world?' The fundamental rule of analysis has as a strict corollary that the patient ignores questions concerning the provenance of the thoughts 'heorshe' has. Children think their parents know all their thoughts; analysands often think that their analysts know all their thoughts – the after-image, one suspects, of the fundamental rule. So whose thought is it? Such questions are expressly put to one side in analysis, to be dealt with later, you might say. Under these circumstances, telepathy, or thought-transference as Freud rebaptises it, seems the natural state of affairs. As Derrida so wittily puts it:

we won't have taken a single step forward in our discussion of the despatch [*envoi*] (the adestination, the wandering of destiny, of destinations, of clandestination) if amongst all these telethings we don't touch on telepathy in person. Or rather if we don't allow ourselves to be touched by it . . . The truth which I find so difficult to get some grip on is: that non-telepathy might be possible. It is always difficult to imagine that one might be able to think of something in separation, within one's interior space, without being surprised by the other, without his being already in on it, as easily as if he had within him a giant screen, just when speaking, with a remote control unit to change the channel and play with the colours, the discourse being repeated in large letters to avoid all misunderstanding . . . This puerile belief of mine, in part mine, can only stem from the foundation – sure, let's call it unconscious, if you want – upon which has been erected objectivist certainty, this so-called provisional system of science, the discourse which is linked to a state of affairs in science which has made us hold telepathy in some respect. It is difficult to imagine a theory of what they still call the unconscious without a theory of telepathy. They can be neither confused nor dissociated.[17]

The fundamental rule of psychoanalysis requires the patient to put to one side the question, 'Whose thoughts are these?', in order to allow these thoughts to emerge as anonymous, almost collective[18] – *already* in the form of hearsay. The distance between what I say of myself as garnered from hearsay and what is said of me by gossip or telepathy is thus, once again, bracketed off by psychoanalytic *technique* – again, I should emphasise this is not so much a question of theory. But the theory that is then elaborated on the basis of the material thus furnished, the theory of the unconscious, and in particular of the dream in its regal relation to the unconscious – or is it rather the unconscious in its regal relation to the dream? – all this theory furnishes a new form of reality, which Freud calls psychic reality. This new reality, which goes beyond anything which I can call simply mine, cannot truly distinguish between the voices of rumour, of gossip, of telepathy, and those voices which are unconscious. Just take the well-worn example of post-hypnotic suggestion: whose thought is it which emerges, telling me to put up my umbrella while giving this lecture? If the super-ego is the voice of my parents, in so far as I have forgotten what they said to me, then why cannot those other voices – whether I feel at ease in their presence or sense them as alien, as foreign, as voices from another world – be those of my neighbours, my *Mitmensch*, even my analyst or fortune-teller,[19] come to haunt me when I am best defended against ghosts?

Of the four means of breaching the membrane that I have mentioned – science, gossip, acting out and telepathy – two of them are already theorised by psychoanalysis: the scientific communication is the form of leakage *permitted* to analysts, and acting out is the form of leakage *expected* of patients. They form a pair. But both gossip and telepathy are not allowed for: they have not been adequately tamed by theory, and maybe cannot be tamed by theory. Not even Freud's papers on telepathy attempt to *tame* it: quite the contrary, in fact, which is one reason why they are so interesting. For Freud, telepathy often represents another *competing* category of phenomena to those psychoanalysis deals in. If the patient's communications come from 'outside' the analysis, from someone else, what sense will it have to talk of his or her specific unconscious? It is also no accident that he deals more with what he calls 'thought-*transference*' than telepathy proper.[20] The question implicit in all of his papers on the topic is: is the transference psychoanalysts deal in similar to thought-transference, and, if so, which is the more fundamental category?

So we have two illicit modes of transmission or communication: gossip and telepathy. Gossip is the underbelly of analysis, telepathy its shadow. However, there is another way of approaching the analytic dyad, which treats them analytically: this is as a dyad, not as two individuals. Then the question of the permeability of the membrane leads to the question: how does psychoanalysis itself get transmitted across this membrane? What guarantees that the discursive dyad is engaged in analysis, rather than the gossip that Freud feared Dora was seducing him into?

There is a very straightforward answer: the analyst brings with her her own experience of a similar dyad that she had herself experienced. Analysts bring with them the fruit of their own transference to their own analysts. That is, analysis is not transmitted from one dyadic 'cell' to another either via gossip or via the scientific communication: it is transmitted via the transplanting of the conditions for generating a transference-neurosis – the essential experience of analysis.

However, this chain of the analytic discourse, passed down from analytic parent to analytic child, has as its point of origin the original analysis: Freud's own analysis. Everyone claims analytic descent from Freud. And what some see as a complicating factor in training analyses, but which I regard as an essential factor, like the transference itself, is the question of the analysand's relation to Freud – what Granoff calls the transference to Freud.[21] It has enormous consequences for the cultural characteristics of psychoanalysis, which I will now explore.

What I am about to discuss will, to some of you, seem like gossip. Historically, both critics and defenders of psychoanalysis behave as if they were dealing with a whole series of skeletons locked up in cupboards – skeletons that throw revolutionary or unwanted new light on the lives and practices of the early analysts. They treat what other people would regard as material for gossip as if it were truly the repressed secret, the hidden motor of their science. Let me mention some examples. Masson's book, *The assault of truth*, tries to paint Freud as an intellectual coward who refused to look reality in the face when confronted with it, and dressed up the evidence so that he could conceal the horrible reality he had discovered. One part of the horrible reality was connected with the near-fatal surgical error that Freud's friend Fliess perpetrated on one of Freud's most important patients, Emma Eckstein, and Masson traces, with little comprehension, the interesting way in which she became the first person to cross the analytic Rubicon by switching from patient to analyst.

Where Masson thinks the moral of this story is that Freud from then on repressed the real causes of neurosis, the sexual assaults on children, I judge it far more pertinent to point out that the other features of the analysis of the dream arising out of the Emma case which Freud left unmentioned were to do with his sexual feelings for his patients.[22] The *indeterminacy* of knowing whether it is past seductions by the parents or present seductions by the analyst is what is interesting – because unspoken – when it comes to these skeletons in the closet.

Gossip, telepathy and/or science?

The theme continues into the next piece of gossip, which concerns Freud's relation to his daughter, Anna. Rumour has it that Freud analysed his own daughter, Anna – and this piece of analytic incest is meant to explain how and why she and the other guardians of the Freudian legacy have acted in order to protect his memory from being besmirched. The gossip runs: how could the founder of analysis think he could analyse his very own daughter?

When we turn to Anna Freud's great rival, Melanie Klein, we find similar gossip. Phyllis Grosskurth's biography reveals how the first child patients Klein had were her own children.[23] And the tantalising ethical and epistemic problem raised – and all gossip is addressed to both questions – by this gossip is: is this connected with the fact that Klein's most virulent and passionate analytic critic for many years was her own daughter, Melitta Schmideberg? And with respect to questions concerning the *internal* space of analysis: what connection might this practice of the mother analysing her own children have with the theoretical disputes Klein was famous for as to the irrelevance for analytic purposes of the child's 'real' relations to its parents?

This sort of gossip, gossip by analysts about other analysts, in particular about the founding analysts, seems to me to be more than just gossip. It points to that which is unanalysed in analysis itself. This sounds like the attitude of the more purist analysts themselves: yes, Freud shouldn't have analysed Anna, Melanie Klein should not have analysed her own children – they obviously 'needed' more analysis! As if the unanalysed, the unconscious, could be *done away with* by more analysis. Instead of this blind prescription, I am suggesting that there is always an irreducible residue of each analysis, which is passed on through the genealogy of analysts, manifesting itself in those symptoms that now masquerade as theory.

Even without knowing the gossip about Freud and his daughter, or about Klein and her children, we would know that the central analytic question raised by their work revolves respectively around the father–daughter relationship,[24] or the mother–child relation. In this sense, the gossip amongst analysts is exactly what one might expect it to be: the making explicit of the unconscious of their psychoanalytic theories, through its being the discourse of their other, as Lacan defines the unconscious. The discourse of Freud's other is the gossip about his daughter; the discourse of Klein's other is the gossip about her children. In this sense, the gossip is the *analysis* of their respective psychoanalytic parents/theories.

255

The destiny of psychoanalysis

Lacan meditated very deeply on these questions, as is demonstrated by the following lengthy passage from *Seminar II* that makes some theoretical points pertinent to these considerations of analysis in general and gossip about analysts in particular. He also makes the link with Freud's interest in telepathy:

Think back on what we said in preceding years about those striking coincidences Freud noted in the sphere of what he calls telepathy. Very important things, in the way of transference, occur in parallel in two patients, whether one is in analysis and the other just on its fringes, or whether both are in analysis. At that time, I showed you how it is through being links, supports, rings in the same circle of discourse, agents integrated in the same circle of discourse, that the subjects simultaneously experience such and such a symptomatic act, or discover such and such a memory.

Here we rediscover . . . that the unconscious is the discourse of the other. This discourse of the other is not the discourse of the abstract other, of the other in the dyad, of my correspondent, nor even of my slave, it is the discourse of the circuit in which I am integrated. I am one of its links. It is the discourse of my father, for example, in so far as my father had made mistakes that I am absolutely condemned to reproduce – that is what we call the super-ego. I am condemned to reproduce them because I am obliged to pick up again the discourse he bequeathed to me, not simply because I am his son, but because one can't stop the chain of discourse, and it is precisely my duty to transmit it in its aberrant form to someone else. I have to put to someone else the problem of a situation of life or death in which the chances are that it is just as likely that he will falter, in such a way that this discourse produces a small circuit in which an entire family, an entire coterie, an entire camp, an entire nation or half the world will be caught.[25]

The discourse in which my life, my thoughts, my desires are caught up is what Lacan calls the symbolic order: the stories that I hear as a child, stories of the sins of my fathers and mothers, the uncle who tells me that my mother really wanted a girl, all these stories which Freud called the family romance, all of this is the discourse of gossip – when seen from a particular perspective of being a subject outside the circuit who becomes implicated through the very fact of the existence of the circuitry. 'Gossip' may not be a very grand name for Lacan's grand vision, but we are referring to the same thing: the phenomenon in which the discourse of the other, which is what the analyst says to me, is my unconscious – in the end the analyst only echoes back the gossip that inhabits the subject without his knowing it. And it is the specific circuit of discourse that analysts inhabit in their gossip about their forebears that is the unconscious of analysis.

Gossip, telepathy and/or science?

Having mentioned Lacan, it is only fair to do some gossiping about him. And here we encounter a most curious fact: when it comes to Lacan's clinical practice, the only form of knowledge we have is gossip. Lacan's so-called scientific communications were never, with one exception I will come to, about his patients – they were always reflections on other people's cases, or on analytic concepts in general. Yet there has never been an analyst whose practice has been so discussed, so interrogated. In 1962, the London Committee investigating Lacan's suitability as analyst went to Paris, were installed in the Westminster Hotel there, and spent days interviewing Lacan's analysands about his way of conducting analysis. As well as telling this story in her second volume of the history of psychoanalysis in France, Elizabeth Roudinesco gives page after page of transcribed interviews with ex-patients of Lacan. One piece of gossip about Lacan will suffice to back up my Lacanian claim about the discourse of the other.[26]

The gossip concerns the one exception to Lacan's practice of never recounting case-histories from his practice. Lacan's medical thesis of 1932 was based upon his study of one woman patient who had been psychiatrically interned after she had stabbed a famous actress backstage. This paranoid woman, christened Aimée by Lacan, was his analytic muse, just as Anna O. was Breuer's, or the crowd of female hysterics were Freud's. Roudinesco goes so far as to claim that Lacan's 'analysis' of her was more constructive for his own personal development as both patient and analyst than his own, roughly contemporaneous, training analysis with Rudolph Loewenstein. This magnificent lengthy thesis, devoted primarily to Aimée, is certainly testimony to her importance to him.

Some twenty years later, Aimée's son – who, after her hospitalisation, had been brought up by an aunt – entered analysis with Lacan, without knowing that Lacan was his mother's analyst. Nor, Lacan afterwards claimed, did he, Lacan, recognise Didier Anzieu as the son of his patient, having either never known, forgotten or failed to recognise the family name as that of his ex-patient. For an analyst who became celebrated as the advocate of the importance of the name-of-the-father, this is an extraordinary fact – but it fits in perfectly with my claim that the unanalysed residue, pinpointed here by gossip, is the motor of psychoanalytic theory. Indeed, the story does not end there.

At about the same time as Anzieu completed his analysis with Lacan, in 1953, his mother, who had been released from hospital during the war, and had since become a cook, entered service with

Lacan's father in Boulogne. On meeting her former analyst and psychiatrist when he came to visit her employer, his father, she asked him to return the writings of hers which he had used to construct his thesis about paranoia. He refused. Certainly one is tempted to interpret this refusal as an intervention – or a refusal to intervene – within the circuit of discourse now established between mother, son, analyst, analyst's father, theses, writings and so on. Meanwhile, Lacan supplied the son, Didier Anzieu, with help towards the project he, Didier, was engaged upon: answering the question whether self-analysis is possible. Published in a first edition in 1959, enlarged in 1975, this work, now entitled *Freud's self-analysis*, has finally been translated into English – it is the definitive work on the subject. None the less, it bears the traces of its genesis, in that various ideas and arguments which are clearly based upon Lacan's seminars, which Anzieu attended in the 1950s, are presented there without any mention of Lacan's influence. Telepathy, plagiarism – certainly the circuit of analysis – what question is this, might you well ask.

I hope these examples give a sense of the importance of the gossip about analysts, in so far as it throws light on the unanalysed residue of analysis, and is thus absolutely essential to the writing of a history of psychoanalysis. Given my model of cells of discursive dyads, connected together at the official level by scientific communications between analysts, at the unofficial level by gossip between analysts and between patients, it is clear that it may well be as much the gossip that goes on between and within these cells that constitutes a psychoanalytic culture as the diffusion and acceptance or rejection of the 'science' of psychoanalysis. And this is in addition to the suggestion I have made that psychoanalysis be seen as, in part, the science of gossip. These two levels – gossip mediating *between* analytic dyads, and gossip as what goes on *within* those dyads – emerge clearly in a remark of Serge Leclaire's.[27] He notes that, in a sufficiently psychoanalysed culture, such as contemporary Paris, the question as to what is being said by friends and lovers on their respective couches can take on a greater analytic significance than the traditional Oedipus complex. The structure of gossip here replaces the family structure, the structure of blood and lineage, which is the norm assumed by psychoanalysis. This remark connects neatly, you may say too neatly, with the history of the word 'gossip'. 'Gossip' stems originally from 'God-sib' – siblings in the sight of God. From the fourteenth century on, there developed three primary senses of gossip:

258

1 godparent: third party that oversees the future moral development of newborn babe;
2 gossip: women who gather together at the lying-in of a woman;
3 gossip: light-hearted and idle talk, especially of women (by implication, of women gathered at a lying-in).

An explanation which is not in the *Oxford English Dictionary*, and for which I am grateful to a friend who has worked on the history of midwifery,[28] is the following. In the seventeenth century, the gossips who attended the lying-in were all women, men being barred. The gossip was then called on to bear witness in church to the fact that this baby being christened was the baby she had seen born; in doing so she became the god-parent.[29] In this way the gossip mediated between the all-female mystery of birth and the patrilineal world of the church, of the christening. Not a bad lineage for a word which I take to describe the cultural unconscious of psychoanalysis.

11

TRANSFERENCE AND THE STENOGRAPHER: ON DOSTOEVSKY'S *THE GAMBLER*

I

What else could one expect from the detailed examination of the soul of a gambler but the anatomy of a neurosis? Should we follow this rhetorical question to the point of proposing that there are certain topics and certain authors which cannot but, between them, produce texts ripe for the psychoanalysts – texts which, to use the felicitous expression of Paul Ricœur's lend themselves to the exercise of the psychoanalyst's methodology of perpetual suspicion?[1] We might even be tempted, in a bout of enthusiastic intellectual extremism, to call these literary works neurotic – not because they depict neurotic characters, but because there are certain human activities that cannot but be permeated by the structure of neurosis. We know immediately who will be the masters of this genre: Sade, Poe, Baudelaire, Dostoevsky, Joyce, Genet, Mailer, Highsmith, Tournier. All those who, in the words of a critic writing in 1979 in the *TLS* ' – alas! – in the modern fashion, are taken seriously'.

Let us leave to one side such thoughts, save to note that if we want to discard the notion that there are neurotic authors, or that there are psychopathic topics, we might then feel obliged to introduce the concept of the neurotic text. But before we get to grips with this concept, we must clarify some of the issues raised by the project of a psychoanalytic reading. What would make a reading of a literary work a psychoanalytic reading? How do I know when the thoughts I have about a text, when the meanings I confer on it, owe something to psychoanalysis? Does the *sotto voce* muttering of the words 'lost object', or 'regression onto the anal-sadistic level' confer a new quality upon the unravelling of my reading, as it slips its way over and in between the words of the text in front of me? Certainly it would be correct to say that I am employing psychoanalytic terminology. But is that enough to say that I am reading psychoanalytically?

Transference and the stenographer

This question has affinities with another: how do I know when I am being psychoanalysed?[2] To this question, we might well receive some such aphoristic answer as: the patient tells lies while the analyst makes mistakes. Such an answer helps us to see that we perceive some asymmetrical element as constitutive of the relation; it is the patient whose transference is in question, and it is the psychoanalyst who is able to give interpretations and write the case-history, the history of this transference. Surely it is this which is constitutive of psychoanalysis? If we want to give a psychoanalytic reading, how can we do it if not through this relation of asymmetry with another, organised around the asymmetry of the transference and its writing?

It has certainly been attempted. We are all familiar with the glee with which psychoanalysts have seized on texts as evidence of the unconscious intentionality of their authors, so that in writing *Hamlet* Shakespeare was working over the death of his son, and in writing *The gambler* Dostoevsky was drawing upon the prohibitions placed upon masturbation in his childhood.[3] The genre of pathography to which such analysis leads one no longer captures our interest, though I might point out that one such pathography, Manuel's biography of Isaac Newton, indicates clearly the paradox to which such works lead: namely, we are interested in great men and women for their works, not for their neuroses.[4] As Freud said, before the problem of the creative artist, or the creative scientist, 'analysis must, alas, lay down its arms'.[5] But the creative artist only becomes a problem once one has assumed that he is a neurotic like any other; he is only a problem once one has postulated that there are madmen who get away with it. If psychoanalysis is helpless in the face of the creative artist, it is not only because of the elusiveness of the creative act; it is also because we are interested in the creative artist only for his creation, so that every time we flee from the obscurity of the text in search of enlightenment to the psyche of the author, the logic of our own interest forces us back to the text. More to the point, no analysis of an author's intentionality can tell us more about the text: it can only tell us more about the author. The illusion that such intentions enrich our reading is only our attempt to wriggle out of our obligation as reader. And, *en fin d'compte*, we are interested in the texts for something they tell *us*, not for something they tell us about *him* or *her*.

The aim of reading is thus not the establishing of a reciprocal relation between equals, where the reader and author can be alternately identified as subjects of a neurotic (or otherwise) text.

261

Taking the asymmetry of the psychoanalytic relation seriously means precisely not identifying the author as a reader who pre-empted one in that position, who got there first. Certain narrative techniques – perhaps best seen in the murder stories of Agatha Christie – produce this mirage-effect. But the psychoanalytic critic is not a detective solving a textual mystery, as if the narrative form of the murder mystery were his or her only methodology. The psychoanalytic critic, for example Shoshana Felman in her virtuoso reading of *The turn of the screw*,[6] will show *how* a text produces its effects of mystery, suspense – or of neurosis and madness.

So we turn away from the analysis of the author to the analysis of the text. We have been shown this way by the generation of psychoanalysts and critics influenced by Lacanian analysis. But what do we find in their analyses? Firstly, the text is decentred, so that its linear narrative form, derived from the obligation placed upon meaning to arrange itself in irreversible temporal order, is seen as the resultant of forces that act within the text, sometimes acting retroactively, so that the text now becomes a geological terrain, only capable of being understood as the product of the combination and separation of linguistic strata. The model here is Freud's practice in *The interpretation of dreams* – his analysis of dream-texts rather than of authors. Secondly, we find a relatively traditional thematic analysis, one which gives over the dynamic force that underlies narrative form to the perpetual striving (repetition) of a 'lost object' to find representation in the text. The narrative becomes the rewriting of a primal scene; but it is no longer the primal scene of the author or even of the characters – it is the primal scene of meaning itself (as if there were only one). Thirdly, we are all aware that the new interest of psychoanalysis for literary critics depends upon a closeness of fit between the methods and objects of analytic and literary practice. This closeness of fit resides in the perceived homology of the notions of style, narrative and device with the mechanisms that the psychoanalyst presumes to be at work in the products of neurosis. Much has been made of the Lacanian/Jakobsonian reinterpretation of the dream-work's mechanism as being identical to the traditional figures of speech to be found in Aristotle and Quintilian: metonymy, metaphor, trope, catachresis, etc. It is on the basis of the homology that the new assimilation of psychoanalysis and literary analysis has been made.

At this point let us return to the question I raised earlier: what makes a literary reading psychoanalytic in character? In his paper on 'The theme of the three caskets', Freud offered an analysis of *King Lear* which turned around the identification of Cordelia with Lear's (and Freud's) own death, so that in refusing her, in taking her silence for absence of love, Lear was refusing to recognise that her love for him was also the death that awaited him. In this refusal he both refused his own death and – by the magical process common to literature and neurosis – brought his own death down on *her*. By refusing the necessity of death, Lear was closing off the only human possibility open to him: the choice of death. In this short paper, which has been much admired by his readers, Freud was careful to point out that he was offering a 'superficial and allegorical interpretation' – 'eine flächenhafte, allegorische Deutung'[7] – in contrast with the deep and literal interpretation available to psychoanalysis. We certainly should not read 'The theme of the three caskets' as psychoanalytic in character – we have Freud's word on the matter. Now, the urgency of my question is heightened: what makes a reading psychoanalytic? It would seem, to start off with, that invoking metaphor and metonymy, the figures of speech, as the processes at work in both psychoanalysis and literary texts, does not make such a reading psychoanalytic: rather, it makes psychoanalysis literary. If we then find that a text that yields an interpretation of the father's refusal of his daughter's love in the service of a wish to avoid death, if this interpretation is allegorical and cannot be called psychoanalytic, even when given by the founder of psychoanalysis, even when given by someone whose plaque on the door arouses no suspicion of charlatanry, then what are we to call a psychoanalytical reading?

One answer would be the following. A psychoanalytical reading must involve some crucial reference to the causal efficacy of sexuality. One simple way in which to introduce such a reference is to mobilise the psychoanalytic theory of symbolism – the standard reductions of swords to penises, of journeys through wooded country to clambering over the mysteriously vast expanse of the mother's body. Some have come to see such reductions as the hallmark of the psychoanalytical reading. But I will ignore this method of the introduction of the body sexual into the reading of literature in order to suggest that we need another way of introducing sexuality into the text, without committing ourselves to the theory of language which underlies the notion of sexual symbolism – the theory that language is originally and fundamentally sexual in character, so that the movement of interpretation finds a vouchsafed resting place once the word has been attached (back) onto the body.

But if we dispense with the reductive theory of symbolism, we must find another way to attach sexuality to our interpretations. The referent is not always sexual. To help find this way, let me ask another question: whose sexuality is at issue? We have already put to one side the issue of the author's intentions, and we are surely reluctant to reintroduce them under the guise of his sexual desire. We might possibly be talking of the sexuality of the characters. If such were the case, then we would be treating these characters as if they were 'real people', as Freud effectively did in his analysis of Jensen's *Gradiva*, as he did when he employed *Oedipus Tyrannos* so as to give clarity to his discovery of the nuclear complex of the neuroses, or, in a slightly different mode, when Lacan employed the story of Edgar Allan Poe to illustrate the circuits of repetition, exchange and desire. (We might want to amend this formula when we apply it to Lacan, and say rather that he treats real people as if they were fictional characters, rather than vice versa. Either way, the conventional distinction between fictions and reality is under-mined.) And there is much to be said for this practice. That it leads to asking oneself questions of the type: 'How many children had Lady Macbeth?' does not seem to be a decisive argument against the method, since the opposition between the fictional and the real has already been undermined by the very possibility of the ques-tion.[8] That the dispute as to the answer to the question will revolve around the interpretation of a textual dislocation – that introduced by Macduff's cry 'He has no children!' – should reassure the faint-hearted that we are not threatening to populate this over-crowded world with any more characters than it already possesses. Certainly we should feel no qualms about deciding upon internal textual evidence that there is a central absence in a text, hypotheses about which may prove fruitful in the elucidation of what is already there laid down.

But the logic of my argument leads further than the investigation of the sexuality of characters met with in fiction. If we continue the purification procedures I outlined above, we will be drawn towards the following answer to the question 'Whose sexuality?' – the sexuality of the text. Immediately, we want to say that this sexuality involves the reader, just as exhibitionism involves the onlooker, and masturbation involves relation to a fantasy-object. To be more precise, it is not so much that the text is the sexual object of the reader, though there is always a dimension of the pleasuring reader. Rather, it is the reader who is the sexual object of the text: quite simply, reading is being seduced by the text.[9] Switching back briefly to the parallel with the psychoanalytic situation, we can recognise this notion as the equivalent of the concept of transference: when the subject in analysis addresses the analyst directly with a demand or a desire, that demand or desire not only specifies the fantasy as it coalesces around the figure of the analyst, but also specifies a position of the subject in that fantasy. Transference constitutes the scene of desire into which the patient has already been seduced.

We can make sense of the essentially sexual character of psychoanalytic readings of literature by enlisting the concept of the transference: but we must make a detour to ensure that the link is clear. Up to this point, my argument has implicitly opposed sexuality and meaning: the theme of sexuality disrupts the system of meaning from the outside, so that the system of language is both an attempt to master the disruptive force of the sexual and is its extension, a pursuit of the sexual by other means. The sexual is what cannot be represented, yet this very impossibility is what yields the necessity for the continuing attempt to do so. This model, however, is based upon the early Freudian theory of a past traumatic moment, of which the system of signifiers (or symbols), organised as a symptom, is the distorted representation. But, with the concept of transference, Freudian theory produced a second version of the relation between sexuality and representation. In this second version, it is sexuality which is 'present', and it is towards a future representation that the analyst's efforts are directed. The effect of psychoanalysis is to reproduce the trauma in the analytic setting – reproduce the trauma of representing the sexual. Transference is now the symptom; analysis is conducted on the analytic scene itself, analysis of analysis; now this *particular* symptom no longer has the structure of some *other* scene. Yet this other scene comes 'clear', and appears in the analysis, only in this traversal: the transference is a repetition, but one pared down to the barest minimal conditions: repeating itself, as 'its self' appears in the repetition. The sexuality which was the motive power of distorted representation now is relocated (theoretically speaking) as the force of transference, emerging as its own primal scene in the very nakedness of its appearance as repetition.

So, what if, in following the second phase of Freud's theory, from sexuality to transference, we take to talking of the transference of the text? There are already two paths carved out for us here: the notion of a reading-effect, which has a similar ambiguity to the transference, since it has a structure of always being already there, 'waiting' for the reader to feel the text's effect, whereas the other side of the theoretical advance represented by the transference is the abolition of the already-thereness associated with the analysis of memory. As Freud put it: 'When the transference has risen to this significance, work upon the patient's memories retreats far into the background.'[10] The second way is sketched by Shoshana Felman when she refers to the literary critic's ascription of authority to the work of literature: 'the text has for us authority – the very type of authority by which Jacques Lacan indeed defines the role of the psychoanalyst in the structure of transference . . . the text is viewed by us as a "subject presumed to know" – as the very place where meaning, and *knowledge* of meaning, reside'.[11] Yet this Lacanian transference may lead us back to the question of meaning all-by-itself, the concept which we are attempting to go beyond – as if Lacan's supplementing of Freud's conception of transference, by adding the passion for knowledge to the other two great transference-passions of love and hate, were being taken as surpassing and eliminating love and hate.[12] The passion for knowledge may well have intimate ties with the search for and the generation of meaning. But the reading-effects of the text are often as akin to love and hate as they are to meaning: fascination, suspense, repulsion, satiation, frustration, titillation, seduction – all organised according to the structure of the Symbolic, if you will. These are not just the imaginary concomitants of reading: these are the real effects of reading.

What the notion of the transference of the text will help us to achieve is what the practice of analysis takes as its task: the repetition, in another form, in analysis, of the 'original' reading-effects induced by the text. It is this enterprise that makes Lacan's reading of *The purloined letter* epoch-making: demonstrating that the reading of the text always induces the same effects of blindness, insight, illusion of mastery, the same movements of the signifier – and not only in Lacan's text, but in Derrida's, in Johnson's . . . and so on.[13] These effects will not always be epistemological in character – not always, as Felman implies, to do with the knowing subject. The subject is also a feeling subject: the effects of suspense of an Agatha Christie story are, of course, epistemological in form, as the reader engages in the quest for the identity of the killer and the certainty of knowing how it was done; but the suspense, surprise and wonder are effects of a question that unfolds via a system of imaginary identifications (corpse-detective, detective-reader) by which the anxiety of death is transformed into the pleasuring suspense of not-knowing.

Transference and the stenographer

I will have further remarks to make about the transference of the text in part V of this chapter. At this point, let us turn to *The gambler*.

II

The gambler returns to Roulettenburg, having successfully fulfilled his mission of obtaining further funds for the General and his entourage, to whom he is attached as tutor.[14] The General is infatuated with a Parisian concubine, Mademoiselle Blanche, who is accompanied by the devious and power-hungry Marquis de Grieux. Blanche is angling to become the wife of the General, on the expectation that he will inherit the estates of his aunt, the formidable Grand'maman, who is dying in Russia. The General has mortgaged his estates to de Grieux and is penniless while waiting for the wealth her death will bring him. In his entourage we also find Polina, the General's step-daughter, who is slavishly loved by the gambler and is being courted by Astley, the honourable and reasonable English businessman. De Grieux has an unspecified hold over Polina. We discover later that Polina loved him, and yielded to his advances – again in some unspecified manner. Remonstrating with Polina that he is her plaything, that he will do anything for her, including jumping off a mountain, the gambler is ordered to demonstrate his fidelity by accosting a typical Prussian couple. The scandal that threatens to erupt as a consequence reveals to him and us the delicate nature of the General's position in relation to Blanche and the hold that de Grieux has over both the General and Polina. The appearance of Grand'maman, seemingly risen from her death-bed, restores the position of the gambler, who becomes the old lady's accomplice at the gaming tables, where she manages to gamble away the inheritance that the General was banking on receiving, having done which she returns to Russia. The General's finances are in a hopeless position; Blanche throws him over and prepares to depart for Paris; de Grieux leaves to claim the General's estates, since there is now no prospect of the General's ever paying off the debt. Before doing so, he makes arrangements so that Polina will receive 50,000 francs, the value of her estates, which the General had also mortgaged to de Grieux. In this act of generosity, the latter attempts to restore to Polina what he had taken from her, thus proving that he is a man of honour. In her distress at this act of reparation, she turns to the gambler for help, who, in turn, suggests that she turn to Astley for help. 'What, do

you yourself really want me to go from you to that Englishman?',
she replies (p. 127). At that moment, in the realisation that she
loves him, the gambler is inspired with an idea, tells her to wait for
him, and makes his way to the casino, where he gambles and wins
200,000 francs. He returns to Polina and offers her 50,000 francs,
with which she will be able to buy back her honour from de Grieux
by returning his gift. With Polina in tears alternating with joyful
happiness, they both fall, on the bed . . .

The next morning Polina throws the 50,000 francs in the
gambler's face, and flees. Contemplating this action, and slowly
making his way after her, he finds the entourage in turmoil
following the departure of Grand'maman and de Grieux, and
discovers that the honourable Astley is protecting the stricken
Polina, to the point of threatening to murder the gambler if he does
not depart for Paris at once. All Russians spend their winnings in
Paris. Blanche assists the now aimless gambler in making up his
mind, by enticing him into slipping stockings onto her legs; he
leaves with her immediately, their contract having been made
explicit: she is to receive 50,000 francs, and promises to help him
spend the rest of his winnings inside a month. In Paris, she
introduces him to some remarkable women, and he, bored, entirely
aware of his position as her compliant object, desultorily assists in
the spending of his winnings. The General arrives and marries
Blanche. The gambler departs, once again poor. After twenty
months of frequenting the gambling spas of Germany, during which
time he has a spell in prison and works as a servant, he comes across
Astley, who has come on Polina's behalf to ascertain how he is
faring. This affirmation of her enduring love for him prompts the
gambler to the formation of further good intentions: once he has
mobilised his indomitable courage for the last time at the roulette
tables, he will leave to join Polina in Switzerland. Tomorrow,
tomorrow – he will bring his life as a gambler to an end.

III

Let me call this the narrative reading of the story. Embedded in it,
there are a series of themes that will form the next level of the
reading. Firstly, there is the theme of the exchange of women. The
price of a woman is set at 50,000 francs. Polina is exchanged by de
Grieux for 50,000 francs; the gambler aims to wipe out the effect of
this transaction by winning 50,000 francs and giving them to Polina,
so that she can undo the effects of de Grieux's letter to her, thereby

freeing herself from the law of 50,000 francs. But, in her eyes, the gambler's action only embeds her forever within that circuit of exchange. That it is a circuit, and a circuit established between men, is made clear by the gambler's first response to Polina's demand for help: he suggests she turn to Astley. Blanche's value is also 50,000 francs, although, given her profession, she is not particularly concerned to stick to a fixed price. If the price of a woman is pegged at 50,000 francs, it is no less the case that marriage receives a fairly well-defined exchange-value in the Roulettenburg market: its price is an estate. The crisis that interrupts this system of exchanges – the crisis set in motion by the roulette wheel – does not prevent Blanche from marrying the General when Grand'maman finally dies, leaving him the estates; this happy ending underlines the fact that the system of marital exchange is not disturbed by the roulette crisis. Nor does that crisis disrupt the exchange of women; rather, it reveals it, the way a rise in the price of key commodities reveals the underlying character of the exchange relations in capitalism.

Part of the narrative technique of the story consists in using roulette as a 'device' for uncovering the 'true' state of affairs between the various parties in the relationships of exchange – de Grieux and Polina, the General and Blanche, Astley and de Grieux. One of the functions of Astley's appearance in the final chapter is to 'round off' the story by showing how the legacy eventually *did* come to Polina, that Blanche eventually *did* receive the estate she was angling for. And Astley's aversion to the 'coupling' of names – Polina's and de Grieux's – only reaffirms that the state of economic affairs has not changed: Polina's status as possible consort depends upon a repudiation of the reality of the law of 50,000 francs, in favour of the marriage law of the estate.

Astley's refusal to let the two names 'couple' is symptomatic of the hypocrisy with which the exchange of women is negotiated in Roulettenburg. While it is Blanche who most clearly spells out that she is to be had by anyone putting up the necessary 50,000 francs – 'Quant à moi, je veux cinquante mille francs de rente et alors . . . ' (p. 143) – she ends up as what she planned to be: the General's rich widow. It is Polina who has been exchanged – from de Grieux, via the gambler, to Astley.[15] It is as if her refusal to recognise the law entails that it be exercised on her with excessive force. One of the other effects of the law of 50,000 francs is that love is always misplaced; when Polina addresses herself to the gambler for help, she exclaims of de Grieux: 'I have found him detestable for a long,

long time. Oh, he was not the same man before, a thousand times, no, but now, now! . . . Oh, with what joy I would have flung that fifty thousand in his nasty face now, and spit at him . . . ' (pp. 126–7). This passionate declaration, including a declaration of former love for de Grieux that exceeds any other expression of Polina's throughout the novella, is then acted out with the gambler, after they have spent the night together. But Astley also experiences the same consequences of the law of 50,000 francs: Polina's preoccupation with the next to last man in the chain of exchange, the gambler. Astley tells him: 'Yes, you unhappy man, she loved you, and I can tell you so because you are a lost soul!' (p. 160). One can almost picture the scene in which Polina hurled 50,000 francs in the face of Astley, the next in line to experience the deferred effect of the law of love by which Polina is ruined.

There are two different conceptions of love at work here. The first is love as the unconditional demand. Polina comes to the gambler to ask for help, which she knows full well he is not in a position to give. According to Lacan's definition of love as the gift of something one does not have, that is precisely what she is asking. And that is how the gambler comes to realise she loves him; when he suggests that Astley, rather than he, will be able to help, she says:

'What, do *you yourself* really want me to go from you to that Englishman' . . . She had called me 'thou' for the very first time . . . I felt as though I had been struck by lightning; I stood there unable to believe my eyes or my ears! What? So she loved me! She had come to *me*, not to Mr Astley! She, a young girl, had come alone to my room, in a hotel – which meant she had publicly compromised herself – and I could only stand before her un-comprehendingly. (pp. 127–8)

He could not imagine that she loved him; he could only deduce it, by eliminating the alternative hypotheses, explaining her action. And it is necessarily so, with the demand for love – since it cannot specify its object without denying its reality. Specifying the 50,000 francs would pervert the absolute demand into a request to be bought and reinserted back into the circuit of exchange defined by the law of 50,000 francs.

The second conception of love invoked is idealisation: the conception that requires Astley to refuse the coupling of names, to maintain the suitable distance between sacred and profane. But this dimension of love is more extensively depicted in the form of the master–slave relationship, so prominent in the first half of the novella. It is also within the context of slavery and servitude that we see the concept of freedom emerge, as well we might, given the period in which Dostoevsky was writing, just after the abolition of serfdom. Servitude, it is implied, is the natural condition of Russians. We find the theme of servitude described in the following variations, amongst others: in the couple Polina and de Grieux (the episode in which Polina allows the gambler to conceal from de Grieux that he was gambling on her behalf, thus indicating that she needs to keep secrets from him (p. 39), and then: 'I can see that Miss Polina is his slave (because she begs even my pardon)' (p. 68)); in the vacillations of the gambler's relation to the General, to whom he refuses to be servile ('I only wish to clear up the offensive suggestion that I am under the tutelage of a person who is supposed to have authority over my free will' (p. 57)). Later in the story, the General's only tactic for persuading the gambler to stop Grand'maman playing roulette is servility: 'Save us, Alexis Ivanovich, save us! . . . .'; 'I beg you, I implore you, I bow down humbly like a true Russian . . .' (pp. 101–2). And in the very first paragraph the gambler simply records, 'I even thought the General was a little ashamed to see me' (p. 19).

However, the central master–slave relationship is that of the gambler and Polina. Let us briefly plot its shifts. In their first reported conversation, Polina says to him: 'You ought to be made to pay for the mere fact that I allow you to ask such questions and make such suppositions.' The gambler replies: 'I am ready to pay for them any way you want, and don't think my life of any value now' (p. 26). She terminates the interview by ordering him to play roulette for her (his first time at the tables); he reflects:

Yes, I hated her. There were moments (to wit, at the end of every one of our conversations) when I would have given half my life to strangle her! . . . And yet I swear by all that's holy that if on the fashionable peak of the Schlangenberg she had indeed said to me, 'Cast yourself down', I would have done so immediately and even enjoyed doing it. I knew that one way or another the matter must be settled. (p. 27)

He concludes:

I think that up to now her attitude to me has been like that of the empress of antiquity who would undress in front of her slave, not considering him a man . . . (p. 27)

The gambler did win at roulette for her; nevertheless, Polina felt resentful. Disturbed that he had been playing for someone else, she issues the following typical pronouncement to him:

. . . you really must go on playing in partnership with me and – of course – you will. (p. 33)

Undoubtedly this order is carried out – the interminability of his gambling is testimony to his fidelity to her imperial will.[16] What his obsessional fidelity to her command conceals, as is often the case with obsessionals, is its opposite: his wish to degrade and humiliate her, as he so successfully does when he wins the gold which will allow him to buy her, the gold intended to help her cancel out her debt to de Grieux. He is thus able to reproduce in relation to himself her relation of servitude to de Grieux.

But their relation develops gradually. By chapter 3, while not understanding it, the gambler recognises his function as 'slave or errand-boy' (p. 33). However, in chapter 4, he lies on her behalf, to allay de Grieux's suspicions – the tables are beginning to turn, it seems. But it is exactly at this moment that the gambler mounts his tirade on paternity – the German *Vater* in this instance – which he concludes as follows: 'I would rather be a Russian rake or make my pile at roulette. I don't want to be Happe and Co. after five generations. I need money for myself, and I don't look on myself as merely an indispensable factor in the acquisition of wealth' (p. 42). Having perceived that his function as slave might be in danger, he wants to make sure that no other relationship for a man is possible for him. Paternity and family life are out of the question since they imply an abnegation of self which he, with the slave-mentality, can conceive of only as mortal annihilation; hence he will accept no other relation to woman than that of master and slave.

We might say, as a tentative hypothesis, that this emphasis on mastery and slavery corresponds to the phenomenology of gambling, while the dialect of exchange and the law of 50,000 francs is what governs the articulation of gambling with the real. Why phenomenology? Gambling highlights not only the opposition 'win/lose', but also the themes of fate, chance and freedom. Dostoevsky scholars have contrasted the impersonal *automaton* of roulette with the idea of personal destiny, of fate, which gambling then reduces down to the value of luck, of *tuché*. The typical Dostoevskian theme taken up here is put well by Savage:[17] The man who loses God loses himself, and thus finds himself abandoned in a deterministic universe. To this calculating Law, he can only oppose Chance:

Watching the spinning roulette wheel, the gambler is, as it were, at the metaphysical source of being, and what he sees in front of him is nothing other than a symbolic model of the cosmic mechanism. The seduction which draws his soul is that of an ultimate, irrational and groundless freedom . . . [18]

This, the 'metaphysical' reading of the novella, is quite accurate, but insufficient: it fails to point out that the master–servant dialectic is what such a conception of mechanism *versus* freedom is founded on. Nor would it be entirely misplaced to think that what I am offering here is a Hegelian-inspired sociology of knowledge.[19] The concept of freedom as contentless and random action is what the slave ends up opposing to the master's will. And it is this conception that the gambler offers the General and Polina:

Upstairs in my little cell I have only to remember and imagine the merest rustle of your dress and I am ready to gnaw my hands off. And why are you angry with me? Because I call myself a slave! Take advantage of my slavery, profit by it, make use of it! Do you know, one day I shall kill you? Not because I shall stop loving you, or out of jealousy, but – I'll simply kill you, just like that, because sometimes I long to devour you. (p. 48)

'Just like that' – the arbitrariness of the act is the inevitable resolution of the state of slavery. The act of freedom that the slave dreams of is always a *useless* one – one whose uselessness is opposed to the use-value that is extracted from the permanent labour to which his servitude condemns him (even when in his little cell, so that it becomes a labour of love to imagine). The slave's act of free will is very much the philosopher's conception of the refutation of determination: raising one's arm, a pointless action, to *show* freedom. An action that had a point would be 'useless' here – the demonstration depends upon its pointlessness. The gambler's equivalent is throwing himself off the Schlangenberg, and Polina's reply colludes in the irrationality of this act of slavery, which is on the point of turning over into its opposite, absolute freedom, absolute resistance to the master. Polina replies: 'It would be no use to me' (p. 49). The gambler quite clearly perceives this as the master's refutation of his bid for freedom: 'Magnificent! You said that magnificent "no use" on purpose to crush me' (p. 49). Her subsequent reply then elicits the same murderous impulse in the gambler – and he recognises that Polina knows it – 'She was running a risk' (p. 49). But she goads him, not into a fall from the heights, but into something equally useless: he approaches a German Baroness and says 'Madame, j'ai l'honneur d'être votre esclave'

(p. 50). As the gambler himself says, aghast at Polina's order, which he is obliged to obey: 'What a thing to take into one's head, to go and insult a woman' (p. 51).

The dialectic sketched here between the gambler and Polina is manifestly that of the master and slave in the *Phenomenology* of Hegel: the labour of the slave, the risk of death run by the master, a risk that is fantasised as symbolising freedom by the slave. But the master–slave relationship is knotted to a dialectic of sexual exchange and of seduction, as well as being in apposition to the bourgeois virtues of the *Vater*, alluded to in the economics of gambling and the marriage market. This knot is the formal achievement of Dostoevsky's text: to knit the three themes together via the roulette wheel. Yet there is something left over, which I will come to later, which is not entirely subordinated to the eternal return of the wheel.

One theme that all three levels share is waiting. The abhorred *Vater* waits till the twilight of middle age to marry, and his waiting is inherited by his sons as they try to make up for lost time; as Hegel puts it, the slave's being is a waiting-for-death. It is this waiting which gamblers, obsessionals and slaves share and which Lacan has linked together in his theory of obsessional neurosis.[20] What Dostoevsky's gambler also does is wait on the desire of a woman: he promises to give up his life for Polina. But, once accepted, his desire fades – when Polina calls him 'thou', when she gives herself to him, and also once he has helped Blanche on with her stockings. He can sustain desire only in so far as he is waiting for the total sacrifice that may, that *will*, be asked of him, at any moment. As narcissistic character, the gambler loves that which promises his own freedom to him, in an indefinite future: he loves the *expectation* of another's act of freedom, another's pure desire; we can give the name 'attendant' to this type of erotic character.

So far, I have not given any interpretation that I would qualify as psychoanalytic in character. True, I have talked of exchange and of mastery, both concepts that figure largely in certain genres of the psychoanalytic literature. But we would not wish to see these as specific to psychoanalysis: the first four chapters of *Das Kapital* are as illuminating on the exchange relations of which Dostoevsky writes as are the *Three essays on the theory of sexuality*. And concentrating on the character-type of the gambler, while of great interest – indeed, maybe of supreme interest as the model of gamblers for the analyst – can only lead away from literary analysis, not towards it. No, we must look to the heart of the story for our psychoanalytic reading. We must look to the psychoanalysis of gambling.

IV

Given the difficulties I have already mentioned, it is interesting to note that neither the literature on Dostoevsky's *The gambler* nor the psychoanalytic literature on gambling approaches the crucial question, 'What is the significance of gambling?' It is true that in the Dostoevsky literature we find references to the obsessive character of gambling, to the fact that the gambler wastes his life-energy on gambling, instead of allowing his love for Polina to grow. The tension between impersonal determinism and personal destiny, between Fate and Chance, is played out in gambling. But it is rare that the question, 'Why gambling?' is asked.

On the other hand, the psychoanalytical literature on gambling fails to treat gambling in its specificity, assimilating gambling to play and then play to fantasy. The conclusion is thus that gamblers are dominated by fantasy: their neurosis is like every other. Certainly there have been other hypotheses aired: that the gambler, rather than wanting to win, actually wishes to lose, so that his seemingly irrational persistence at the tables is a very successful means of bringing about his desired end.[21] This end is a repetition of a primary rejection by the mother, so that its achievement is a way of binding him back, once again, to her, in a relationship that is always about to come to a traumatic end. In the earlier analytic literature, we find the hypothesis that gambling represents the sexual act played out and symbolised in the anal-sadistic phase, so that the gambler's losses represent ejaculation, defecation and castration.[22] The repetitious and compulsive aspects of gambling were what led Freud, in his paper on Dostoevsky, to derive it from infantile prohibitions on masturbation.[23] Yet even there we see that, as Shoshana Felman puts it, literature is the unconscious of psychoanalysis,[24] since Freud can find no better way of revealing the relation of gambling to masturbation than by recounting a Stefan Zweig story, 'Four-and-twenty hours in a woman's life', in which a woman falls in love with a young man's hands gambling.

My thinking will follow Felman's argument in the inverted form: the psychoanalysis of gambling is the unconscious of *The gambler*. But it is gambling in its specificity, not as a derivative of something else – play, masturbation, or whatever. How are we to characterise this specificity?

275

Firstly, gambling is a highly rational way of achieving an irrational end. The juxtaposition of rational and irrational is achieved through its unique temporality. Everyone knows that in the long run we must lose – a fact that has a deep relation to Keynes' dictum that in the long run we are all dead. Everyone also knows that it is possible to win large amounts of money gambling; one can make something out of nothing (or almost nothing – one needs a residue from previous exchange relations in order to start or continue playing – a fact about gambling that may be exploited for novelistic purposes, for instance in the opening scene of Balzac's *La Peau de chagrin*). Out of this juxtaposition of inevitable loss and possible gain arises the idea that if one does one's gambling in the shortest time possible – preferably one huge bet – one has the best chance of winning. Given the inexorable character of the time proper to gambling, if one can do it in a timeless moment – quick, now, here, now, always – one will have eliminated one's chances of losing. Of course, the gambler is smitten with doubt as to whether he has chosen the *correct* timeless moment, from whence the intimate relationship of gambling and superstition – how to read the future. However, a gambler does not read the future in order to know whether he will win; rather, he wishes to know what time it is. Hence, it is not only his attending to Blanche's stockings that draws Dostoevsky's gambler to Paris. He makes up his mind, he finds the right moment, when she says to him: 'Je te ferai voir des étoiles en plein jour.' And the gambler says to himself: 'If it's to be Paris, very well, let's go to Paris! Evidently it was written in my stars!' The roulette wheel now doubles up as a quasi-Ptolemaic time-piece.

Blanche offers the gambler the annihilation of the natural order of temporality, as marked out by night and day. She offers him the possibility of annihilating time if he will make a decision. But the theme of the stars is immediately read by the gambler within the system of determinism and freedom proper to the paradoxes of Calvinism. Paris is written in his stars – since it is written, it will be so. By making it be so, by leaving with Blanche, the gambler reaffirms the existence of the temporal order, that temporal order which exists in so far as it is made to exist, by acting in spite of it. This structural relation between action and the temporal order is argued by Lacan to be the relation proper to the Symbolic – and gambling (and its concomitant, superstition) is the Symbolic at its most merciless.[25] The gambler's fate – the question of his subjectivity, the question he poses to Destiny – can be decided only by the set of numbers on the roulette wheel, as a fading of the subject. The gambler binds up his subjectivity with this fading. But the temporality of the fading – a temporality linked to the mortality of the body and the immortality of the Symbolic (dead father) – is achieved in the bet.

This unique temporality is brought out well by the gambler's ruminations on what brings success in gambling:

> It appeared to me that pure calculation means fairly little and has none of the importance many gamblers attach to it . . . they lose exactly the same as we poor mortals playing without calculation . . . on the other hand I drew one conclusion, which I think is correct: in a series of pure chances there really does exist, if not a system, at any rate a sort of sequence – which is, of course, very odd. (p. 35)

A system of probabilities will indicate nothing in roulette. But if the subject can only insert himself into the sequence of numbers *at the correct moment*, then success is guaranteed. The peculiar tension between the notion of system – a Laplacean, deterministic, timeless universe – and the brevity of the temporal sequence is what characterises the relation of the subject to the symbolic system laid out on the roulette wheel.

Let me now introduce two key phrases from the gambler's vocabulary. Firstly, 'keeping one's head', opposed to which we find the terms 'tornado', 'vortex', 'my head was spinning', 'being snatched up in its skirts' (p. 115). All of these terms are evocations of the movement of the *boule* in the roulette wheel. The second phrase is: 'dare to decide'. The gambler needs courage in order to decide. But then, in a subtle shift, we find that the continuum runs from 'keeping one's head' through to standing firm: 'Yes! I have only to be prudent and patient for once in my life – and that's all! I have only to stand firm once, and I can change the whole course of my destiny in an hour!' (p. 161). And, this moment, this timeless moment, the hour of destiny, is always tomorrow, tomorrow when 'It will all come to an end!' (p. 162). Just once, he must decide to stand firm in order to prove to Polina he is a man. And the consequence, entirely expected to connoisseurs of obsessional neurosis, is timeless waiting for death. 'Polina! Give me only one hour! Wait here only an hour . . . ' It is the last time the true Polina figures 'onstage' . . . except to seduce him into their night of love. His response to this seduction? 'I no longer thought of anything or heard anything. My head was spinning . . . ' Majestically and characteristically, Dostoevsky marks this exit with a trademark: an ellipsis . . .

Hence the very figures of speech employed testify to the fact that the logic of the roulette wheel is the means by which the themes of love, exchange and authority are articulated with each other. Gambling represents both the subversion and the glorification of the exchange system. It mocks the logic of the something for something else, by its insistence on the possibility of 'something for nothing'. But such a promise of escape from the iron law of exchange is quite clearly totally dependent on that law. Gambling is parasitical on the unambiguous clarity of exchange relations, and not only because of the sacrosanctity of numbers. The Monte Carlo system of gambling – said to be a fool-proof method of winning – consists in the player doubling the evens stake he lost on the previous turn of the wheel: if he wins he is back to quits and his *next* bet may then bring him out ahead. But, if one suffers a long sequence of losses, one can continue to double one's stake only if one has infinite capital; in which case, 'gambling to win' could never be a reasonable motive. Fool-proof gambling winnings depend on prior accumulation within the 'normal' system of exchange relations; the Monte Carlo system is entirely parasitic on these relations. We also find this word 'parasite' as a frequent epithet for gamblers in psychoanalytic case-histories (in, for instance, Edmund Bergler's *The psychology of gambling*). Gambling mocks at these exchange relations by proving that, in one moment, the dreadful virtues of the *Vater*, the dreadful virtues of honesty and thrift that result in the sale of all the sons of the father with the aim of amassing a few hundred more guldens for the family capital, with one bet, these virtues can be revealed as the means by which the bourgeois is enslaved to the capitalist ethos. Thus gambling is both the subversion and the celebration of the logic of exchange.

But the logic of exchange continually attempts to co-opt and coerce the wilful ignorance and mocking defiance embodied in gambling. We date the beginnings of a rational science of probability from the moment when the Chevalier de Méré presented two gambling problems to Pascal, who could triumphantly claim them as annexed 'à l'empire de la raison', in redefining them as follows. If two players are engaged in a game, how do we calculate what is owing to each of them at any determined point in the game, given that one of them wishes to withdraw before the game has finished? That is, if each gambler gives up his money on entering the game, how do we *retranslate* back into money the chances he possesses of winning or losing at any future time?[26] Such is not the way we now think of chance. In so arguing, Pascal was revealing the close affiliation of gambling to the primitive theory of exchange in the mid seventeenth century. He, and many others since, conceived of a chance in the game as something one possessed and could exchange. Similarly, the underlying concept of Huygens' treatment of the theory of the lottery was that neither the gambler nor the lottery-owner should be able to profit without risk.[27] We are not far from Keynes' dictum that only gamblers should interest themselves in the Stock Exchange.[28]

The achievement of *The gambler* is to show how this subverted logic of exchange offers an answer, just as a neurotic symptom offers an answer, to an agonising dilemma in the domain of love. But it is a perverse answer – perverse in the sense Masud Khan defines as follows:

the pervert puts an impersonal object between his desire and his accomplice; this object can be a stereotype fantasy, a gadget or a pornographic image. All three alienate the pervert from himself, as, alas, from the object of desire.[29]

The roulette wheel with its impersonal time is this gadget. How does it work in love?

When Polina comes to the gambler for help, she comes to him as someone already inserted into the system of exchanges by de Grieux. She looks to the gambler to extricate her from this system, to offer her a love that exists outside of the system; she expects from him an absolute and romantic *Aufhebung*: release from the law of 50,000 francs. He can only offer her *either* a further exchange with Astley – which is in fact the end result – *or* the waiting of the gambler, the waiting for the gambling to stop which Dostoevsky himself forced on his young wife. But the gambler wishes to accede to her demand, and it is through roulette that he seeks to do so, precisely because roulette both obeys and subverts the iron law of exchange. The possibility of love outside of the law is truthfully represented within the system of gambling: the something for nothing. But this system also closes off the possibility of leaving this field; once he is caught up in the spinning of the roulette wheel, as the means by which to stop his head spinning, the gambler cannot stop. The gambler must 'keep his head'. His profligacy on the level of monetary and personal exchange is matched by the castration anxiety at the level of phallic exchange. As an attendant, the gambler could anticipate with eagerness the prospect of throwing himself off the mountain, of 'plunging into space' (p. 53), to satisfy Polina's whim. But, in the casino, when faced with the choice between setting the *boule* in motion forever and returning to Polina, 'there was, however, one instant's expectant pause, perhaps sensation for sensation the same as that experienced by Madame Blanchard in Paris while she was plunging to the ground from the balloon' (p. 130). The gambler experiences himself as a woman falling – like Blanche the fallen woman. Since the feminised swoon can be accepted only within the timeless walls of the casino, waiting for the movement of the *boule*, the gambler is pledged to remain an attendant.

It is at this point that we finally gain access to the sexuality of the text. There is no doubt that the reader is caught up in the crisis, in the cycle of tension and return that the gambler undergoes, both on the level of the roulette wheel and in the relations with Polina, the General and Blanche. But, underlying this movement, there is a static quality to the text, so that the post-textual sadness that one experiences in the latter third of the story is due not so much to the fact that we are all supposedly sad after making meaning, as to the fact that we are always in the same place, trying, with the gambler, to keep our heads. The story has no movement; we are trapped in one of the gambler's timeless moments. The first sentence of the novella fixes us in time, a time of the in-between: 'I am back at last after my absence of two weeks' (p. 19). And the last sentence leaves us there: 'Tomorrow, tomorrow it will all come to an end!' (p. 162). The text repeats the perverse time of gambling. The opening and closing movement of the unconscious can synchronise, in ideal circumstances, with the flow of desire and the opening and closing of our bodily orifices; this text suppresses this movement and replaces it with an impersonal object, a gadget: a narrative without movement. At one level, we encounter this perversity in the character of the gambler, who, to Astley's displeasure, remains as cheerful and high-spirited under conditions of adversity as he was in happier 'times'. At another level, the possibility of a non-perverse relation of reader to text is closed off by this double layering, in which the reader is seduced into expecting a movement, a temporality, that never materialises. The reader replicates the gambler's expectant relation to the future, and is thus co-opted into the position of attendant. Like the gambler, the reader attempts to step outside the system of exchanges. Instead, he or she is captured by the perpetual timeless crisis of gambling, its illusion of 'now or never'. The trouble is: now *and* never, in this story, both turn out to be tomorrow.

So the frenzied movement of the text produces a narrative that defies its own law of temporal progression. This freezing of movement is also one of the effects of gambling on a capitalist economy. In the 1940s and 1950s, much of the sluggishness of Brazil's economy could be attributed to the illegal game of *bichot*. It was estimated that over 30 per cent of all disposable income was committed to gambling, so that 'the game practically immobilizes an appreciable part of disposable income, *by causing it to circulate too quickly*'.[30] But this feature has also been noted by Bakhtin as characteristic of Dostoevsky's work: it is a world of space, not time, a world with the atemporality of tragedy.[31] Dostoevsky's characters do not develop: they unfold. And they are grouped as different, often contradictory, facets of an idea around a timeless moment in which action is concentrated. The world of the convict and the gambler are similar – lives withdrawn from life, a world of timeless crisis time, of the 'final moments of consciousness before execution or suicide'.[32] Hence we can suggest that one reason why Dostoevsky's story *The gambler* is so successful is that the inherent logic of gambling is very close to the polyphonic atemporality of Dostoevsky's writing. His formal technique thus reveals the heart of gambling, because it is homologous with it.

V

Finally, what are we to make of the question of the relationship between the author and the text, a relationship which we recommended, in good company, should be treated in the most phobic of manners? After all, *The gambler* is a text whose links with Dostoevsky's 'life' are undeniable – surely it takes a peculiar blindness to ignore them entirely? It is not just the fact that Dostoevsky's own experiences at the gaming tables are drawn upon, to the point where phrases from his letters to his brother describing his own gambling are transferred almost word for word into the story.[33] Rather, it is the curious scene of writing of this story – which 'repeats' Dostoevsky's gambling, his gambling with his own writing as stake, and the manner in which he fell in love with the woman who transcribed the story – which tempts us to this inquiry. The story deserves retelling.[34]

Dostoevsky had spoken in a letter of 30 September 1863 of his intention to write a story depicting 'a type of Russian abroad', all of whose 'vital juices, strength, aggressiveness, boldness go into roulette'.[35] The reader's attention was to be drawn by the '*graphic* and most detailed description of roulette'. By 1866 Dostoevsky's financial affairs were in a desperate state. He had signed a contract in 1865 with Stallovsky, with the condition that he deliver a new novel to him by 1 November 1866: if the novel were not in Stallovsky's hands by that date, Stallovsky would have the right for nine years to publish anything Dostoevsky had written without paying Dostoevsky anything. By 1 October he had not written a line, and, in desperation, hired a young student from a school of stenography. The novel *The gambler* was dictated in twenty-five days, Anna Grigorievna Snitkina writing up each day's work overnight. On 30 October, with the manuscript ready to be delivered, the stenographer saved Dostoevsky from the final stratagem of the publisher, who had absented himself from the city to make delivery impossible. She suggested they register the manuscript at a police station and thereby meet the conditions of the contract.

Dostoevsky fell in love with his stenographer while dictating *The gambler*. What more clear-cut instance of transference-love could one find? And this is the pure Lacanian transference – that transference mobilised in the very act of saying, by the very structure of speech. Does the autobiographical fact that *The gambler* was 'originally' destined for a listener who then became the object of the author's love affect – enrich or impoverish – our reading?

My reading of *The gambler* has emphasised the subversion of three codes that are intertwined in the circular movement of the roulette wheel: the code of rational calculation of self-interest (de Grieux), the code of master/slave obligations (Russians, the General, Polina) and the code of feminine seduction (Blanche). The gambler is importuned by representatives of each of these codes when reports of the death on which each had banked, Grand'maman's, turned out to be, in Twain's famous phrase, greatly exaggerated. For the gambler, Polina embodies all three of these codes: as seductress in a master/servant relation, and as herself subject to the law of 50,000 francs. Yet there their ways part: the solution the gambler offers to this knot is the timelessness (both punctual and eternal) of roulette. Polina's solution is love: 'she loved you, and I can tell you so because you are a lost soul! Moreover, even if I tell you that she loves you to this day, you know you will stay here all the same!' (p. 160). So Polina's love comes to reflect his timeless gambling, appearing in the equally timeless guise of fidelity. Roulette and love are coupled with one another, as different and as inseparable as two sides of the same coin.

Transference and the stenographer

Dostoevsky was gambling with his own words: staking his future words on one novella, one date. Dostoevsky scholars may surely recognise this as the 'crisis time' of the Menippean satire and carnival interpretations offered by Bakhtin ('consistent unfinalizability' and 'final moments of consciousness' before execution or suicide).[36] But the unique achievement of Dostoevskian time recounted by Bakhtin – unfinalisability in the service of the inner, individual truth of each voice in the novel, never subject to domination by the authorial voice – is itself subverted by the hope of love that Polina so unexpectedly offers the gambler. Such unexpected love is also the consequence of the desperate wager Dostoevsky made with the publisher – in the form of the stenographer. Yet this stenographer is the 'authorial' voice by means of which Dostoevsky envisions the truth of confessional self-utterance emerging:

first he speaks to himself, then he addresses an invisible listener, as if addressing a judge. And so it is in reality. If a stenographer could have overheard him and taken down all that he said, the result would have been a little rougher and less polished than I represent it, but the psychological sequence would, it seems to me, remain the same. This assumption of a stenographer taking notes (which I would then put into polished form) is what I call the fantastic in this story.[37]

We even have the stenographic record of a conversation between Dostoevsky and the stenographer who took down *The gambler*, in which the author outlines the plot of a novel about an artist, a failure, who meets a young woman called Anya; the record continues:

'Put yourself in her place for a minute . . . Imagine that I am this artist, that I am confessing my love for you and ask you to be my wife, tell me what would you answer'?
'I would answer that I love you and shall all my life.'[38]

It is not at all clear who is speaking now. Are the final words of this passage put into the mouth of Anya by Dostoevsky? Are these words put into the mouth of Anya by Anna Grigorievna Snitkina, in order to complete Dostoevsky's story sketch? Are these words that Anna Grigorievna Snitkina spoke to Dostoevsky, speaking them out of turn, as it were, from the heart, having refused to put herself in Anya's place, and answering *as if* she had been addressed these words by Dostoevsky himself rather than *qua* stenographer? How do these words, 'I would answer that I love you and shall all my life', manage to figure in this diary or notebook – are they a mistake, words that formed part of a life that managed to find their way into a diary that forms a record of things Dostoevsky said to the stenographer?

These questions are, of course, unresolvable. I ask them only because they are in many ways more interesting than any answers we might receive, even if the biographer's nightmare were to come true, and he or she ended up in heaven asking Dostoevsky and Anna Grigorievna Snitkina who *really* said what in those stenographic sessions. What we do know is that Dostoevsky 'proposed' to Anna Grigorievna Snitkina nine days after they had delivered the manuscript to the police, and they were married a couple of months later.

When did the writing of this life stop? At what point do we say: we have passed over from writing into reality? To be more specific: is this snippet of recorded dialogue the *sequel* to *The gambler*, its prolongation? Or is that just an effect of the textual organisation I impose? We can take this opportunity to remind ourselves that *The gambler*'s organisation was also imposed – by the terms of a publishing gamble, and by the stenographic and legal ploys by which Dostoevsky won the gamble with Stallovsky. In all manner of ways, the stenographer enabled Dostoevsky – through her presence, her faith, her writing, her turning to the police – to meet his contract with the publisher: she then enabled him to meet his contract with 'the stenographer', maybe that self-same stenographer who makes 'A gentle creature' a fantastic story. Here, surely, we recognise the transference – that 'intermediate region between illness and real life through which the transition from one to the other is made'.[39] The structural position of the stenographer is exactly that between illness (perversion) – the text of *The gambler* – and real life.

What are the effects in the text itself which bear witness to this stenographic transference? As Jackson has argued,[40] Polina and 'Lady Luck' (his name for the fantastic woman aimed at through the gambler's play at the roulette wheel) occupy structurally homologous positions. Yet Polina *in reality* possesses one more feature – she loves the gambler. This love is supplementary to all the other codes – of exchange, seduction, mastery. It is, I would suggest, the 'real' residue of the transference to the stenographer. The gambler's double, Astley – an approximate anagram of Alexei – reveals the permanence of this love, as permanent as the time created by gambling, the no-time, crisis-time of the Dostoevskian universe, in an episode that is supplementary to the time of the story, twenty months later. Polina's love is thus posited as a 'beyond' of the text, within a concluding section that is an indefinite prolongation of that text: a prolongation repeated (extended) in the stenographic proposal the author made nine days after delivering '*The gambler*' to the police station. Now our psychoanalytic reading brings us not to the idea that *The gambler* repeats some other scene (Dostoevsky's love of Appolinaria Suslova, his episodes of gambling in the early 1860s), but to the scene of writing of *The gambler* as an engendering of the structures of gambling and love involving Dostoevsky and the stenographer, Alexei and the reader of his diary (undoubtedly a woman), the text (this Penguin text) and its reader – as the transference in action. The time of writing of *The gambler* was a gamble; the crisis-time of its story is the punctual, endless repetition of roulette; its effect – its transference – is to posit gambling and love as opposites, while in reality love is the promised supplement of the text: what is promised as its after, once the book is closed. Just as it worked for Dostoevsky, so the story can work for a reader – the transference-effect of the stenographer.

12

MICHEL FOUCAULT AND THE HISTORY OF PSYCHOANALYSIS

What I have studied are the three traditional problems: (1) What are the relations we have to truth through scientific knowledge, to those 'truth games' which are so important in civilization and in which we are both subject and object? (2) What are the relationships we have to others through those strange strategies and power relationships? And (3) what are the relationships between truth, power and the self? . . . What could be more classic than these questions and more systematic than the evolution through questions one, two and three back to the first? I am just at this point.

Michel Foucault[1]

I

I was not always a grateful admirer of Michel Foucault's. In 1970, when I first opened and read a book of his, *Madness and civilization*, my reaction was one of mystified irritation. I set the book aside, impatient, confused, all the while not being able to forget some of its most poignant images or its most brilliant passages: the Ship of Fools, the sense of oppressive order and silence descending over the asylum as Pinel struck off the chains of the insane, the enigmatic last pages in which Foucault describes the final modern attempt to come to terms with Unreason, that of Freud – an attempt that founders, he surmises, because of the inescapable alienation that is built into the doctor–patient relation upon which the psychoanalytic situation is built.[2]

Those images – they do remain with you, however disdainful and dismissive one's overall attitude to Foucault. Each of his books has a passage that serves as a kind of mnemonic in talking with others about them. The 'death of man' passage from *The order of things* – 'like a face drawn in sand at the edge of the sea', the virtuoso laying out of the space of *Las Meninas*, as the ground plan for the space of representation of the Enlightenment, that opens that book. The opening description of Damien's corporeal destruction, the plans and schemes of the Panopticon in *Discipline and punish*. Images that are not so much unforgettable as riveting – they draw the sensibility tight to them and will not let go; as images they rivet the imagination and the abstract arguments of the books to them, with as much force as that needed to rivet the plates of a ship together. Certainly it takes a specifically dogged though common enough Puritanism to distrust and deprecate the power of Foucault's images. But, once read and understood, the images return almost involuntarily, as if they represented a coded, shorthand version of what one has learned, an image that sums up the argument the way a mathematical equation is thought to sum up, to 're-present' an argument. Hence discussions and criticisms of Foucault's texts may well be couched in terms of an analysis or attack on his images – the debate over his interpretation of *Las Meninas* that enlivened the pages of *Critical Inquiry* some years back seemed to stand in for a more difficult and arduous judgement on his account of the theory of representation in the eighteenth century. Even the empiricist historian's discomfort is often, like my own initial reaction, a rather irritated and dismissive one, coloured and complicated by the difficulty of weighing the significance of these images, behind which is masked a density of argument that historians are not used to confronting.

When I turned once again, after a lapse of some four years, to Foucault, my mental landscape had been transformed by a study of Freud and, with great resistance, of Lacan. And now, it was an entirely different author I was reading – those sentences of Foucault's on Freud and the doctor–patient relationship, together with *The birth of the clinic*, revealed an entirely new way of thinking about the history of medicine and science: the logic of the gaze, the architecture, the ordering and cataloguing of diseases within the hospital, the creation of the clinical space of hospital medicine, indicated how perception, material, practices and knowledge were articulated together. When, in 1974, I read them, as I then did, alongside *The order of things*, it was clear that Foucault's metahistory,[3] as I thought of it then, or archaeology as he began to talk of it, was an unrivalled, unprecedented attempt at organising systems of knowledge in a historical account which respected both systemic coherence and explanatory force and depicted the profound transformations of such systems, transformations which might well turn around seemingly 'surface' events. Admittedly, I had had an experience which made Foucault especially appealing – I had attempted to grapple with the complexities of eighteenth-century physiology.[4] I had got substantially nowhere tracing the chains of influence of one theory on another, one school on another, one eminent group of doctors on another, one individual text upon another. And nor, so it seemed, from looking at the scholarly literature, had anyone else. Foucault's work on the eighteenth century gave – and still gives – a framework to the amorphous mass of eighteenth-century material in the life sciences and medicine, a framework which could be argued over, but was without precedent in its overarching scope and depth of illumination.

Yet my concerns had become and have remained elsewhere – with psychoanalysis and its history. So, I asked myself, where does psychoanalysis fit in to the various narratives Foucault gave? Tantalising at the end of *Madness and civilization*, implicit in *The birth of the clinic*, where a rigorous account of the 'modern' forms of the doctor–patient relationship was given,[5] and explicit in *The order of things*, as one of the two new sciences (the other being ethnology) that broke up the order of nineteenth-century sciences' *episteme*. What was more, Foucault's chapters on philology in the nineteenth century gave me moral and material support in my own attempt to argue the kinship, the genealogical relation, between philology and psychoanalysis.[6] But even then, Foucault seemed to me to be a little too coy about the historical position which Freud can be accorded, and, more to the point, the historical significance of the interpretative strategies of psychoanalysis. Yet I had little reason to think that this sense of dissatisfaction was anything more than a derivative of my own desire that Foucault, who was so magisterial and encyclopaedic in other areas, address the domain which I was trying to make my own.

However, when *La Volonté de savoir* came out, some of my questions were answered: it seemed as if psychoanalysis was the grandest and purest of those apparatuses for the generation of knowledge-power – the modern confessional discipline *par excellence*, and generator of a discourse that proclaimed evangelically that the truth of the subject was to be found in his or her secret discourse on sexuality. Indeed, Foucault wrote in that book that his enterprise could be read as the archaeology of psychoanalysis.[7] Yet there was something too neat about the project: if the book was the archaeology of psychoanalysis, why was there so little textual reference, so little explicit addressing of themes in psychoanalysis? To me, it seemed clear that many arguments were implicitly aimed at psychoanalysis (amongst other things) – yet sometimes the other things were so vaguely evoked, so tangential, while the unnamed object was so obviously psychoanalytic, that I felt that there was something odd, refracted and displaced about the book. My curiosity was aroused.

My next step in tracking down Foucault's relation to psycho-analysis was to go and ask him about it. Remarkably enough, that was no help at all – our quite lengthy discussion, while confirming and adding a new dimension to my admiration for him, gave me no sense whatsoever of what I deduced was a complex relation, even a complex genealogy. He proved genuinely evasive on this topic. So I turned scholar instead of journalist, and read with the secret glee of the would-be detective an early work of Foucault's, one that I have never seen discussed. I know of no other piece of his which prevents me from assuming that it was Foucault's earliest publication: the Introduction to a French translation of Ludwig Binswanger's *Traum und Existenz* (*Le Rêve et l'existence*).[8] Here I came upon a sense not only of Foucault's relation to psychoanalysis, but also of the seeds of other, probably more important, themes in his work.

Foucault's *Introduction*, published in 1954, included a lengthy discussion both of Freudian interpretation (focused, as the occa-sion clearly demanded, on the dream) and of the theory of the subject in psychoanalysis. Here are two themes which are immedi-ately apparent in Foucault's later work – the criticism of a variety of metaphysics of interpretation (the most obvious text here is *The archaeology of knowledge*,[9] but one should not forget the critique of the techniques of the confessional targeted in *The history of sexuality. Vol. I*) and of the concept of the subject it generates: the project to which Foucault would turn in what were to be his final books.[10]

Foucault's *Introduction* aims to show how Binswanger's dream analysis goes beyond both Freudian hermeneutic techniques and Husserlian phenomenology. The main weight of criticism of the Freudian technique falls on its failure to give sufficient account of the innate expressivity of the image prior to, or beyond, any semantic, representational analysis. Freudian semantic analysis completely overlooks the morphological and syntactic structure proper to the image in itself, and never succeeds in 'reconstituting the expressive act itself in its necessity'.[11] Foucault perceives Freud, and psychoanalytic techniques following him, as funda-mentally evading a confrontation with the subjectivity expressed in the image, the morphology proper to the imaginary:

what counts is that the image has its own dynamic powers, that there is a different morphology of imaginary space when what is at issue is free, light-filled space, or when the space at work is that of the prison of obscurity and of suffocation. The imaginary world has its own laws, its specific structures – the image is a bit more than the immediate fulfilment of meaning; it has its own density, and the laws of the world are not solely the decrees of a single will, were that one divine. Freud has furnished the world of the imaginary with Desire, just as classical metaphysics had inhabited the physical world with the divine will and understanding: a theology of significations in which truth anticipates its own formulation, and entirely constitutes it. The significations exhaust the reality of the world through which it makes itself known.[12]

To the question, 'Why does meaning express itself in images in the dream?', Foucault points out that Freud has two responses. Firstly, that repression necessitates the veiling, the covering over of the original semantic, verbal meaning of the dream. Secondly, Freud has recourse to a concept of the 'primitively imaginary character of the satisfaction of desire' (p. 23), an important connection but one which is only partial in that Foucault overlooks the fact that the meaning of the original image (the hallucinated breast, or the perception of the primal scene) is conferred on it only retrospectively. Hence, he continues, the inadequacy of Freudian analysis stems from its defective theory of the symbol, which it regards either as a limpid signification or as an image conceived of as a 'transformed and transformable residue of perception' (p. 24), a thin pellicule which separates, through joining, the outside and the inside, the unconscious drive and the conscious perception, the implicit language and the sensible image.

Foucault sees no resolution of this problem in the historical development of psychoanalysis. One wing of this development, represented by Melanie Klein, centres on the analysis and tracing of the development of fantasies, of images, conceived of as the primitive matter of psychological experience; but for the Kleinians, at bottom, meaning is simply the mobility of the image, the furrow of its trajectory. The other wing is represented by Lacan, who

seeks in language the dialectical element in which is constituted the entire set of the significations of existence, and in which they come to fruition . . . Lacan has done everything possible to show in the Imago the point where the significatory dialectic of language is located and where it leaves itself fascinated by the interlocutor by which it is constituted.   (p. 27)

But as a consequence, in Lacan's work, 'the Imago is only an enveloped speech, a silent moment' (p. 27). Hence the failure of psychoanalysis, represented at the time of Foucault's writing by the one-sided, complementary double failures of the Kleinian and

Lacanian schools, was that it 'had never managed to make images speak' (p. 28).

On the other hand, Husserlian phenomenology fares little better, suffering from an opposite problem. While it recognises 'signification in the context of the expressive act which grounds it' and, 'to that extent, a phenomenological description is capable of revealing the presence of meaning in an imaginary content, (pp. 37–8), it leads to a total interiority and therefore the question of the other becomes insoluble for it. Jaspers had recognised this problem, but his only answer to it had been to introduce what Foucault calls a 'mystical concept of communication between doctor and patient'.[13] In Foucault's eyes, Binswanger manages to make up for these complementary lacks of Freudian psychoanalysis and Husserlian phenomenology.

The uncharacteristic flavour of Foucault's critique of psychoanalysis becomes even clearer in Foucault's account of Dora's successful termination of her analysis with Freud. Freud misunderstood Dora's second dream, which announces her means of escape, her plan to go on alone, without him, without Herr K., free from the iron law of Freud's theory of identification, in which every image of herself and of the others is just a representation, and a representation of something else. What Foucault cannot allow Freud is his practice of interpreting everything that Dora might avow as if it might stand for someone else's desire:[14] beyond Freud's interpretations, Dora's dream refers to a

mode of existence of which this history is, finally, only the chronology: an existence in which the foreign sexuality of men appears solely under the sign of hostility, of constraint, of an irruption which culminates in rape; an existence which doesn't even become actualised in the sexuality of women, however close and parallel it is, but which inscribes its most profound significations in acts of rupture, one of which, and it is the most decisive, will put an end to her psychoanalysis. One can say that Dora was cured, not despite the interruption of her analysis, but because, in taking the decision to interrupt it, she fully and completely took on herself her solitude. (p. 77)

What is most deficient in Freud's interpretations is not his overlooking the fact that she was giving notice to him as much as to Herr K., so much as the radical objectification of the subject Freud assumes in the dream: the subject is always at the mercy of the game of some other,[15] 'suspended in some way between the dreamer and that of which he dreams' (p. 79).

The proof of this is that for Freud, this game can, through an effective alienating identification, represent others, or that another person can, through a sort of *héautoscopie*, represent the dreamer himself. (p. 79)

What has to be counterposed to this interpretative strategy – which we can, with hindsight, immediately recognise as what Lacan calls the fading of the subject, the perpetual covering over of the subject by the signifiers, ultimately the signifiers of the Other – is Binswanger's starting-point:

This subject is not described as one of the possible significations of one of the characters, but as the foundation of every single one of the eventual significations of the dream, and to that extent, it is not the re-edition of a prior form or an archaic stage within the personality, rather it appears as the unfolding and the totality of its existence itself. (p. 80)

Although the critique of psychoanalysis based upon the ineffability of the image might well surprise, given that it comes from the pen of an author who would later be capable – in his virtuoso interpretations of *Las Meninas*, of Bentham's Panopticon, of Magritte's paintings – of unwinding the expressivity of an image till it could sum up the thought, the experience of space and power of an age, that very virtuosity may well render it understandable.[16] When, however, it is also coupled with what, with hindsight, looks like a defence of the self-determining responsible subject, we should reflect further. After all, this is a critique from the pen of an author who wrote, in his 'What is an author?', of the necessary simultaneous dispersion of (at least) three egos by the 'author-function'; this is a critique to be placed alongside his famous words: 'I am no doubt not the only one who writes in order to have no face. Do not ask who I am and do not ask me to remain the same: leave it to our bureaucrats and our police to see that our papers are in order. At least spare us their morality when we write.'[17]

The brilliance of Foucault's analysis should not hide the fact that here, in 1954, he is fighting something of a rearguard action against the power of psychoanalytic discourse. Throughout, he admits the force of Freud's interpretative strategies. Yet Freud's discourse is recognised as imperialistic: it would take into itself the expressivity of the image without recognising the language peculiar to the visual, and it would brush aside all claims of the subject to be distinct from its various others, to be a subject capable of being solid, being a subject in solitude. The subject must be grounded, Foucault seems to be saying, and it must be grounded prior to and within the act of interpretation; maybe, even, the two critiques are linked and

Foucault would have wished to have grounded the subject in a direct relation to the image. This, given the state of Lacanian theorisation, and of Foucault's obvious awareness of it,[18] would have been an idiosyncratic, almost Canute-like position, as the Lacanian discourse, year by year, in the seminars at Sainte-Anne which Foucault attended, articulated the manner in which the ego was an effect of the subject's fascination with the image.

II

Having established that Foucault's relationship to psychoanalysis was already complex in the early 1950s, before he wrote *L'Histoire de la folie*, in this section I shall be concerned with two entirely distinct arguments concerning the history of psychoanalysis to be found in his later writings. The first, easier to discuss, but conceptually more difficult, arises from the history of scientific ideas that is to be found in his *The order of things* (1966). In this account, psychoanalysis takes up a key position in the history of the development of what, for convenience's sake, I will call the human sciences. What is of interest to Foucault in psychoanalysis is the system of concepts associated with the unconscious: meaning, signification and the system of significations.[19] Foucault relates the crucial function of psychoanalysis to its nodal point in the anatomy of the human sciences at the end of the nineteenth century. His argument is as follows. The space within which the human sciences were constructed, from about 1800 onwards, was determined by the formation of three separate sciences: biology, economics and philology. Each of these was founded upon one central concept: for biology, the concept of function; for economics, the concept of conflict; for philology, the concept of sign. The specifically *human* sciences were then constituted by borrowing models from these three forms of knowledge, and the shift from one to another borrowed model can be seen to have taken place within any given human science. But it seems that there existed some sort of 'natural' affinity between the biological concept of function and the concepts elaborated in psychology, between the economic concept of conflict and the concepts found in sociology, and, thirdly, between the concept of sign and the science of literature. Exciting and controversial moments of crisis for practitioners of, say, sociology occurred when they switched from one borrowed model to another: for instance, from that of conflict to that of the sign. When this 'event' took place the result was a debate between those who founded sociology upon a notion of the function of institutions and those who founded sociology upon the system of signs that make up society. The passage from Durkheim and Malinowski to Lévi-Strauss might be conceived of in this manner.

Each of these three concepts could thus be borrowed from sciences that, through their formation, had created the possibility of an imaginary point which the concept of man was to fill. The space defined by the three conceptual dimensions, when visualised as three axes defining such a three-dimensional space, is that occupied by the human sciences. The point of origin, where the dimensions 'meet' or 'originate', is the concept 'man', a concept which did not exist before these three separate dimensions came into existence at the end of the eighteenth century. As Foucault puts it, 'the human being, with his power to represent himself with representations, arises in a space hollowed out by living beings, objects of exchange, and words . . .'[20]

These three sciences reveal to man his own finitude: the end of life, the disappearance of desire, the last word. Foucault implies that the human sciences do not confront the consequences of this finitude. In a sense they attempt to construct analyses that will make such a limit disappear, so that biology and psychology analyse life as if death were just a contingent event; economics and sociology analyse the system of conflicts and laws as if desire were the permanent substrate that is their *sine qua non*; and philology can never countenance the possibility that a word will one time be uttered that does not call for a further word, an answer, a reply. The significance that Foucault gives to psychoanalysis can then be specified as follows:

(1) Firstly, Freud broke down the distinction between the abnormal and the normal, between the significant and the insignificant. In psychoanalytic theory, a continuum replaces the break that biology had introduced with the contrast between the pathological and the physiological.[21] Are we abnormal or are we normal? Within psychoanalysis, the question can no longer be answered: it has become foolish. Similarly, there is nothing that is insignificant to the psychoanalyst, a feature of common knowledge well represented by the fact that unimportant speech defects are called 'Freudian slips'. But we can put this feature of psychoanalysis into a more striking perspective when we recognise that psychoanalysis is interested in two sorts of phenomena: the little things, like 'Freudian slips', dreams and jokes – things too insignificant to be worthy

of attention. And it is also interested – in exactly the same way, with exactly the same degree of free-floating attention – in lovers who commit murders, or in little boys who want to have sexual intercourse with their mothers; in other words, in those people who are mad enough to die for love, mad enough to love until death brings a final disruption of the union between subject and object – those tragedies for which the term 'hubris' indicates that we are dealing with phenomena mid-way between the acts of gods and those of men.

This 'modernist' move of Freud's establishing the continuum of significance, heralded the switch-over from the nineteenth-century concern with function to a concern with its paired concept, the norm; from the concern with conflict to a concern with the rules that resolve or represent the conflict; from the concern with the sign to a concern with the system of signification that determines the value of the sign, its meaning. True to the concerns of intellectual life in post-war France, Foucault lays most emphasis on the last of these three, the system, since it is the system that codifies rules and determines norms, as well as determining all that can be said. Freud thus becomes the harbinger of all that was to happen in the twentieth century in the human sciences, since he could take the logic of the biological (what preserves life), the logic of the economic (conflict lies at the heart of all manifestations of value), and wed them to the logic of language, to a system of signification: 'Freud more than anyone else brought the knowledge of man closer to its philological and linguistic model'.[22]

(2) Freud also made explicit a feature of the new sciences that until then had lain in shadow: the unconscious. Of course, the biological concept of function or the economic concept of conflict – not to mention the concept of sign – entailed that the unconscious be posited, that these conflicts, functions and signs act outside of consciousness. But the human sciences derived from these concepts hoped to avoid the concept of the unconscious. It always seemed possible that the concept of need, which is the corollary of the concept of function, would prove itself capable of representation in consciousness, so that psychology could hope to observe the projection of its founding biological concepts by surveying the contents of consciousness. Hence, with Freud, a resolute attempt to pare back the claims of consciousness to be a privileged court of appeal in the human sciences seems to set itself against the very notion of man.

(3) Thirdly, and most importantly, what Foucault calls 'a perpetual principle of dissatisfaction, of calling into question',[23] is to be found in psychoanalysis. Foucault regards this as the chief value of psychoanalysis, making it a unique human science, almost the meta-human science – the science that is continually criticising the very possibility of there ever being a human science.[24] As Lagrange succinctly describes Foucault's view: 'Camped amongst the Sciences of Man like the Trojan Horse, [psychoanalysis] comes to disturb the latter in their anthropological sleep.'[25] Psychoanalysis directly addresses the question of the *possibility* of representation – whether of conflict, of desire, or of signification – by expecting it precisely in that most contradictory of places, the unconscious, and can thus go beyond the level of function, rule and sign to find below them the figures that represent man's finitude, the figures that represent the limits and the principles that both sustain and undermine the human sciences: mute death, naked desire and a language that is the supreme delegate of the law.[26]

Much of this account was distinctly under the influence of a particular reading of psychoanalysis, that conducted by Jacques Lacan.[27] Setting out this influence on Foucault should, however, by no means preoccupy us. Rather, let me just try and indicate what Foucault finds of value in psychoanalysis: the concept of the unconscious as the limiting concept of all the human sciences, from which emanates a perpetual suspicion, extending over all the sciences that construct the object 'man', but which can only borrow their conceptual armouries from elsewhere. We may even be able to give to psychoanalysis a social dimension that further illuminates this perpetual suspicion, this sense of its always being at a distance from those comfortable concepts that give man a nature. We can recognise that psychoanalysts have constructed for themselves an institutional affiliation that is independent of the universities, that is independent of the state apparatuses of health and happiness, and that is even suspicious, at least in Britain, of those who cast themselves as a cultural elite, the intellectuals. The effects of the psychoanalysts' suspicion – which will thus appear, according to which of these institutions is examining its 'outside', as flabby unsubstantiated theory, as middle-class self-indulgence, or as anti-intellectualism – paranoid as it may sometimes seem, are perhaps not only their means of survival, but also their most priceless possession.

The other science that finds a special critical status in Foucault's account, ethnology, is isolated for another reason. It is founded upon the notion of an undiscoverable Other, obeying an imperative to search it out, looking at every face in every country to see if this might be the one that will be just a face, and only a face, thus giving the anthropologist an end to her search, having found another who is so inhuman that she can be recognised as oneself, like Narcissus looking at his reflection. Put psychoanalysis and ethnology together, and we have the wandering Jew, or, perhaps, the urban gypsy.

Let us now turn to the second of Foucault's books that I wish to discuss in some detail: *La Volonté de savoir*, translated as *The history of sexuality. Vol. I: An introduction*. Foucault's initial question is: why, since the eighteenth century, have we talked so much about sex? And we can immediately see that, behind every argument in this book, Foucault will be conducting an interrogation of psychoanalysis, which has given the purest expression to the notion that the subject's truth is to be found through a discourse on his or her sexuality. What is more intimate seems to be most important and precious. But, in this new work, Foucault's emphasis has shifted: he is not so much interested in the historical and epistemological foundations of the sciences, in an archaeology of knowledge as he called it. Rather, he is interested in the strategy of power that knowledge embodies; he is interested in what he calls *savoir-pouvoir*, knowledge-power.[28] And, in consequence, instead of being a critical event in the history of the human sciences, psychoanalysis will be only one element in the entire apparatus of knowledge-power.[29] The forms of knowledge that one finds in pedagogy, psychiatry, sexology, criminology, etc., are interesting in so far as they are bound up with relations of power, and psychoanalysis will, it seems, be of interest because of its *similarities* to psychiatry, to criminology, to paediatrics, because it has a place in this new apparatus, rather than because it is their privileged critic. Let us turn to this discourse on sexuality.

Foucault's claims are two-fold: first, the form of discourse on sexuality that has become obligatory for us moderns is a transformation of the pastoral confession of medieval Christianity, which became slowly detached from the aim of spiritual guidance and obedience, and in the eighteenth century became affiliated to institutions that employed it for the purposes of regulating the lives of their confined inmates: convents, schools, military academies. In the nineteenth century, the confession became incorporated in those forms of knowledge that can be called human sciences:

pedagogy, medicine, criminology, psychiatry – those I called the professional apparatus for health and happiness. Through this movement, 'sexuality', as a property of bodies and as an object of knowledge, was created, and eventually became the secret of all secrets, the essential truth about that other concept that was generated in the same movement: the individual. The argument, compressed, thus runs: in giving birth to the individual, the professionals of man installed a truth within him, as the secret core of his being – his sexuality. It is this secret that must at all times be sought out if knowledge of humans is to be had. And the feeling we have, as objects of this compulsion to yield up our secret truths, is that we can never say enough, that we are necessarily too timid, fearful, anxious or suspicious. The essential always manages to escape us.

Before we turn to the second major claim that Foucault makes, we can see that psychoanalysis is here cast in quite another light. It appears as the purified modern form of the confessional, and it embodies more clearly than any other discipline the conception of man's truth as being a sexual secret, of our truth being embodied in a tale of two bodies: mine and the other's. Foucault's second major claim also implicates psychoanalysis. He disputes the reality of that wave of sexual repression that supposedly overtook Western society in the nineteenth century, from which psychoanalysis has often been claimed, and certainly has claimed itself, as helping to rescue us. Rather, Foucault sees the superficial layers of Victorian prudery as incidental to the main historical movement, which installed discourses on sexuality as among the chief agents of social control, and which constructed and gave body to the individual who was to be controlled. (In contrast, where later there would be individuals imbued with criminality, or patients with dispositions, before the nineteenth century, there were crimes the agents of which were to be punished, and there were illnesses to be cured.)[30] Going further, Foucault questions the value of the model of power that the concept of repression involves, which he calls the 'juridico-discursive' model. The notion of power modelled upon repression calls on two ideas for its support: firstly, law is taken as the exemplary institution in which power is exercised; secondly, its privileged mode of operation is negation. Foucault wishes to replace this juridical model with a more military notion, one in which the strategy and tactics of the exercise of power are paramount, where the exercise of power is positive as well as negative, in which incorporation, annexation and infiltration are more important modes of operation than suppression. 'Should we turn the expression round, then, and say that politics is war pursued by other means?'[31] And his next step is to dispute a model of the relations between the subject and power that involves an opposition between desire and the law, between the free and individual energy that constitutes the subject, and the codified system that mirrors, reflects and enfolds this desire.[32] We must dispense with the humanistic faith that truth is on the side of freedom, rising above the brutish manifestations of power, to replace it with an idea that truth and power cannot be separated, that domination produces truth as well as truth domination.

One has a strange feeling as one reads this book of Foucault's. It is like reading Freud, but with all the signs changed. When Freud outlined his concept of repression, he described it as an exclusion, a negation, a forceful setting apart. In so far as desire wells up from within the repressed, this desire is also constituted in the moment in which the repressed is distanced from the 'official', 'censoring' system. So it seems as if Foucault is borrowing Freud's undoubtedly clear concept of repression and turning it inside out. The tradition that comes to fruition with Freud, from Hegel to Marx and beyond, a tradition that partakes of the key notion of conflict that Foucault had earlier analysed, and which is dialectical in so far as this conflict is constituted through a sequence of successive negations – this tradition is now subjected to an attack that bears similarities to the 'deconstruction' that Nietzsche carried out on Hegel.

Foucault's two arguments thus seem to bear directly upon psychoanalysis and thus make one see the absence of discussion of psychoanalysis as requiring comment, if not explanation. One senses that this lack of explicitness is a cunning tactical device. Let us now examine one of Foucault's claims, in order to see what it will do for our perception of psychoanalysis and its history.

Perhaps the largest and vaguest claim is that the discourse on sexuality that is so peculiar to our century is the consequence of manoeuvres involving the practice of confession, that this discourse is due to the successful fusion of the seemingly radically dissimilar sacred procedures of confession and scientific canons of acceptable discursivity. Notice that this is a much more interesting claim than saying, as has often been said, that psychoanalysis is 'like' confession. In his earliest writings on psychoanalysis, Freud himself drew the analogy, at a time when he believed that simply putting experiences into words amounted to a discharge of what had been dammed up by repression. Since then, many others have used the analogy for the unlikely purpose of showing that psychoanalysis is more like a religion than a science. Foucault's much more interesting point is that traditional methods for the welding of a soul on to the body of the church were transformed when they were assimilated into the canons of scientific discourse.[33] How was this achieved?

Foucault gives four conditions that made this achievement possible:[34]

(1) A clinical codification of the procedure for making someone talk: anamneses, a system of questions, a system of interpretation akin to that practised on bodily signs and symptoms.

(2) A general and diffuse notion of causality, acting as a guarantee that, no matter how far off it might seem at first sight, the concentrated causal power of sexuality is there to be discovered. How can we not recognise here that distinctive combination of 'pansexualism' linked to the rigorously dogmatic doctrine of psychic determinism, so characteristic of psychoanalysis?

(3) The premise that the truth of sexuality is essentially clandestine, elusive and latent. Note that this argument, when found in psychoanalysis, appears both at the level of the biological phases – the 'latency' phase, which at times Freud seemed to regard as the crucial causal factor in human beings' vulnerability to neurosis – as well as in the notion that sexuality is 'the secret' *par excellence*, so that there is an opposition between sexuality and language.[35]

(4) The logic of the censor, by which the not-permitted, the not-said, and the non-existent support and confuse one another.[36]

Each of these arguments, which Foucault wishes us to take as describing a historical movement which gained momentum from the eighteenth century onwards, corresponds to a feature of the practice of psychoanalysis that psychoanalysis itself theorises. Firstly, the 'clinical codification' found in psychoanalysis is simple, and, quite rightly, is known as the fundamental rule: say whatever comes into your head. No simpler or purer method of making the subject speak could be found.[37] Secondly, as we have already noted, the pansexualism and the psychic determinism of Freud are the necessary conditions for the interminably hopeful inquiries undertaken in the search for the secret of secrets – the moment when sexuality inflicted itself upon the subject. Thirdly, the latency of all that is important and all that is sexual in psychoanalysis is no secret. 'What is hidden is probably sexual' is the rule of thumb of the working psychoanalyst. And fourthly, in the world of fantasy, where all is sexual, there is no distinction between the non-existent and the existent, between the permitted and the not permitted, between the said and the not said (since all can and should be said): in consequence the logic of the censor in psychoanalysis passes via 'all is possible' to 'all is impossible': what is technically known in psychoanalysis as the unconscious sense of guilt evoked by deeds performed in fantasy.

So it is as if Foucault had read Freud and turned his account of the *science* of psychoanalysis on its head, turning it into a *historical* account of how we, all of us, are subject to this need, this compulsion, or perhaps, simply this *desire* to talk out the mystery of mysteries. In place of Freud describing what occurs in psycho-analysis, we have Foucault describing what goes on in our everyday discourse. Their arguments are strictly homologous. Yet there is a difference. It is clear that, by the time that he wrote *La Volonté de savoir*, Foucault's admiration for psychoanalysis, at its height in the mid 1960s, had somewhat diminished. Instead of a paean of praise, he has surreptitiously and obliquely lifted the framework of psycho-analysis out of its institutional and conceptual bracket and has turned it into a historical account through which one should understand the set of conditions by which the chaos of history could have come to produce a configuration of desire, power and know-ledge that exists 'within' us.

Along the way, some of the claims that psychoanalysis made for itself are shown to be inaccurate: infantile sexuality was recognised as something dangerous, as something to be regulated, way back in the eighteenth century. Freud can lay no claim to have discovered it. Foucault also sets out the frame of knowledge and power that governed the theory of the perversions from the mid nineteenth century on: the classification and discovery of homosexuality, maso-chism, sadism, narcissism, fetishism. All these were the work of psy-chiatrists in quest of the essential nature of the pathology of human-ity. At this point, Foucault's account of psychoanalysis in *The order of things* proves useful: Freud never claimed to have discovered the perversions. What he did to them was, firstly, to remove them from the realm of the pathological, by dislocating the distinction between the normal and the pathological, and, secondly, to have shown them to be the mirror images of the various infantile sexualities, and pre-cisely not the exclusive property of those who were forced to submit to the scrutiny of the psychiatrists. What Freud *did* do was to generalise the investigative methods of psychiatrists so that these could be brought to bear upon those previously thought to be normal, in consequence discovering the same series of essences – the masculine, the feminine, the passive, the active – and the same perverse desires, wherever the subject could speak his secret.

Having undermined the claims of psychoanalysis to be original in the minimally significant sense of 'having priority', Foucault's argument then undergoes one of the strange reversals that he is so adept in detecting elsewhere. He *borrows back* the structure of psychoanalytic theory and transforms it into a historical account of the conditions that underlie the coming into being of the sexual apparatus in which the body and truth are knitted together. If imitation is a form of flattery, one cannot but detect a profound admiration lurking behind the version of psychoanalysis that Foucault has produced. But change the inflection slightly and imitation is transformed into mockery, whose consequences are important.

The first consequence is that Foucault displaces the scientific arguments of psychoanalysis, transforming them into the conditions under which a historical system of discourses, of knowledge-power, came into existence. The investigator of the psyche is revealed as a closet metaphysician of history, as if he were a modern-day Kant, who had forgotten to rewrite the *Critique of pure reason* as philosophy instead of as psychology. The mode of discourse which we find so compelling and natural is that whose possibility is outlined clearly in psychoanalytic theory. We live within a culture defined by psychoanalysis. Psychoanalysis is not confined to the relation between armchair and couch; it is not a privileged form of speech that can exist only in one room, in one space, under limited and specifiable material conditions. Rather, the micro-political web in which we ourselves can hope to find the relations of truth, knowledge and sexuality is precisely that which psychoanalysis has thrown to catch us in. One is reminded of the thesis presented some years ago by Philip Rieff, in his excellent book, *Freud. The mind of the moralist*.[38] Rieff centres his account of Freud and his impact on the twentieth century round the notion of 'psychological man', the type created by, supported by and susceptible to psychoanalysis. Foucault's idea is similar, but is that much more rigorous – and critical. His work could well have been retitled, *An archaeology of psychoanalysis*; indeed, he closes the main part of the book with the sentence: 'The history of the deployment of sexuality [*dispositif de sexualité*], as it has evolved since the classical age, can serve as an archaeology of psychoanalysis.'[40] And he is always finding new historical functions to assign to psychoanalysis. At one point, it is the one institution in the 'great family of technologies of sex' that 'rigorously opposed the political and institutional effects of the perversion–heredity–degenerescence system'.[41] At another, Foucault finally determines that the radical aspect of Freud's work resides in his opposition to the heavy weight of hereditary degeneration that soldered the individual to his progenitors and his progeny. And there is no doubt that this is the case: as Freud noted in a letter to Fliess in 1897, he had made it his 'business to oust hereditary predisposition from the explanation of neurosis'.[42] While Freud came later to spell out the importance of a residual concept of 'constitution',[43] the aim of psychoanalysis always remained the examination of those 'accidental' factors that determine the character of neurosis, constitution serving as the last resort and boundary limit of its explanatory procedures.

Foucault again seems quite correct when he argues that psychoanalysis, following the logic of its refusal to link neurotics, perverts, onanists and syphilitics into one unit of 'bad blood' – namely the family – underwent a curious reversal in returning its clients back to mummy and daddy:

But it was precisely here that psychoanalysis, whose technical procedure seemed to place the confession of sexuality outside family jurisdiction, rediscovered right at the heart of this sexuality, as the principle of its formation and as the key to its intelligibility – the law of alliance, the confused workings of marriage and kinship, incest.[43]

Foucault argues that one of the major achievements of psychoanalysis was to bind back together the two great systems, that of alliance, and that of sexuality, through the linking concept of the Oedipus complex, in which the father as sovereign, as legislator, as pure negation of desire, is reinstated alongside the eternal and never to be forgotten embodiment of all possible sexualities, the mother. The Oedipus complex thus managed to stitch back together what was falling apart, to keep sewn together the pre-industrial law of the family and the knowledge-power embodied in the new discourses on the *individual*'s sexuality. But, Foucault argues, this could be done only by employing a concept of power that did not correspond to the new realities: it could only 'surround desire with all the trappings of the old order of power': 'the law of alliance, tabooed consanguinity and the Sovereign-Father'.[44]

This achievement of psychoanalysis, still worthy of Foucault's political approval in so far as it was continually suspicious of the new proliferations of power, lays the foundation for the critique of psychoanalysis that Foucault mounts. The repressive hypothesis, embedded deep within psychoanalysis, was originally borrowed from the juridico-discursive discourse elaborated by the Absolutist State from the medieval period onwards. Here, again, Foucault's argument has a certain plausibility when applied to psychoanalysis. As Reich remarked, the early Freud, when elaborating the concept of repression in the 1890s and early 1900, was a far more 'radical' social thinker than the later pessimistic proponent of the concept of the death instinct. A paper such as his '"Civilized" sexual morality and modern nervous illness' (1908) directly equated the processes of psychic repression and the forces of moral repression represented in law and convention.[45] Despite the good intentions with which Freud generated the hypothesis of repression and the Oedipus complex, it is exactly upon those concepts that Foucault's critique bears.

However, perhaps Foucault is making an error in taking the psychoanalytic concept of repression to be so crucial to the widespread theory of the negative character of power and its climatic triumph in the nineteenth century. His critique may well be apposite when directed at three specific targets: those social theorists who conceive of power as essentially negative, juridical and 'nay-saying' in character; those French psychoanalysts who employ the Lacanian equations of authority, the father and the Law (whether the latter be natural or social); and, thirdly, those analysts who regard repression as constituting the relation between desire and the unconscious. But in 'classical' psychoanalysis, repression is only one of the defence mechanisms. It was the first one to receive Freud's detailed attention, and thus become a theoretical element, but it was eventually only one amongst several others: reaction-formation, isolation, undoing what had been done, projection, etc. In recognising this fact, and in thus replacing the concept of repression by that of defence in 1926, Freud noted the following:

Our first observations of repression and of the formation of symptoms were made in connection with hysteria . . . Later on, when we came to study the obsessional neuroses, we found that in that illness pathogenic occurrences are not forgotten. They remain conscious but they are 'isolated' in some way that we cannot as yet grasp, so that much the same result is obtained as in hysterical amnesia.[46]

We can draw two consequences from this passage. Firstly, the defences invoked by psychoanalysis are much more varied than the simple negative absence connoted by repression; indeed, they correspond quite closely to the broader, more positive forms of power that Foucault wishes to accentuate. Secondly, Freud's suggestion that repression is specific to hysteria might help us to give greater historical specificity to some of Foucault's discussion of the constitution of the hysterised woman, who was both completely sexual and also without sex (the virgin and the prostitute). But we shall be able to do this only if we can admit that repression is indeed *one* of the manifestations of *savoir-pouvoir*, a claim that Foucault would probably not have denied. And, having made this claim, we begin to wonder whether Foucault's critique of the repressive hypothesis was not a little beside the point, a little too strong for the purposes for which it was designed. After all, many recent works by historians, both in the English- and French-speaking worlds, have concentrated on forms of social control and discipline that are not simply variations on the theme of a repressive Victorian epoch. Certainly psychoanalysis, including that variety still holding centre-stage in France, describes a rich variety of mechanisms by which desire is deflected from its aim, thus receiving its diffuse transformations. And the French structuralists' programme always emphasised the 'system', the network of linkages, the webs of relations, rather than the simple refusal and metaphorical death that Foucault imputed to the theorists of the repressive society. Shorn of its antithetical references to the weight of negative law, and to the absolute right of refusal of the Sovereign, Foucault's espousal of a positive concept of power does not seem so strikingly novel.

The critical dimension of Foucault's argument lies in his perception that the twin pillars of the 'deployment of sexuality' – the notion that the truth of the subject is to be found hidden in his sexuality and the notion that repression is the model of models by which to describe power relations – these two pillars are a major support for whatever forms of domination presently exist. Psychoanalysis is of great interest for two reasons: it actually supplies this conceptual apparatus with which to analyse how this 'apparatus' (*dispositif*) of sexuality, this Sexual Talking Machine, produces its effects. Secondly, it is the purest and the most economical version of the whole apparatus of domination. It dominates employing only two rules: the 'fundamental rule', 'say it aloud', and the rules of the contract that is drawn up between analyst and analysand. Psychoanalysis claims to have no ruling ideology. Rather, as Foucault had argued in his earlier work, it embodies a principle of perpetual suspicion, such that it eschews the truth-values as represented by academic discourse, the moral values as represented by the professions of care (medicine, social work, prison officers), and the values of reasoned domination that make up political thought. The only value it will explicitly allow itself is the belief in positivistic science that Freud thought was the least distorted expression of 'the soft voice of the intellect'[47] – and some of the sterner analysts would regard this residual belief of Freud's as something of an aberration. But it is in so far as it does conform to the canons of scientific discursivity implied by the notion of Reason (*logos*) that Foucault can find there the purified form of confession, now so purified that no pardon, no admonition, no advice, not even a response is to be expected from the confessor. And, seemingly, precisely because of that, the subject is that much more profoundly subject to the strategy of domination inherent in the Sexual Talking Machine.[48]

What has happened to the theses of Foucault's earlier work? We have seen that the principle of perpetual suspicion now acts in the direction of making psychoanalysis the purest and most powerful example of the new mechanism of power that Foucault has set out to describe. Whereas in *The order of things*, the principle of perpetual suspicion aligned psychoanalysis on the side of critical thought, thought critical of the claims to hegemony of the human sciences, in *The history of sexuality* its principle of suspicion is the clearest embodiment of the conditions without which the deployment of sexuality would not be possible.[49] But what of the notion of the unconscious, what of the figures of man's finitude whose recognition appeared to be unique to psychoanalysis? In an interview that Foucault gave in 1977, a confrontation between him and the Lacanian school of psychoanalysis, he stated that the importance of Freud was twofold: firstly, his firm shift away from the hereditarian and racist theories of abnormality characteristic of the late nineteenth century; secondly, and more importantly, the concept of interpretation and the hermeneutic of the unconscious that one finds in *The interpretation of dreams*.[50] But one should be careful to separate out two components from this latter judgement. Firstly, as we have seen, Foucault's critique bears down very forcibly upon the notion that truth is secret and is to be found at the heart of the subject's most forgotten and private inner discourse – as we have seen and as we shall see when we examine the concluding volumes of *The history of sexuality*, throughout his œuvre, Foucault's hostility to such hermeneutical strategies was unwavering. Secondly, Foucault also casts critical light upon the notion that truth is a means of liberation, that truth is always on the side of the repressed, of the oppressed, of the dominated – a final consolation for God's always being on the side of the big battalions. What he can still find of value in the psychoanalytic theory of the unconscious is – and this is where he remains 'French' in a way that is perhaps still foreign to us Anglo-Saxons – the fact that it entails a displacement of the subject from its position at the centre, from its position as a desiring, judging, dominating and eternally efficacious origin. Foucault introduces the concept of the subject, not as a foundation, but as a part of a play of forces, a play of forces of domination and discourse, so that the subject is first and foremost subject to, rather than subject of. It is this innovation of psychoanalysis, what Freud called his 'Copernican revolution', that Foucault can still find of value. It was this idea that was crucial to the critique of the concept of man in his earlier book, and thus to the subversion of the possibility of the sciences of man. Yet, in his defence of Dora in 1954, it was his close identification of the Freudian strategies of interpretation with this dispersed, decentred subject that led him to reject the latter, and psychoanalysis with it. However, it is now, in *La Volonté de savoir*, this notion that underlies his new theory of the strategies of power, in which the skirmishes pass via the subjects of knowledge, themselves continually shifting as knowledge shifts in response to the guerrilla tactics of those being dominated. In these new strategies, to speak of the juridico-discursive subject as the central point in the relations of domination is to be blind to the actual play of forces. In this new reality, Foucault argues, it is psychiatrists as much as judges who exert *savoir-pouvoir*, as much bureaucrats as legislators who decide on the points of concentration of power. It is these newer forces that have created the family as the privileged locus of sexual feelings, their hothouse, and that have subjected us to those familiar familial sentiments of coercion, subversion and despair, rather than such sentiments being due to the father functioning as domestic legislator, or to the mother functioning as a charitable agent, doing daddy's dirty work for him.

We have shifted, with Foucault, from surveying the grand sweep of the sciences, marked out by proper names such as Cuvier, Marx, Freud, Durkheim, Goldstein, Watson and Lacan, to a different sort of science of man:[51] that practised by psychiatrists in clinics and asylums; that found at work in schools, coded in rules of conduct and elaborated in heated staff-room discussion rather than in the faculty of philosophy; that science of man embodied in the architecture of prisons, whose practitioners are probation officers, welfare workers, the governors of borstals, rather than professors of criminology. Yet again psychoanalysis has a special place in this schema, since it figures on both lists. It figures on the first list as representing the crucial term in the elaboration of the metaphysics of the disappearance of man which Foucault discussed in *The order of things*. It figures on the second list as the purest version of the social practices that exercise domination in and through discourse, whose power lies in words, whose words can never be anything other than instruments of power. Foucault came to judge the second list of more importance, since it allows one to analyse not only the conditions of the possibility of a given historical configuration of knowledge, but also the shape of the power relations that are inherent in knowledge. Unconscious there may well be, but what is more important is to establish the epistemological spaces across which the play of knowledge-power creates and dissolves subjects, and creates and dissolves the knowledge that is constitutive of their position in a universe in which there is no liberty outside and no repression within.

How do these two different accounts of psychoanalysis affect the sort of history we will give it? Firstly, the account in *The order of things* will affect our history on the level of ideas; it will affect what used to be called 'internalist' history of science. The first 'internalist' consequence is that a new set of affiliations and historical relations can immediately be perceived. Up to now, the history of psychoanalysis has been written by historians of science who have taken into account the medical and biological contexts of its inception and development.[52] If Foucault's emphasis on economics and philology is correct, we may do well to search other sources and fields of knowledge adjacent to psychoanalysis. The concepts of sign, system of signification, meaning: the array of methods elaborated by philologists, mythologists and comparative anthropologists designed for the deciphering of texts; the perpetual dissolution of the boundary between the significant and the insignificant, between common sense and nonsense, paralleling the breakdown of the boundary between the normal and the pathological – all these were crucial features of psychoanalysis borrowed from and built upon the methods and findings of nineteenth-century linguistic science.[53] A profitable area for further investigation of this historical configuration would be in the relations between archaeology and anthropology, and between 'physical' and 'social' anthropology – a study of the differential analytic modes brought to bear on material artefacts and on kinship and ritual terms.

The implications to be drawn from *The history of sexuality. Vol. I*, and from its predecessor, *Discipline and punish*, are of a different order. Instead of bearing upon the history of ideas (even conceived as abstractly and generously as it was by Foucault in *The order of things* and *The archaeology of knowledge*), these books point to the importance of the social and institutional relations of the sciences of man. Rather than filling in the historical vicissitudes that a concept of 'race' underwent, whether it was conceived on a biological (hereditary) or a cultural (linguistic) level, one will investigate the relations of knowledge and power entailed by the production of the 'discourse' on race, by examining the social relations of the 'men of knowledge'. We will be drawn to compare the different 'epistemological environments' of Charcot and Freud, as well as their conceptions of the relation between psychical and physical aetiology. For example: what is the significance of the dramatic mode of the Salpêtrière, wherein Charcot demonstrated, in a most magisterial fashion, to hundreds of disciple-spectators, the pliability and elusiveness of the hysterical woman? How are we to compare this with the dramatically austere but literarily baroque methods evolved in Freud's quiet consulting-room? Or: How are we to assess the differing significances of various discursive methods for the questioning of the object's truth that proliferated at the turn of our century: the anamnesis, the psychoanalytic monologue, the questionnaire, the free association experiment, the case history? Once we accept the form of Foucault's analysis, even though we may leave in abeyance the deletion of the parentheses that might be taken for assent, we are encouraged to enquire as to the conditions under which, say, the questionnaire, and its accompanying apparatus of statistics, can be a method for ascertaining the objective truth of utterances.

Another path opens up. Let us put two arguments alongside one another. Firstly, Foucault's claim that the repressive hypothesis of psychoanalysis, and its concomitant identification of power with the patriarch *qua* law-giver, was generated at the threshold of our modern age, precisely when the patriarchal law was being surpassed and supplanted by the positive mechanisms of knowledge-power. 'We must not forget that the discovery of the Oedipus complex was contemporaneous with the juridical organisation of the downfall of the father.'[54] Secondly, there is a theme that lies embedded in psychoanalytic theory since Freud's elaboration of the Oedipus complex, namely that modern neurosis is intimately bound up with a failure in relation to the father, whether this be a failure of 'nerve' (a staying of the hand), or a failure to appreciate his lack of omnipotence (his installation as master). We find this theme at opposite ends of the spectrum of psychoanalytic hetero-doxy: in Reich's idea that neurosis is the consequence of the incompatible demands made on 'fathers', who take up the position of wage-slaves within capitalist industry, and who attempt to function as absolutist heads of households *en famille*,[55] and also in Lacan's conception, first elaborated in the 1930s, that neurosis is linked to a 'certain concrete abasement . . . of the image and figure of the father', and to the 'effacement by the decline of our history' of the 'figure of the moral master', the Socratic ideal.[56] Are we to assent to the implication of Foucault's argument, that this Nietzschean crisis of authority of the law and its makers is the mythical skein under which is played out the 'true' relations of the individual to power? And, if this is so, how do we write the history of discourses on authority, on moral imperatives, on guilt, and on the various 'oughts' that the social sciences produce, and have produced, continuously and insistently, for a century? Can we, finally and definitively, declare, not only that God is dead, but also that we have begun to sketch out the historical conditions which made possible his exact, clinical and scientific murder?

III

How surprised should we be by the turn that Foucault's work took in the last phase of his writing, in volumes II and III of *L'Histoire de la sexualité*? Should we regard them as simply a broadening of the question raised in his earlier, introductory volume: what are the paths by which the truth of the subject has historically been constituted, apart from our modern regime of knowledge-power, the purest embodiment of which is psychoanalysis? Foucault's espousal of the cause of Dora is now, thirty years on, translated into an investigation of the Greeks and Romans, which, if never becoming quite a search for allies, at least was the discovery of an ethic which was founded neither on religion (as in Christianity), law (as in Kantianism) nor science (as in psychoanalysis), but on an aesthetic of existence.[57] Yet these books do seem decidedly unexpected coming from Foucault, almost at odds with what we have known up to now of his work; what are the elements of this unexpected final turn?[58]

Firstly, the question of power, which seemed so important in his work in the middle to late 1970s, is almost totally absent; it has become transformed and dispersed into a series of other concerns: something far more akin to traditional political theory, what Foucault called a study of governmentality:

'Government' . . . designated the way in which the conduct of individuals or of groups might be directed . . . To govern, in this sense, is to structure the possible field of action of others. The relationship proper to power would not therefore be sought on the side of violence or of struggle, nor on that of voluntary linking . . . but rather in the area of the singular mode of action, neither warlike nor juridical, which is government.[59]

And secondly, Foucault's reflections on power, when they are to be found, had become far more abstract and programmatic, or retrospectively clarificatory, in the way that *The archaeology of knowledge* was a programmatic reflection on Foucault's previous practices, prior to launching out onto what is universally regarded as a new path. Even the sweeping, inspiring arguments of 'The subject and power' home the concern with power in on the distinctively modern struggle against the forms of subjection (in contrast with domination and exploitation) that the novel political agency, the State, fostered through its recuperation of Christian pastoral power, indeed through the State itself becoming coterminous with the matrix of individualisation of intimate knowledge, produced by pastoral techniques.

What replaces the relation of subject and power is ethics: how is a sexual ethics constituted and what is the 'technology of the self' associated with it? The claim that Foucault accepts is that such an ethics contains two elements: a code of prohibitions and a method of subjectivation – a method of producing a subject of moral truth and action. The code has remained remarkably constant from the Ancients, through Christianity, to today. What changes is the ethic and the self that is produced by this ethic. However, for the Greeks and the Romans, it is practices of self-mastery that have precedence over the exact contents of the code of prohibitions, and the function of this self-mastery is in relation to social ideals, rather than sacred truths; in contrast with 'Christian' ethics – and I use scare quotes because Foucault has modern preoccupations in mind as well as specifically Christian ones – the Ancients are concerned with mastery, not purity. It is only a later ethic founded on purity that gives rise to the endless deciphering and interpretation, the concern with the truth of the subject, so characteristic of the 'Christian'. Hence, it seems as if these books are directed to ethical ends in the present, rather than epistemological, historical or political ends, and that the method no longer includes the 'making strange' of the past (and the present) in order to reorient our articulation of past and present, but is more straightforwardly comparative: the juxtaposition of the discursive and governmental environments in which the Greeks, the Romans, the early Christians, the Reformers, the Enlightenment bourgeoisie all found themselves.

Certainly what seems to have disappeared from these final books is any concern with epistemology and with truth. The contrast between an Ancient *ars erotica* and the modern *scientia sexualis* had already been advanced in Volume I of *The history of sexuality*. The main line of cleavage between these two traditions had arisen, Foucault argued, with the scientisation of the Western practice of confession, 'one of the main rituals we rely on for the production of truth'.[60] Via the confession, sex becomes elevated onto the plane of truth, becomes, indeed, a principal focus for the truth of an individual. But Foucault had also recognised that the link between truth and sex was crucial for the Greeks, albeit in a different manner than for us:

In Greece, truth and sex were linked, in the form of pedagogy, by the transmission of a precious knowledge from one body to another; sex served as a medium for initiations into learning. For us, it is in the confession that truth and sex are joined, through the obligatory and exhaustive expression of an individual secret.[61]

In Volumes II and III of *The history of sexuality*, this focus on knowledge and truth, this linking together of the Greek *ars erotica* and the modern sciences of sexuality, is abandoned; indeed, the very notion of a Greek *ars erotica* is admitted to be a mistake.[62] Instead, Foucault analyses discussions of sexual practice almost entirely within the register of precept and pleasure, of honour, self-mastery and the ulterior practical ends of sexual acts. True, he did point out that, for Aristotle, 'one could not form oneself as an ethical subject in the use of pleasures without forming oneself at the same time as a subject of knowledge'.[63] But this essential relation of truth to moderation is always retained within the context of questions as to what the good man will do; it is always the ethic of moderation that orients the dimension of truth. As if to remind us how far away we are from the metaphysics of truth and desire, of the endless spiral of interpretative virtuosity to which – as Foucault, some thirty years before, had perceived – psychoanalytic subjects are condemned, he spells out in *The use of pleasure* that this relation to truth:

never took the form of a decipherment of the self by the self, never that of a hermeneutics of desire. It was a factor constituting the mode of being of the moderate subject; it was not equivalent to an obligation for the subject to speak truthfully concerning himself; it never opened up the soul as a domain of potential knowledge where barely discernible traces of desire needed to be read and interpreted. The relation to truth . . was not an epistemological condition enabling the individual to recognize himself in his singularity as a desiring subject and to purify himself of the desire that was thus brought to light. (p. 89)

Instead, this relation to truth opened up onto an 'aesthetics of existence . . . a way of life whose moral value did not depend either on one's being in conformity with a code of behaviour, or on an effort of purification, but on certain formal principles in the use of pleasures' (p. 89). Even though the ideal of being 'stronger than oneself' required an austerity in the constitution of the self-disciplined subject, the means to achieving this ideal were 'not presented in the form of a universal law . . . but rather as a principle of stylization of conduct for those who wished to give their existence the most graceful and accomplished form possible' (pp. 250–1). It is only later, with Christianity, that we see appear in place of this aesthetics, on the theoretical level, those themes of universality and eternalisation which, thanks to Foucault and others, are now noticeable by their absence in Greek thought; it is this Christian novelty that sketches out a link between eternity, death, immortality, marriage and truth. And, on the level of practices, 'what was now at the core of the problematization of sexual conduct was no longer pleasure and the aesthetics of its use, but desire and its purifying hermeneutics' (p. 254).

Desire and its purifying hermeneutics: we know the best modern example of this practice. And we should not allow ourselves to be lulled into accepting that the awesome historical weight of the confessional practices associated with Christianity, both Catholic and Reformed, lessens the importance of their modern incarnation; as Foucault himself wrote:

we should distinguish between two aspects of pastoral power – between the ecclesiastical institutionalization which has ceased or at least lost its vitality since the eighteenth century, and its function, which has spread and multiplied outside the ecclesiastical institution . . . [P]ower of a pastoral type . . . suddenly spread out into the whole social body . . . [I]nstead of a pastoral power and a political power, more or less linked to each other, more or less rival, there was an individualizing 'tactic' which characterizes a series of powers: those of the family, medicine, psychiatry, education, and employers.[64]

However much it might appeal to point to the figure of Christ, or to the relation of priest and penitent, as already presaging the individualising 'tactic' that pastoral power was eventually to disseminate, Foucault makes it quite clear that we are more concerned with the *novelty* of the modern individualistic hermeneutics of the self than with its Christian ancestors. Foucault's project is not – emphatically not – the uncovering of the religious warp across which the caring professionals of today shuttle so many docile selves. Religion, science (read: psychoanalysis!), law are indifferently repudiated underpinnings for what Foucault, in these later works, recognises as a legitimate *positive* hope: guidance in addressing the question, how should I live?

Yet, irony of ironies, is not psychoanalysis precisely the modern practice that has most closely identified *this* question as implicit in the myriad demands – distorted, true, and requiring 'interpretation' – made on its practitioners since its beginnings with this century? Is not psychoanalysis precisely the practice that has repudiated at least two of Foucault's three agencies: religion ('an illusion') and law (through the very fact of being a 'higher' agency, the super-ego has the 'general character of harshness and cruelty', 'its dictatorial "Thou shalt"')?[65] And Lacan had, in a text with which Foucault was already familiar when he wrote his first critique of psychoanalysis, already placed the analyst in an ethically *mediating* relation to knowledge, to science:

Of all the undertakings that have been proposed in this century, that of the psychoanalyst is perhaps the loftiest, because the undertaking of the psychoanalyst acts in our time as a mediator between the man of care and the subject of absolute knowledge. This is also why it requires a long subjective ascesis, and one which can never be interrupted, since the end of the training analysis is itself not separable from the engagement of the subject in its practice.[66]

In short, are these not Foucault's *most* psychoanalytic works, precisely where he seems to be engaged in a project that repudiates the 'endless self-analysis', 'the hermeneutics of suspicion', the unholy alliance of the truth of the subject and its secret sexuality, by seeking an ethic of the aesthetic and the beautiful life? Is he not *most* in tune with our century's psychoanalytic ethos when he recognises in the search for such an ethics, independent of Church and State, Law and Laboratory, the most authentically modern demand that an individual makes of the self?

314

Finally, and in conclusion, I wish to air a speculative hypothesis as to why Foucault's last writings are so humble and austere, a hypothesis that is also a reflection upon the personal trajectory of a man whose work evokes in me deeper admiration the more familiar I become with it. It is the thought that Foucault, as a historian of the present, was first and foremost a historian of the intellectual failures and crises of the present. The shift from philosophy to psychopathology of the young Foucault, of the late 1940s and early 1950s, was a recognition of philosophy's failure to deliver on its promises. The text I have discussed on 'Dream and existence', then *Mental illness and psychology*, which makes explicit the programmatic function of his study of the history of madness, and later *Madness and civilization*, the fulfilment of the programme, were constructed on the failure of psychopathology and philosophy to encompass madness, a failure he recognised out of an experience of 'great personal discomfort'.[67] The failures of Marxism and structuralism are mapped out in *The order of things*. And the failures of *gauchisme*, of liberationist politics, are what give *Discipline and punish* its bite, with its dizzying, but secretly satisfying, masochistic analysis of the ubiquity of power. Quite clearly, *The history of sexuality. Vol. I* is both an analysis of the failure of the movements of sexual liberation and of the emptiness of psychoanalysis' claims to be the discourse that has privileged access both to all other discourses and to each and every secret of the body.

So, what is the failure being addressed in these last two books? I think it is the failure of the intellectual himself – Foucault's own failure. His refusal to be a guru did not prevent him from according a critical function to the intellectual – witness the myriad interviews which were avidly recorded and transcribed, commented upon and treasured. With these last two books, the only trace left of the historian of the present is to be found in the initial question: how are the paths to becoming a subject of the practice of living to be mapped? And the domain here is no longer political or strategic, despite Foucault's continuing development, in shorter works, of these concepts; this is the moral quest, the *ascesis* Foucault talks of at the beginning of Volume II – an exercise of the self, maybe even the exercise of mastery over the self that Foucault finds in the Greeks and which he nowhere, to my knowledge, repudiates as a goal. Perhaps these austere books were Foucault's own exercise of self-restraint, in which the style of the intellectual and the image of the promise of a freedom beyond the reach of interpretative recuperation were given up, without reluctance or nostalgia, in returning to Socrates, Aristotle and Phidias.

The destiny of psychoanalysis

Given that such may have been Foucault's own path, we can now discern only too clearly that the ideal of the intellectual he sketched in an interview published in 1977 was not only a portrait of how he wished to be but also revealed him as he was. I will close this book with those moving words of his, as a small tribute to one of the great thinkers of our time, and to a man who has had a most profound influence on my work.

I think that intellectuals – if this category exists or if it should still exist, which is by no means certain, which is perhaps by no means desirable – are renouncing their old prophetic functions. By that, I am not only thinking of the pretention they have for saying what is going to happen, but of the legislating function to which they have aspired for so long: *This is what has to be done, this is what is good, follow me. In your uncertainty in which you all find yourselves, here is the fixed point, here where I am.* The Greek philosopher, the Jewish prophet and the Roman legislator have always been the models which haunt those who, today, make a profession out of speaking and writing. I dream of an intellectual who is destructive of what is self-evident and of what is universal, someone who can discern in the inertias and the constraints of the present the points of weakness, the cracks which form openings, the lines of force, someone who is forever in motion, never knows quite where he will be nor what he will think tomorrow, because he is too attentive to the present; someone who makes his contribution wherever he happens to be, asking the question whether the revolution is worth the effort, and which (I mean which revolution and which effort), it being understood that only those who are prepared to put their lives on the line are qualified to reply.[68]

NOTES

Unless they are already specified in the notes, full bibliographical details are to be found in the Bibliography.

Introduction

1 For a profound meditation on the encounter of reader, author and Other Reader, see Calvino, *If on a winter's night a traveller*.

2 I once introduced myself to Michel Foucault precisely so as to ask him why *he* was interested in psychoanalysis – so interested that he described his *The history of sexuality. Vol. I* as an 'archaeology of psychoanalysis' – whilst never addressing it directly. His answer was evasive; he maintained a dignified, sympathetic and – dare I say it? – analytic silence on this question throughout a lengthy conversation. However, it is his works that, suitably interpreted, give as accurate an indication of the ground for such an interest as any others of recent years. Chapter 12, 'Michel Foucault and the history of psychoanalysis', a homage to his memory, attempts this interpretation.

3 Lacan, 'Function and field of speech and language', E 321/105, quoted on p. 314 below.

4 Ellenberger, *The discovery of the unconscious. The history and evolution of dynamic psychiatry*, pp. 41–2, 895–6.

5 For a sociological view of this history, see Turkle, *Psychoanalytic politics: Jacques Lacan and Freud's French revolution*.

6 See Roudinesco, *La Bataille de cent ans, Histoire de la psychanalyse en France. Vol. 2. 1925–1985*, esp. pp. 288–379.

7 See in particular the predominantly psychoanalytic works published in Derrida, *The post card. From Socrates to Freud and beyond*, and the collection of more recent work in *Psyché*.

8 Lacan, 'Function and field of speech and language', E 258–9/49–50'

9 See Steiner, *After Babel*, p. 143.

10 Sterba, *Reminiscences of a Viennese psychoanalyst*, p. 119. Of course, Anna's point could be recuperated from a Kleinian perspective, by pointing out that a patient who induces in a prospective analyst his own sense of despair can still legitimately expect the analyst to offer something.

11 'Introduction au commentaire de Jean Hyppolite sur le *Verneinung* de Freud' (1954), E 373n1.

12 Koestler, *The sleepwalkers*.

13 James, *The golden bowl*, p. 107.

14 That the genre is no longer the exclusive domain of the hagiographers, as I somewhat condescendingly referred to them in *Language and the origins of psychoanalysis*, is demonstrated by Peter Swales' meticulous researches, which are devoted to a character-assassination of Freud. Sulloway's demythologising is also an attempt at character-assassination, but takes the path of emptying out all of Freud's claims to originality – indeed demonstrates that he was not a psychoanalyst. McGrath shoulders the cloak of the psychoanalytic detective in order to demonstrate the insertion of political concerns into the development of Freud's thought, while Balmary is psychoanalytic character-assassination at its purest: showing how an unconscious lacuna of Freud's, his relation to his father, lies at the heart of psychoanalytic theory. (For all these works, see full references in the Bibliography.)

15 'Rarely have you *understood* me, and rarely too have I understood you. Not until we both found ourselves in the *mud* did we promptly understand each other.' See (1900a) SE V 513.

16 Leading inevitably to a shabby and small-minded recasting of Freud's character, when made into the guiding thread around which to organise his entire personal and theoretical development, as it was in the BBC2 series *Freud* (see Swales' articles in the Bibliography; Harrison, *Freud*).

17 Though it has been suggested to me by Michael Shortland that Freud marks a sea change in the history of hypocrisy; see his 'Setting murderous Machiavel to school: hypocrisy in politics and the novel'.

18 Here, I am only touching on the wider – and deeper – question of the fictionality of case-histories, the relation between the scientific status of psychoanalysis and its singular relations (both philosophical and historical) to fiction and faction. The wittiest of these 'idle' analysts was undoubtedly Lindner, *The fifty-minute hour*.

19 Freud, *Civilization and its discontents* (1930a [1929]), SE XXI 70–1.

20 Cf. Freud, 'A note upon the "Mystic Writing-Pad"', the telescope analogy employed in chapter 7 of *The interpretation of dreams*, and Derrida, 'Freud and the scene of writing'.

21 Freud, 'A disturbance of memory on the Acropolis' (1936a), SE XX 239–43.

22 T.S. Eliot, 'Burnt Norton', in *Collected poems. 1909–1962*, London: Faber & Faber, 1963, p. 189.

1 The true story of Anna O.

This chapter was written a week after the birth of my daughter, Katrina; it is dedicated to her.

1 Freud, 'Remembering, repeating and working-through' (1914g), SE XII 150.

2 Breuer, 'Das sexuale Element war erstaunlich unentwickelt; die Kranke, deren Leben mir durchsichtig wurde, wie selten das eines Menschen einem andern, hatte nie eine Liebe gehabt, und in all den massenhaften Halluzinationem ihrer Krankheit tauchte niemals dieses Element des Seelenlebense empor', in *Studies on hysteria* (1895d), SE II 21–2; *Studien über Hysterie*, p. 20.

3 *Letters*, pp. 409–10, letter dated 2 June 1932.

4 *Ibid.*

5 Earlier in the letter, Freud remarks: 'If things had been as your text maintains, then everything else would have taken a different turn [this indicates the sense in which Freud saw the early history of psycho-analysis as *crucially dependent* on how this incident turned out]. I would not have been surprised by the discovery of sexual aetiology, Breuer would have found it more difficult to refute this theory, and if hypnosis could obtain such candid confessions, I probably would never have abandoned it.' Freud here forgot that it was not the sexual aetiology of the neuroses that Breuer objected to but rather to the seduction theory and its subsequent development in the theory of infantile sexuality. In his biography of Freud, Jones reinforced this view of Breuer's distaste for sexuality. One aim of this chapter is to remind us that the crucial factor was never sexuality, but was rather the transference and its implications for therapeutic technique.

6 SE II 246; emphasis in original.

7 SE II 246n1. In the conversation with Breuer quoted below in the letter from Freud to Martha, Breuer asked Freud to repeat certain things only after he was married, an injunction that foreshadows the picture of the veil of secrecy drawn by senior doctors over the subject of sexuality. Freud's response to this injunction is also a foreshadowing: in claiming that he can already say anything to his wife, he implicitly refuses to obey any such injunction to secrecy, a position he will vigorously defend in the Dora case-history as necessary in any scientific study (see SE VII 9). In the story Freud recounted later (see note 16 below; SE XIV 13), Breuer expressed himself as follows: 'These things are always *secrets d'alcôve!*', and when asked by the young Freud what he meant, explained what the word *alcôve* (marriage bed) meant – again, Breuer took this topic to be one in which the dialectic of the knowledge of experience and the ignorance of innocence was paramount. Freud's conception was altogether differently oriented.

8 In his new edition of the Freud/Fliess correspondence (*The complete letters of Sigmund Freud to Wilhelm Fliess. 1887–1904*), J.M. Masson includes a lengthy note translating some comments of Breuer's on Freud's theories concerning the sexual aetiology of the neuroses, delivered to the Vienna College of Physicians on 4 November 1895, when he supported Freud in public but told Freud in private: 'But all the same, I don't believe it.' At the public meeting, Breuer had said: 'Especially in the case of the female sex, the complaint about the

underestimation of the sexual factor is justified. It is not right, for example, that in the case of girls who suffer from insomnia, etc., one simply prescribes iron for anemia, without even thinking of masturbation, while in the case of young men we immediately look for pollutions. In this respect we are in a state of hysteria; we repress this feeling which is unpleasant to us. We simply know nothing about the sexuality of girls and women. No physician has any idea what sorts of symptoms an erection evokes in women, because the young women do not want to talk about it and the old ones have already forgotten' (p. 151n1). Breuer thus repeated the same structure of argument, with some of the terms changed: where he had talked of older and younger doctors, he now talked of old and young women. And the 'unpleasant feeling' that he is referring to seems likely to have been the unpleasantness of recognising the sexuality of women. It is this unpleasantness that Freud was to imply had prevented Breuer from recognising the importance of the dramatic events which terminated his treatment of Bertha. Breuer's harping on the axis of 'older/younger' – something Freud was never once to do, throughout his writings on sexuality – indicates that he attributed some change in his position over the period 1882 to 1895 to his having become a 'senior' in the mean time.

9 Letter of 31 Oct. 1883. It is a mystery why this letter was not published in the original edition of Freud's correspondence, since it is of great historical and personal interest; the hypothesis of a general cover-up of the Freudian skeletons will not explain its omission, since all the important elements had been at least alluded to in Jones' account in his biography of Freud. This letter was quoted in an appendix to the manuscript of the complete edition of the Freud–Fliess correspondence prepared by J.M. Masson, but unfortunately this appendix was not published. Masson discusses at some length the question of the fluctuations of Freud's relations with Breuer, and the vexed question of the origin of the various stories about the abrupt end of Anna O.'s treatment. He concludes that the matter is not decided by the survey of the available evidence, nor by the new evidence he introduces: namely, the previously unpublished letters to Fliess made available in his edition of the *Complete letters*, the unpublished letters to Breuer from which he quotes, and the unpublished letters between Sigmund and his fiancée, which he also quotes and cites from at length. I would like to thank Sigmund Freud Copyrights for permission to quote from these letters.

10 Letter of 2 Nov. 1883; translation slightly adapted.

11 Letter of 4 Nov. 1883.

12 'Es ist merkwürdig, der armen Bertha ist nie ein anderer Mann näher getreten als ihr jeweiliger Arzt, das heisst die hätte als Gesunde schon das Zeug dazu, dem vernünftigsten Manne den Kopf zu verdrehen, ist das ein Unglück mit dem Mädchen, nicht wahr.'

13 'Josef Breuer' (1925g), SE XIX 280: 'I found reason later to suppose that a purely emotional factor, too, had given him an aversion to further

work on the elucidation of the neuroses. He had come up against something that is never absent – his patient's transference on to her physician, and he had not grasped the impersonal nature of the process.'

14 'On the history of the psycho-analytic movement' (1914d), SE XIV 12.

15 In the unpublished Appendix cited above (note 9).

16 A reference to the three stories told Freud by these three senior colleagues when he was a young man, each implying that sexuality was the key to the neuroses. See 'On the history of the psycho-analytic movement' (1914d), SE XIV 12–15.

17 Cf. Lacan's account of the Breuer–Bertha–Freud scene, in Sem X, Session 4, 5 Dec. 1962 (unpublished): 'Breuer bit the bait that Anna O. offered him, whereas Freud was neurotic. And since he was both intelligent and courageous, he knew how to make use of his own anxiety when faced with his desire – which was at the bottom of his ridiculous attachment to this impossible fine lady who, what is more, buried him and who was known as Frau Freud – and knew how to make use of it in order to project onto the X-ray plate of his fidelity to this fantasised object, so as to be able to recognise there without even blinking for one moment what it was necessary to do, namely to understand what all this was for and to admit straight off that Anna O. had her sights perfectly trained on him, Freud, but clearly he was a little harder to get than the other, Breuer. It really is because of this that we owe our entry into analysis through fantasy and a rational employment of the transference.'

18 'On the history of the psycho-analytic movement' (1914d), SE XIV 17.

19 *Five lectures on psycho-analysis* (1910a [1909]), SE XI 9. Freud adapted and in part retracted this version of the origins of psychoanalysis, when he came to write 'On the history of the psycho-analytic movement' in 1914. Strachey supplies useful notes on this subject, appended to the texts quoted from here. See also some remarks in chapter 9, this volume, pp. 235ff.

20 See *The interpretation of dreams* (1900a), SE IV 106–21. This 'specimen dream' of psychoanalysis, as Freud called it, has been the object of a great deal of attention and analysis; I will deal with it, together with many of the themes raised in this chapter, in my forthcoming book, *The dream of psychoanalysis*.

21 This manner of treating the history of psychoanalysis can be further developed, which I will not be able to do in this chapter. It will suffice to signal a further hypothesis offered by Anzieu in his *L'Auto-analyse de Freud*, pp. 690ff., with respect to the '*Table d'hôte*' dream (SE V 638), where the woman friend who figures in the dream is identified with Bertha Breuer, sister of Dora Breuer, and sister-in-law of Anna Hammerschlag (Irma of the Irma dream), and is linked up with the roughly contemporaneous Dora case – to the extent that Anzieu surmises that Dora's name is taken from Dora Breuer, so that Dora

becomes a revenant of Anna O./Bertha Pappenheim. Herr K. in Dora's story then corresponds to Breuer: the man 'seduced' by a young hysteric (just as the friend in the dream seduces Freud) – see *L'Auto-analyse*, p. 732.

22 SE II 103. Or note the close collaboration between Freud and Breuer in the treatment of Frau Emmy von N.: see, for instance, SE II 54–5, where Breuer pops in and out of the treatment room, while Freud quickly takes over the position of authority that Breuer had previously occupied for the patient, by telling her 'a white lie', thus aiding the increase of Freud's influence over her.

23 *Letters*, pp. 55–6, letter dated 13 July 1883.

24 Letter dated 5 Aug. 1883.

25 Ellenberger, 'The story of "Anna O."', pp. 267–79.

26 See chapter 2, pp. 38ff.

27 In his comprehensive account of Freud's dreams and self-analysis, Anzieu remarks on the importance of the theme of responsibility, making remarks that support the thesis advanced here. See, in particular, *L'Auto-analyse*, pp. 609 and 659.

To take only one example among the many dreams concerned with responsibility, and medical responsibility in particular: One of the key dreams in Freud's 'self-analysis' was the dream of a memory of taking money from a doctor's wife wrongfully, and thus revolved around the theme of Freud's stealing from his patients the money they pay him for treatment; this led back to a childhood scene in which he stole money from his mother at the behest of his nurse, who was sacked and imprisoned when it was discovered (see *Complete letters*, letter of 3/4 Oct. 1897). Or, in the dream '*Autodidasker*' (SE IV 298–302), Freud's perennial concern to be right about a diagnosis of the sexual aetiology of the neuroses allows the 'deeper' wishes, concerning the fate of his children, to find expression.

One of the other major dreams discussed in the book, the dream of the botanical monograph, can also be seen as a repetition of the Irma dream (see SE IV 176, where Freud wonders what would have happened if the woman in this botanical/floral dream had been called Anna [Irma's real name], not Flora), and is also a dream preoccupied with medical responsibility (made explicit by Freud, in SE IV 173): the dream was in the nature of 'a self-justification, a plea on behalf of my own rights'.

28 The theme of responsibility is far larger than I have time and space to devote to it here. My thinking on this subject is very close to that of Cottet, *Freud et le désir du psychanalyste*. For example, in discussing the relation between countertransference and the responsibility of the analyst, Cottet remarks (p. 169): 'The notion of countertransference has for a long time taken the place of a conceptual response to this question, and has relegated to second place considerations concerning the responsibility of the analyst in the conduct of the cure.'

29 SE IV 108.
30 Ellenberger, 'The Story of "Anna O."'.
31 It is not certain that Breuer ceased seeing her in July 1882, when she
   was moved to Bellevue, at Kreuzlingen, until 29 October 1882. But he
   wrote out her case, which formed the basis for the report in *Studies on
   hysteria*, probably shortly after the latest date mentioned in the report,
   June 1882, which is also when his account of his treatment of Anna O.
   in the *Studies* ends. It seems most plausible, then, given the available
   evidence, to date Breuer's flight from Anna O. in June 1882. This does
   not explain all the elements of the history: we have yet to discover how
   Freud managed to believe that Breuer's daughter, Dora, was conceived
   on a second honeymoon decided upon in order to escape from the
   threat that Anna O. posed to his marriage. See the letter to Stefan
   Zweig quoted above (note 3), esp. p. 408.
      There is a further coincidence in the history of psychoanalysis
   associated with the hospital at Bellevue, in the town of Kreuzlingen, in
   Switzerland, also previously unremarked upon. The Binswanger family
   were the doctors in charge of the sanatorium there over several decades
   – at the time when Bertha was placed there by Breuer, and then in 1912
   when Ludwig Binswanger was a patient there, in danger of death.
   Freud went to visit him in secret there, and Jung took this rapid
   weekend visit to a town close by Zurich of which he was uninformed as
   a gesture of rejection. It became known as the 'Kreuzlingen gesture',
   and was the moment from which Freud and Jung dated the beginning of
   their estrangement. See *The Freud/Jung letters*, pp. 509–10.
32 The fact that Bertha was a friend of Martha's, the fact that Anna
   Hammerschlag as well as her friend in the Irma dream, Sophie
   Schwab-Paneth, were members of the Freud circle of friends, the fact
   that the Breuers and the Hammerschlags were intermarrying – all these
   overlappings between medical and family ties are of great significance,
   but can only be mentioned here rather than analysed in detail. See my
   forthcoming *The dream of psychoanalysis*.
33 *Letters*, p. 236, letter dated 24 Oct. 1887.

2 Contracting the disease of love

1 Castel, *Le Psychanalysme*, p. 55.
2 *Ibid.* p. 87.
3 On the history of these aspects of hypnotism, see Didi-Huberman,
   *Invention de l'hystérie. Charcot et l'iconographie photographique de la
   Salpêtrière*; Ellenberger, *The discovery of the unconscious*.
4 Modell, *The relief of symptoms*, p. 55, cited in Brody, *Placebos and the
   philosophy of medicine*, p. 37.
5 Freud, 'Review of August Forel's *Der Hypnotismus*' (1889a),
   SE I 94.
6 *Ibid.* p. 94.

7 The idea of doctor as drug is discussed in illuminating detail in Balint, *The doctor, the patient and the illness*.

8 See Johnston, *The Austrian mind; an intellectual and social history, 1848–1939*; Lesky, *Die Wiener Medizinische Schule im 19. Jahrhundert*.

9 Freud, 'A case of successful treatment by hypnotism' (1892–93), SE I 119.

10 *Ibid*. p. 120.

11 *Ibid*.

12 Freud, 'Psychical (or mental) treatment' (1890a), SE VII 295.

13 *Ibid*. p. 296.

14 *Ibid*. p. 298.

15 *Ibid*. p. 293.

16 Freud, 'Preface and footnotes to the translation of Charcot's *Leçon du mardi*' (1892–94), SE I 141.

17 See Foucault, *HS I*.

18 The literature on this dream is by now voluminous. The following are most useful: the text itself, with Freud's discussion, in Freud, *The interpretation of dreams* (1900a), SE IV 106–21; for its place in Freud's self-analysis, Anzieu, *Freud's self-analysis*; on additional previously unpublished important background material, Schur, 'Some additional "day residues" of the specimen dream of psychoanalysis'. For interesting, controlled speculation, see Schneider, *Blessures de mémoire*, pp. 31–135; Cottet, *Freud et le désir du psychanalyste*; Hartman, 'A reappraisal of the Emma episode and the specimen dream'. Controversial and dubious claims are to be found in Masson, *The assault on truth: Freud's suppression of the seduction theory*.

19 Freud, 'The aetiology of hysteria' (1896c), SE III 202ff. See pp. 76–82 and pp. 161ff. below.

20 *Ibid*. p. 204.

21 Freud and Abraham, *A psycho-analytic dialogue. The letters of Sigmund Freud and Karl Abraham, 1907–1926*, p. 20 (letter dated 9 January 1908).

22 Freud, *Origins*, p. 206 (letter 64, dated 31 May 1897).

23 Breuer and Freud, *Studies on hysteria* (1895d), SE II 301–4.

24 See also chapter 4, pp. 85–8.

25 Giraudoux, *Amphitryon 38*, in *Théâtre*, vol. 1, p. 128: 'The main problem, with honourable women, isn't seducing them, it's to get them behind closed doors. Their virtue consists in open doors.'

26 Kierkegaard, *Either/or*, vol. 1, p. 100.

27 Freud, 'Observations on transference-love' (1915a), SE XII 162.

28 *Ibid*. p. 163.

29 *Ibid*. p. 165.

30 Austin, *How to do things with words*, pp. 13ff. See chapter 7 below.

31 Freud, 'Notes upon a case of obsessional neurosis' (1909d), SE X 166.

32 Freud, 'Two encyclopaedia articles' (1923a), SE XVIII 250–1.

33 Freud, 'On beginning the treatment' (1913c), SE XII 135–6n1.

34 Eissler, 'The payment of fees', p. 101.

3 The untold pleasures of psychoanalysis

1 *Letters*, letter to Martha Bernays, 20 December 1883, p. 96.
2 *Ibid.* p. 96.
3 Freud, 'Fragment of the analysis of a case of hysteria' (referred to hereafter as *Dora*) (1905e), SE VII 96.
4 *Letters*, p. 96.
5 *Dora* SE VII 51.
6 Montrelay, 'Inquiry into femininity', quoted in Willis, 'A symptomatic narrative', pp. 46–60. The Spring 1983 issue of *Diacritics* is devoted to Dora and includes a translation of Hélène Cixous's *Un Portrait de Dora* and a useful bibliography.
7 *Dora* SE VII 35–6; Stud VI 112.
8 Cf. Slipp, 'Interpersonal factors in hysteria: Freud's seduction theory and the case of Dora', which discusses Dora's predicament in inter-actional and transactional terms.
9 Lacan, 'Intervention on transference', in Mitchell and Rose, eds., *Feminine sexuality. Jacques Lacan and the Ecole Freudienne*, p. 65.
10 Willis, 'A symptomatic narrative', p. 47, especially n.2, quoting Cixous and Clément, *La Jeune Née*, p. 104. Like her, I am much indebted to the complex and decisive arguments of Gearhart, 'The scene of psychoanalysis: the unanswered questions of *Dora*', pp. 114–26.
11 Lacan, 'Intervention on transference', p. 68; Lacan, Sem III 191–203. See also the subtle discussion of Dora's desire in Rose, 'Dora – a fragment of an analysis'.
12 Hertz, 'Dora's secrets, Freud's techniques'; Moi, 'Representation of patriarchy: sexuality and epistemology in Freud's Dora'.
13 It was Krafft-Ebing who, in 1896, thought Freud's seduction theory sounded like a scientific fairy-tale; see Freud, *Complete Letters of Freud to Fliess*, April 26, 1896, p. 184. For the 'serious stamp of science', see Freud and Breuer, *Studies on Hysteria* (1895d), SE II 160.
14 Cf. Moi, 'Representation of patriarchy', on the theme of oral and written sources of sexual knowledge.
15 Scharfman, 'Further reflections on Dora', p. 55.
16 Freud, *Origins*, Letter of 11 March 1900, p. 312.
17 *Ibid.*, Letter of 14 October 1900, p. 325.
18 Marcus, 'Freud and Dora: story, history, case history', p. 12.
19 *Dora* SE VII 59–60.
20 *Origins*, pp. 325–6.
21 *Ibid.* p. 327.
22 *Dora* SE VII 120n1.
23 Collins, Green, Lydon, Sachner and Honig Skoller, 'Questioning the unconscious: the Dora archive'.
24 The dismissal of Dora's mother has been discussed by a number of authors, e.g. Gearhart; Collins *et al.*; Ramas, 'Freud's Dora, Dora's hysteria', pp. 72–113.

25 *Dora* SE VII 119.

26 *Dora* SE VII 51: 'The less repellent of the so-called sexual perversions are very widely diffused among the whole population, as every one knows except medical writers upon the subject.'

27 *Dora* SE VII 49.

28 Moi, 'Representation of patriarchy'.

29 *Dora* SE VII 62.

30 *Dora* SE VII 109; cf. Stud VI 175: the phrase in German is 'wenn ich mich selbst in eine Rolle gefunden . . . hätte', which is more ambiguous than the English; it tends towards my interpretation that Freud was reflecting not so much on *not* acting a part as on finding what role he *had* been playing.

31 *Dora* SE VII 119; Stud VI 183.

32 Gallop, *Feminism and psychoanalysis. The daughter's seduction*, chapter 9, 'Keys to Dora', esp. pp. 141–7; Cixous and Clément, *La Jeune Née*, pp. 276ff.

33 Freud, 'The psychogenesis of a case of female homosexuality' (1920a), SE XVIII 164.

34 Jones, *Sigmund Freud, life and work*, vol. III, p. 197. Jones omitted the final sentence from this passage; it has been restored in Masson, *The assault on truth: Freud's suppression of the seduction theory*, p. 137.

35 Granoff, *Filiations*, pp. 185–6.

36 Freud, 'Sándor Ferenczi' (1933c), SE XXII 227.

37 *Dora* SE VII 109.

38 See chapter 4 and 8 below.

4 Rape, seduction, psychoanalysis

I would like to thank Sylvana Tomaselli for her aid in writing this paper, from the preliminary draft prepared in April 1981, as a paper read to a conference on 'Sex and language', held in New York, to this final version; at every step she contributed enormously both in discussions and in formal criticisms of the style and argument. I would also like to thank Roy Porter, Jennifer Temkin and Ross Harrison for incisive criticisms of earlier drafts, which made me aware that I still had much thinking to do.

1 Brownmiller, *Against our will: men, women and rape*, 1976 edn, p. 192. On the same page, Brownmiller writes: 'Freud himself, remarkable as this may seem, said nothing about rapists . . . His confederates were slightly more loquacious, but not by much . . . [E]ven among the Freudian criminologists there was a curious reluctance to take rape head on . . . no Freudian or psychoanalytic authority has ever written a major volume on rape. Articles on rape in psychology journals have been sparse to the point of nonexistence . . .'

2 For a similar discussion of the impact of psychoanalysis on rape trials, see Edwards, *Female sexuality and the law*, esp. pp. 100–8. Edwards pinpoints masochism and the rape fantasy as the two areas where

psychoanalysis has had the greatest detrimental impact. She argues that a Lacanian psychoanalysis can 'save' rape from these consequences: 'A patriarchal language imposes itself on the individual who acquires a conscious and subconscious sexual identity and at the same time a language by which others are perceived' (p. 107).

3 Brownmiller, *Against our will*, p. 350.

4 *Ibid.* p. 251.

5 *Ibid.* p. 351.

6 *Ibid.* p. 346.

7 Abrahamsen, *The psychology of crime*, p. 165, quoted in Brownmiller, *Against our will*, pp. 194–5. See also West, Roy, and Nichols, *Understanding sexual attacks. A study based upon a group of rapists undergoing psychotherapy*, pp. 127–8, for a different perspective on Abrahamsen's argument.

8 Brownmiller, *Against our will*, p. 195.

9 *Ibid.* p. 192.

10 *Ibid.* p. 228.

11 For a similar, though by no means infertile, defence, see Mitchell, *Psychoanalysis and feminism*, esp. p. 353 (*contra* Millett on the reality of rape), p. 342 on the 'common feminist anti-Freudian habit of amalgamating Freud with Helene Deutsch', and p. 354: 'Desire, phantasy, the laws of the unconscious or even unconsciousness are absent from the social realism of the feminist critiques.'

12 Brownmiller, *Against our will*, p. 350. 'Lust' is Brownmiller's translation of the German *Lust*, invariably translated in SE as 'pleasure'.

13 Freud, 'The economic problem of masochism' (1924c), SE XIX 162, 167.

14 Freud, *The psychopathology of everyday life* (1901b), SE VI 181n1.

15 This feature is well attested in the literature on rape, and is not regarded as being in need of explanation. Thus Amir, *Patterns in forcible rape*, pp. 166–71, gives 51 per cent of rape victims as having shown submissive behaviour. Many sources take the fact that rapists are often armed and threaten murder or serious injury as accounting for this response. It should be noted that other studies (e.g. West, Roy and Nichols, *Understanding sexual attacks*) divide rapists into various categories, some of whom would self-confessedly have been dissuaded from continuing with the assault if they had encountered resistance, while others – the 'sadistic rapists' – would have regarded resistance as an opportunity to escalate the degree of violence already employed, so as to secure the pleasure of the victim's pain that is a part of their aim.

16 Freud, *The interpretation of dreams* (1900a), SE V 620.

17 Freud, *Introductory lectures on psycho-analysis* (1916–17), SE XVI 433.

18 Brownmiller, *Against our will*, p. 359; emphasis in text. Brownmiller follows Deutsch's discussion of rape fantasies, finding it an 'amazing' combination of perception and dogma. She does not, however, quote

the following passage, which is commenting on triangular scenes in which the woman is forced by another woman to submit to a man, which is of interest in demonstrating how Deutsch's psychoanalytic method breaks rape down into other components which are less 'objectionable': 'The superficial elements of these fantasies are easy to grasp: the pain decreases the guilt feeling produced by the pleasure, the rape frees the girl from responsibility, the compulsion exerted by the woman, who represents the mother, is a counterweight to the latter's prohibitions . . . It is no doubt only by sanction of pain and by negation of the object's identity that these fantasies can come before consciousness.' To give a sense of the different focus of Deutsch's interest in these fantasies, we may quote the passage that follows: 'The rape and seduction fantasy, with its primitive sexual content directly relating to the body, is less dangerous than other masochistic fantasies, mostly unconscious, that do not work directly toward the gross sexual goal. If the rape fantasies were directly gratified they would lead to perversion, but this is extremely rare; it is known that the masochistic perversion is less frequently found in women than in men. Where it exists, its content is completely different from that of the rape fantasy: its essence is the wish to be beaten.' Even here, the fantasy is in the service not of direct gratification but is indulged in for the sake of the lover. Deutsch regards the more dangerous fantasies as being those of prostitution. See Deutsch, *The psychology of women*, vol. 1, p. 202.

19 Williams, *Criminal law. The general part*, pp. 33ff. quote from p. 33. The second edition of 1961 repeats this section with one slight addition.

20 *Ibid.* pp. 34–5. The final paragraph of his discussion reads: 'The field of the unconscious is irrelevant to responsibility where it pertains merely to motives, for even conscious motives are ruled out. To illustrate, a man may steal because of an early antagonism to his father, since repressed, which unconsciously leads him to do something of which his father would disapprove. The stealing is deliberate; it is only the motive that belongs to the unconscious. The analysis of neurotic motives is, of course, important in the realm of treatment.'

21 Williams, *Textbook of criminal law*, pp. 196–7.

22 Smith, *Trial by medicine. Insanity and responsibility in Victorian trials*.

23 See Zeitlin, 'Configurations of rape in Greek myth'.

24 The price of consent is a theme that emerges from the story of the rape of Lucretia and the many and various commentaries on it, excellently discussed and documented in Donaldson, *The rape of Lucretia: a myth and its transformation*, p. 26.

25 McCahill, Meyer and Fischman, *The aftermath of rape*, p. 106.

26 *Ibid.* p. 104.

27 See Temkin, 'Women, rape and law reform' and her important paper, 'Towards a modern law of rape'.

28 See Rush, 'Freud and the sexual abuse of children', pp. 31–45, and her *The best kept secret; sexual abuse of children*.

29 Schusdek, 'Freud's seduction theory: a reconstruction'; Sulloway, *Freud. Biologist of the mind*, pp. 110ff.; and the biographies of Freud by Ernest Jones, Max Schur, Ronald W. Clark and Peter Gay.

30 Freud, *The complete letters of Sigmund Freud to Wilhelm Fliess*, ed. Masson; letter of 30 May 1893, p. 49.

31 *Ibid.*, letter of 2 November 1895, p. 149.

32 *Ibid.*, letter of 3 January 1897, p. 219. See also letter of 11 January 1897, pp. 222–3.

33 Masson, *The assault on truth*; Alice Miller, *For your own good. Hidden cruelty in child-rearing and the roots of violence*, and *Thou shalt not be aware. Society's betrayal of the child.*

34 See *Abstracts of the scientific writings of Dr. Sigm. Freud* (1897), SE III 254.

35 Freud, 'The aetiology of hysteria' (1896c), SE III 200–1. This is the single occasion, noted above, on which Freud uses the term 'rape'.

36 *Ibid.* SE III 202.

37 *Ibid.* SE III 202.

38 *Ibid.* SE III 213.

39 *Ibid.* SE III 204.

40 *Ibid.* SE III 207.

41 *Ibid.* SE III 207.

42 *Ibid.* SE III 208.

43 *Ibid.* SE III 208.

44 *Ibid.* SE III 214.

45 *Ibid.* SE III 215. It should be noted that the same is true of a considerable number of first-hand descriptions of sexual relationships between adults and children, a significant feature that is not discussed by commentators on these descriptions. See, for example, Bass and Thornton, eds., *I never told anyone. Writings by women survivors of child sexual abuse.*

46 Legally speaking, the child is able neither to consent nor to withhold consent – which seems a satisfactory way of avoiding having to discuss the nature of the relationship between adult and child, in favour of the presumption that children have the absolute legal right to be protected from sexual contact with adults.

47 Consciousness is not the criterion, since convictions of rape may follow from rendering a woman unconscious with alcohol or having inter-course with her while she is asleep. Under such circumstances, the presumption of unconsciousness stands in for memory. See Smith and Hogan, *Criminal law*, pp. 406 and 409 (on administering drugs to obtain or facilitate intercourse).

48 McCahill, Meyer and Fischman, *The aftermath of rape*, p. 216. See also Griffin, 'Pornography and silence', p. 134n, and Smart and Smart, 'Accounting for rape. Reality and myth in press reporting', which offers an explanation for this doubt, shame and guilt (p. 93): 'In those cases where there is a lack of congruence between cultural expectations or

understandings of rape and the rape itself, there may well follow a reticence on the part of the victim to define the assault as rape, doubts may intrude into the victim's understanding of her ordeal as to whether she unconsciously or unknowingly "encouraged" or precipitated the assault. Thus the rape victim may begin to engage in a process of self-criticism and blame . . . ' See also Walker and Brodsky, eds., *Sexual assault. The victim and the rapist*, and Hursch, *The trouble with rape*, pp. 96–7.

49 Freud, 'Observations on transference-love' (1915a), SE XII 168.

50 *Ibid*. SE XII 170.

51 Mannoni, 'L'amour de transfert et le réel', pp. 7–13, esp. p. 13.

52 See Freud, *Introductory lectures* (1916–17), SE XVI 443: 'It is out of the question for us to yield to the patient's demands deriving from the transference; it would be absurd for us to reject them in an unfriendly, still more in an indignant, manner.'

53 Breuer and Freud, *Studies on hysteria* SE II 301–2.

54 *Ibid*. SE II 302–3. See also chapter 2, pp. 41–2, chapter 7, pp. 160–2 and chapter 9, pp. 235–7. This wish that the other 'take the initiative', noted by Deutsch as an important feature of rape fantasies (see note 18 above), has the same paradoxical quality as masochism: a handing over of responsibility (and maybe even of pleasure) to the other. This feature of the erotic lives of women should not be underestimated – it certainly has not been by feminists, who urge women to independence and into taking responsibility for their sexual lives, while indicting male society for depriving women of the opportunity to do so. In a curious fashion, the theme emerges in the passage in Brownmiller's book in which she uses one of her own dreams to 'refute' the Freudian rape symbolism found in dreams: 'Freudian dream interpretation, in which a host of plausible, real-life situations [note the weight of a call upon the real here] are assigned sexual symbolism, can certainly add to one's insecurity. Years ago I once had a dream in which I walked up the stairs to my apartment and was about to open the door when a male figure emerged from the shadows and struck out at me with a hammer. Inundated with popular Freudian psychology, I was distressfully convinced that this dream had to represent a hopeless fear of men and sex – until my Adlerian analyst drew from me the information that I hadn't paid my rent that month and had gotten a dispossess notice from the landlord!' (Brownmiller, *Against our will*, p. 356). Noticing in passing the manner in which the 'real-life situation' presses in on this account, pushing aside any deeper or more internally oriented theme, it is curious that the dream-thought the landlord-interpretation expresses is the following: 'If you don't give it to them, then they will steal it!' It is exactly such a view that, when transposed to the domain of sexual relations, Brownmiller is attacking: the obligation to give, under duress if necessary, or under the weight of utterances of the sort, 'All women want to be raped.'

55 Freud, 'Observations on transference-love' (1915a), SE XII 165.
56 Freud, *Introductory lectures* (1916–17), SE XVI 444. Cf. SE XVI 446: 'in our technique we have abandoned hypnosis only to rediscover suggestion in the shape of transference'. Or, SE XVI 455: 'we get hold of the whole of the libido [of the patient] which has been withdrawn from the dominance of the ego by attracting a portion of it on to ourselves by means of the transference'.
57 See SE XVI 443: 'The hostile feelings [concerning the analyst] are as much an indication of an emotional tie as the affectionate ones, in the same way as defiance signifies dependence as much as obedience does, though with a "minus" instead of a "plus" sign before it.'
58 The 'first' transference-seduction is often taken to have been that between Breuer and Anna O., in which Breuer took it 'for real' and ran away. Cf. the 'second' occasion, narrated in Freud, *An autobiographical study* (1925d), SE XX 27: 'As [the patient] woke up [from hypnosis] on one occasion, she threw her arms round my neck . . . I was modest enough not to attribute the event to my own irresistible personal attraction, and I felt that I had now grasped the nature of the mysterious element that was at work behind hypnotism.' Note that it is this 'modesty' which determines Freud's position as being 'analytic'; under other circumstances, it might be another emotion (pride, fear) that would create it. For further discussion of this episode and the mythical history it inevitably gives rise to, see chapters 1 and 9.
59 The possibility of rape having a future is found in certain abduction stories, principally those of the rape of the Sabines and the rape of Lucretia, discussed in Bryson, 'Two narratives of rape in the visual arts: Lucretia and the Sabine women': the future lies in the gradual annulling of the extent of the violation of the property relations through the marriage of the Sabine women and in their having children by their abductors. The futureless character of rape, in contrast, renders it eminently suitable as the founding myth (or occasion) for blood feuds that never end (as in Sicilian society; see also the original myth of rape in the biographies of bandits such as Pancho Villa).
60 For a profound discussion of the idiosyncratic dialectics of Freud's concepts, see Derrida, 'Spéculer – sur "Freud"'.
61 See Kundera, *The book of laughter and forgetting*, p. 210.
62 Baudrillard, *De la séduction*. See also two numbers of the journal *Traverses* (nos. 17 and 18, 1979/80) devoted to Baudrillard's book and the general topic of seduction, in particular the articles by Monique Schneider, Conrad Stein and Vincent Descombes in no. 17 and by Mario Perniola, Louis Marin and Alain Arnaud in no. 18.
63 A naturalistic conception of sexuality informs most if not all work in this area oriented around biological concepts, as in Thornhill, Thornhill and Dizinno, 'The biology of rape'.
64 The *locus classicus* for the relation between love and seduction is Plato's *Symposium*, whose 'content' is love (various discourses, includ-

ing Socrates' on the virtues of loving as opposed to being loved) and whose frame is seduction – by 'frame' I mean the final scene, in which Alcibiades' story of the night he spent with Socrates is interpreted as a seductive manœuvre designed to tear Agathon away from Socrates. See *Symposium* 222c–e.

65 On this point, Baudrillard is following, while at the same time questioning, Foucault, *The history of sexuality. Vol. I.* Baudrillard characterises pornography as a fantasy of a real in which representation does not exist, i.e. a real without seduction. See *De la séduction*, p. 45.

66 See Edwards, *Female sexuality and the law*, pp. 144–8. Edwards assimilates rape and seduction as follows: 'it is probable that many [of these breach-of-promise actions] were not simple cases of broken engagements after lengthy courtships but involved instances where marriage was promised to secure a submission to intercourse. This situation was not rape, but the carefully planned intimidation involved in the seduction does not fall far short. The distinctions depend on the complainant's submission and the defendant's intent' (p. 147). This idea, that seduction is tantamount to rape, is expressed in a number of works, especially those dealing with sexual harassment. See, for example, Mackinnon, *Sexual harassment of working women*. Note that in the early half of the twentieth century, many American states had seduction statutes, expressly designed to penalise cases in which intercourse was achieved by trickery or with promises of marriage.

67 Feild and Beinen, *Jurors and rape*, p. 339.

68 *Ibid.* p. 167.

69 Williams, *Textbook of criminal law*, p. 199.

70 Feild and Bienen, *Jurors and rape*, p. 168.

71 West, Roy and Nichols, *Understanding sexual attacks*, p. 136, quotes Kinsey: 'the difference between a good time and a rape often largely depends upon whether the girl's parents happened to be awake when she returned home'. Kinsey seemingly thought that the reported 'no' depended on the wakefulness of the parents – or maybe even of the super-ego, as in Glanville Williams' citing of shame as a motive for her believing she had said 'no' (see Williams, *Textbook of criminal law*, pp. 196–7). It should also be noted that the distinction between 'against the will' and 'without consent' hinges on the difference between the absence of 'no' and the presence of 'yes'. See Smith and Hogan, *Criminal law*, pp. 403–4 and 407.

72 Kierkegaard, 'Diary of the seducer', p. 337. On champagne, contrast Kierkegaard's description of the champagne aria in *Don Giovanni*: 'He is here, as it were, ideally intoxicated in himself. If every girl in the world surrounded him in this moment, he would not be a source of danger to them, for he is, as it were, too strong to wish to deceive them . . . ' ('Immediate stages of the erotic or the musical erotic', p. 133).

73 Kierkegaard, 'Immediate stages', p. 100.

74 Forcibly argued by Lacan, Sem II 260–4/222–6.

75 See Harrison, 'Rape – a case study in political philosophy', where he points out a related special feature of those rape trials in which consent is the principal issue, namely that the identification of the act at the same time entails that the defendant committed the act.

5 ' . . . a perfect likeness of the past'

The opportunity for writing on this topic arose when I was asked to organise a session at a Conference held at the University of Warwick Centre for Research in Literature and Philosophy in the summer of 1986. The organisers, David Wood and Andrew Benjamin, had chosen for the conference the arcane title: 'Writing the future'. My paper, originally conceived as discussing the concept of the past in psychoanalysis, came to address the conference title far more appositely than I could have expected. I wish to thank them for stimulating this unexpected turn.

1 SE V 621.
2 *allerdings*, unfortunately translated by Strachey as 'after all'.
3 SE V 623–5. First published in 1940.
4 SE V 623.
5 In what follows, I am much indebted to the sensitive analyses to be found in Granoff and Rey, *L'Occulte, objet de la pensée freudienne*.
6 Cf. the phrase that Freud employs in his correspondence with Jung, when discussing superstition and magic: 'the compliance of chance'. Naturally, this entire topic should be discussed in relation to the theory of repetition and transference as mapped out by Lacan in 'The four fundamental concepts of psychoanalysis'; there, his key reference is to the Aristotelian concepts of *tuché* and *automaton*. Aristotle gives the name *tuché* to such events as Freud calls 'remarkable coincidences' – both Aristotle and Freud regard such remarkable coincidences as empirical facts that need to be taken into account in any description of human affairs. See chapter 8, pp. 207–14.
7 Freud, *Interpretation of dreams*, p. 624.
8 Auden, 'As I walked out one evening', in *Collected shorter poems*, p. 85.
9 'Some additional notes on dream-interpretation as a whole' (1925i), SE XIX 137.
10 *Ibid*. SE XIX 138.
11 And therefore less dangerous than the 'intentional' wild analysts Freud discussed in Freud (1910k).
12 Lacan, 'Function and field of speech and language', E 302/88; translation modified.
13 See Aristotle, *Physics*, Book II, v, 196b, his account of the causality of luck and good fortune, where he describes lucky events as those which 'would have been recognised' as intended 'and would have determined the action, had it been anticipated'.
14 The target in these passages written in 1901 in *The psychopathology of*

everyday life is clearly Wilhelm Fliess, whose theories, it should be remembered, predicted the individual's future in terms of biological cycles. Such a biological writing of the future became anathema to Freud.

15 *The psychopathology of everyday life* (1901b), SE VI 257.
16 *Ibid*. SE VI 258.

A note on translation

1 Sem I 229/204–5.
2 According to the *OED*, 'enjoy' stems either from Old French *enjoie-r*, 'to give joy to', or Old French *enjoir*, 'to enjoy, rejoice'. For further discussion of the apparent difficulties of translating *jouissance*, see Macey, *Lacan in contexts*, pp. 201–5, and Gallop, 'Beyond the *jouissance* principle', *Representations* 7 1984.
3 Either in the form of a yearning for a means of expression which will not be subject to misunderstanding, which will not allow the reader the freedom to interpret, or in the excessive astonishment at the polysemy of language, at the fact that all terms have *at least* two meanings.

6 'In place of introduction'

This essay was originally intended as an introduction to the translations of Seminars I and II which Sylvana Tomaselli and I prepared, published by Cambridge University Press in Great Britain and Norton in the United States in 1988; for full details see the bibliography. Jacques-Alain Miller, the editor of the original French editions, insisted that the English translation of the Seminar should appear without any sort of introduction for the English reader, just as the French and other language editions had done. None the less, it seemed and still seems to be worth while to provide some such introduction to the text of an author who has a reputation in the English-language world for being formidably difficult. I hope that the historical remarks will be particularly useful to an audience unfamiliar with a history that has become nigh on mythical in French psychoanalytic circles. For an extensive account of these historical events, see Roudinesco, *La Bataille de cent ans. Histoire de la psychanalyse en France. Vol. 2. 1925–1985*, and the extremely informative book by Macey, *Lacan in contexts*, neither of which I was able to draw upon or footnote in detail in writing this introduction. I would like to thank Sylvana Tomaselli, Jacqueline Rose and Sebastian Gardner for their advice and comments on earlier versions of the essay.

1 In fact, Lacan refers to seminars that took place before 1953 in Seminar I and in the following seminars – in particular to his analysis of the *Wolfman* and *Ratman* (part of which found its way into his paper on 'The neurotic's individual myth', a 1953 lecture published in a corrected

version in English in 1979, listed in the bibliography), and to the discussion of *Dora*, which one can presume was reworked for the paper Lacan gave to the Congress of Romance-language speaking psychoanalysts in 1951, 'Intervention on the transference', translated in Mitchell and Rose, eds., *Feminine sexuality*, pp. 62–73.

2 Personal communication from Dr Ilse Hellmann.

3 Letter dated 14 July 1953, in Miller, ed., *La Scission*, p. 131.

4 The following section is in part derived from two previously published articles of mine ('The linguistic and the psychotic' and 'Lacan, Jacques').

5 Lacan's original paper was listed in the reports of papers read to the Congress as 'The looking-glass phase'. It is better known in the version dating from 1949, published in *Ecrits* and translated in *Ecrits: a selection* as: 'The mirror stage as formative of the function of the I'.

6 See Lacan, 'La psychiatrie anglaise et la guerre'.

7 Lacan, 'Le temps logique et l'assertion de certitude anticipée' and 'Le nombre treize et la forme logique de la suspicion'; for detailed discussion of these papers, see chapter 8, pp. 178–92.

8 The documents relating to this 'excommunication' (as Lacan termed it, in the opening session of *Seminar XI*, in January 1964) have been published; see Miller (ed.), *L'Excommunication*; for a full account of these events, see Roudinesco, *La Bataille, Vol. 2*, and the useful 'Jacques Lacan: curriculum vitae' in Macey, *Lacan in contexts*, pp. 236–46. From the original documents, one gains some sense of the issues concerning Lacan's practice and teaching that led the IPA to regard him as 'unacceptable': the arguments that were offered defending the variable lengths of the session had no weight – no one could 'predict' the duration of the session; Lacan was said to avoid the negative transference, playing havoc with the analysis of transference, to the point where he manipulated it; Lacan was said to see himself as the source of rewards and punishments; he was seen to have too great an influence on the clothes and vocabulary of his pupils. Yet the Advisory Committee, reporting in 1963, also recognised that 'Lacan is the interpreter of Psychoanalysis for a large public.' They added: 'But his pupils must rewrite what he is doing.' These points are taken from what became known as the Perrier document: François Perrier's 'compte-rendu' of Pierre Turquet's supposedly confidential verbal report to certain officers of the SFP. Turquet, who chaired the Advisory Committee of the IPA which reported on the SFP, and who transmitted these views, protested that this 'compte-rendu' in no way reflected the 'real tenor' nor the 'esprit' of the Committee's Report. The Report remains unpublished, and is not available for consultation. Further extensive material on these events, and on analysands' experiences of Lacan's short sessions, can be found in Roudinesco, *La Bataille de cent ans*, vol. 2, esp. pp. 427–34. For a recent debate by Lacanians and non-Lacanians on the use of variable length sessions, see *Etudes Freudiennes 25* April 1985.

9 Foucault, 'Introduction' to Binswanger, *Le Rêve et l'existence*. In this, his first publication, a weighty introduction to a French translation of Ludwig Binswanger, *Traum und Existenz*, Michel Foucault addressed the Lacanian version of psychoanalytic theory alongside the Kleinian, making it clear that he reserved his weightiest consideration for the new approach to psychoanalysis being developed each week at the Hôpital Sainte-Anne. See chapter 12, pp. 289–93.

10 Ricoeur, *Freud and philosophy* (1961). Later in the 1960s, Ricoeur was involved in vitriolic debates with the Lacanians, in part over the extent of his supposed debt to Lacan. See Roudinesco, *La Bataille de cent ans*, vol. 2, pp. 398–405, for an even-handed account of these debates.

11 Lacan, 'The Freudian Thing' (1957), E 436.

12 Freud, 'Psychical (or mental) treatment' [(1890a), SE VII 283–302], in what has become a celebrated passage: 'A layman will no doubt find it hard to understand how pathological disorders of the body and mind can be eliminated by "mere" words. He will feel that he is being asked to believe in magic. And he will not be so very wrong, for the words which we use in our everyday speech are nothing other than watered-down magic. But we shall have to follow a roundabout path in order to explain how science sets about restoring to words a part at least of their former magical power.'

13 See Freud, *The question of lay analysis* GW XIV 281; Stud Erg 337; SE XX 246.

14 There are two translations of this work, 'The function and field of speech and language in psychoanalysis': that produced by Wilden, *The language of the self*, in 1968, with extensive notes and a long commentary on the themes and influences of Lacan's work – as a book Wilden's is *still*, remarkably, the best introduction to Lacan's work; and that by Alan Sheridan in Lacan, *Ecrits: a selection*.

15 For example, in two sentences discussed in *Seminars I & II*: 'the concept is the time of the thing'; 'the word is the murder of the thing'.

16 For a subtle recent consideration of Lacan's reading of Freud, see Bowie, *Freud, Proust and Lacan: Theory as fiction*.

17 A pun that is not possible in French, but one that is entirely in keeping with Lacan's thought, and allows one to see even more clearly the bridge between Lacan's version of the mirror stage, concentrating explicitly on the other, and Winnicott's contemporaneous notion of the mother (in particular her eyes, or her gaze) as mirroring the child (back) to itself.

18 Sem I 10; references are to the pagination of the English edition of *Seminars I & II*.

19 E 242–3/35.

20 It originally appeared in *Evolution Psychiatrique* 1956, pp. 225–52. The extent of the rewriting of Lacan's articles from the 1950s into the form in which they are almost universally read and cited, in the *Ecrits* of

1966, has not often been noted, and has certainly not been analysed in detail. It is obviously of importance if one is wishing to gain a sense of the details of the development, year by year, of Lacan's thought.

21 'Two aspects of language and two types of aphasic disturbance', in Jakobson and Halle, *Fundamentals of language*, p. 90.

22 E 207–8; see pp. 178–92 below, in particular p. 359n77.

23 Sem I 52–3.

24 Sem I 74.

25 Sem I 127–8.

26 Sem I 115.

27 Sem I 141.

28 E 208.

29 See the papers in Wollheim and Hopkins, eds., *Philosophical essays on Freud*, in particular the paper by Donald Davidson.

30 An exception in this respect, as in so many others, is Bion, *Attention and interpretation*, chapter II, 'Lies and the thinker', pp. 97–105.

31 *captation*, translated by 'captation', is a distinctive term by which Lacan signals this dimension of deception and fascination by the image. Many have thought his use of the term to be original and idiosyncratic. In fact, it probably stems from his response to a sympathetic criticism by Pichon, 'M. Lacan devant la famille', recently reprinted with a commentary by Roudinesco, 'Monsieur Pichon devant la famille'. There Pichon referred to the term *captatif* introduced into psychoanalytic terminology by M. Codet, and which was then used by Pichon, Laforgue and Codet. Pichon criticises Lacan for not employing the term, since he thinks it is most apt to describe what Lacan places so much emphasis on in his article on 'La famille', namely narcissistic identification. It seems plausible that Lacan took this rebuke to heart, but went on to make 'captation' very much his own term.

32 Sem I 138.

33 For a fascinating discussion of these paradoxes, stimulated by Lacan's work, see Eco, 'Mirrors'.

34 Sem I 170.

35 See Laplanche and Pontalis, *The language of psychoanalysis*, entries on ideal ego/ego ideal.

36 Sem I 205.

37 Sem I 217.

38 Sem I 222.

39 Sem I 230.

40 *Studies on hysteria* GW I 293, Stud Erg 82; SE II 289.

41 Opening address to Caracas Conference, July 1980, published in *L'Ane 1*, April–May 1981, pp. 30–1.

42 Sem I 320.

43 Since Lacan's seminar of 1954–5 there have been other such specu-

lative interpretations, clearly founded upon the sea-change in general view to which his work led; the most important and original of these is Derrida, 'Spéculer – sur "Freud" '.

44 See E 462–3.

45 E 242/35.

46 E 463.

47 In *Seminar II*, Lacan puts a related point in the following ironic fashion:
Post-analytical paranoia is a long way from being a mythical problem . . . You don't need a very good psychoanalyst to get this to come about, it's sufficient to believe very fervently in psychoanalysis. I have seen paranoias one can call post-analytical, and which can be said to be spontaneous. In an adequate environment, where there's a very strong preoccupation with psychological facts, a subject can succeed, on condition nonetheless of having some inclination for it, in girdling himself with problems which without any doubt are fictive, but to which he gives substance, within a ready-made language – that of psychoanalysis, which everyone talks about. It generally takes a very long time for a chronic delirium to get built up, the subject must put a lot into it – generally, he invests a third of his life in it. I must say that, to some extent, the analytic literature constitutes a ready-made delirium, and it isn't rare to see subjects dressed up in it, ready-to-wear. The style, if I may put it like this, of those silent devotees of the ineffable mystery of the analytic experience is an attenuated form of it, but its foundation is homogeneous with what for now I am calling paranoia. (Sem II 242)
One might conclude that, to the extent that a culture becomes infused with psychoanalysis such that it takes on the paranoid form of a system of knowledge, that culture becomes immune to the specifically psychoanalytic effects of psychoanalysis.

48 Sem II 296.

49 Though the reference to Condorcet in Seminar II is an indication that the source may well be an eighteenth-century one. About the same time, Lévi-Strauss was elaborating a distinction between 'mechanical' and 'statistical' explanations (see Lévi-Strauss, *Structural anthropology*); however, Lacan's distinction is a more radical one.

50 Further development of Lacan's thinking here may be found in Lacan, *Seminar XI*, in the discussion of Aristotle's doctrines of causality, and the place of *tuché* as a causal concept proper to human affairs; see chapter 8, pp. 207ff.

51 See 'Function and field of speech and language' E 284–9/73–77; nor was it to be the last – the reference is sustained in Sem XI.

52 Sem II 234ff.

53 Sem II 31–2.

54 'Seminar on *The purloined letter*', p. 44, and Sem II 203.

55 Sem II 306.

56 Sem II 307.

57 'Function and field of speech and language' E 285/73.

58 Freud, 'Remembering, repeating and working-through' (1914g), SE XII 150, emphasis in original; see chapter 9, p. 241.

59 That it is exemplary is not, to my mind, denied by its having been subverted, and undercut, by the criticism of Derrida, 'Le facteur de la vérité', as is indicated by Barbara Johnson's article on Lacan and Derrida: the chain of readings also repeats the transmission (dissemination) with which Lacan and Derrida concern themselves. See Johnson, 'The frame of reference: Poe, Lacan, Derrida' and Felman, 'To open the question'.

60 Dennett, 'The abilities of men and machines', in Dennett, *Brainstorms*, p. 257.

61 For an introduction to this area, see Hofstadter, *Gödel, Escher, Bach*, esp. chapter 7; Boden, *Artificial intelligence and natural man*; and Dennett, 'The abilities of men and machines', in Dennett, *Brainstorms*.

62 See Lacan, *Le Séminaire. Livre IX. L'Identification. 1961–62; Le Séminaire. Livre XIII. L'Objet de la psychanalyse. 1965–66*; see also 'La science et la vérité' (1965), E 861.

63 Freud, *Introductory lectures (1916–17)*, SE XVI 320–57.

64 Sem II 326.

65 Prigogine and Stengers, *Order out of chaos*; see also Wiener, *The human use of human beings*, for the first element of such a global re-interpretation.

66 Sem II 74.

67 Sem II 125.

68 Sem II 228.

69 Sem II 254.

70 Sem II 153.

71 See Forrester, *Language and the origins of psychoanalysis*, pp. 84–96.

72 The first published version of the 'Seminar on *The purloined letter*', which appeared in *La Psychanalyse 2* 1956, included a compressed synopsis of some of the themes that made *The purloined letter* pertinent to the work of the seminar that year: the analysis of sequences of signifiers (letters, numbers) displaying the properties of repetition and creativity. An extended version of the paper and synopsis was reprinted in *Ecrits*. It is unfortunate that this version of 1966 was not translated in full in the *French Freud* number of *Yale French Studies* of 1972, because it has allowed the 'Seminar' to be read in Britain and America out of the context of Lacan's discussion of repetition, of the machine and cybernetics.

73 Sem II 244–5.

74 See Wiener, *The human use of human beings* (1954, second edition), New York: Bantam, 1968, pp. 33–4. Lacan's view that the lie and deception are crucial to psychoanalysis and its practice predates the

cybernetic influence, for example: '[language] manifests this truth as intention, through eternally opening it up on to the question of knowing how what expresses its particular lie can end up formulating the universal of its truth' (Lacan, 'Propos sur la causalité psychique' (1946), E 166).

75 Sem III 48.

76 See chapter 7, esp. pp. 153ff.

77 Freud, *Jokes and their relation to the unconscious* (1905c); GW VI 165; Stud IV 139; SE VIII 148.

78 *Ibid.* GW VI 207; Stud IV 170; SE VIII 181. 'In a joke this third person is indispensable for the completion of the pleasure-producing process; but on the other hand the second person may be absent . . .'

79 Sem II 264.

7 What the psychoanalyst does with words

An earlier version of this paper was given to a conference on the theme 'Langage et psychanalyse', at a Journée de Travail of the Centre de Recherches en Psychanalyse et Psychopathologie, Université Paris VII, 29 September, 1984; I would like to thank Pierre Fedida for the opportunity of presenting these ideas to such a sympathetic and knowledgeable audience. With the aid of the linguistic gifts of Michelle Tran Van Khai, that version appeared, under the title 'Quand dire, c'est faire: Austin, Lacan et les actes de parole en psychanalyse', in *Psychanalyse à l'Université 10* 1985 pp. 350–67. Papers on similar themes, including earlier versions of the ideas included here, were given to: the Department of Psychology, University of Manchester, in January 1982, thanks to John Churcher's invitation; the Faculty of Humanities, University of Kent, in November 1983, thanks to Martin Stanton's invitation; to a Graduate Students' Research Seminar, Social and Political Sciences, Cambridge University, on 23 February 1988, thanks to Anthony Giddens' invitation. I would like to thank all these audiences for their comments and criticism, in particular J.-B. Pontalis, Anthony Giddens and Jacques Nassif.

1 'Function and field of speech and language' E 247/40.

2 Sem III 255.

3 Wittgenstein, *Philosophical investigations*, § 38.

4 *Ibid.* § 255.

5 *Ratman* SE X 162.

6 *Ratman* SE X 178–9.

7 Harvey Sacks, 'Everyone has to lie', in B. G. Blount and Mary Sarches, *Sociocultural dimensions of language use*, New York: Academic Press, 1975, pp. 57–79.

8 Nor did he think that the correct solution of these 'linguistic' confusions is an advance in itself for the treatment. He notes that his patient responded to his clarifications and explanations by admitting 'that all of this sounded quite plausible, but he was naturally not in the very least convinced by it' (SE X 181).

9 Cf. Janik and Toulmin, *Wittgenstein's Vienna*, which emphasises the importance of the philosopher and essayist Mauthner for Wittgenstein's theories of language. Nor should we forget that the sort of concerns that prompted Freud to write his *Psychopathology of everyday life* might quite properly be found discussed in a daily newspaper – see Meringer, 'Wie man sich versprechen kann'. What is more, Lacan's advice to a young psychoanalyst was: 'Do crossword puzzles' (E 266/56).

10 *Ratman* SE X 181n1.

11 To see this, note how Freud's sentence 2 allows the substitution of 'anyone' by 'I', yielding: 'If I say /my father is dead/, 'I' will have me to contend with' – the punitive (and divided) function of the 'me' emerges clearly.

12 There are many excellent descriptions of this world; amongst the most evocative are Leclaire's series of papers from the 1950s, reprinted in his *Démasquer le Réel*; two of these chapters, 'Jerome, or death in the life of the obsessional', 'Philo, or the obsessional and his desire', are translated in Schneiderman, *Returning to Freud. Clinical psychoanalysis in the school of Lacan*.

13 The Ratman did not succeed in satisfying Freud on this point; however, the next memory he produced did culminate in his being surprised, since his own ideas implied that he compared his father's death with someone else's and discovered that he cared less about his father's death than he thought.

14 The importance of this '(not) knowing one's thoughts' is discussed at further length by Lacan in Sem VI 269–70, where he points out that the discovery that the Other (parents) does not know my thoughts is the moment when the not-said is brought into my being – the moment when one becomes a subject possessing the dimension of the unconscious. The formulation, 'my parents know my thoughts', is the foundation of speech – all of thought is to be found in the Other (the discourse of the Other). Lacan notes: 'then the child realizes that the adult does not know its thoughts – there lies the path of repression'. One crucial means of transition from 'my parents know my thoughts' to 'the Other doesn't know what I am thinking' is the lie; as Lacan writes: 'even if it is destined to deceive, the discourse speculates on faith in testimony' (E 251–2/43; translation modified). See my *Lying on the couch. Truth, lies and the epistemology of psychoanalysis*.

15 There is the distinct possibility that Foucault's formulation of psychoanalytic procedures and its theorisation was written under the influence of Lacan; as Foucault said in an interview granted just after Lacan's death, Lacan's writings in the 1950s had helped to liberate him from the 'completely traditional conception of the subject' on which philosophy and the human sciences depended, by showing him that 'the apparently simple use of the pronoun "I"' masked the fact that the subject is, in reality, 'a complex, fragile thing, of which it is so difficult to speak, but

without which, however, it is not possible to speak' ('Lacan, il liberatore della psicanalisi', p. 1).

16 Including in this idea the derivatives of the various persons of the verbs or pronouns, such as 'my', 'my father', as in the Ratman passage.

17 See Todorov, 'Freud sur l'énonciation'.

18 Cf. 'Function and field of speech and language' E 303/89: 'In order to know how to reply to the subject in analysis, the procedure is to recognise first of all the place where his *ego* is, the *ego* that Freud himself defined as an *ego* formed of a verbal nucleus; in other words, to know through whom and for whom the subject poses *his question*.' This formula is at once a *clarification* of the technique, a standby of virtually all analytic schools, of the analysis of identifications, and a *reminder* that what constitutes an identification is the substitution of the 'you' by the 'I'. But this passage also asserts that, once one knows who is being addressed (the other's object) and by whom (the other, the 'you') – the procedure I have concentrated on by discussing pronouns – the path is clear for the most important aspect: the specification of the *question* – what I would call the speech act – which the symptom embodies.

19 Lacan describes the super-ego's discourse as fundamentally summed up by the sentence 'You are that.' See Sem III 312, 322.

20 Cf. *The interpretation of dreams* (1900a), SE V 534–5: '"If only Otto were responsible for Irma's illness!" The dream repressed the optative and replaced it by a straightforward present: "Yes, Otto is responsible for Irma's illness." . . . The present tense is the one in which wishes are represented and fulfilled.' See also 'On dreams' (1901a), SE V 647, for an even more emphatic statement of the general principle.

21 Linguists themselves have shown that the tenses of European languages are largely dependent on the subject of the utterance rather than on some objective relation to an external or objective chronology: the difference in tense usages between different languages indicates this (e.g. the French future tense is much less used than it would be in corresponding English cases; a simple present tense is used when the future would be required in English).

22 A famous claim this, one spelt out in 'The unconscious' and discussed in 'Negation'. The operation of negation is bound up with the subject of the utterance and rarely if ever corresponds to a logical operation of 'not *p*'. Lacan argues this at some length with respect to the peculiar particle *ne* in French, which is not only superficially semantically redundant, but has certain usages which are semantically inexplicable: 'J'ai peur qu'il ne vienne.' In English, we can understand some of the peculiarity of the negative by considering double negatives, whose formal result may seem to be to arrive back at simple affirmation, but whose discursive function is never that. Compare 'he is not unintelligent' and 'he is intelligent'. The difference between these statements points to a different posture of the 'I' in the act of uttering, in which the double negative sentence increases the concentration of

interest, of self regard, upon the 'I', rather than focusing on the 'he', the subject of the statement.

23 *Ratman* SE X 222. See below for a further discussion of this passage.

24 See Forrester, *Language and the origins of psychoanalysis*, pp. 141–65.

25 *Dora* SE VII 116; Forrester, *Language*, p. 163.

26 See Wilden, *The language of the self*, Ragland-Sullivan, *Jacques Lacan and the philosophy of psychoanalysis*, Benvenuto and Kennedy, *The works of Jacques Lacan*; a similar, but now searchingly critical, concentration on this aspect of Lacan's work, by no means of an introductory sort, is to be found in Lacoue-Labarthe and Nancy, *Le Titre de la lettre (Une lecture de Lacan)*.

27 See Wollheim, 'The cabinet of Dr. Lacan', for a critique of the signifier/signified model in psychoanalysis.

28 Indeed, *la langue* hardly played a part in his lexicon in the 1950s: his Rome Report was entitled 'Fonction et champ de la parole et du *langage* [not *langue*] en psychanalyse'; his emphasis on *langage* was on the combinatory, on the quasi-mathematical basis that Lévi-Strauss supplied for the human sciences (a basis that he later downplayed in the selective rewriting of certain passages, e.g. the four paragraphs of E 285, for the *Ecrits* of 1966), on the mathematics of the code. The opposition in Lacan is thus between *langage* and *parole*, an opposition that has entirely different connotations from that of *langue* and *parole*.

29 See Benvenuto and Kennedy, *The works of Jacques Lacan*, p. 85.

30 I am aware of two other works that draw attention to the importance of speech acts for psychoanalysis: Felman's virtuoso *Le Scandale du corps parlant*, and Bellemin-Noël, 'Psychanalyse et pragmatique'. There are many points of convergence between Felman's account and mine: the appreciation of Austin's humour and a recognition of its conceptual importance; the fundamental starting-point, seeing the theory of speech acts and psychoanalysis as unwitting allies in specific debates within linguistics and the philosophy of language; the *rapprochement* between Lacan's theories and Austin's; a sense that Austin's work has often been ill used, and that recognising its kinship with psychoanalysis is not only clarifying for the latter but will enable us to remain aware of the subversive force of Austin's work (its elimination of any justificatory grounds for acting as if certain speech acts were privileged through being devoted to denoting their own truth and reality). My use of speech act theory differs from hers in that I am more specifically interested in characterising the *conversation* of the analytic session and the distinctiveness of the analyst's conversational style.

Bellemin-Noël takes the Lacanian theory of language to be the exemplar of a formalist linguistic analysis that runs the danger of falling back into the substantialism against which it so vigorously argues, and takes the fetishism of the signifier found in Lacanian theory (of a certain date and age) to be exactly this positivistic and formalistic theory which the theory of speech acts will help psychoanalysis to avoid. While agreeing with the thrust of his argument, it will be clear that I view Lacan's theory of speech and language as far richer than a narrowly conceived theory of the signifier; while endorsing Bellemin-Noël's overall project, I think he has mistaken the object of criticism.

31 'Function and field of speech and language' E 251–2/43; translation modified. An interesting text of Freud's also puts the emphasis entirely on the dimension of communication, even when what is communicated appears to be nothing of the kind: 'Let us suppose, then, that someone – a patient in analysis, for instance – tells us one of his dreams. We shall assume that in this way he is making us one of the communications to which he has pledged himself by the fact of having started an analytic treatment. It is, to be sure, a communication made by inappropriate means, for dreams are not in themselves social utterances, not a means of giving information. Nor, indeed, do we understand what the dreamer was trying to say to us, and he himself is equally in the dark . . . We [make] – quite arbitrarily, it must be admitted – the assumption, adopt as a postulate, that even this unintelligible dream must be a fully valid psychical act, with sense and worth, which we can use in analysis like any other communication. Only the outcome of our experiment can show whether we are right. If we succeed in turning the dream into an utterance of value of that kind, we shall evidently have a prospect of learning something new and of receiving communications of a sort which would otherwise be inaccessible to us . . . How do we propose to transform the dream into a normal communication and how do we explain the fact that some of the patient's utterances have assumed a form which is unintelligible both to him and to us?' (*New introductory lectures on psycho-analysis*, 'Lecture XXIX. Revision of the Theory of Dreams' (1933 [1932]), SE XXII 8–9).

32 For what follows see E 279–80/68–70. I also discussed these in chapter 6, pp. 116ff.

33 One sees an additional reason why Freud found the method of grammatical transformation appropriate to the analysis of Schreber's psychosis: as is clear from the outset of his book, Schreber does not wish to be recognised; he is simply stating how the world appears to him, for the purpose of obtaining his freedom from legal detention.

34 See, amongst several passages, 'Function and field of speech and language' E 265/55–6; Sem I 100/85.

35 Cast your mind back to the passage from the Ratman case-history (*Ratman* SE XII 62ff.), where Freud contrasts obsessional thinking and 'every sort of psychical act' once the 'affective index' has been restored to it. This distinction is very similar to one that Austin draws between statements examined simply on the basis of whether they are true or false (these would be Freud's patients' 'obsessional ideas'), and those statements which are acts rather than descriptions of states of affairs (Freud's list includes 'wishes, temptations, impulses, reflections, doubts, commands, or prohibitions'). Freud comes back to this distinc-

tion between ideas and psychical acts at the end of his theoretical discussion of obsessions: 'A thought-process is obsessive or compulsive when, in consequence of an inhibition . . . at the motor end of the psychical system, it is undertaken with an expenditure of energy which . . . is normally reserved for actions alone; or, in other words, an obsessive or compulsive thought is one whose function it is to represent an act regressively.' (SE X 246).

36 Felman, *Le scandale du corps parlant*, gives a brilliant extended analysis of the significance of Austin's wit.

37 Austin, 'Performance utterances' (1956), in: *Philosophical papers*, p. 249. The passage continues by making it quite clear that a whole class of discourses, particularly those that advertise themselves as 'scientific', are being targeted here: 'What we need to do for the case of stating, and by the same token describing and reporting, is to take them a bit off their pedestal, to realize that they are speech-acts no less than all these other speech-acts that we have been mentioning and talking about as performative' (pp. 249–50). Felman also recognises the force of this passage (quoting it at least twice in her book – see *Le Scandale du corps parlant*, p. 20).

38 The promise is the linch-pin of Felman's *rapprochement* of Molière's *Don Juan* and Austin's theory of performatives: Don Juan is devoted to an examination *en acte* of the meaning of promises and the ways in which they can be made to misfire, not perform: the promise of marriage being a key stage in the dialectic of seduction (these remarks could be read alongside chapter 4, this volume). Felman also points out the temporal logic of the promise: 'the promise is linked to a temporality of speed and haste, to what Lacan called – in an entirely different context – "the function of haste", giving rise to "the assertion of anticipated certainty" ' (*Le Scandale du corps parlant*, p. 66); see chapter 8, this volume.

39 This sort of example indicates why introducing a distinction between sincere and insincere speech acts creates more problems than it solves.

40 Bellemin-Noël begins his article on speech act theory and psycho-analysis by noting the striking lack of interest on the part of psychoanalysts in 'recent advances in linguistics' – by which he means both Chomsky's transformational grammar and speech act theory (called *pragmatique* in France). For her part, Felman emphasises the manner in which Austin's work has been recuperated and neutralised by both philosophers and linguists (Grice, Searle, Benveniste, Katz *et al.*).

41 The prevalent model of communication invoked a closed circuit between speaker and hearer, with a message passing via the linguistic code. This model fits quite easily into the functionalist account that we find in sociolinguistics: language always communicates, so this account runs, even when you have a couple of goons saying, 'How're you doin', 'I'm doing fine, man.'

42 Indeed, he was acutely aware of the development of information and communications theory (discussed at length in *Seminar II*) and took up the former's concept of redundancy so as to make explicit the following assumption on which his conception of speech, and that of psycho-analysis, is built: 'the more the function of language becomes neutralised as it moves closer to information, the more language is imputed to be laden with *redundancies* . . . This is highly instructive for us, for what is redundant as far as information is concerned is precisely that which does duty as resonance in speech. For the function of language is not to inform but to evoke. What I seek in speech is the response of the other' ('Function and field of speech and language' E 299/86).

43 Austin, *How to do things with words*, p. 17.

44 In *Le Moment lacanien*, p. 71, Sichère recognises the interesting convergence of argument of Austin and Lacan in their use of the marriage ceremony as the exemplar of speech, and attacks Felman, *Le Scandale du corps parlant*, for seeing their arguments as parallel. Sichère considers Austin and Lacan to be arguing the exact opposite of each other: 'c'est précisément dans la possibilité que la promesse ne soit pas tenue qu'elle révèle son efficace, que se manifeste le plus ouvertement la dimension indépassable et contraignante de la Loi incarnée en l'occurrence dans la puissance à jamais d'un "Tu es ma femme" où le sujet se modifie dans son être même de se lier lui-même à sa partenaire depuis ce lieu tiers et transcendant qui ne le contraint pas moins, à la seconde même, que celle qu'il nomme ainsi.' As is clear, I do not contrast Austin and Lacan on this point, though it is clear that Lacan (and Freud) are more aware than Austin of the profound importance of the failure of promises for understanding their true character.

45 Bellemin-Noël, 'Psychanalyse et pragmatique', p. 414, emphasises the mutual implication of speaker and hearer in speech acts, pointing out the importance of this for understanding the analytic conversation.

46 See 'Function and field of speech and language' E 296/84. It might also be an error fostered by too great an emphasis on identification. If the analysis of transference were exclusively modelled on the analysis of identification, there would be no other model of 'full speech' possible save the 'recognition' of the reality of the analyst's person. Too exclusive a reliance on the 'pronominal' method outlined above might foster this unfruitful preoccupation with the analyst's reality.

47 In his papers in the 1950s, Lacan made some use of the concept of the 'shifter', introduced into structural linguistics at about that time, while a very similar conception was proposed in 1954 by Bar-Hillel in Anglo-Saxon philosophy under the name 'deictics'; it was this latter concept that was much employed in ethnomethodology's preoccupation with the standpoint of a speaker, whether observer, participant or both. Shifters are terms in sentences which require specification by relating them to the interlocutors; otherwise they fail to refer (often

enough provoking anxiety). The pronouns are important members of this category, and so are certain adverbs and prepositions which mark time, place etc.: tomorrow, here, now. In this way, it was thought, the necessary interpretation of a specific subject of discourse in the statements uttered was secured, in much the same way as Austin secured the position of a subject by noticing that utterances are acts rather than quasi-scientific statements about the world. While this function of the shifter is discussed by Lacan, one should not over-emphasise its influence in his work: it makes Lacan into more of a follower of Jakobson's than he was. Lacan's use of the shifter was tied to his introduction of the distinction between the subject of the *énoncé* and the subject of the *énonciation*. We will return to this distinction.

48 He also called it 'elective speech' in *Seminar III* and 'votive speech' in *Seminar VI*; see note 58 below.

49 'Function and field of speech and language' E 298/85.

50 Muller and Richardson, *Lacan and language: a reader's guide to Ecrits*, pp. 118–19.

51 In fact, Austin did construct a category that includes this special feature: what he called the 'perlocutionary force' of an utterance measures the effect that an illocutionary act has on the other; when I say, 'I convinced him', the effect of conviction is necessary to the utterance, whereas when I say, 'I promised him', the accent falls entirely on the speaker. But Austin did not enter into much detail concerning the binding effect of these instances of 'founding speech'. Yet these are the most delicate and significant of utterances.

52 'Function and field of speech and language' E 298/85.

53 Sem I 125/107. This exegesis of Lacan's theory of speech indicates why I chose Austin's neologism 'performative' to translate Lacan's ideas in this section of the English version of Seminar I.

54 To counteract this tendency to interpret psychoanalysis as simultane-ously not-serious and not-real, Lacan often emphasised Freud's declaration ('Observations on transference-love' (1915a), SE XII 168) that the love that goes under the name transference-love is as genuine a love as any other.

55 Sem I 126/108.

56 See Sem I 244/219; Sem II 190–2/169–70. In this context, it would be fruitful to reconsider the psychoanalytically exemplary self-naming of Odysseus as 'no one', as does Granoff, in *Filiations*, 'C'est personne, c'est moi: l'espace du contre-transfert' (pp. 84–109).

57 Lacan grants two different functions to the second person, the *tu*: the first is that of founding speech, the second is the specification of the depersonalised 'no one' (see Sem III 311).

58 'Function and field of speech and language' E 285/73; translation modified. See also Sem I 126/108: 'Two planes have always been distinguished within which the exchange of human speech is played out – the plane of recognition in so far as speech links the subjects together

into this pact which transforms them, and sets them up as human subjects communicating – [and] the plane of the *communiqué*, [in which] the emphasis is placed on the object considered as external to the action of speech, which speech expresses.'

An even more extreme contrasting of two planes of speech is to be found in Sem VI 271: 'We distinguish two planes. One is immediate, that of the call (*bread! help!*): the subject is for a moment identical to its need – this is the *quesitive level of demand* (which one first finds articulated in the relation of the child to its mother). The other is the *votive* level, on which the subject, throughout its entire life, has to find itself, in whatever has escaped the form of language as it develops in transforming, in rejecting that element of need that tends to get expressed. It is this second degree of articulation which is sought in analysis.'

59 Sem III 343.

60 Searle, *Speech acts: an essay in the philosophy of language*, p. 71. And isn't that what we mean by convention – the idea that there is an *unspoken* rule governing the use of the words?

61 'La psychanalyse et son enseignement' (1957), E 439.

62 Warnock, *The object of morality*, pp. 96ff., considers the notion that a promise is a prediction.

63 Bachelard, *The philosophy of no*, p. 18.

64 In this sense, it would not make much sense to call the Bank of England's promise either sincere or insincere; see the distinction Searle introduces, *Speech acts*, p. 62.

65 Sem II 371–2/323–4.

66 Searle, *Speech acts*, pp. 50–3.

67 'La psychanalyse et son enseignement' (1957), E 454.

68 See *Being and nothingness. A phenomenological essay on ontology*, pp. 86–96, and the numerous discussions it has spawned in the Anglo-American philosophical literature, particularly the essays in Wollheim and Hopkins (eds.), *Philosophical essays on Freud*, and Sebastian Gardner, 'Sartre's critique of Freud; irrationality and the philosophy of psychoanalysis'.

69 Sem I 197/174–5.

70 That this is also a legitimately Freudian view of the hysteric is indicated by the Lewis Carroll-like observation he made on the topic of the lies hysterics tell. 'The mendaciousness of hysterics calls to mind the old paradox of the Cretan [Epimenides]: if a hysterical woman asserts that she has lied, it may be precisely this assertion that is a lie' (Nunberg and Federn, eds., *Minutes of the Vienna Psychoanalytic Society, Vol. III: 1910–1911*, 'Scientific Meeting on 19 October 1910', p. 23).

71 Searle, *Speech acts*, p. 58: '"I promise" and "I hereby promise" are among the strongest illocutionary force indicating devices for *commitment* provided by the English language.'

72 Sem I 254–5/229–30.

73 Sem II 326–7/282–3.

74 Sem II 371/323.

75 *Studies on hysteria* (1895d), SE II 115.

76 This imaginary example has some interesting points in common with a piece of analytic gossip that has gone the rounds about an analytic intervention of Lacan's. The man in question had had great difficulty in making up his mind to get married, had spent many sessions struggling with his doubts and his second thoughts. One day, he stretched out on the couch and said to his analyst: 'Donc, je me marie demain.' [So, I'm getting married tomorrow.] To which Lacan replied: 'Avec qui?' [To whom?] The force of the interpretation in part depends upon the fact that the verb *marier* can be used both transitively and reflexively. The analysand had chosen to use it reflexively, thus accentuating his anticipated change of marital status, without specifying the partner who was to collaborate in this change of status – one assumes that he thought that that went without saying. Lacan's intervention might well be seen as a gentle, if rather surprising, enquiry as to whether the subject was attempting to squirm out of the commitments of founding speech – as if his absorption in the 'I am your husband' had made him forget the necessary correlative 'You are my wife.'

77 One might say we have never left him; these considerations of pronouns could be immediately cashed out by noting that the fundamental rule of association, 'Say whatever comes into your head', carries with it the implicit assurance, or guarantee, of the fundamental anonymity of the analyst: 'It doesn't matter who you think I am, you may say anything to me.' That is, 'I am no one' (cf. Odysseus).

78 Sem I 127/109. Lacan refined this formulation in Sem XI 133/146: 'the transference is the enactment [*mise en acte*] of the reality of the unconscious.' This 'enacting' should not be confused with 'acting out'. Schneiderman (*Rat Man*, pp. 15–16) notes usefully: 'Whatever ritual character the analytic session maintains serves as a frame that permits the *staging* of what we may call non-events. The analyst owes it to his patient as well as to himself to maintain this frame rigorously to assure that whatever is enacted in the session remains in function of the act of speech.' This chapter attempts to avoid the implicit opposition of speech and action (which Schneiderman would be amongst the first to admit is unsatisfactory) while recognising that the 'events' or 'speech acts' found within the analytic session are defused of their character of 'events' or 'actions'. It is the specific mode of intervention of the analyst that achieves this end.

79 Although this is a simple, operational definition, it is much criticised, since it is said to downgrade the importance of the reality of the analyst's individuality and the analysand's 'truthful' or 'realistic' reaction to it. I think that this criticism is based on a misconception, which I hope the rest of this chapter will clear up.

80 One which I have used for a slightly different purpose elsewhere: see chapter 2, this volume, which also alludes to some of the arguments concerning speech acts developed more fully here.

81 *Studies on hysteria* (1895d), SE II 302–3.

82 Freud was later to make this line of thought more explicit by employing the terms *Ich* and *Es*, 'I' and 'it', for two of his major concepts ('ego' and 'id') – there are complications in this development, though; I do not want to give the impression that I concur with Bettelheim's rather naïve account of Freud's humanistic psychology as an extension of his facility with the German language, or with other commentaries that would make the reference of the *systems 'das Ich'* and *'das Es'* coincide with the uses of the pronouns *Ich* and *Es*.

83 *Studies on hysteria* (1895d), SE II 304.

84 On this point, Searle's stricture is a useful and important one: 'So we must not suppose, what the metaphor of "force" suggests, that the different illocutionary verbs mark off points on a single continuum. Rather, there are several different continua of "illocutionary force"' (*Speech acts*, p. 70). Felman, *Le scandale du corps parlant*, pp. 104ff., has very pertinent remarks on the importance of 'force', and of the way in which readers of Austin (Benveniste and others) have evaded the force of Austin's theory of 'illocutionary force'.

85 *Ratman* SE X 221–2.

86 *Ratman* Stud VII 83.

87 As opposed to describing or 'constating' – though as soon as one tries to make 'noting', 'observing', 'seeing' into non-performative verbs, we see how implausible it is to claim that there can be a pure non-performative verb.

88 *Ratman* SE X 166.

89 *Ratman* SE X 169.

90 I quote from the opening line of the account of the first session:

> The next day I made him pledge himself to submit to the one and only condition of the treatment – namely, to say everything that came into his head . . .

(SE X 159)

Here, the German is important:

> Nachdem ich ihn am nächsten Tage auf die einzige Bedingung der Kur verpflichtet, alles zu sagen . . .

(Stud VII 38)

I would translate this as:

> The next day, I bound him to the unique condition of the treatment, to say everything . . .

In his translation, Strachey employed a perlocutionary formulation. However, it is not Freud who bound himself, as in Austin's phrase, 'our word is our bond', though that is the rubric under which this utterance falls. What Freud did was to bind *someone other* than himself – a most strange linguistic phenomenon. But it highlights one of the themes I am

uncovering: the 'I' and 'you' created by the illocutionary and perlocutionary acts, by the founding speech, by the opening pledge, which
creates the analytic situation and which opens the analytic dialogue (in a
similar way as the move P–K4 might open a game of chess). The peculiarity of Freud's binding the Ratman can be clarified, using the chess
analogy, by imagining a game in which the first player opens for the other
– as if Freud made the first move for white, then turned the board around
and said: see, you have the advantage, you're playing white.

91 *Ratman* SE X 166.

92 There are numerous other interpretations we could offer of this
incident. I will mention two:

1 The Ratman addresses Freud in the manner appropriate to confus-
ing him with his friend (who Freud definitely does stand for, in some
senses), and ends up addressing him as if he were his father. Of
course, this is precisely what the interpretation is intended to do:
shake up the identifications, *and* allow them to come forward,
rather than being hidden through a conscious or unconscious
collusion by the analyst with the patient – that is why Freud cannot
play the part of the friend.

2 The Ratman, through this manoeuvre, plays the part of the
Captain, and Freud is obliged to undergo the torture of listening to
the story of the rat torture. In this line of thought, it is the narrative
structure which provokes the dependence of the listener on the
hearer – the Ratman is torturing Freud by not finishing the story, by
not telling him the punchline.

93 See Langs, 'The misalliance dimension in the case of the Rat Man'. See
also the condensed and sophisticated discussion of Freud's 'errors' of
interpretation in Lacan, 'Function and field of speech and language'
E 302–3/88–9.

94 See the comments on 'playing a part' in chapter 3, this volume,
pp. 58–61.

95 The ideal of the objective observer of the contents of the mind might
seem to be the attitude recommended to his patients by the formulation
of the fundamental rule Freud offered in 'On beginning the treatment'
[(1913c), SE XII 135]: 'Act as though, for instance, you were a traveller
sitting next to the window of a railway carriage and describing to
someone inside the carriage the changing views which you see outside.'
Leaving to one side the ironic fact that one of Freud's most conspicuous
neurotic symptoms was an anxiety about travelling by rail, even the
seemingly objective relation to the travelling companion is undermined
once one asks: 'Who is this other? And what sort of descriptions will he
be interested in? Will he want to hear about the changing fauna and
flora, the colours of the sky, or the geology?' (Geology is, in fact, the
rather bizarre example that Glover mentions in his commentary on this
passage from Freud in his masterful *The technique of psycho-analysis*.)
By raising the question of what the other wants to hear about, one

opens the question of transference – one turns away from the views through the window to take a look at one's travelling companion.

96 Cf. a similar line of argument with respect to the relation of psycho-analytic discourse to others – legal, medical, political, etc. – in chapter 2, this volume.

97 See Lacan, 'Le mythe individuel du névrosé'.

98 Another of Freud's interpretative *tours de force*, the central dream of 'On dreams', also revolved around the question 'for love or money?' condensed into the phrase *beaux yeux*; see SE V 636–40, 649–50, 655–7, 671–3, and Anzieu's lengthy discussion of the dream in *Freud's self-analysis*, pp. 531–49.

99 *Ratman* SE X 213.

100 Bearing in mind that his fiancée was unable to have children.

101 Freud's 'On beginning the treatment' deals primarily with the following questions: a trial period before the beginning begins; time; money; the communication of the fundamental rule of psycho-analytic technique and associated questions; the attitude to adopt towards transference; the analyst's first communications.

102 English in the original.

103 Sem VII 337.

8 Dead on time

An earlier draft of this chapter, entitled 'Hobbling and hesitating: on the temporality of the unconscious', was given in March 1979 to the Seminar in Social and Political Sciences, University of Cambridge, organised by Anthony Giddens. I would like to thank him and John Thompson for their comments, and I would like to thank Malcolm Bowie for his comments on the later drafts, and Mark Cousins for the title.

1 Lacan, Sem XI 67/69–70.

2 Freud, *The question of lay analysis* (1926e), SE XX 220.

3 Winnicott, *Maturational processes and the facilitating environment*, p. 122.

4 Derrida, 'Freud and the scene of writing', pp. 96–7.

5 Sem XI 33/32.

6 Allouch, 'Enfants du parladit', p. 122: 'There is no theory of punctuation (only some empirical rules, which are, moreover, debatable and debated) and scarcely a theory of reading . . .'

7 Roudinesco, *La Bataille de cent ans, vol. 2*, p. 428.

8 Although countless stories can and have been told about many analysts that illustrate their unconventional and bizarre behaviour. This is not quite my point here . . .

9 Roudinesco, *La Bataille de cent ans, vol. 2*, p. 428.

10 Clearly the question of the *rendez-vous* as discussed in chapter 5, '. . . a perfect likeness of the past', is speaking to the same issues here. These chapters should be read in parallel, maybe even at the same time.

11 Including there an implicit agreement between patient and the institution, given that the International Psycho-analytic Association found itself obliged, in response to Lacan, to introduce the condition that only people who stick to a fixed time limit for sessions can call themselves psychoanalysts.

12 'Function and field of speech and language' E 244/37.

13 It is a theme that dominates the 1938 essay on *The family*; for example: 'Notre expérience nous porte à désigner la détermination principale [de la grande névrose contemporaine] dans la personnalité du père, toujours carente en quelque façon, absente, humiliée, divisée ou postiche' (*La Famille* 8. 40.16, *Les Complexes familiaux*, p. 73).

14 In the passage that Strachey singles out as presaging the later discussion, in *Inhibitions, symptoms and anxiety*, of this defence so characteristic of obsessional thought and action, Freud refers to the Ratman's transferring his obsessional fears to the next world as 'designed – in defiance of reality, and in deference to the wish which had previously been showing itself in phantasies of every kind – to undo the fact of his father's death' ((1909d), SE X 235–6).

15 *Inhibitions, symptoms and anxiety*, SE XX 119.

16 *Ibid.* SE XX 120.

17 'Function and field of speech and language' E 314/99–100.

18 *Ibid.*

19 *Ibid.*

20 *Ibid.*

21 *Ibid.* Lacan continued: 'However, I am not here to defend this procedure, but to show that it has a precise dialectical meaning in its technical application.

'And I am not the only one to have remarked that it ultimately becomes one with the technique known as Zen, which is applied as the means of the subject's revelation in the traditional ascesis of certain Far Eastern schools.'

Lacan spent some of the Second World War learning Chinese and acquiring a diploma at the School of Oriental Languages in Paris.

22 One may well reflect on the ambivalence with respect to the labour of the obsessional shown by Lacan (his 'disdain' for the analysts, his awareness of the 'passionate quest' of the obsessional) via a technical procedure I heard advocated, late one night, over wine, by an 'orthodox' Lacanian analyst, recommending that those objects that patients forgetfully leave in the waiting-room of their analysts should be thrown in the dustbin ('à la poubelle').

23 'Function and field of speech and language' E 315/100.

24 *Ibid.* E 310/95.

25 Bataille, 'D'une pratique', p. 30.

26 One might also voice a Lacanian criticism of this Lacanian practice: Why this reticence? Why this unease with the word, with speech, when one might legitimately claim that the analyst is precisely someone whose very existence depends upon his or her ability to find the right

word? – though, to be sure, at the right time. But if the analyst is not at ease in the art of conversation, surely something has gone fundamentally astray?

27 Indeed, this question could be raised at a number of points throughout this discussion, in particular when I turn to discuss the Freudian concept of deferred action – is this not precisely one of the psychoanalytic concepts that makes the relation between Derrida's thought and psychoanalysis so intimate, so intertwined? Is not the intermingling of space, of spacing, and time, of delay and deferral, which Derrida's *différance* crystallises, and which this chapter reflects upon, one major source of the intuition that Derrida's thought is so profoundly at one with analysis?

28 'Function and field of speech and language' E 252/44.

29 Particularly that presented to him by Karl Abraham, his main interlocutor on this topic.

30 *The ego and the id* (1923b), SE XIX 58. See also *Inhibitions, symptoms and anxiety* (1926d), SE XX 129–30: 'the unconscious seems to contain nothing that could give any content to our concept of the annihilation of life . . . nothing resembling death can ever have been experienced; or if it has, as in fainting, it has left no observable traces behind'. Pontalis, 'On death-work in Freud, in the Self, in culture', remarks (p. 90): 'As for the assertion so often reiterated by Freud that "our unconscious can not imagine our own mortality", wouldn't this be a denial? A curious "oversight" or slip in any case for someone who was able to recognize the function of the double and to spot so many symbolic figurations of death in dreams or in tales . . . Unless the formula "the unconscious does not know the negative" should be understood in this way: it doesn't know the negative because it *is* the negative . . . And it is the negative to the extent that its very constitution, as a heterogeneous system, is correlative to the loss, absence, and negation of the object of satisfaction.'

31 Only to modify this opinion in a footnote, added in 1919, a significant year for Freud's thinking about death, in which a child pointed out that the difference lies in the fact that a dead person will not come back again – thus suffering a punishment which 'admits of no degrees [*nicht dosierbare*]' (Stud II 259n2; SE IV 255n1), as Freud glossed it.

32 'Thoughts for the times on war and death' (1915b), SE XIV 292–3.

33 Cf. 'The fear of death in melancholia only admits of one explanation: that the ego gives itself up because it feels itself hated and persecuted by the super-ego, instead of loved' (*The ego and the id* (1923b), SE XIX 58).

34 *Ibid.*

35 See *Inhibitions, symptoms and anxiety* (1926d), SE XX 136ff.

36 'Function and field of speech and language' E 315/100.

37 See Hyppolite, 'Spoken commentary on Freud's *Verneinung*' and Thom, '*Verneinung, Verwerfung, Ausstossung*: a problem in the interpretation of Freud'.

38 Sem II 202/169.
39 'Function and field of speech and language' E 319/104. The passage continues: 'The first symbol in which we recognize humanity in its vestigial traces is the sepulture, and the intermediary of death can be recognized in every relation in which man comes to the life of his history.' This is a perennial theme in Lacan's writing: for instance, Sem XVII (8 April 1970), where Lacan affirms that we can mark the origin of speaking man with the sepulchre: 'where a species, affirms that in contradiction to any other, the dead body retains what gives the living being its bodily character.'
40 Cf. Sem XVII (20 May 1970): 'if there is a possibility of seizing reality, it is on a blackboard'.
41 'Function and field of speech and language' E 320/105.
42 As Lacan would put it in his seminars of the late 1960s, developing a theme that had been distinctively his since the 1930s, the father is, in his very nature, already dead.
43 'The further development of an active therapy in psycho-analysis' (1920), in *Further contributions*, p. 198; my emphasis.
44 *Ibid.*; my emphasis.
45 *Ibid.* pp. 200–1, my emphases. In later works, as Laplanche and Pontalis point out (*Language of psycho-analysis*, p. 7), Ferenczi argued against active techniques, on the grounds that 'it is the patient himself who must decide the *timing* of activity, or at any rate give unmistakeable indications that the *time* is ripe for it' (my emphases). Laplanche and Pontalis underline that active techniques are specifically aimed at repetition: 'in order to overcome the compulsion to repeat and at last make recollection possible – or at least let the treatment proceed – Ferenczi judged it needful not merely to permit but actually to encourage repetition' (p. 7). Whilst this may be generally true, it overlooks the fact that Ferenczi is referring to a third situation, above and beyond the repetition and the remembering that are classically alluded to here: Ferenczi was trying to think about the temporality of *stagnation*: if repetition was required to avoid stagnation, so be it.
46 Lacan's criticism of the false opposition between active and passive techniques, based as it often was on a crude conception of passivity, may be placed early in his career. Lacan was thinking along lines similar to Ferenczi's and beginning to develop his own original conception, which we will be examining in detail, when he commented, in his 1935 'Review of E. Minkowski, *Le Temps vécu*': 'The original conception of waiting [*l'attente*] as the authentic antithesis of activity (instead of passivity, "as our reason would wish it") is ingenious and required by the system' (p. 430).
47 In this sense, Lacan's portrayal of the obsessional is a faithful extension and filling-in of Freud's description of the obsessional's major defence as 'undoing what has been done' – making sure that nothing ever gets done.

48 In his discussion of traumata and secrets, Abraham aphoristically noted: 'Hysterics are those interesting people to whom something is always happening' ('The experience of sexual traumas as a form of sexual activity', p. 57). We might define obsessionals as those boring people to whom nothing ever happens.

49 'Function and field of speech and language' E 314/99.

50 And thus becomes an alternative way of deriving character traits to that essayed by Freud in his 'Character and anal erotism'.

51 E 289/77. This passage is the final paragraph of Section II of 'Function and field of speech and language in psychoanalysis': it sums up where Section II had got to, and announces the aim of the third and last section, headed: 'The resonances of interpretation and the time of the subject in psychoanalytic technique'.

52 These are the opening paragraphs of Lacan's paper, 'Le temps logique et l'assertion de certitude anticipée' – 'Logical time and the assertion of anticipated certainty'; my translation, slightly amended in the light of a forthcoming translation by Bruce Fink and Marc Silver, whom I would like to thank for showing me their version before its publication. My discussion follows Lacan's paper closely at the beginning.

53 We should note one of the governor's prohibitions on the means of solving the problem, precluding any communication between the subjects, is transcended, since the conditions of the problem *also* determine that *involuntary* communication takes place. The very act of waiting is equivalent to a communication to the other subjects, in so far as the waiting is a consequence of a process of thought which comes to a preliminary impasse in the realisation of each that there is no instantaneous method for eliminating certain combinations of discs. Having seen two whites, each knows that he could be a white *or* a black. The subject's scansion of the logical time of the problem thus amounts to a communication that he does not see a black and a white. Thus the logical problem of the possible combinations of discs becomes converted from a problem of the individual logical imagination into a problem in which three different possible times are governed by the intersubjectivity of communication. And indeed, we find on further examination of the problem that *two* suspended temporal moments are necessary for an unequivocal solution of the problem.

54 'Le temps logique' (1945), E 205–6.

55 See *Group psychology and the analysis of the ego* (1921c), SE XVIII 111–16, 143.

56 We have in this notion of a 'common measure' the conception of an objective unit of time, but one which has no fixed duration. This objective unit of time is one which is engendered in the relation of the individual subject to the collective: it is the objective time of the unconscious.

57 One can correlate these three steps with Freud's *Group psychology* schema:

1 formation of ego ideal
2 identification of ego with others on the basis of having the same ego ideal
3 formation of the subject, in haste

58 To the best of my knowledge, accusations of cheating in bridge are rarely directed at the waiting period when a player is obliged to play a card, but remains locked in thought. On the face of it, such objectively different times of waiting could be used as a signal to the partner. But, experienced from within the game, such waiting periods are not matched against objective time. The time of understanding in bridge, just as in the problem of the prisoner, receives its objective meaning once the decision has been taken. If a player attempted to manipulate this time for understanding, he could only re-evoke in himself (or revoke himself), and in the others, doubts which he thought he had resolved when he 'completed' the true time for understanding and entered – without pause – the travestied time that followed. He might himself, in retrospect, have to recognise that what he believed to be a travesty of waiting was, truly, a real period of waiting. I put this question to one of the leading bridge players in this country, who replied: 'I doubt, however, whether changes in tempo by defenders are a likely method for the exchange of illegal information. More likely, declarers will complain that they have been misled unfairly. There must be simpler ways of conveying a message, and in general why should a defender who is subjected to finesse want to tell his partner anything that is not obvious?' (letter from Terence Reese, 8 April 1980). A counter to this argument is perhaps to be found in Terence Reese's column in *The Observer*, dated 19 October 1980, which deals with rules that require players to wait, under certain circumstances, before making a bid, so as to render meaningless any periods of waiting that might give information to the other players (whether it be true information intended for partners or information intended to mislead opponents).

59 See Von Neumann and Morgenstern, *Theory of games and economic behavior*, and Rapaport, *Two-person theory. The essential ideas*.

60 Or, as Lacan spelt its original German title, *Massen: Psychologie und Ichanalyse*, to emphasise the term *Massen*, so characteristic of the political thinking and the historical practice of the first half of the twentieth century, whether in the First World War, the rise of Nazism or the victory of Bolshevism.

61 His conception of the centrality of the rule in social activity is similar to that of his contemporary, Ludwig Wittgenstein. See chapter 7.

62 Cf. the treatment of the machine that produces novel sequences in the Appendices to the 'Seminar on *The purloined letter*'.

63 'Le nombre treize et la forme logique de la suspicion', *Cahiers d'Art* 1945. The paper was not included in the collection *Ecrits* (published in 1966) and has not, to my knowledge, been reprinted with Lacan's

authorisation. It is included in a collection of Lacan's entitled *Travaux et interventions*, non-paginated.

64 *Ibid*. 'Elle fait partie de nos approches exemplaires pour la conception des formes logiques où doivent se definir les rapports de l'individu à la collection, avant que se constitue la classe, autrement dit avant que l'individu soit specifié' (n.p.).

65 *Ibid*. He also mentions that if, at the Last Judgement, with its myth of the chosen, there were 100 million souls, letting n be 26 would be sufficient to isolate the singly different soul.

66 'Le temps logique' (1945), E 213.

67 It is not included in *Ecrits*, but may be found in *Travaux et interventions*.

68 He mentioned Lewin's vectorial mathematics and the conception of the Oedipus complex as a three-body problem. This is a reference to a paper of John Rickman's, whom Lacan was to cite with great respect in Sem I, only to reserve some acerbic and often repeated criticisms for a conception of psychology as a two- or three-body problem. See Sem I 17/11; 'Function and field of speech and language' E 304–5/90–1; 'The Freudian thing' E 429/139.

69 A reading of Bion's *Experiences in groups* indicates the objective source of Lacan's realisation of a miraculous new beginning, recapturing the Freudian spirit.

70 *Unité* also means 'unity', so the phrase could also mean 'return to unity'.

71 'Function and field of speech and language' E 276–7/65–6.

72 See chap. 7, 'What the psychoanalyst does with words'.

73 Yet even the system of language may be the prime mover of certain temporal rhythms: 'Servitude and grandeur in which the living being would be annihilated, if desire did not preserve its part in the interferences and pulsations that the cycles of language cause to converge on him . . .' ('Function and field of speech and language' E 279/68). The enigmatic reference to 'pulsation' recurs extensively throughout Seminar XI.

74 Sem II 336/291; translation modified in the light of Lacan's allusion to Marvell's poem.

75 See Schneiderman, *Rat Man*; Mahoney, *Freud and the Rat Man*; Lacan, 'The individual's neurotic myth'; and the discussion in chapter 7, 'What the psychoanalyst does with words', where full references will be found.

76 One of the later legitimate offspring of Lacan's subjective logic was his theory of the four discourses of the late 1960s: the discourses of the master, hysteric, analyst and the academic. This project offered a formal analysis of the relations between subjects, involving four terms: the subject, two signifiers and the *objet petit a*. In a sense, it was the psychoanalytic correlative to the analysis of discourse that Michel Foucault was offering – whilst incorporating, within an essentially Hegelian schema, the power relations that Foucault then felt obliged to

incorporate in his later work, the genealogies of *Discipline and punish* and *The history of sexuality. Vol. I.* See chapter 12, this volume.

77 There is also the question, which is so ambiguous in the original paper on 'Logical time', of the relation between 'psychology' and logic: Lacan appears to resolve this question by postulating a parallelism: 'This movement of the logical genesis of the "*I*" through a clarification of the logical time proper to it is closely parallel to its psychological origin. Just as, let us remind ourselves, the psychological "*I*" frees itself from an undetermined specular transitivism, through the contribution of a trend awakened as jealousy, the "*I*" in question here is defined through the "making subjective" [*subjectivation*] of a *competition* with the other through the function of logical time. As such, it thus appears to us to give the essential logical form (rather than the so-called existential form) of the psychological "*I*" ' ('Le temps logique' (1945), E 208).

78 See 'Constructions in analysis' (1937d), SE XXIII 265–6.

79 Lacan, 'Seminar on *The purloined letter*', p. 44 (translation modified).

80 Sem II 213–14/180–1. See the parallel discussion in Introduction to 'Le Séminaire sur "La Lettre volée"' (1956), E 57–60.

81 For the cascade of texts Lacan's seminar has given rise to, see Muller and Richardson, *The purloined Poe, Lacan, Derrida and psychoanalytic reading*, and the provocative reflections of Major, 'La parabole de la lettre volée. De la direction de la cure et de son récit', following Derrida, 'Le facteur de la vérité'.

82 Sem II 231/180.

83 'It's not out of the question that there may have been such a young child who won more frequently than his turn should allow – . . . But the heart of the matter lies in a completely different register from that of imaginary intersubjectivity' (Sem II 213/181). Cf. E 59.

84 Sem II 214/181.

85 *Ibid.* 217/184.

86 See 'Introduction' to 'Le Séminaire sur "La Lettre Volée"' (1956), E 46. This is another of the texts which, like 'Logical time' and 'The number thirteen', is an attempt at, or even a pastiche of, a formal, mathematical theory of certain properties of the subject – properties which are usually thought of as 'psychological', rather than formal or mathematical. Yet again, this is a text which is very rarely commented upon.

87 *Ibid.* E 48.

88 *Ibid.* E 49.

89 It is straightforward to collate the time for understanding and the moment for concluding with the recognisably Freudian concepts of 'working through', as Lacan explicitly pointed out in 'Function and field of speech and language', E 249/41.

90 The term still requires delicate handling in English, where Strachey's 'deferred action' is not an adequate translation of a term that has a straightforward adjectival form, one which Freud often makes use of.

In this instance, the standard French translation, *après coup*, is far more pithy and accurate.

91 Lacan, Sem XI 33/32.

92 Freud, 'Findings, ideas, problems' (1941f [1938]), SE XXIII 300.

93 Freud points out this continuum in his paper on 'Dostoevsky and parricide' (1928b), SE XXI 180.

94 One might cite Sartre and Merleau-Ponty as major figures leaning to this view.

95 One may regard the 1938 passage as a correction of this generalisation.

96 'Some general remarks on hysterical attacks' (1909a [1908]), SE IX 233–4.

97 For discussion of this theme in Freud's work with hypnosis, see chapters 2 and 4.

98 See the discussion of 'Being in love and hypnosis' in *Group psychology and the analysis of the ego* (1921c), SE XVIII 111–16.

99 See Freud's discussion of the relation between psychoanalysis, transference and suggestion in *Introductory lectures on psycho-analysis* (1916–17), SE XVI 446–55. For the relations between hypnosis, love and the ego-ideal, see Borch-Jacobsen's important book, *Le Sujet Freudien*.

100 For these metapsychological developments, see *Project for a scientific psychology* (1895), SE I 295–387 and *Beyond the pleasure principle* (1920g), SE XVIII 7–64.

101 Though one should not underestimate the extent to which analysts are still concerned with, are confronted by and theorise in terms of traumata; see the exemplary work of Khan, 'The evil hand' in his *Hidden Selves. Between theory and practice in psychoanalysis*, pp. 139–80.

102 Ellenberger, *The discovery of the unconscious*.

103 Abraham, 'The experiencing of sexual traumas', p. 61.

104 Charcot, 'Cas d'hystéro-neurasthénie survenue à la suite d'une collision de train chez un employé de chemin de fer âgé de 56 ans', in *L'Hystérie*.

105 *Ibid*. p. 135.

106 Cf. Freud, *The complete letters of Sigmund Freud to Wilhelm Fliess*, p. 144, 15 October 1895: 'Have I revealed the great clinical secret to you, either orally or in writing? Hysteria is the consequence of a presexual *sexual shock*. Obsessional neurosis is the consequence of presexual *sexual* pleasure which is later transformed into [self-] reproach. "Presexual" means actually before puberty, before the release of sexual substances; the relevant events become effective only as *memories*.'

107 Charcot, 'Paralysie hystéro-traumatique', in *L'Hystérie*, p. 92.

108 Charcot, 'A propos de six cas d'hystérie chez l'homme', in *L'Hystérie*, pp. 155–6; emphasis added.

109 SE II 134; Freud gives a reference to Charcot, *Leçons du Mardi*, 1888, vol. I, p. 99. Breuer elaborates further on this finding on SE II 213, particularly for traumatic hysterias, again citing Charcot: 'the renewal of the affect in *memory* is often also enough, if the recollection is repeated rapidly and frequently, immediately after the trauma and before its affect has become weakened'.

110 *Studies on hysteria* (1895d), SE II 6.

111 This is not unlike the practice Lacan described as Freud's annulling the times for understanding in favour of the moments of concluding – the temporal passage between events is annulled in favour of the narrativity of the story – in the way a classic novel can blithely introduce the passage of five or ten years in order to move on to the next event (or chapter).

112 Such a continuity could be provided by the concept of disposition, so that the surface account, a string of accidents, is bound together by the substratum of disposition. Thus as a characteristic statement concerning disposition, 'the true masochist always turns his cheek whenever he has a chance of receiving a blow' (1924c), SE XIX 165, brings together all these separate incidents of masochistic behaviour, and also allows *us* not to be *surprised* by any future, seemingly causeless, masochistic behaviour.

113 *Studies on hysteria* (1895d), SE II 173. The case under discussion is that of Rosalia H., which Freud introduced precisely in order to make more 'plausible' his claim that symptoms do 'not occur while the patient [is] experiencing the impressions of the first period, but after the event [*nachträglich*], that is, in the second period, while she [is] reproducing those impressions in her thoughts. That is to say, the conversion does not arise from the fresh impressions, but from the memories of them [*Die Konversion sei erfolgt nicht an den frischen Eindrücken, sondern an den Erinnerungen derselben*].' Breuer and Freud, *Studien über Hysterie*, p. 138; SE II 169; translation considerably modified.

114 The personal significance of the case will hang on the identity of the patient. The identity of Emma, as Freud called her in the *Project*, has not been the occasion for much speculation; however, it seems plausible to me that she is Emma Eckstein, the joint patient of Freud and Fliess, about whom so much has been written since Max Schur in 1966 quietly revealed her story, as found in the unpublished correspondence between Freud and Fliess (Schur, 'Some additional "day residues" of the specimen dream of psychoanalysis'), and since Jeffrey Masson, with much noise signifying very little (in his *The assault on truth*), made her his heroine-victim of the early history of psychoanalysis. If this hypothesis is correct, the very concept of an event, psychoanalytically speaking (i.e. a trauma), may well have owed something to the 'events' of March 1895, when Emma nearly lost her life to Fliess' 'irresponsible' surgical treatment, *and their aftermath*. If

she was Emma, then it is extremely interesting that Freud developed the fine detail of his argument concerning deferred action apropos of the patient who earlier that year had been a victim of Freud's friend Fliess' near-fatal surgical error. We might then have to thank Freud's personal reactions to this incident with his female patient for both his definitive theory of wish fulfilment and of causality in the neuroses.

115 *Project* SE I 353; emphasis in the original.

116 *Ibid.* SE I 354.

117 *Ibid.*

118 *Project* SE I 356.

119 *Ibid.*

120 'Further remarks on the neuro-psychoses of defence' (1896b), SE III 166–7n2; emphasis in the original. A few weeks after sending this paper off to the journal, Freud summed up his 'theory of the neuroses' to Fliess as follows: 'it occurs to me that the limits of repression in my theory of the neuroses – that is to say, the time after which sexual experiences no longer have a posthumous but an actual effect – coincide with the second dentition' (*The complete letters of Sigmund Freud to Wilhelm Fliess*, 1 March 1896, p. 174).

Similarly, in a letter dated 6 December 1896: 'If [event] A, when it was current, released a particular unpleasure, and if when it is reawakened it releases fresh unpleasure, then this cannot be inhibited. In this case the memory is behaving as though it were some current event. This case can occur only with sexual events, because the magnitudes of the excitations which these release increase of themselves with time (with sexual development).

'Thus a sexual event in one phase acts in the next phase as though it were a current one and is accordingly uninhibitable. What determines pathological defence (repression) is therefore *the sexual nature of the event and its occurrence in an earlier phase*' (*Ibid.* p. 209). In this letter Freud makes use of Fliess' theory of periodicity in order to derive the different epochs upon which his account of repression relies: he attempts to give an account of these epochs in terms of round number multiples of the Fliessian π (period).

121 *Project* SE I 356n1; the passage dates, it should be pointed out, from 1966.

122 Laplanche and Pontalis, *Language of psychoanalysis*, pp. 111, 113.

123 Sem XI 197/216. In a paper, 'Position de l'inconscient', also, like Seminar XI, dating from 1964, Lacan reaffirms his priority in this matter: see the passage from E 839 quoted below in note 137.

124 'Function and field of speech and language' E 256/48, referring to SE XVII 45n1 and text. In a footnote to this passage, Lacan notes that 'après coup' is a weak translation of this term, a rather ironic comment given the almost fetishistic use of this term in the tradition of French psychoanalysis much influenced by Lacan.

125 'Function and field of speech and language' E 256/48.

126 It would be equally true to say that the creation of his infantile neurosis was his way of understanding the primal scene; this is certainly the way Freud puts it in his account. Cf. Lacan's remarks about the return of the repressed and the repressed being the same thing (Sem I 215/191).

127 See Freud, 'From the history of an infantile neurosis' (1918b), SE XVII 35–6.

128 'Function and field of speech and language' E 257/48; translation slightly adapted.

129 Not only in *Language of psychoanalysis*, but also in their (by now) classic paper, 'Fantasy and the origins of sexuality'.

130 Sem I 242/217.

131 Sem IV Session of 6 March 1957, p. 851.

132 Sem XI 61/63.

133 *Ibid*.

134 Sem XI 62/64. See also a similar formulation, in 'On a question preliminary to any possible treatment of psychosis' (1956), E 354/197: 'In effect, this schema [schema R] enables us to show the relations that refer not to pre-Oedipal stages, which are not of course non-existent, but which cannot be conceived of in analytic terms (as is sufficiently apparent in the hesitant, but controlled work of Melanie Klein), but to the pregenital stages in so far as they are ordered in the retroaction of the Oedipus complex.'

135 The question as to who it was who was the principal promoter of the classical developmental stages in analytic theory is a disputed one; Lacan sometimes casts Ferenczi as the analyst who engaged Freud in this particular misconception, as in his article 'Stages in the development of the sense of reality': 'Ferenczi is the one who started to put the famous stages into everyone's heads' (Sem I 146/127). It is at least as plausible to claim that Abraham was the theoretical mainstay of this line of development of psychoanalytic theory.

136 Lacan's explicit use of the mathematics of knots is to be found in his work of the 1970s, but the metaphor of a knot, and specifically the idea of a symptom as a knot, is to be found from the early 1950s on.

137 Perhaps it is appropriate, to avoid misunderstanding at this juncture, to point out that Lacan used the term 'retroactivity' to describe another essential concept in his account of psychoanalysis: the retro-action of meaning in a phrase, whereby the meaning is created only with the last term of the phrase, reading backwards. Lacan explicitly distinguishes this type of retroaction from that used by Freud: '[The closing of the unconscious] also indicates the kernel of a reversible time, which it is entirely necessary to introduce to account for any efficacity of discourse; it is already quite discernible in the retroaction, upon which I have for a long time now insisted, of meaning in a phrase, which requires its last word so as to be closed.

'*Nachträglich* (remember that I was the first to unearth it from

Freud's text), *nachträglich* or deferred action, in accordance with which the trauma is implicated in the symptom, displays a temporal structure of a higher order than . . . the reversible time of discourse' ('Position de l'inconscient' (1964), E 838–9).

138 The complexity of the idea of accident will be explored below; one could at this point, however, at least indicate the line of thought in Freud's work upon which Lacan draws here: the opposition that Freud sets out between 'constitution' and 'experience', between 'necessity' and 'accident'.

139 A phrase taken from Freud's surmises as to the identity of the three Moerae, the Fates, the three senses of 'fate': 'Lachesis, the name of the second, seems to denote "the accidental that is included in the regularity of destiny" – or as we should say, "experience"; just as Atropos stands for the "ineluctable" – Death. Clotho would then be left to mean the innate disposition with its fateful implications' ('The theme of the three caskets' (1931f), SE XII 298).

140 What follows is in part a commentary on Freud's remarkable letter to Else Voigtländer (*Letters*, dated 1 October 1911, pp. 292–4), which it is worth quoting from at length:

We find in psychoanalysis that we are dealing not with *one* disposition but with an infinite number of dispositions which are developed and fixed by accidental fate. The disposition is so to speak polymorphous . . . The question as to which is of greater significance, constitution or experience, which of the two elements decides character, can in my opinion, only be answered by saying that δαίμων καὶ τύχη [daimon kai tuché] (fate and chance) and not one *or* the other are decisive . . . If in our analytical work we concentrate more on the accidental influences than on the constitutional factors, we do so . . . because on the basis of our experience we know something about the former, while about the latter we know as little as – non-analysts . . . We are also of the opinion that by appreciating the importance of the accidental we have taken the right road towards the understanding of constitution . . . What remains inexplicable after a study of the accidental may be put down to constitution.

The relation between this move towards defining the field of the psychoanalytic as that of the accidental, and Freud's earlier move, in *The psychopathology of everyday life*, defining the field of the psychoanalytic as that in which there is no chance, is a very important one, but one I cannot develop here. An indispensable guide for so doing is Derrida, 'My Chances/*Mes Chances*: a rendezvous with some Epicurean stereophonies'.

141 *Letters*, p. 293.

142 *Ibid.* Somewhat unexpectedly, one might even say perversely, Michel Foucault attributed to psychoanalysis an important historical position only insofar as it resolutely opposed the variety of hereditarian and

degenerative discourses of the late nineteenth century. See chapter 12.

143 A dimension completely overlooked in Grünbaum's misconceived *The foundations of psychoanalysis*.

144 Much could, clearly, be said of this: again, I refer the reader to the work of Jacques Derrida, for instance his critique of the notion of truth as a disclosing, in 'Le facteur de la vérité' (1975), pp. 412–96, esp. the discussion of Freud's commentary on 'The emperor's new clothes', pp. 414–19, and pp. 468–83. It raises a question concerning the typically Freudian gesture of dissolving the object (the dream, the memory) through the process of interpretation, a process which offers itself as the guarantor of the *safety* of the object, while it is intimately related to finding, at the end of the process, that the original object has lost all *interest* (the exemplary instance of this, one whose timing is extremely educational, is the discovery by Freud, the day *The interpretation of dreams* was published, of the meaning of premonitory dreams (see chapter 5 above); the discovery was that premonitory dreams are constructed in the moment that they are remembered: they are forms akin to *déjà vu*; and, most significantly, their being rendered null as dreams demonstrates clearly how, for Freud, the dream is *dissolved* by the interpretative narrative).

145 Freud, 'Screen memories' (1899a), SE III 322; GW I 553–4.

146 '[Psychotherapy's] task is to make it possible for the unconscious processes to be dealt with finally and be forgotten' (*The interpretation of dreams* (1900a), SE V 578).

147 'Function and field of speech and language' E 256/48; see also 'Subversion du sujet et dialectique du désir dans l'inconscient freudien' E 808/307.

148 'Function and field of speech and language' E 302/88; translation modified.

149 The influence of Heidegger was probably at its height in these passages discussing the historicity of analysis. Space will not allow me to enter into this more fully; Macey gives a useful sketch of the relations linking Lacan, Sartre and Heidegger and their common conception of the temporality of the subject, in *Lacan in contexts*, pp. 104–6.

150 I am obliged to pass over another of the themes, that of death, which clearly belongs here: 'Indeed, this limit [death] is at every instant present in what this history possesses as achieved. This limit represents the past in its real form, that is to say, not the physical past whose existence is abolished, nor the epic past as it has become perfected in the work of memory, nor the historic past in which man finds the guarantor of his future, but the past which reveals itself reversed in repetition' ('Function and field of speech and language' E 318/103). This 'reversal found in repetition' can be put phenomenologically as follows: following Freud's dictum that 'Vor allem beginnt er die Kur

mit einer solchen Wiederholung' (Before anything else, the patient begins the treatment with a repetition) (SE XII 150; GW X 130; Stud Erg 210; translation modified; see my commentary on this sentence in chapter 9), event 1 appears on the horizon of analysis prefiguring the event it is *already* repeating, namely event 2, the event to be discovered. Analysis is the site of repetition; it is methodologically impossible for it to be anything other than this site for repetition. Hence the seeming chronological time of event-1-follows-event-2 is reversed in analysis, where event 2 has always-already-happened, and event 1 is only an event in so far as it repeats event 2. Yet, analytically speaking, event 1 happens before event 2 can possibly be heard of. This impossibility of the event's being sufficient in itself to *be* an event is characteristic of Derrida's meditations on the 'event'; it perhaps also accounts for the repeated convergence of his thought with Freud's, and hence – to the extent that Lacan is also on Freud's track – with Lacan's. See the final pages of chapter 9.

151 Attrib.

152 For, as we have seen, Freud refers to these questions and had even invoked *tuché*, the Greek term upon which Lacan was to centre his discussion; see note 140 above.

153 This was a distinctive feature of Freud's methodology from early on in his work; for instance, in the case of little Hans: 'what emerges from the unconscious is to be understood in the light not of what goes before but of what comes after' ('Analysis of a phobia in a five-year-old boy' (1909b), SE X 66; see Forrester, *Language*, p. 221n33).

154 We might well appropriate a Neoplatonic model of the creation with which to think about this: view the creation of the world of a person's character as the withdrawal of the Godhead, a self-imposed limitation, self-negation – a model which Michael Balint used when he described every character-trait as due to a limitation on the capacity for love and enjoyment, a restriction of the 'original' subjective plenitude (see Lacan, Sem I 228/204).

155 Stud III 383; SE XXI 152; translation slightly modified.

156 Sem XI 51/52.

157 I have found the writings of Sorabji indispensable as a guide to the relations between classical philosophy and modern philosophy of science, in particular *Necessity, cause and blame. Perspectives on Aristotle's theory*. Another profoundly stimulating work is Nussbaum, *The fragility of goodness. Luck and ethics in Greek tragedy and philosophy*.

158 Lacan explicitly notes that they have been incorrectly translated as 'le hasard' and 'la fortune'.

159 Sem XI 51/52. It is probably no accident that Aristotle's example of the action of *tuché* is a chance encounter; see the passage quoted below from *Physics*, II.iv.196a1–8.

160 Sem XI 51/52.

161 Sem XI 54/53–4.
162 Aristotle, *Physics*, II.vi.197b1–3; 19–24.
163 *Ibid.* II.iv.196a1–8.
164 *Ibid.* II.iv.196b1–7.
165 Nussbaum, *Fragility of goodness*, p. 319.
166 Aristotle, *Physics*, II.v.197a7.
167 *Ibid.* II.v.196b34–5.
168 Cf. Shafer, *A new language for psychoanalysis*, and Wittgenstein, 'Conversations on Freud', amongst several texts.
169 Aristotle, *Physics*, II.v.197a6–8. The whole passage reads: 'Clearly then luck itself, regarded as a cause, is the name we give to causation which incidentally inheres in deliberately purposeful action taken with respect to some other end but leading to the event we call fortunate. And the significant results of such causes we say "come by luck".'
170 *Beyond the pleasure principle* (1920g), SE XVIII 21–2; Stud III 231–2; GW XIII 20–1; translation modified. At the point where the passage ends, there is a footnote to Jung's paper, 'The significance of the father in the destiny of the individual' – such footnotes to Jung were, by this date (1920), rare in Freud's work; much rarer still were notes, of which this was one, expressing a *debt*, *recommending* the paper to the reader. The passage which Freud wishes his reader to find is the following: 'An instructive and well-known example of the ambivalent behaviour of the father-imago is the love-episode in the Book of Tobit. Sara, the daughter of Raguel, of Ecbatana, desires to marry. But her evil fate wills it that seven times, one after the other, she chooses a husband who dies on the wedding night. It is the evil spirit Asmodeus, by whom she is persecuted, that kills these men . . . Unfortunately medical etiquette forbids me to report a case of hysteria which fits this pattern exactly, except that there were not seven husbands but only three, unluckily chosen under all the ominous signs of an infantile constellation' (Jung, 'The significance of the father in the destiny of the individual', pp. 322–3).

   The 'demon' who enters into the passage from *Beyond the pleasure principle*, to which we will return, has already been noted and commented upon by Derrida, in his 'Spéculer – sur "Freud" ', esp. pp. 341ff.
171 Sem XI 53–4/53–4.
172 Sem XI 54/54.
173 Sem XI 54–5/54–5.
174 Aristotle, *Metaphysics*, 1065a31.
175 I am thinking of the sort of philosophical reflection inspired by modern biology, to be found in Monod's *Chance and necessity*, or Jacob, *Le Jeu des possibles*, and his *The possible and the actual*.
176 Derrida, 'Spéculer – sur "Freud" ', *passim*.
177 Sem XI 54/54.
178 Sem XI 53/53.

179 On Lacan's relations with surrealism, see Roudinesco, *La Bataille de cent ans, Vol. 2*, and Macey, *Lacan in contexts*, pp. 44–74; I would like to thank the Tate Gallery, Liverpool, for, seemingly by chance, obliging me to confront the relation between the chance encounter in Lacan and the necessity of making use of chance that the surrealists advocated, by inviting me to give a lecture on 'Psychoanalysis and surrealism' in November 1988.

180 I recall two points from the first part of this chapter: Lacan's anger with the analysand who failed to knock him up in his consulting-room, and the analysand's consequent decision to organise his *own rendez-vous*; Lacan's variable length sessions entailed that his analysands spent a variable length of time in the waiting-room, unsure as to when – and whether – the *rendez-vous* would be kept.

181 Sem XI 61/63.

182 SE V 509; Stud II 488; GW II/III 513.

183 SE V 510; Stud II 489; GW II/III 514.

184 I refer to the child as 'it' since the original text leaves unspecified the sex of the child, referring to *das Kind*.

185 Freud, *The interpretation of dreams*, SE V 510; Stud II 489; GW II/III 514.

186 Sem XI 56–7/57.

187 Indeed, Freud takes so seriously the speech of the child that his first comments on the dream are directed to this point: 'the words spoken by the child must have been made up of words which he had actually spoken in his lifetime and which were connected with important events in the father's mind' (*The interpretation of dreams* (1900a), SE V 510). This relates to the 'replay' hypothesis, and Freud's preoccupations with the source of speeches in dreams, touched on in my *Language and the origins of psychoanalysis* (and examined in detail in Heynick's meticulous monograph, 'Theoretical and empirical investigation into verbal aspects of the Freudian model of dream generation'). Curiously enough, becoming aware of Freud's general preoccupation with the source of speeches in dreams lessens one's sense that the reason why he pays so much attention to the child's words is because of their oracular quality; or rather, Freud treated *all* speeches in dreams as having this oracular quality, a quality which he was particularly eager to undercut and render quotidian by referring them back to specific waking occasions of utterance. On this occasion, Freud bluntly puts it as follows: 'The dead child behaved in the dream like a living one: he himself warned his father, came to his bed, and caught him by the arm, just as he had probably done on the occasion from the memory of which the first part of the child's words in the dream were derived. For the sake of the fulfilment of this wish the father prolonged his sleep by one moment' (SE V 510). But perhaps Freud's compulsive searching for the real event of the utterance of these words, of all spoken words in dreams, was an attempt to

undercut any intuition on our parts that words – especially such words – spoken in dreams may be oracular in the sense of their being direct communications from the locus of death. See the continuation of this line of thought in note 193 below.

188 Edgar Allan Poe, 'The facts in the case of M. Valdemar'. See Barthes, commentary on the fictional realisation of this impossible speech act, 'I am dead', in 'Textual analysis of Poe's "Valdemar"', pp. 152–4.

189 Sem XI 58/59. The preceding sentence, which we will discuss later, reads: 'But what, then, was this accident – when everybody is asleep, including the person who wished to take a little rest, the person who was unable to maintain his vigil and the person of whom some well intentioned individual, standing at his bedside, must have said, *He looks just as if he is asleep*, when we know only one thing about him, and that is that, in this entirely sleeping world, only the voice is heard, *Father, can't you see I'm burning?*'

190 Sem XI 57/58: 'Freud lui-même ne nous dit-il pas que, dans cette phrase, il faut reconnaître ce qui perpétue pour le père ces mots à jamais séparés de l'enfant mort qui lui auront dits, peut-être, suppose Freud, à cause de la fièvre . . .' (Doesn't Freud himself tell us that one must recognize in this phrase what perpetuates for the father those words forever separated from the dead child that were said to him, perhaps, Freud supposes, because of the fever . . .'; translation modified).

191 SE V 509; note that Freud does not attribute the man's awakening to this light; rather, he mentions this light as being the clue that led the man, *whilst still asleep*, to conclude that 'a candle had fallen over and set something alight in the neighbourhood of the body'.

192 Sem XI 58/57; translation modified.

193 The pressure that Freud exerts, pushing the reality of the dream towards a memory, towards the occasions in reality when the child spoke the words, 'Father, can't you see . . . ?' and 'I'm burning', is an index of the importance of this dream as another example of the class of dreams Freud later called 'premonitory dreams': Freud is eager to ensure that no hint of an *occult* explanation enters into our understanding of the dream: it is not a dream of a supernatural communication, in which a dead child communicates to its father that its *body* is in reality, in the next room, burning, while the father sleeps. Compare the discussion of the 'premonitory dream' in chapter 5 above, where Freud forces the interpretation away from any occult one, towards its being an interpretation based upon the memory of a *rendez-vous*. Lacan's idea of the encounter is an intriguing *rapprochement* with this theme of Freud's.

194 Sem XI 57/58; translation modified.

195 Sem XI 66/68; I have left uncorrected Lacan's slip, his assumption that the child is male, is the father's son.

196 Sem XI 66/69.

197 A rhythm that Winnicott introduced in a most subtle manner in his remarkable 'A child psychiatry case illustrating delayed reaction to loss'.

9 Who is in analysis with whom?

This chapter was originally a paper delivered at a conference on 'Philosophy in modern France', held jointly by the British Society for Phenomenology and the Human Sciences Seminar of the Institute for Advanced Studies of Manchester Polytechnic, at Manchester Polytechnic, 23–5 September 1983. I have extended and rewritten sections, but have preserved much of the original spoken flavour.

1 Jung, 'A contribution to the psychology of rumour', p. 45.
2 'Du tout', in Derrida, *La Carte postale*, pp. 525–49. This was originally published in *Confrontation I* 1978, where it was prefaced by the following editorial note:
> On the 21 November 1977, a session of 'Confrontation' with Jacques Derrida was organised around *Glas* and other texts which have a thematic relation with the theory, the movement or the institution of psychoanalysis, notably 'Freud and the scene of writing', 'The purveyor of truth', *Fors, Eperons*. In reply to the opening questions of René Major, Jacques Derrida put forward several introductory propositions. We are reproducing them here as they were recorded. Only the title is an exception to this rule.

The *Confrontation* group is a forum for debate between psychoanalysts and others which crosses the various barriers created by the analytic societies, institutes and training 'kinship-systems'; as Derrida remarks in 'Du tout', '*Confrontation* says by means of antiphrasis what will neither take place here nor, I suppose, in analysis, namely the face-to-face face-off, a speaking affrontment' (p. 535).
3 There is an interesting parallel to the question raised by Derrida, the non-analyst speaking to *Confrontation*, and that raised by Jacques-Alain Miller, also a non-analyst, when speaking to Lacan's seminar in 1965:
> No one without those precise conceptions of analysis which only a personal analysis can provide has any right to concern himself (or herself) with it . . . If, contravening this injunction, it is of psychoanalysis that I am going to speak – then, by listening to someone whom you know to be incapable of producing the credentials which alone would authorise your assent, *what are you doing here*?
> Or, if my subject is not psychoanalysis – then you who so faithfully attend here in order to become conversant with the problems which relate to the freudian field, *what are you doing here*? . . . . The justification lies in this . . . that *the freudian field is not representable as a closed surface*.
> (Miller, 'Suture (elements of the logic of the signifier)', p. 24)

4 Derrida, 'Le facteur de la vérité'.

5 This subversion of a concept and its exterior is the classic Derridean move: he has operated it successfully on speech/writing, absence/presence – we may well describe it as the displaced transcendental move. Yet its application to the couple analytic/non-analytic has a specificity of interest, in that the effects of analysis on philosophy, or perhaps on the possibility of reading texts, will be transformed by this leakage of the analytic onto its outside.

6 Leclaire, *Démasquer le réel*, p. 35. One may well be able to trace a historical development of this theme of the disruptive effects of third parties to analysis, from the early unorthodox triangles of Freud (Freud–Loe–Jones, etc.) to the sophisticated notion of Leclaire's that the primal scene is the other couch/armchair. For further entertaining and illuminating detail on the Jones/Freud triangles, see Young-Bruehl, *Anna Freud*, pp. 65–70, concering Jones' courtship of Anna, and Freud's reaction. A document which marks an intermediate stage between the era of Freud and that of Lacan is Melitta Schmideberg, 'A contribution to the history of the psychoanalytic movement in Britain', which includes the following passage concerning the state of affairs in the British Psycho-analytic Society during the 1930s:

> The Society was still small, and we knew each other well, and often each other's patients. Edward Glover once stated in a discussion that he saw and referred in initial consultation one third of all London patients who were being analysed, and had a follow-up on two thirds. There was an uneasy silence . . . Paradoxically, a listener sometimes knew more about the patient in question than did his analyst. Analysts tend to ignore environmental factors and rarely know what becomes of their patients. I once listened comfortably to a case presentation by a leading Kleinian, who described how her analysis of 'deep anal material' had produced 'almost delusional' reactions of jealousy. The patient in question happened to be the boy-friend of a patient of mine, and I knew only too well that his jealousy was founded on fact and was not produced by analysis. It was this experience more than any other which started me on the path of questioning seriously how much we really know about our patients, and how often what we assumed to be 'endopsychic' or 'phantasy' or 'related to analysis' was actually stark reality.

What is distinctive, and of theoretical interest, here is the relation between gossip, privileged secrets and 'strict reality'; the 'environment' or 'reality' now functions as the third party. For modern theoretical developments along these lines, see the revival of the seduction theory, in Masson, *The assault on truth*; Alice Miller, *The drama of the gifted child and the search for the true self*, and *For your own good*, and *Du sollst nicht merken, Variationen über das Paradies-Thema*; and Balmary, *Psychoanalyzing psychoanalysis*.

7 Derrida, *La Carte postale*, p. 536.
8 Granoff, *Filiations*; Roustang, *Un destin si funeste*.
  Guntrip, 'My experience of analysis with Fairbairn and Winnicott'.
10 Compare a parallel statement of Winnicott's: 'Direct observation does
   not confirm the degree of importance given to the Oedipus complex by
   the psychoanalyst. Nevertheless, the psychoanalyst must stick to his
   guns, because in analysis he regularly finds it' (Winnicott, *The child, the
   family and the outside world*, p. 149).
11 Guntrip, 'My experience of analysis', p. 151.
12 *Ibid.* p. 153.
13 Compare Lacan, 'Proposition du 9 Octobre 1967 sur le psychanalyste
   de l'Ecole', p. 27: 'I would like to point out that, in conformity with the
   topology of the projective plane, the interior circle which we trace out
   as the gap of psychoanalysis in intension is at the very horizon of
   psychoanalysis in extension.'
14 Derrida, *La Carte postale*, p. 313.
15 Lacan, Sem XI 209/230.
16 *Ibid.* 211/232; translation modified.
17 Freud, '"Wild" psychoanalysis', SE XI 221.
18 *Ibid.* SE XI 226.
19 Jones, *Sigmund Freud*, vol. III, p. 22.
20 Derrida, *La Carte postale*, p. 353.
21 Freud, 'Remembering, repeating and working-through', SE XII 150;
   GW X 130; Stud Erg. p. 210. Strachey's translation – 'Above all, the
   patient will *begin* his treatment with a repetition of this kind' – catches
   the importance of this beginning, which is a repetition by italicising
   'begins' – an emphasis not in the original; but the 'proper' translation of
   Vor allem as 'above all' loses the temporality of *vor* (literally, 'before').
22 Derrida, *La Carte postale*, p. 324.
23 See Derrida, *Of grammatology*.
24 Derrida, *La Carte postale*, p. 345.
25 Not 'the subject supposed to know', as it has been translated.
26 Cited in Malcolm, 'Annals of scholarship (Psychoanalysis – Part I)',
   p. 85. The letter is misquoted in Jones, *Sigmund Freud*, pp. 280–1.
27 Little, 'Counter-transference and the patient's response to it'.
28 Though he confused the author's name – he called her 'Annie Reich',
   instead of Margaret Little. Reich's paper on countertransference is to
   be found in the same number of the *Int. J. Psa.*
29 Lacan, Sem I 40–3/30–3.
30 Lacan, Sem I 41/31.
31 Little, *Transference neurosis and transference psychosis*, p. 278.
32 Racker, *Transference and countertransference*.
33 See Lacan, 'Function and field of speech and language', pp. 44–5: 'the
   supervisor manifests a second sight, make no mistake about it, which
   makes the experience at least as instructive for him as for the person
   supervised . . . the supervised person acts as a filter, or even as a
   refractor, of the subject's discourse, and in this way there is presented

to the supervisor a ready-made stereograph, making clear from the start the three or four registers on which the musical score constituted by the subject's discourse can be read.'

34 Lacan, Sem XI 16/12.

35 A by-now-famous quotation from a letter to Marie Bonaparte quoted in Jones, *Sigmund Freud*, vol. 2, p. 468. The fact that Freud's early work with patients was collaborative (taking its model from Breuer's collaboration with Anna O.) is substantiated by the complex relations between Freud and one of his most important patients of the 1890s, Emma Eckstein. See Masson, *The assault on truth*, *The complete letters of Sigmund Freud to Wilhelm Fliess* and Chapter 1.

36 Foucault, *HS I* pp. 146–7.

37 Derrida, *Positions*, pp. 116–17.

38 *Ibid.*

39 See Johnson, 'The frame of reference', and Kofman, 'Ça cloche'.

40 Derrida replaces this phrase in the context of the compulsion to repeat; see *La Carte postale*, pp. 341ff.

10 Psychoanalysis: gossip, telepathy and/or science?

1 Derrida, 'Télépathie', p. 216.

2 All translations are from Lionel Salter's version.

3 James, *A taste for death*, p. 258.

4 See chapter 3, where other accounts arguing similar views are cited.

5 The problems of being Lacan's translator over the past few years have led to a singular intellectual phenomenon for me: an incapacity to remember whether certain ideas, when expressed in English, are 'mine', my version of Lacan's ideas, or my translation of Lacan's French. Perhaps it is not surprising that this has been my lot, given that the act of translation is specifically aimed at repressing the original and replacing it with an exact replica. On the psychoanalytic theme of the 'exact replica' see chapter 5.

6 Freud, *An outline of psycho-analysis* (1940a [1938]), SE XXIII 173: 'The analytic physician and the patient's weakened ego form a pact with each other. The sick ego promises us the most complete candour – promises, that is, to put at our disposal all the material which its self-perception yields it; we assure the patient of the strictest discretion and place at his service our experience in interpreting material that has been influenced by the unconscious . . . This pact constitutes the analytic situation.'

7 The idea that the analyst encourages the patient *in any way*, either implicitly or explicitly, may seem to some unduly interventionist; the issue forms part of the substance of the debates concerning active technique instigated primarily by Ferenczi. It is clear that Freud agreed with many of the techniques Ferenczi created – for instance, forbidding certain actions within analysis which had the function of substitutive masturbatory activities, or encouraging phobics to place themselves in

situations which elicited the anxiety associated with the phobia. But avoiding discussing the analysis 'outside' is not the only question here; there is also the analyst's working assumption that the family and friends of the patient will, at some point, prove to be enemies of the treatment.

8 See chapter 9, Lacan's 'Seminar on *The purloined letter*', the sections devoted to *The purloined letter* in Lacan, Sem II 175–205, and Derrida, 'Le facteur de la vérité'.

9 Freud, *Jokes and their relation to the unconscious* (1905c), SE VIII 181–6. It is also plausible to argue that gossip and joking are tools of the oppressed; on this, and other analogies with Freud's discussion of jokes, see Spacks, *Gossip*.

10 This may give a further insight into Dora's putative intentions; for a similar line of thought concerning these, see Foucault, 'Introduction' to Ludwig Binswanger, *Le Rêve et l'existence*, discussed in chapter 12, pp. 291ff.

11 This is the solution to so many of the quarrels about whether or not analysis deals with real or fantasied events.

12 See Olinick, 'The gossiping psychoanalyst', p. 439.

13 Person, 'Women in therapy: therapist gender as a variable': 'Although neither had reacted negatively at the time of the discovery, in re-analysis each expressed the feeling that he had been "raped"' (p. 201).

14 It is not feasible to justify in this chapter calling the seduction of a woman patient the 'original sin' of psychoanalysis. See chapters 1, 2, 4 and 9, including the passage quoted from Lacan on p. 240 above, and my forthcoming *The dream of psychoanalysis*. For an account of the early history of Freud's theories explicitly in terms of 'original sin', see Balmary, *Psychoanalyzing psychoanalysis*.

15 This point is expanded upon in chapter 9.

16 Freud, 'Dreams and occultism', in *New introductory lectures on psychoanalysis*, Lecture XXX (1933 [1932]), SE XXII 55–6. The brief paragraph which then follows – 'And this brings us back to psycho-analysis, which was what we started out from' – ends the lecture.

My thinking on the topic of telepathy is very much in line with that of Granoff in *Filiations*, and the more detailed studies by Granoff and Jean-Michel Rey, *L'Occulte, objet de la pensée freudienne*, and by Derrida in a series of papers, including 'Télépathie', to be found in his *Psyché*.

17 Derrida, 'Télépathie', pp. 209–10; my translation. Cf. also the passage on p. 211: 'Because here is my last paradox, which only you will fully understand: it is because there will have been telepathy that a post card may not arrive at its destination. The final naivety would be to think that Telepathy guarantees a destination that the "Post Office" [*postes et télécommunications*] fails to assure.'

18 See Lacan's discussion of the acephalic subject and the 'collective unconscious' in Sem II 202–4/170–1.

19 For the story of the fortune-teller and the analyst, see Freud, 'Psycho-analysis and telepathy' (1941d [1921]), SE XVIII 185–90, and chapter 5, this volume.

20 The distinction he draws between them is a fine one: telepathy is the report of an *event* coming to the consciousness of a person in a different place (and perhaps time), by means of some mysterious process of transmission; thought-transference is the transmission of a *thought* from one mind to another. Note that this may be transmission to the *unconscious* mind of another person – which is where psychoanalysis is in a privileged position to investigate the phenomenon.

21 Granoff, *Filiations*.

22 This is explored in detail in my *Dream of psychoanalysis*. See also a series of fine books by Monique Schneider, including *La Parole et l'inceste. De l'enclos linguistique à la liturgie psychanalytique*, Paris: Aubier Montaigne, 1980, and *'Père, ne vois-tu pas . . . ?' Le père, le maître, le spectre dans l'interprétation des rêves*, and also Michel Schneider (no relation), *Blessures de mémoire*.

23 Grosskurth, *Melanie Klein. Her world and her work*, esp. pp. 95–100.

24 See chapters 1, 2 and 4.

25 Lacan, Sem II 112/89–90.

26 See Roudinesco, *La Bataille de cent ans*, pp. 135–6.

27 Leclaire, *Démasquer le réel*, esp. pp. 33–41. I discuss Leclaire's argument at greater length in chapter 9, pp. 226ff.

28 Adrian Wilson.

29 This fact also adds a surprising twist to the claim that paternity is always subject to a doubt that can never be raised concerning maternity. At a time when a sizeable proportion of children born became foundlings, abandoned to various institutions, this is perhaps not so surprising.

11 Transference and the stenographer

A first version of this paper was given at the British Comparative Literature Association's Workshop Seminar on 'Psychoanalysis and literature', at the University of Reading, 17–19 December 1979. Another version was given to the French Seminar organised by Malcolm Bowie at Queen Mary College, London, in December 1983. I would like to thank these two audiences for their helpful and stimulating comments, and to other readers who have offered comments and suggestions, in particular, Frank Kermode, André Green, Robert Young, Marian Hobson, Edward Bonds, Colin MacCabe and Felicity Baker. I have special debts to Chris Prendergast and Sylvana Tomaselli.

1 Paul Ricœur, *Freud and philosophy*, pp. 32ff.

2 See chapter 9.

3 Freud, 'Dostoevsky and parricide' (1928b), SE XX1 177–94. On Hamlet, see Jones, *Hamlet and Oedipus*.

4 Manuel, *A portrait of Isaac Newton*. See Kuhn, 'The relations between history and history of science', pp. 157–8.

5 Freud, 'Dostoevsky and parricide' (1928b), SE XXI 177.

6 Felman, 'Turning the screw of interpretation'.

7 Freud, 'The theme of the three caskets' (1913c), SE XII 291–301.

8 Knights, 'How many children had Lady Macbeth'? Knights does not mention that the text in which this question is explicitly posed as the key to the interpretation of *Macbeth* is Freud's 'Some character-types met with in psycho-analytic work, II Those wrecked by success' (1916d), SE XIV 311–33. It is not clear from his text whether his attack was directed at psycho-analytic criticism or whether Knights hit that mark 'by accident'.

9 See Eagleton, *Formations of pleasure*.

10 Freud, *Introductory lectures on psycho-analysis* (1916–17), SE XVI 444.

11 Felman, 'To open the question', p. 7.

12 Lacan, Sem XI 209–14/230–6, and Sem I 297–8/271; 306–7/277–8.

13 Lacan, 'Seminar on *The purloined letter*'; Derrida, 'Le facteur de la vérité'; Johnson, 'The frame of reference: Poe, Lacan, Derrida', all now conveniently collected in Muller and Richardson (eds.), *The purloined Poe*.

14 I have used the Penguin edition of *The gambler*, translated with an introduction by Jessie Coulson; page references in the text are to this edition (pp. 19–162). I have made reference to *The gambler with Polina Suslova's diary*, edited by Edward Wasiolek (who provides a very useful introduction) and translated by Victor Terras. There is a considerable tradition in Russian literature of tales about gambling; see in particular Gogol's play *The gamblers*. The other story about cards, chance and destiny with which *The gambler* is often compared is Pushkin's *The queen of spades*; see Jackson, *The art of Dostoevsky. Deliriums and nocturnes*. The character of de Grieux is directly based on des Grieux in Abbé de Prevost's *Histoire de Manon Lescaut* (1733); see Debreczeny, 'Dostoevskij's use of *Manon Lescaut* in *The gambler*'. Astley is taken from Thackeray's 'The Cickleburys on the Rhine'; see also Hoffmann, 'Gambler's fortune'.

15 Cf. pp. 66–7, when Astley and Alexei discuss Polina's relations with de Grieux, Astley scolding the gambler for linking their names, and then defending her by saying 'we form connexions even with people we loathe, if necessity forces us. There may be relations here you know nothing about, which depend on extraneous circumstances . . . ' What Alexei then supposes, asking Astley, who refuses to answer, is that Polina and Astley have *already* discussed these matters, without his knowing.

16 Jackson, *Art of Dostoevsky*, chapter 8, 'Polina and Lady Luck in *The gambler*', pp. 208–36. Jackson argues that Polina is the combination of the ordinary woman whom Alexei refuses and the imperial Goddess Fortuna whose slave he is.

17 Savage, 'Dostoevski: the idea of *The gambler*'; see also Carroll, *Breakout from the Crystal Palace. The anarcho-psychological critique: Stirner, Nietzsche, Dostoevsky*, pp. 155–66.

18 Savage, 'Dostoevski', p. 292; the theme is reiterated in Jackson, *Art of Dostoevsky*.

19 The failure to note that freedom is the ideal of the slave, rather than being one pole of a quasi-Platonic and neo-existentialist framework of pure ideas which the characters espouse or represent, accounts for the finally unsatisfactory account of Alexei's relations with Polina in Jackson's essay. Their relation is as much ruled by the master–slave dialectic as any other of the 'Russian' social relations in the novella, and Polina is entirely complicit in it. Jackson, however, posits a normative function of a wholesome or realistic relationship with Polina, the 'authentic Praskovya', 'a confused and troubled Russian girl' who seeks Alexei as a friend and confidant, who expresses 'tenderness and love', allied with 'doubts and uncertainties'. Jackson allows her to escape the demonic Alexei, finding some sort of 'positive resolution' with the 'family of the eminently decent Astley'. Such a reading of Polina imposes a normative conception of an ideal relationship from the outside; Polina within the story is as much a party to mastery and servitude as Alexei, though her final constancy – with Astley as her new slave – offers a glimpse of something beyond the imperial majesty she had previously incarnated. I return to this 'glimpse beyond' in the final section of this chapter.

20 Lacan, 'Function and field of speech and language'; Leclaire, 'L'obsessionel et son désir'; Roublef, 'Le désir de l'obsessionel dans la théorie de Jacques Lacan', pp. 78–98. A paper that combines discussion of the theory of obsessional neurosis and the theory of gambling from a Lacanian perspective is Tostain, 'Le joueur, essai psychanalytique'. See chapter 8, pp. 171–6 for further discussion of the obsessional, time and waiting.

21 The most important psychoanalytic work on gambling is Bergler, *The psychology of gambling*. Halliday and Fuller, eds., *The psychology of gambling*, is a very useful collection, including an extensive and stimulating introduction by Peter Fuller, and Elvio Fachinelli's 'Anal Money-Time', pp. 272–96.

22 Simmel, 'Zur Psychoanalyse des Spielers'.

23 Freud, 'Dostoevsky and parricide' (1928b), SE XXI 191–4.

24 Felman, 'To open the question'.

25 Lacan, 'Le temps logique'. See also E 241, 252, 287, 310ff.

26 Pascal, Letter to Fermat on 'La Règle des partis', 29 July 1654, in *Oeuvres complètes*, p. 43. For a general history of the relations between gambling and probability theory and modern conceptions of chance, see Hacking, *The emergence of probability*; Todhunter, *A history of the mathematical theory of probability from the time of Pascal to that of Laplace*; for a professional gambler's philosophical ruminations, see

the very interesting Richardson, *Memoir of a gambler*, esp. pp. 146–76, 191–2. It is also of interest that the first solutions to the dicing problems in the sixteenth century were parts of devices intended for reading the future. See Pearson and Kendall, *Studies in the history of statistics and probability*.

27 Hacking, *Emergence of probability*, pp. 92ff.

28 Keynes, *The general theory of employment, interest and money*, pp. 155–7.

29 Khan, *Alienation in perversions*, p. 9.

30 Caillois, *Man, play and games*, p. 156; see also Caillois's remarks on gambling and Argentinian *coups d'états* in *Quatre essais de sociologie contemporaine*, 'L'usage des richesses. Economie quotidienne et jeux de hasard en Amérique Ibérique', pp. 27–46.

31 Bakhtin, *Problems of Dostoevsky's poetics*, pp. 21ff.

32 *Ibid*. p. 144.

33 See, in particular, the letter to N.N. Strachov, Rome, 18(30) September 1863, in *Letters of Fyodor Michailovitich Dostoevsky to his family and friends*. On Appolinaria Suslova as the model for Polina, see the Wasiolek edition of Dostoevsky, *The gambler with Polina Suslova's Diary*.

34 See Waşiolek edition; also see Anna Dostoevsky, *Reminiscences*.

35 Letter to Strachov (cited in note 33), and in Wasiolek edition of *The gambler*.

36 Bakhtin, *Problems*, pp. 92ff. and 143–4.

37 Preface to 'A gentle creature' (1876), cited in Bakhtin, *Problems*, pp. 44–5. English editions of 'A gentle creature' often omit the Preface.

38 Quoted in Mochulsky, *Dostoevsky, his life and work*, p. 322.

39 Freud, 'Remembering, repeating and working-through' (1914g), SE XII 154.

40 Jackson, *Art of Dostoevsky*. Jackson's thesis repeats the attitude of Dostoevsky's brother, who wrote to him in 1862, when Dostoevsky had stopped off at Wiesbaden to gamble (for the first time) when travelling to meet Appolinaria Suslova in Paris: 'I cannot understand how you can gamble while travelling with a woman with whom you are in love' (quoted in Grossman, *Dostoevsky. A biography*, p. 296).

12 Michel Foucault and the history of psychoanalysis

This chapter is a considerably expanded version of my article with the same title, first published in *History of Science 18* 1980 pp. 285–303; it also includes material drawn from my 'Foucault and psychoanalysis', originally published in Lisa Appignanesi (ed.), *Ideas from France. The legacy of French theory*, London: ICA Publications, Documents 3, 1985, pp. 24–6.

1 'Truth, power, self: an interview' (25 October 1982), p. 15.

2 'To the doctor, Freud transferred all the structures Pinel and Tuke had set up within confinement. He did deliver the patient from the existence

of the asylum within which his "liberators" had alienated him; but he did not deliver him from what was essential in this existence; he regrouped its powers, extended them to the maximum by uniting them in the doctor's hands; he created the psychoanalytic situation where, by an inspired short-circuit, alienation becomes disalienating because, in the doctor, it becomes a subject'. Foucault, *Madness and civilization. A history of insanity in the Age of Reason*, p. 278.

3 Before I had read Hayden White's admirable *Metahistory*.

4 Forrester, 'An essay in intellectual, institutional and educational domination: English and Scottish medicine, 1740–1800' (unpublished, 1971).

5 A framework that enabled me to write my only almost entirely Foucaultian paper, entitled 'The eye and the ear in the doctor–patient relationship', when I addressed a group of general practitioners at a Colloquium on the Doctor–Patient Relationship, organised by the Wellcome Unit for the History of Medicine, Cambridge, in June 1975.

6 See chapter 5 of my *Language and the origins of psychoanalysis*.

7 Foucault, *La Volonté de savoir* (hereafter *VS*), p. 172; *The history of sexuality. Vol. I: An introduction* (hereafter *HS I*), p. 131.

8 Foucault, Introduction to Binswanger, *Le Rêve et l'existence*.

9 See the following passage, from 'What is an author?' (1969), in Foucault, *Language, counter-memory, practice. Selected essays and interviews*, p. 120, which marshals an array of critical remarks in the service of an attack on Derrida's concept of writing: 'To say that writing, in terms of the particular history it made possible, is subjected to forgetfulness and repression, is this not to reintroduce in transcendental terms the religious principle of hidden meanings (which requires interpretation) and the critical assumption of implicit significations, silent purposes, and obscure contents (which give rise to commentary)?

10 One of the phrases he used to characterise the area of concern was 'technologies of the self'.

11 Foucault, Introduction to *Le Rêve et l'existence*, p. 22.

12 *Ibid.* p. 20–1.

13 The relation to the overarching structure of *Mental illness and psychology* and later of *Madness and civilization* becomes clearer here, with the centrality of the question of the doctor–patient relationship; in those works, Freud's failure stems from his having *built into* psychoanalysis a charismatic and sacerdotal version of that relation.

14 In this sense, Foucault's interpretation of Dora is very similar to Lacan's (in 'Intervention on transference'); but whereas Lacan cites this practice of Freud's as exemplary of how the analyst *should* operate, Foucault finds it pre-eminently an *obstacle*, the obstacle created by psychoanalysis itself, to the subject acceding to a true desire.

15 Again, Lacan makes of this the defining characteristic of the hysteric's mode of being, whereas Foucault attributes it to Freud's interpretative strategy.

16 However, where this analysis differs from those is in its apparent uncritical attitude to the image. This text would seem to bely the analysis of Foucault's attitude to vision given by Jay, 'In the empire of the gaze: Foucault and the denigration of vision in twentieth-century French thought'. Foucault here would appear to be endorsing the possibility of a 'more revelatory visual experience' that Jay attributes to Heidegger and others, but which he argues Foucault had from the start repudiated.

17 Foucault, *The archaeology of knowledge*, p. 17.

18 In an interview given at the time of Lacan's death ('Lacan, il liberatore della psicanalisi', quoted in Lagrange), Foucault mentioned that reading Lacan in the early 1950s had helped liberate him from the 'very traditional conception of the subject', by showing him that 'the apparently straightforward use of the pronoun "I" ' masked the fact that the subject is, in reality, 'a complex, fragile thing, of which it is so difficult to speak, and, without which, however, it is not possible to speak'.

19 Foucault, *OT*. The passages most relevant to psychoanalysis are to be found in the two final chapters, 'Man and his doubles' and 'The human sciences'.

20 *OT* 313.

21 The 'physiological/pathological' distinction was peculiar to the late nineteenth and early twentieth centuries; it corresponded roughly to the later 'normal/pathological' distinction, but had the advantage of placing 'physiological' within the discipline 'physiology', and 'pathological' within 'pathology'.

22 *OT* 361.

23 *OT* 373.

24 The critical function that Foucault assigns to psychoanalysis has affinities with the critical self-reflexivity that Jurgen Habermas looks to psychoanalysis to provide; see his *Knowledge and human interests*, pp. 214ff. See also chapter 2, this volume, which points out how the rules governing psychoanalytic technique effectively place it in a meta-position with respect to all other discourse of truth and knowledge.

25 Lagrange, 'Versions de la psychanalyse dans le texte de Foucault', p. 105.

26 Again, Lagrange puts this succinctly and well: 'In addition, psychoanalytic concepts will not be invoked in analysing empirical contents of the sciences of man, since they work at a different level, that of the conditions which make possible functions and their norms, conflicts and their rules, significations and their systems. That is why psychoanalysis cannot be just one human science amongst the others' (pp. 106–7).

27 The question of the extent of Lacan's influence on Foucault's reading of psychoanalysis is a difficult one to resolve, and, in the end, may not be of great significance. Compare an interesting assessment by Foucault from the year of publication of *Les Mots et les choses*: 'Lacan's importance stems from the fact that he has demonstrated how, through

the discourse of the patient and the symptoms of his neurosis, it is the structures, the very system of language – and not the subject – which speaks . . . before there is human existence, there would already be a knowledge, a system that we are rediscovering . . . What is this anonymous system without a subject, who is thinking? "The subject" has exploded (take a look at modern literature). It's the discovery of the "there is". There is a "one"' (Foucault, 'Entretien', quoted in Ogilvie, *Lacan le sujet*, p. 42). As Ogilvie elegantly demonstrates, this characterisation of the structuralist position on the subject, attributed centrally to Lacan, is more royalist than the king – indeed, it is very good evidence that Foucault, despite his later indignant repudiations, was, at this time, very much enamoured of the extreme structuralist positions on the subject (one of the central topics on which one might be judged as to the extent of one's structuralism). Three years later, at a discussion of the Société Française de Philosophie of Foucault's lecture, 'What is an author?', Lacan made it quite clear that the Foucaultian position on the death of the author, death of the subject, death of man was in no way derived from his own view, nor was it consonant with his development of psychoanalysis: 'I would like to point out that, structuralism or not, in the field that has been vaguely delineated by this label, there is absolutely no question of the negation of the subject. What is in question is the dependence of the subject, which is a very different matter; and quite specifically, at the level of the return to Freud, the dependence of the subject in relation to something truly elementary, which we have tried to bring out with the term "signifier".' As to Lacan's view of Foucault, an excerpt from an interview granted in December 1966 gives some flavour of it: 'As for Foucault, he follows what I do, and I like his work, but I don't see him as being very interested in Freud's position' (*Figaro Littéraire*, 29 December 1966).

28 The shift of interest is even more clearly seen in Foucault's previous book, *Discipline and punish* (*Surveillir et punir*), in which the historical shift discussed in more general terms in *VS* – from the subject as constituted by law to the subject as constituted by a set of essential properties which are the objects of knowledge embodied in various sciences of man – is demonstrated to be part of the development of various legal and punitive measures from the eighteenth to nineteenth centuries.

29 See Lagrange, 'Versions de la psychanalyse dans le texte de Foucault', p. 112.

30 These two themes – illness and crime – had been the objects of study of two previous works of Foucault's: respectively, *The birth of the clinic* and *Discipline and punish*. The manner in which Foucault characterises the shift from eighteenth- to nineteenth-century modes of knowledge has not essentially changed from the early works of the 1960s: the idea of a *hidden cause*, the seat of disease, the seat of criminal desires, has

been central to his account of nineteenth-century science, and can be seen argued most clearly in *The order of things*.

31 *HS I* 93; *VS* 123.

32 This particular discussion is particularly relevant to recent psychoanalytic debates in France, a debate which Foucault was well aware of: 'the assertion that sex is not "repressed" is not altogether new. Psychoanalysts have been saying the same thing for some time' *HS I* 81ff.; *VS* 107ff.

33 Lagrange, 'Versions de la psychanalyse', p. 270 considers Foucault's characterisation of psychoanalysis as a variety of confession, noting in passing an early passage (*Studies on hysteria* (1895d), SE II 282) in which Freud likens the psychotherapist to 'a father confessor who gives absolution, as it were, by a continuance of his sympathy and respect after the confession has been made' – though it should be noted that Freud here introduces confession as simply one of the means the therapist has at his disposal, these means including 'almost all those by which one man can ordinarily exert a psychical influence on another'. Lagrange remarks that this reference to confession indicates firstly a debt to the multiplicity of previous discourses from which psychoanalysis borrows; secondly, a tactic whereby one refers to this religious practice and posture so as to provide a counterweight to the medical model which threatens the uniqueness of psychoanalysis – a pragmatic tactic of discursive subservience whereby psychoanalysis will eventually find a truer, more critical independence.

34 *VS* 87–90; *HS I* 65–9.

35 The idea that there is something about sex that is linguistically recalcitrant is often found in Freud; see Forrester, *Language*, pp. 33–6. Lacan makes it more explicit by tying the division of the subject created by language to the operation of castration.

36 For an incisive reflection on this theme and its relation to psychoanalysis, see Descombes, *L'Inconscient malgré lui*.

37 For a more extensive discussion of the fundamental rule, see chapter 7.

38 Rieff, *Freud. The mind of the moralist*, chapter 10.

39 *VS* 172; *HS I* 131.

40 *VS* 157–8; *HS I* 119. The first line of this paragraph includes a mistranslation, 'psychiatry' being given for *psychanalyse*.

41 Freud, *Origins*, p. 216; letter of 21 September 1897.

42 Although on this point see the remarkable letter cited at length in chapter 8, p. 205 & p. 364n140.

43 *VS* 148–9; *HS I* 112–13; translation modified.

44 *VS* 198; *HS I* 150.

45 Freud, '"Civilized" sexual morality and modern nervous illness' (1908d), SE IX 181–204.

46 Freud, *Inhibitions, symptoms and anxiety* (1926d), SE XX 163–4.

47 Freud, *The future of an illusion* (1926c), SE XXI 5–56, this passage from p. 53.

48 We might generalise Foucault's argument, and expose it to immediate criticism, by pointing out that what he means by confession is *both* a historically continuous, whilst continually transforming, set of social and religious practices, *and* a form of discourse whose specificity can be formally defined, as he in fact does: 'The confession is a ritual of discourse in which the speaking subject is also the subject of the statement [*enoncé*]; it is also a ritual that unfolds within a power relationship, for one does not confess without the presence [or *virtual presence* cf. the analyst?] of a partner who is not simply the interlocutor but the authority who requires the confession, prescribes and appreciates it, and intervenes in order to judge, punish, forgive, console, and reconcile; a ritual in which the truth is corroborated by the obstacles and resistance it has had to surmount in order to be formulated; and finally, a ritual in which the expression alone, independently of its external consequences, produces intrinsic modifications in the person who articulates it' (*VS* 82–3; *HS* I 61–2). Such a formulation, eminently in keeping with the tenor, even the rhetorical pacing, of the Lacan of the early 1950s, would be accepted by many analysts, Freudian, Lacanian or both. Such a formulation would also, as I demonstrate by discussing the possibilities of reflexivity of the power relations wheeled into the consulting room by the patient ('judge, punish, forgive, console and reconcile') in chapter 2, and by discussing the specific forms of speech act the analyst adopts in relation to such transferences (which is what analysts call these imported figures of speech, these figures of authority, resolution and reconciliation) in chapter 7, be open to specifying more fruitfully the *differences* between analytic discourse and confession. It is these differences, this perpetual stance of *evasion* of the speech acts of 'judgement, of punishment, forgiveness, consolation, and reconciliation', which, whilst it may well be the culmination of the tradition of confession, ensures that psychoanalysis can retain its essentially critical function. Yet it is crucially only a partial formulation; one cannot stop at the identification of the confessional subject with the subject of the statement; stopping there amounts to denying that there is anything more to be said, implicit in what the subject says – it amounts to denying the existence of an unconscious subject, awareness of which, in its multiplicity, Foucault had earlier, in 1966, attributed to Lacan's influence ('What is this anonymous system without a subject, who is thinking? "The subject" ['this complex, fragile thing'] has exploded . . . '). Stopping there amounts to lapsing into a sociolinguistic determinism, in which the position of the other (confessor, doctor, judge, meter-maid) constrains completely the discourse proffered to them.

49 See Lagrange, 'Versions de la psychanalyse', p. 112, for an alternative formulation of this point, and p. 115 for a discussion of the negativity credited to sexuality by Foucault.

50 Foucault *et al.*, 'Le jeu de Michel Foucault', pp. 62–93, translated as 'The confession of the flesh' in *Power/knowledge*, pp. 194–228.

51 It was the criticism of this peculiar use of the proper name in *The order of things* that prompted Foucault to reflect on the question 'What is an author?' in 1969. He certainly gave up, in his later work, the manner of invoking proper names of *The order of things*. But, as I indicate in the text, he *replaced* it with a different conception of the relation of 'author' and discursive practice – the two concepts explored in 'What is an author?' Significantly, much of the latter part of that paper addressed the distinctive relations of the names Freud and Marx to the discursive practices to which they had given rise.

52 Representative examples of these historical works are: Amacher, 'Freud's neurological education and its influence on psychoanalytic theory'; Andersson, *Studies in the prehistory of psychoanalysis*; Cranefield, 'The organic physics of 1847 and the biophysics of today'; Ellenberger, *The discovery of the unconscious*. Despite its claims to be demythologising, it is this conventional internalist slant that makes Sulloway's *Freud. Biologist of the mind* seem so dated when compared with a Foucaultian approach.

53 See chapter 5 of Forrester, *Language*, and Burrow, 'The uses of philology in Victorian England'.

54 *VS* 172; *HS I* 130; translation modified.

55 See for instance Reich's *The mass psychology of fascism* (1933).

56 Lacan, 'Le mythe individuel du névrosé ou "Poésie et vérité" dans la névrose' (1953 (mimeo), p. 4); a revised version has been published as 'The neurotic's individual myth'. A longer discussion of the occlusion of the ideal father will be found in the article Lacan wrote in 1938 for the *Encyclopédie française*, under the title 'La famille'.

57 Foucault, 'On the genealogy of ethics' (1983): 'Well, I wonder if our problem nowadays is not, in a way, similar to [that of the Greeks], since most of us no longer believe that ethics is founded on religion, nor do we want a legal system to intervene in our moral, personal, private life. Recent liberation movements suffer from the fact that they cannot find any principle on which to base the elaboration of a new ethics. They need an ethics but they cannot find any other ethics than an ethics founded on so-called knowledge of what the self is, what desire is, what the unconscious is, and so on. I am struck by this similarity of problems' (p. 231).

58 I will not address the most obviously surprising feature of these books: their style – there are far fewer lyrical and awesome passages – the 'gleaming words' that Alan Sheridan talks of in his book on Foucault; there are no striking images, as if the Aristotelian precept and practice of moderation Foucault describes and analyses had also infused his own writing.

59 Foucault, 'The subject and power' (1982), p. 221. Note how this new conception is linked to a redefinition of power into which is built the freedom of the other: 'a power relationship can only be articulated on the basis . . . that "the other" (the one over whom power is exercised)

be thoroughly recognized and maintained to the very end as a person who acts' (p. 220).

60 *HS I* 58.

61 *HS I* 61.

62 'On the genealogy of ethics', pp. 234–5: 'The Greeks and Romans did not have any *ars erotica* to be compared with the Chinese . . . They had a *techne tou biou* in which the economy of pleasure played a very large role. In this "art of life" the notion of exercising a perfect mastery over oneself soon became the main issue. And the Christian hermeneutics of the self constituted a new elaboration of this *techne*.' I may be mistaken, but this final sentence seems to be in considerable tension with Foucault's arguments elsewhere (particularly in *The history of sexuality Vol. III*) that the Christian examination of the self is in sharp contrast with, rather than a prolongation of, the Greek care of the self.

63 *The use of pleasure*, p. 86.

64 Foucault, 'The subject and power', pp. 214–15.

65 Freud, *The ego and the id* (1923b), SE XIX 55.

66 'The function and field of speech and language' (1953) E 321/105.

67 Foucault, 'Truth, power, self: an interview', p. 11.

68 *Le Nouvel Observateur* 12 March 1977, quoted in *Magazine Littéraire* September 1977, p. 26. Also translated as 'Power and sex: an interview', in *Telos 32* 1977. The passage continues: 'As for all the questions as to classification, as to programmes that people ask us: *Are you a Marxist? What would you do if you were in power? Who are your allies and what do you belong to?* these are questions which are clearly secondary when compared with the ones I've just pointed out, because these are the questions of today.'

BIBLIOGRAPHY

Abraham, Karl, 'The experiencing of sexual traumas as a form of sexual activity' (1907), in *Selected papers on psycho-analysis*, with an introductory memoir by Ernest Jones, trans. by Douglas Bryan and Alix Strachey, London: Hogarth Press and the Institute of Psycho-analysis, 1927, pp. 47–63.

Abraham, Nicolas, and Maria Torok, *Le Verbier de l'homme aux loups*, Paris: Aubier Flammarion, 1976.

Abrahamsen, David, *The psychology of crime*, New York: Columbia University Press, 1960.

Allouch, Jean, 'Enfants du parladit', *Etudes Freudiennes*, 'Incidences de l'œuvre de Lacan sur la pratique de la psychanalyse' No. 25, April 1985 pp. 97–113.

Amacher, Peter, 'Freud's neurological education and its influence on psychoanalytic theory', *Psychological Issues 4* 1965, monograph 16.

Amir, Menachem, *Patterns in forcible rape*, Chicago: University of Chicago Press, 1971.

Andersson, Ola, *Studies in the prehistory of psychoanalysis*, Stockholm: Scandinavian University Books, Svenska Bokförlaget/Norstedts-Bomiers, 1962.

Anzieu, Didier, *L'Auto-analyse de Freud*, Paris: Presses Universitaires de France, 1975; trans. as *Freud's self-analysis* by Peter Graham, London: Hogarth Press and the Institute of Psycho-analysis, 1986.

Appignanesi, Lisa, ed., *Ideas from France. The legacy of French theory*, London: ICA Publications, Documents 3, 1985.

Aristotle, *Metaphysics*, ed. W.D. Ross, Oxford: Clarendon Press, 1924.

Physics, Loeb Classical Library, London: Heinemann, 1934.

Auden, W.H., *Collected shorter poems 1927–1957*, London: Faber & Faber, 1966.

Austin, J.L., *How to do things with words*, Oxford: Oxford University Press, 1962.

Philosophical papers, ed. J.O. Urmson and G.J. Warnock, second edition, Oxford: Oxford University Press, 1970.

Bachelard, Gaston, *The philosophy of no. Philosophy of the new scientific mind* (1940), trans. by G.C. Waterston, New York: Orion Press, 1968.

Bibliography

Bakhtin, Mikhail, *Problems of Dostoevsky's poetics*, trans. by R.W. Rotsel, Ann Arbor: Ardis, 1973.

Balint, Michael, *The doctor, the patient and the illness*, London: Pitman Medical, 1957.

Balmary, Marie, *Psychoanalyzing psychoanalysis. Freud and the hidden fault of the father* (1979), trans. and with an introduction by Ned Lukacher, Baltimore: Johns Hopkins University Press, 1982.

Barthes, Roland, 'Textual analysis of Poe's "Valdemar" ', in Robert Young, ed., *Untying the text. A post-structuralist reader*, London: Routledge & Kegan Paul, 1981, pp. 133–62.

Bass, Ellen, and Louise Thornton, eds., *I never told anyone. Writings by women survivors of child sexual abuse*, New York: Harper & Row, 1983.

Bataille, Laurence, 'D'une pratique', *Etudes Freudiennes*, 'Incidences de l'œuvre de Lacan sur la pratique de la psychanalyse' No. 25, April 1985 pp. 7–30.

Baudrillard, Jean, *De la séduction*, Paris: Flammarion, 1979.

Bellemin-Noël, Jean, 'Psychanalyse et pragmatique', *Critique 420* May 1982 pp. 406–22.

Benvenuto, Bice, and Roger Kennedy, *The works of Jacques Lacan*, London: Free Association Books, 1986.

Bergler, Edmund, *The psychology of gambling*, New York: International Universities Press, 1958.

Bion, Wilfred, *Experiences in groups*, London: Tavistock, 1961.
Attention and interpretation, London: Tavistock, 1970.

Boden, Margaret, *Artificial intelligence and natural man*, New York: Basic Books, 1977.

Borch-Jacobsen, Mikkel, *Le Sujet freudien*, Paris: Flammarion, 1982.

Bowie, Malcolm, *Freud, Proust and Lacan: theory as fiction*, Cambridge: Cambridge University Press, 1987.

Breuer, Josef, and Sigmund Freud, *Studien über Hysterie* (1895), Frankfurt: Fischer Taschenbuch, 1970.

Brody, Howard, *Placebos and the philosophy of medicine*, Chicago and London: University of Chicago Press, 1977.

Brome, Vincent, *Ernest Jones. Freud's alter ego*, London: Caliban, 1982.

Brownmiller, Susan, *Against our will: men, women and rape*, New York: Simon & Schuster, 1975; Bantam Books, 1976.

Bryson, Norman, 'Two narratives of rape in the visual arts: Lucretia and the Sabine women', in Tomaselli and Porter, eds., *Rape*, pp. 152–73.

Burrow, John, 'The uses of philology in Victorian England', in R. Robson, ed., *Ideas and institutions of Victorian Britain*, London: G. Bell & Son, 1967, pp. 180–204.

Caillois, Roger, *Quatre essais de sociologie contemporaine*, Paris: Olivier Perrin, 1951.
Man, play and games (1958), London: Free Press, 1962.

Bibliography

Calvino, Italo, *If on a winter's night a traveller*, trans. by William Weaver, London: Picador, 1982.

Carroll, John, *Breakout from the crystal palace. The anarcho-psychological critique: Stirner, Nietzsche, Dostoevsky*, London: Routledge & Kegan Paul, 1974.

Castel, Robert, *Le Psychanalysme*, Paris: Editions 10/18, 1976.

Charcot, J.M., *L'Hystérie*, textes choisis et présentés par E. Trillat, Toulouse: Privat, 1971.

Chertok, L., 'The discovery of the transference: towards an epistemological interpretation', *Int. J. Psa. 49* 1968 pp. 56–76.

Cixous, Hélène, and Cathérine Clément, *La Jeune née*, Paris: Editions 10/18, 1975.

Clark, Ronald W., *Freud: the man and the cause*, London: Jonathan Cape/Weidenfeld & Nicolson, 1980.

Clément, Cathérine, *The lives and legends of Jacques Lacan*, tr. A. Goldhammer, New York: Columbia University Press, 1983.

Collins, Jerre, J. Ray Green, Mary Lydon, Mark Sachner, and Eleanor Honig Skoller, 'Questioning the unconscious: the Dora archive', *Diacritics 13* Spring 1983 pp. 37–42.

Cottet, Serge, *Freud et le désir du psychanalyste*, Paris: Navarin, 1982.

Cranefield, Paul, 'The organic physics of 1847 and the biophysics of today', *Journal for the history of medicine 22* 1957 pp. 407–23.

Daston, Lorraine J., 'Probabilistic expectation and rationality in classical probability theory', *Historia Mathematica 7* 1980 pp. 234–60.

'Mathematics and the moral sciences: the rise and fall of the probability of judgments, 1785–1840', in H.N. Jahnke and M. Otte, eds., *Epistemological and social problems of the sciences in the early nineteenth century*, Dordrecht: Reidel, 1981, pp. 287–309.

'Rational individuals versus laws of society: from probability to statistics', in M. Heidelberger, L. Krüger and R. Rheinwald, eds., *Probability since 1800*, Bielefeld: Universität Bielefeld, 1983, pp. 7–26.

Debreczeny, Paul, 'Dostoevskij's use of *Manon Lescaut* in *The gambler*', *Comparative Literature 28* 1976 pp. 1–18.

Dennett, Daniel, *Brainstorms*, Hassocks, Sussex: Harvester, 1979.

Derrida, Jacques, 'Freud and the scene of writing' (1965), *Yale French Studies 48* 1972 pp. 74–117; also in *Writing and difference* (1967), Chicago and London: University of Chicago Press, 1978.

Of grammatology (1967), trans. and with an introduction by Gayatri Spivak, Baltimore: Johns Hopkins University Press, 1974.

Positions, Paris: Editions de Minuit, 1972.

Glas, Paris: Galilée, 1974.

'Le facteur de la vérité' (1975), in Jacques Derrida, *La Carte postale: De Socrate à Freud et au-delà*, Paris: Aubier-Flammarion, 1980, pp. 441–524; trans. as *The post card. From Socrates to Freud and beyond* by Alan Bass, Chicago: University of Chicago Press, 1987, pp. 411–96.

'Spéculer – sur "Freud" ', in Jacques Derrida, *La Carte postale*, Paris:

Bibliography

Aubier-Flammarion, 1980, pp. 277–437; trans. as *The post card. From Socrates to Freud and beyond* by Alan Bass, Chicago: University of Chicago Press, 1987, pp. 257–409.

'Télépathie', *Cahiers Confrontation 10*, Automne 1983 pp. 201–30; reprinted in Derrida, *Psyché*, pp. 237–70.

'My chances/*Mes chances*: a rendezvous with some Epicurean stereophonies', in Joseph H. Smith and William Kerrigan, eds., *Taking chances: Derrida, psychoanalysis and literature*, Baltimore and London: The Johns Hopkins University Press, 1984, pp. 1–32.

Psyché. Inventions de l'autre, Paris: Galilée, 1987.

Descombes, Vincent, *L'Inconscient malgré lui*, Paris: Editions de Minuit, 1977.

Deutsch, Helene, *The psychology of women*, 2 vols., London: Research Press, 1946.

Didi-Huberman, Georges, *Invention de l'hystérie. Charcot et l'iconographie photographique de la Salpêtrière*, Paris: Editions Macula, 1982.

Donaldson, Ian, *The rape of Lucretia: a myth and its transformation*, Oxford: Oxford University Press, 1983.

Dostoevsky, Anna, *Reminiscences*, trans. and ed. by Beatrice Stillman, introduction by Helen Muchnie, London: Wildwood House, 1975.

Dostoevsky, Fyodor, *Letters of Fyodor Michailovitch Dostoevsky to his family and friends*, trans. by Ethel Colburn Mayne, with an introduction by Arrahm Yamolinsky, London: Peter Owen, 1962.

The gambler, trans. and with an introduction by Jessie Coulson, Harmondsworth: Penguin, 1966.

The gambler with Polina Suslova's diary, ed. and with an introduction by Edward Wasiolek, trans. by Victor Terras, Chicago and London: University of Chicago Press, 1972.

Dreyfus, Hubert L., and Paul Rabinow, *Michel Foucault: beyond structuralism and hermeneutics*, second edition, with an Afterword by and an Interview with Michel Foucault, Chicago: University of Chicago Press, 1983.

Eagleton, Terry, *Formations of pleasure*, London: Routledge & Kegan Paul, 1983.

Eco, Umberto, 'Mirrors', in Eco, *Semiotics and the philosophy of language*, London: Macmillan, 1984, pp. 202–26.

Edwards, Susan, *Female sexuality and the law*, Oxford: Martin Robertson, 1981.

Eissler, K. R., 'On some theoretical and technical problems regarding the payment of fees for psychoanalytic treatment', *Int. Rev. Psychoanal. 1* 1974 pp. 73–101.

Ellenberger, Henri F., *The discovery of the unconscious. The history and evolution of dynamic psychiatry*, London: Allen Lane, 1970.

'The story of "Anna O.": A critical review with new data', *J. Hist. Behav. Sc. 8* 1972 pp. 267–79.

Feild, Hubert S., and Leigh B. Beinen, *Jurors and rape*, Lexington, MA: D.C. Heath, 1980.

Bibliography

Felman, Shoshana, *'To open the question'*, *Yale French Studies Nos. 55/56; Literature and psychoanalysis. The question of reading: otherwise*, ed. by Shoshana Felman, New Haven and London: Yale University Press, 1977, pp. 3–7.

'Turning the screw of interpretation', *Yale French Studies Nos. 55/56* 1977 pp. 94–207.

Le Scandale du corps parlant, Paris: Seuil, 1980.

Ferenczi, Sándor, *Further contributions to the theory and technique of psycho-analysis*, London: The Hogarth Press, third edition, 1950.

Forrester, John, *Language and the origins of psychoanalysis*, London: Macmillan / New York: Columbia University Press, 1980.

'The linguistic and the psychotic; Review of Jacques Lacan, *Le Séminaire. Livre III. Les Psychoses*, Paris: Seuil, 1981', in *Times Literary Supplement* 1 October 1982 pp. 1079–80.

'Lacan, Jacques', in Rom Harré and Roger Lamb, eds., *Encyclopaedia of psychology*, Oxford: Basil Blackwell, 1983, pp. 330–1.

'Austin, Lacan et les actes de parole en psychanalyse', *Psychanalyse à l'Université 10* 1985 pp. 349–67.

'Lying on the couch', in Hilary Lawson and Lisa Appignanesi, eds., *Dismantling truth*, London: Weidenfeld & Nicolson, 1989, pp. 145–65.

Lying on the couch. Truth, lies and the epistemology of psychoanalysis, Oxford: Basil Blackwell, 1990.

The dream of psychoanalysis, forthcoming.

Foucault, Michel, Introduction to Ludwig Binswanger, *Le Rêve et l'existence*, trans. by Jacqueline Verdeaux, Paris: Desclée de Brouwer, 1954.

Mental illness and psychology (1954), trans. by Alan Sheridan, New York: Harper, 1976.

Histoire de la folie à l'âge classique (1961), Paris: Gallimard, 1972.

Madness and civilization. A history of insanity in the Age of Reason (1961), trans. by Richard Howard, London: Tavistock, 1967.

The birth of the clinic, Paris: Gallimard, 1963; London: Tavistock, 1973.

The order of things [*Les Mots et les choses*] (1966), London: Tavistock, 1970.

'Entretien', *La quinzaine littéraire* 15 May 1966.

The archaeology of knowledge (1969), London: Tavistock, 1972.

'What is an author?' (1969), in Michel Foucault, *Language, counter-memory, practice. Selected essays and interviews*, ed. and with an introduction by Donald F. Bouchard, trans. by Donald F. Bouchard and Sherry Simon, Oxford: Basil Blackwell, 1977.

Discipline and punish [*Surveiller et punir*], Paris: Gallimard, 1975; trans. by Alan Sheridan, London: Allen Lane, 1977.

La Volonté de savoir, Paris: Gallimard, 1976; *The history of sexuality. Vol. I: An introduction*, trans. by Robert Hurley, London: Allen Lane, 1979.

Bibliography

'Non au sexe roi', *Le Nouvel Observateur No. 644* 12 March 1977; trans. as 'Power and sex: an interview' in *Telos 32* 1977.

Power/knowledge. Selected interviews and other writings. 1972–1977, ed. by Colin Gordon, trans. by Colin Gordon, Leo Marshall, John Mepham and Kate Soper, New York: Pantheon, 1980.

'Lacan, il liberatore della psicanalisi', Interview with Parigi, *Corriere della Sera*, 106th year, no. 212, 11 September 1981, p. 1.

'Truth, power, self: an interview' (25 October 1982), in Luther H. Martin, Huck Gutman and Patrick H. Hutton, eds., *Technologies of the self. A seminar with Michel Foucault*, London: Tavistock, 1988, pp. 9–15.

'The subject and power' (1982), in Dreyfus and Rabinow, *Michel Foucault*, pp. 208–26.

'On the genealogy of ethics' (1983), in Dreyfus and Rabinow, *Michel Foucault*, pp. 229–52.

The use of pleasure. Vol. II. The history of sexuality (1984), trans. by Robert Hurley, London: Viking, 1986.

The care of the self. Vol. III. The history of sexuality (1984), trans. by Robert Hurley, London: Allen Lane, 1986.

Freud, Sigmund, *The origins of psychoanalysis. Letters to Wilhelm Fliess, drafts and notes, 1887–1902*, ed. by Marie Bonaparte, Anna Freud and Ernst Kris, trans. by Eric Mosbacher and James Strachey, London: Imago, 1954.

Letters of Sigmund Freud, 1873–1939, ed. by Ernst L. Freud, trans. by Tania Stern and James Stern, London: The Hogarth Press, 1970.

The complete letters of Sigmund Freud to Wilhelm Fliess. 1887–1904, ed. by J.M. Masson, Cambridge, MA: Harvard University Press, 1984.

The standard edition of the complete psychological works of Sigmund Freud, under the general editorship of James Strachey in collaboration with Anna Freud, assisted by Alix Strachey and Alan Tyson, 24 vols., London: The Hogarth Press and the Institute of Psychoanalysis, 1953–74 [SE].

'Review of August Forel's *Der Hypnotismus*' (1889a), SE I 91–102.

'Psychical (or mental) treatment' (1890a), SE VII 283–302.

'A case of successful treatment by hypnotism' (1892–93), SE I 117–28.

'Preface and footnotes to the translation of Charcot's *Leçons du mardi*' (1892–94), SE I 133–43.

Project for a scientific psychology (1894), SE I 295–387.

'Further remarks on the neuro-psychoses of defence' (1896b), SE III 162–85.

'The aetiology of hysteria' (1896c), SE III 191–221.

'Abstracts of the scientific writings of Dr. Sigm. Freud 1877–1897' (1897), SE III 227–57.

'Screen memories' (1899a), SE III 304–22.

The interpretation of dreams (1900a), SE IV, V.

'A premonitory dream fulfilled' (1941c [1899]), SE V 623–5.

Bibliography

On dreams (1901a), SE V 636–86.

The psychopathology of everyday life (1901b), SE VI.

Jokes and their relation to the unconscious (1905c), SE VIII.

'Fragment of the analysis of a case of hysteria' [*Dora*] (1905e), SE VII 7–122.

'Character and anal erotism' (1908b), SE IX 169–75.

'"Civilized" sexual morality and modern nervous illness' (1908d), SE IX 181–204.

'Some general remarks on hysterical attacks' (1909a [1908]), SE IX 229–34.

'Analysis of a phobia in a five-year-old boy' (1909b), SE X 5–147.

'Notes upon a case of obsessional neurosis' [*Ratman*] (1909d), SE X 155–249.

Five lectures on psycho-analysis (1910a [1909]), SE XI 3–55.

'"Wild" psychoanalysis' (1910k), SE XI 221–7.

'On beginning the treatment' (1913c), SE XII 122–44.

'The theme of the three caskets' (1913f), SE XII 291–301.

'On the history of the psychoanalytic movement' (1914d), SE XIV 7–66.

'Remembering, repeating and working-through' (1914g), SE XII 147–56.

'Observations on transference-love' (1915a), SE XII 159–71.

'Thoughts for the times on war and death' (1915b), SE XIV 275–84.

'Some character-types met with in psycho-analytic work' (1916d), SE XIV 311–33.

Introductory lectures on psycho-analysis (1916–17), SE XV, XVI.

'From the history of an infantile neurosis' [*Wolfman*] (1918b), SE XVII 7–122.

'The psychogenesis of a case of female homosexuality' (1920a), SE XVIII 147–72.

Beyond the pleasure principle (1920g), SE XVIII 7–64.

Group psychology and the analysis of the ego (1921c), SE XVIII 69–143.

'Psycho-analysis and telepathy' (1941d [1921]), SE XVIII 177–93.

'Two encyclopaedia articles' (1923a), SE XVIII 236–59.

The ego and the id (1923b), SE XIX 12–59.

'The economic problem of masochism' (1924c), SE XIX 159–70.

'A note upon the "Mystic Writing-Pad"' (1925a [1924]), SE XIX 227–32.

An autobiographical study (1925d), SE XX 10–70.

'Josef Breuer' (1925g), SE XIX 279–80.

'Some additional notes on dream-interpretation as a whole' (1925i), SE XIX 127–38.

Inhibitions, symptoms and anxiety (1926d), SE XX 87–172.

The future of an illusion (1926c), SE XXI 5–56.

The question of lay analysis (1926e), SE XX 183–250.

'Fetishism' (1927e), SE XXI 152–7.

Bibliography

'Dostoevsky and parricide' (1928b), SE XXI 177–94.

Civilization and its discontents (1930a [1929]), SE XXI 64–145.

New introductory lectures on psycho-analysis (1933 [1932]), SE XXII 3–182.

'Sándor Ferenczi' (1933c), SE XXII 227–9.

'A disturbance of memory on the Acropolis' (1936a), SE XX 239–43.

'Constructions in analysis' (1937d), SE XXIII 257–69.

An outline of psycho-analysis (1940a [1938]), SE XXIII 141–207.

'Findings ideas, problems' (1941f [1938]), SE XXIII 299–300.

Freud, Sigmund, and Karl Abraham, *A psycho-analytic dialogue. The letters of Sigmund Freud and Karl Abraham, 1907–1926*, ed. by Hilda C. Abraham and Ernst L. Freud, London: The Hogarth Press and the Institute of Psycho-analysis, 1965.

Freud, Sigmund, and Josef Breuer, *Studies on hysteria* (1895d), SE II.

Freud, Sigmund, and C.G. Jung, *The Freud/Jung letters*, ed. by William McGuire, trans. by R. Manheim and R.F.C. Hull, Princeton: Princeton University Press, 1974.

Gallop, Jane, *Feminism and psychoanalysis. The daughter's seduction*, London: Macmillan, 1982.

'Beyond the *Jouissance* principle', *Representations* 7 1984.

Gardner, Sebastian, 'Sartre's critique of Freud: irrationality and the philosophy of psychoanalysis', unpublished Ph.D. dissertation, University of Cambridge, 1987.

Gay, Peter, *Freud. A life for our time*, London: Dent, 1988.

Gearhart, Suzanne, 'The scene of psychoanalysis: the unanswered questions of Dora', *Diacritics 9* 1979 pp. 114–26.

Giraudoux, Jean, *Théâtre*, 4 vols., Paris: Bernard Grasset, 1958.

Glover, Edward, *The technique of psycho-analysis*, London: Baillière, Tindall & Fox, 1955.

Granoff, Wladimir, *Filiations*, Paris: Editions de Minuit, 1975.

Granoff, Wladimir, and Jean-Michel Rey, *L'Occulte, objet de la pensée freudienne*, Paris: PUF, 1983.

Griffin, Susan, 'Pornography and silence' (1981), in Griffin, *Made from this earth. Selections from her writing 1967–82*, London: The Women's Press Ltd, 1982, pp. 110–60.

Grosskurth, Phyllis, *Melanie Klein. Her world and her work*, London: Hodder & Stoughton, 1986.

Grossman, Leonid, *Dostoevsky. A biography*, trans. by Mary Meckle, London: Allen Lane, 1974.

Grünbaum, Adolf, *The foundations of psychoanalysis*, Berkeley: University of California Press, 1984.

Guntrip, Harry, 'My experience of analysis with Fairbairn and Winnicott', *Int. Rev. Psa. 2* 1975 pp. 145–56.

Habermas, Jurgen, *Knowledge and human interests* (1968), London: Routledge & Kegan Paul, 1972.

Hacking, Ian, *The emergence of probability*, Cambridge: Cambridge University Press, 1975.

Bibliography

'Was there a probabilistic revolution, 1800–1930?', in M. Heidelberger, L. Krüger and R. Rheinwald, eds., *Probability since 1800*, Bielefeld: Universität Bielefeld, 1983, pp. 487–506.

Halliday, Jon, and Peter Fuller, eds., *The psychology of gambling*, London: Allen Lane, 1974.

Harrison, Carey, *Freud*, Harmondsworth: Penguin, 1985.

Harrison, Ross, 'Rape – a case study in political philosophy', in Tomaselli and Porter, eds., *Rape*, pp. 41–57.

Hartman, Frank R., 'A reappraisal of the Emma episode and the specimen dream', *Journal of the American Psychoanalytic Association 31* no. 3 1983 pp. 555–85.

Hertz, Neil, 'Dora's secrets, Freud's techniques', *Diacritics 13* Spring 1983 pp. 65–76.

Heynick, Frank, 'Theoretical and empirical investigation into verbal aspects of the Freudian model of dream generation', unpublished Ph.D. dissertation, University of Groningen, 1983.

Hoffmann, E.T.A., 'Gambler's fortune', in Hoffmann, *Serapion brethren*, London: Bell, 1886–92, vol. 2, pp. 218–45.

Hofstadter, D.R., *Gödel, Escher, Bach*, Hassocks, Sussex: Harvester, 1979.

Hursch, Carolyn J., *The trouble with rape*, Chicago: Nelson-Hall, 1977.

Hyppolite, Jean, 'Spoken commentary on Freud's *Verneinung*' (1956), E 879–87; trans. in Sem I 289–97.

Jackson, Robert Louis, *The art of Dostoevsky. Deliriums and nocturnes*, Princeton: Princeton University Press, 1981.

Jacob, François, *Le Jeu des possibles*, Paris: Fayard, 1981.

The possible and the actual, New York: Pantheon, 1982.

Jakobson, R., and M. Halle, *Fundamentals of language*, The Hague: Mouton, 1956.

James, Henry, *The golden bowl* (1904), Harmondsworth: Penguin, 1966.

James, P.D., *A taste for death*, London: Faber & Faber, 1986.

Janik, Allan, and Stephen Toulmin, *Wittgenstein's Vienna*, New York: Simon & Schuster, 1973.

Jay, Martin, 'In the empire of the gaze: Foucault and the denigration of vision in twentieth-century French thought', in David Couzens Hoy, ed., *Foucault. A critical reader*, Oxford: Basil Blackwell, 1986, pp. 175–204.

Johnson, Barbara, 'The frame of reference: Poe, Lacan, Derrida' (1977), in Muller and Richardson, eds., *The purloined Poe*, pp. 213–51.

Johnston, William Murray, *The Austrian mind; an intellectual and social history, 1848–1938*, Berkeley: University of California Press, 1972.

Jones, Ernest, *Hamlet and Oedipus*, London: Victor Gollancz, 1949.

Sigmund Freud. Life and work, 3 vols., London: The Hogarth Press, 1953–7.

Jung, C.G., 'The significance of the father in the destiny of the individual' (1909), in *The Collected Works of C.G. Jung*, ed. by Sir Herbert Read,

Bibliography

Michael Fordham and Gerhard Adler, transl. by R.F.C. Hull, London: Routledge & Kegan Paul, 1961, vol. IV, pp. 301–23.

'A contribution to the psychology of rumour' (1910), in Jung, *Collected Works*, vol. IV, pp. 35–47.

Karpman, Benjamin, *The sexual offender and his offenses*, New York: Julian Press, 1954.

Keynes, John Maynard, *The general theory of employment, interest and money*, Cambridge: Cambridge University Press, 1936.

Khan, M. Masud R., *Alienation in perversions*, London: The Hogarth Press and the Institute of Psycho-analysis, 1979.

'The evil hand', in Khan, *Hidden selves. Between theory and practice in psychoanalysis*, London: The Hogarth Press, 1983, pp. 139–80.

Kierkegaard, S., *Either/or*, 2 vols., trans. by David F. Swenson and L.M. Svenson, Princeton: Princeton University Press, 1959.

'Immediate stages of the erotic or the musical erotic', in Kierkegaard, *Either/or*, vol. I, pp. 43–134.

Knights, L.C., 'How many children had Lady Macbeth?' (1933), in Knights, *Explorations*, Harmondsworth: Penguin, 1964, pp. 13–50.

Koestler, Arthur, *The sleepwalkers*, London: Hutchinson, 1959.

Kofman, Sarah, 'Ça cloche', in *Les Fins de l'homme. A partir du travail de Jacques Derrida*, Paris: Galilée, 1981, pp. 89–112.

Kojève, Alexandre, *Introduction to the reading of Hegel* (1947), ed. by Raymond Queneau (from courses 1933–9), trans. by J. Nichols, Jr, New York: Basic Books, 1969.

Kuhn, T.S., 'The relations between history and history of science', in Kuhn, *The essential tension*, London: University of Chicago Press, 1977, pp. 157–8.

Kundera, Milan, *The book of laughter and forgetting*, Harmondsworth: Penguin, 1983.

Lacan, Jacques, 'Review of E. Minkowski, *Le Temps vécu: Etudes phénoménologiques et psychopathologiques*', in *Recherches philosophiques* 5 1935–6 pp. 424–31.

'La Famille', *Encyclopédie française* 1938, vol. VIII, 'La Vie mentale'; reprinted as *Le Complexe familial*, Paris: Navarin, 1984; trans. as *The family* by Cormac Gallagher, Oxford: Basil Blackwell, 1989.

'Le temps logique et l'assertion de certitude anticipée' (1945), E 197–213.

'Le nombre treize et la forme logique de la suspicion', *Cahiers d'Art* 1945, n.p. [not reprinted in *Ecrits*; it may be found in Jacques Lacan, *Travaux et interventions*].

'Propos sur la causalité psychique' (1946), E 151–93.

'La psychiatrie anglaise et la guerre', *L'Evolution psychiatrique* 1947 pp. 293–312; also in Lacan, *Travaux et interventions*.

'Intervention on transference' (1951), in Mitchell and Rose, eds., *Feminine sexuality*, pp. 61–73.

'Le mythe individuel du névrosé ou "Poésie et vérité" dans la névrose', Paris: Centre de la Documentation Universitaire, 1953 (mimeo);

revised version published as 'The neurotic's individual myth', *Psychoanalytic Quarterly 48* 1979 pp. 405–25.

'Function and field of speech and language in psychoanalysis' (1953) ['Rapport de Rome' (Report to the Rome Congress held at the Istituto di Psicologica della Università di Roma, 26–7 Sept. 1953)], a version of which was published as 'Fonction et champ de la parole et du langage en psychanalyse', *La Psychanalyse 1* 1956 pp. 81–166. A revised version was published in *Ecrits*; it is this version that Wilden translated in Wilden, *The language of the self*, and Sheridan translated in Lacan, *Ecrits: a selection* (1977).

Le Séminaire. Livre I. Les Ecrits techniques de Freud. 1953–1954, Paris: Seuil, 1975; *The seminar. Book I. Freud's papers on technique 1953–1954*, trans. and with notes by John Forrester. Cambridge: Cambridge University Press / New York: Norton & Co., 1988.

'Introduction au commentaire de Jean Hyppolite sur la *Verneinung* de Freud' (1954), E 363–99, trans. in Sem I 289–97.

Le Séminaire. Livre II. Le Moi dans la théorie de Freud et dans la technique de la psychanalyse. 1954–1955, Paris: Seuil, 1978; *The seminar. Book II. The ego in Freud's theory and in the technique of psychoanalysis, 1954–1955*, trans. by Sylvana Tomaselli, with notes by John Forrester, Cambridge: Cambridge University Press / New York: Norton & Co., 1988.

'Seminar on *The purloined letter*' (1954), trans. by Jeffrey Mehlman, *Yale French Studies 48* 1972 pp. 39–72.

'Introduction' to 'Le Séminaire sur "La Lettre Volée"' (1956), E 41–61.

Le Séminaire. Livre III. Les Psychoses. 1955–1956, Paris: Seuil, 1981 [translation forthcoming].

'On a question preliminary to any possible treatment of psychosis' (1956), E 531–83/179–225.

'The Freudian thing' (1957), E 401–36/114–45.

'La psychanalyse et son enseignement' (1957), E 437–458.

Le Séminaire. Livre IV. La Relation d'objet et les structures freudiennes. 1956–1957, 'Comptes rendus' by J.-B. Pontalis, *Bulletin de Psychologie 10* 1956–7 pp. 426–30, 602–5, 742–3, 851–4; *11* 1957–8 pp. 31–4.

Le Séminaire. Livre VI. Le Désir et son Interprétation. 1958–1959, 'Comptes rendus' by J.-B. Pontalis, *Bulletin de Psychologie 13* 1959–60 pp. 263–72, 329–35.

Le Séminaire. Livre VII. L'Ethique de la psychanalyse. 1959–1960, Paris: Seuil, 1986.

'Subversion du sujet et dialectique du désir dans l'inconscient freudien' (1960), E 793–827/292–325.

Le Séminaire. Livre IX. L'Identification. 1961–62 (unpublished).

Le Séminaire. Livre X. L'Angoisse. 1962–1963 (unpublished).

Le Séminaire. Livre XI. Les Quatre Concepts fondamentaux de la psy-

chanalyse, 1964, Paris: Seuil, 1973; *The four fundamental concepts of psychoanalysis*, trans. by Alan Sheridan, London: Tavistock, 1977; reprinted in paperback by Penguin, 1986.

'Position de l'inconscient' (1964), E 829–50.

'La science et la vérité' (1965), E 855–77.

Le Séminaire. Livre XIII. L'Objet de la psychanalyse, 1965–66 (unpublished).

Ecrits, Paris: Seuil, 1966.

'Proposition du 9 Octobre 1967 sur le psychanalyste de l'Ecole', *Scilicet 1* 1968 pp. 14–30.

Le Séminaire. Livre XVII. L'Envers de la psychanalyse, 1969–1970 (unpublished).

Le Séminaire. Livre XX. Encore. 1972–1973, Paris: Seuil, 1975. [Untranslated into English, although sessions have appeared in Juliet Mitchell and Jacqueline Rose, eds., *Feminine sexuality. Jacques Lacan and the Ecole freudienne*, trans. by Jacqueline Rose, London: Macmillan, 1982.]

Ecrits; a selection, trans. by Alan Sheridan, London: Tavistock, 1977.

Travaux et interventions, Paris: Association Régionale de l'Education Pérmanente, 1977 (non-paginated).

Lacoue-Labarthe, P., and J.-L. Nancy, *Le Titre de la lettre (Une lecture de Lacan)*, Paris: Editions Galilée, 1973.

Lagrange, Jacques, 'Versions de la psychanalyse dans le texte de Foucault', *Psychanalyse à l'Université 12* no. 45 Jan. 1987 pp. 99–120; no. 46 April 1987 pp. 259–80.

Langs, Robert, 'The misalliance dimension in the case of the Rat Man', in Mark Kanzer and Jules Glenn (eds.), *Freud and his patients*, New York: Jason Aronson, 1980, pp. 215–31.

Laplanche, Jean, and J.-B. Pontalis, *The language of psycho-analysis*, trans. by Donald Nicholson-Smith, London: The Hogarth Press and the Institute of Psycho-analysis, 1973.

'Fantasy and the origins of sexuality', *Int. J. Psa. 49* 1968 pp. 1–18.

Leclaire, Serge, 'L'Obsessionel et son désir', *L'Evolution Psychiatrique* 1959 pp. 383–408; reprinted in Leclaire, *Démasquer le Réel* and translated in Schneiderman, ed., *Returning to Freud*.

Démasquer le réel, Paris: Seuil, 1971.

Lesky, Erna, *Die Wiener Medizinische Schule im 19. Jahrhundert*, Graz-Cologne: Böhlau, 1965.

Lévi-Strauss, Claude, *Structural anthropology* (1958), trans. by C. Jacobson and B. Grundfest Schoepf, Harmondsworth: Penguin, 1968.

Lindner, Robert, *The fifty-minute hour* (1956), London: Free Association Books, 1986.

Little, Margaret, 'Counter-transference and the patient's response to it' *Int. J. Psa 32* 1951 pp. 32–40.

Transference neurosis and transference psychosis, New York: International Universities Press, 1980.

Bibliography

McCahill, Thomas W., Linda C. Meyer, and Arthur M. Fischman, *The aftermath of rape*, Lexington, MA: D.C. Heath, 1979.

McGrath, William J., *Freud's discovery of psychoanalysis. The politics of hysteria*, Ithaca: Cornell University Press, 1986.

Macey, David, *Lacan in contexts*, London: Verso, 1988.

Mackinnon, Catherine A., *Sexual harassment of working women*, New Haven and London: Yale University Press, 1979.

Mahoney, Patrick, *Freud and the Rat Man*, New Haven and London: Yale University Press, 1986.

Major, René, 'La parabole de la lettre volée. De la direction de la cure et de son récit', *Etudes Freudiennes No. 30* 1987 pp. 81–130.

Malcolm, Janet, 'Annals of scholarship (Psychoanalysis – Part I)', *The New Yorker*. 5 December 1983; reprinted in Malcolm, *In the Freud archives*, London: Jonathan Cape, 1984.

Mannoni, Octave, 'L'amour de transfert et le réel', *Etudes Freudiennes 19–20* 1982 pp. 7–13.

Manuel, Frank, *A Portrait of Isaac Newton*, London: Harvard University Press, 1968.

Marcus, Steven, 'Freud and Dora: story, history, case history', *Partisan Review 41* 1974 pp. 12–23, 89–108; reprinted in Marcus, *Freud and the culture of psychoanalysis*, London: George Allen and Unwin, 1984, pp. 42–86.

Masson, J.M., *The assault on truth: Freud's suppression of the seduction theory*, London: Faber & Faber; New York: Farrar Strauss, 1984.

Meringer, R. 'Wie man sich versprechen kann', *Neue Freie Presse*, 23 August 1900.

Miller, Alice, *The drama of the gifted child and the search for the true self* (1979), London: Faber & Faber, 1983.

For your own good. Hidden cruelty in child-rearing and the roots of violence (1980), London: Faber & Faber, 1983.

Du Sollst Nicht Merken. Variationen über das Paradies-Thema, Frankfurt: Suhrkamp Verlag, 1981.

Miller, Jacques-Alain, 'Suture (elements of the logic of the signifier)' (1966), *Screen 18* no. 4 1977/78 pp. 24–34.

Miller, Jacques-Alain, ed., *La Scission*, Paris: Bibliothèque d'Ornicar?, 1976.

L'Excommunication, Paris: Bibliothèque d'Ornicar?, 1977.

Mitchell, Juliet, *Psychoanalysis and feminism*, London: Allen Lane, 1974.

Mitchell, Juliet, and Jacqueline Rose, eds., *Feminine sexuality. Jacques Lacan and the Ecole Freudienne*, trans. by Jacqueline Rose, London: Macmillan, 1982.

Mochulsky, Konstantin, *Dostoevsky, his life and work*, trans. and an introduction by Michael A. Miniham, Princeton: Princeton University Press, 1971.

Modell, W., *The relief of symptoms*, Philadelphia: W.B. Saunders, 1955.

Bibliography

Moi, Toril, 'Representation of patriarchy: sexuality and epistemology in Freud's Dora', *Feminist Review* no. 9 Autumn 1981 pp. 60–74.

Monod, Jacques, *Chance and necessity*, London: Fontana, 1972.

Montrelay, Michèle, 'Inquiry into femininity', *Semiotext(e) 4* no. 1 1981 p. 229.

Muller, John P., and William J. Richardson, *Lacan and language. A reader's guide to Ecrits*, New York: International Universities Press, 1982.

Muller, John P., and William J. Richardson, eds., *The purloined Poe. Lacan, Derrida and psychoanalytic reading*, Baltimore and London: The Johns Hopkins University Press, 1988.

Nunberg, Herman, and Ernst Federn, eds., *Minutes of the Vienna Psychoanalytic Society, Vol. III: 1910–1911*, trans. by H. Nunberg, with the assistance of H. Collins, New York: International Universities Press, 1974.

Nussbaum, Martha, *The fragility of goodness. Luck and ethics in Greek tragedy and philosophy*, Cambridge: Cambridge University Press, 1986.

Ogilvie, Bertrand, *Lacan. La formation du concept de sujet (1932–1949)*, Paris: Presses Universitaires de France, 1987.

Olinick, Stanley L., 'The gossiping psychoanalyst', *Int. Rev. Psa. 7* 1980 pp. 439–45.

Pascal, Blaise, *Oeuvres complètes*, Paris: Seuil, Intégrale, 1963.

Pearson, E.S., and M.G. Kendall, *Studies in the history of statistics and probability*, London: Charles Griffin & Co., 1970.

Person, Ethel, 'Women in therapy: therapist gender as a variable', *Int. Rev. Psa. 10* 1983 pp. 193–204.

Pichon, E., 'M. Lacan devant la famille', *Revue française de psychanalyse 11* 1938, reprinted in *Confrontaton 3* Spring 1980 pp. 179–207.

Poe, Edgar Allan, 'The facts in the case of M. Valdemar', in Poe, *Selected Writings*, ed. by David Galloway, Harmondsworth: Penguin, 1967.

Pontalis, J.-B., 'On death-work in Freud, in the Self, in culture', in Alan Roland, ed., *Psychoanalysis, creativity and literature. A French–American inquiry*, New York: Columbia University Press, 1978, pp. 85–95.

Porter, Theodore M., *The rise of statistical thinking, 1820–1900*, Princeton: Princeton University Press, 1986.

Prigogine, Ilya and Isabelle Stengers, *Order out of chaos*, London: Heinemann, 1984.

Racker, Heinrich, *Transference and countertransference*, London: The Hogarth Press, 1968.

Ragland-Sullivan, Ellie, *Jacques Lacan and the philosophy of psychoanalysis*, London and Canberra: Croom Helm, 1986.

Ramas, Maria, 'Freud's Dora, Dora's hysteria', in Judith L. Newton, Mary P. Ryan and Judith R. Walkowitz, eds., *Sex and class in women's history*, London: Routledge & Kegan Paul, 1983, pp. 72–113.

Bibliography

Rank, Otto, *The trauma of birth* (1924), London: Routledge & Kegan Paul, 1929.

Rapaport, Anatol, *Two-person game theory. The essential ideas*, Ann Arbor: University of Michigan Press, 1966.

Reich, Wilhelm, *The mass psychology of fascism* (1933), trans. V.R. Carfegno, London: Condor, 1972.

Richardson, Jack, *Memoir of a gambler*, London: Jonathan Cape, 1980.

Rickman, John, 'The factor of number in individual- and group-dynamics' (1950), in Rickman, *Selected contributions to psycho-analysis*, compiled by W.C.M. Scott and with an introductory memoir by S.M. Payne, London: The Hogarth Press and Institute of Psycho-analysis, 1957, pp. 165–9.

Ricœur, Paul, *Freud and philosophy* (1961), New Haven: Yale University Press, 1969.

Rieff, Philip, *Freud. The mind of the moralist*, London: Victor Gollancz, 1960.

Rose, Jacqueline, 'Dora – a fragment of an analysis', *m/f* no. 2 1978 pp. 5–21, reprinted in Rose, *Sexuality in the field of vision*, London: Verso, 1986, pp. 27–48.

Roublef, Irène, 'Le Désir de l'obsessionel dans la théorie de Jacques Lacan', *Rivista sperimentale di Freniatria e Medicine Legale della Alienazioni Mentali 89* 1965 pp. 78–98.

Roudinesco, Elizabeth, 'Monsieur Pichon devant la famille', *Confrontation 3* Spring 1980 pp. 209–25.

La Bataille de cent ans. L'histoire de la psychanalyse en France, Vol. 1. 1886–1925, Paris: Editions Ramsey, 1983, reprinted by Editions du Seuil, 1986.

La Bataille de cent ans. L'histoire de la psychanalyse en France, Vol. 2. 1925–1985, Paris: Seuil, 1986.

Roustang, François, *Un destin si funeste*, Paris: Editions de Minuit, 1976.

Rush, Florence, 'Freud and the sexual abuse of children', *Chrysalis 1* 1977 pp. 31–45.

The best kept secret; sexual abuse of children, Englewood Cliffs, NJ: Prentice-Hall, 1980.

Sacks, Harvey, 'Everyone has to lie', in B.G. Blount and Mary Sarches, *Sociocultural dimensions of language use*, New York: Academic Press, 1975, pp. 57–79.

Sartre, Jean-Paul, *Being and nothingness. A phenomenological essay on ontology* (1943), trans. by Hazel Barnes, New York: Washington Square Press, 1956.

Savage, D.S., 'Dostoevski: the idea of *The gambler*', *The Sewanee Review 58* 1950 pp. 281–98.

Schafer, Roy, *A new language for psychoanalysis*, New Haven and London: Yale University Press, 1976.

Scharfman, Melvin A., 'Further reflections on Dora', in Mark Kanzer and

Bibliography

Jules Glenn, eds., *Freud and his patients*, New York: Jason Aronson, 1980, pp. 48–57.

Schmideberg, Melitta, 'A contribution to the history of the psychoanalytic movement in Britain', *British Journal of Psychiatry 118* 1971 pp. 61–8.

Schneider, Michel, *Blessures de mémoire*, Paris: Gallimard, 1980.

Schneider, Monique, *La Parole et l'inceste. De l'enclos linguistique à la liturgie psychanalytique*, Paris: Aubier Montaigne, 1980.

'Père, ne vois-tu pas . . . ?' Le père, le maître, le spectre dans l'interprétation des rêves, Paris: Denoël, 1985.

Schneiderman, Stuart, *Rat Man*, New York and London: New York University Press, 1986.

Schneiderman, Stuart, ed. and trans., *Returning to Freud. Clinical psychoanalysis in the school of Lacan*, New Haven and London: Yale University Press, 1980.

Schur, Max, 'Some additional "day residues" of the specimen dream of psychoanalysis', in Rudolph M. Loewenstein, Lottie M. Newman, Max Schur and Albert J. Solnit, eds., *Psychoanalysis. A general psychology: Essays in honor of Heinz Hartmann*, New York: International Universities Press, 1966, pp. 45–85.

Freud. Living and dying, London: The Hogarth Press and the Institute of Psycho-analysis, 1972.

Schusdek, Alexander, 'Freud's seduction theory: a reconstruction', *Journal of the History of the Behavioral Sciences 2* 1966 pp. 159–66.

Searle, John, *Speech acts: an essay in the philosophy of language*, Cambridge: Cambridge University Press, 1969.

Shannon, Claude E., 'A mathematical theory of information', *Bell System Technical Journal 27* 1948 pp. 379–423, 623–56.

Shannon, Claude E., and Warren Weaver, *The mathematical theory of communication*, Urbana: University of Illinois Press, 1949.

Sheridan, Alan, *Michel Foucault: the will to truth*, London: Tavistock, 1980.

Shortland, Michael, 'Setting murderous Machiavel to school: hypocrisy in politics and the novel', *Journal of European Studies 18* 1988 pp. 93–119.

Sichère, Bernard, *Le Moment lacanien*, Paris: Grasset, 1983.

Simmel, Ernst, 'Zur Psychoanalyse des Spielers', *Int. Zeitschrift für Psychoanalyse 6* 1920 p. 397.

Slipp, Samuel, 'Interpersonal factors in hysteria: Freud's seduction theory and the case of Dora', *Journal of the American Academy of Psychoanalysis 5* 1977 pp. 359–76.

Smart, Carol, and Barry Smart, 'Accounting for rape. Reality and myth in press reporting', in Smart and Smart, eds., *Women, sexuality and social control*, London: Routledge & Kegan Paul, 1978, pp. 89–103.

Smith, J.C., and Brian Hogan, *Criminal law*, fourth edition, London: Butterworth & Co., 1978.

Bibliography

Smith, Roger, *Trial by medicine. Insanity and responsibility in Victorian trials*, Edinburgh: Edinburgh University Press, 1981.

Sorabji, Richard. *Necessity, cause and blame. Perspectives on Aristotle's theory*, London: Duckworth, 1980.

Spacks, Patricia Meyer, *Gossip*, Chicago: University of Chicago Press, 1985.

Steiner, George, *After Babel*, Oxford: Oxford University Press, 1975.

Sterba, Richard, *Reminiscences of a Viennese psychoanalyst*, Detroit: Wayne State University Press, 1982.

Sulloway, Frank, *Freud. Biologist of the mind*, London: Burnett Books, 1979.

Swales, Peter, 'Freud, Minna Bernays and the conquest of Rome: new light on the origins of psychoanalysis', *The New American Review 1* 1982 pp. 1–23.

'Freud, Johann Weier, and the status of seduction; the role of the witch in the conception of fantasy', privately printed, 1982.

'Freud, Fliess and fratricide; the role of Fliess in Freud's conception of paranoia', privately printed, 1982.

'A fascination with witches', *The Sciences* vol. 22 no. 8 November 1982 pp. 21–5.

'Freud, Krafft-Ebing and the witches. The role of Krafft-Ebing in Freud's flight into fantasy', privately printed, 1983.

'Freud, Martha Bernays and the language of flowers: masturbation, cocaine, and the inflation of fantasy', privately printed, 1983.

'Freud, cocaine, and sexual chemistry: the role of cocaine in Freud's conception of the libido', privately printed, 1983.

'Freud, his teacher, and the birth of psychoanalysis', in Paul E. Stepansky, ed., *Freud. Appraisals and reappraisals. Contributions to Freud studies. Vol. I*, Hillsdale, New Jersey: The Analytic Press, 1986, pp. 3–82.

'Freud, Breuer and the Blessed Virgin', privately printed, 1986.

Temkin, Jennifer, 'Towards a modern law of rape', *The Modern Law Review 45* 1982 pp. 399–419.

'Women, rape and law reform', in Tomaselli and Porter, eds., *Rape*, pp. 16–40.

Thom, Martin, '*Verneinung, Verwerfung, Ausstossung*: a problem in the interpretation of Freud', in Colin MacCabe, ed., *The talking cure. Essays in psychoanalysis and language*, London: Macmillan, 1981, pp. 162–87.

Thornhill, Randy, Nancy Thornhill, and Gerard A. Dizinno, 'The biology of rape,' in Tomaselli and Porter, eds. *Rape*, pp. 102–21.

Todhunter, I., *A history of the mathematical theory of probability from the time of Pascal to that of Laplace*, London: Macmillan, 1865.

Todorov, T., 'Freud sur l'énonciation', *Langages 17* 1970 pp. 34–41.

Tomaselli, Sylvana, and Roy Porter, eds., *Rape*, Oxford: Basil Blackwell, 1986.

Bibliography

Tostain, René, 'Le joueur, essai psychanalytique', *L'Inconscient 2* 1967 pp. 117–32.

Turkle, Sherry, *Psychoanalytic politics: Jacques Lacan and Freud's French Revolution*, London: Burnett Books, in association with André Deutsch, 1979.

Von Neumann, J., and O. Morgenstern, *Theory of games and economic behavior*, New York: Wiley, 1945.

Walker, Marcia J., and Stanley L. Brodsky, eds., *Sexual assault. The victim and the rapist*, Lexington, MA: D.C. Heath, 1976.

Warnock, G.J., *The object of morality*, London: Methuen, 1971.

West, D.J., C. Roy, and Florence L. Nichols, *Understanding sexual attacks. A study based upon a group of rapists undergoing psychotherapy*, London: Heinemann, 1978.

White, Hayden V., *Metahistory. The historical imagination in nineteenth-century Europe*, London and Baltimore: The Johns Hopkins University Press, 1973.

Wiener, Norbert, *Cybernetics: or control and communication in the animal and the machine*, Cambridge, MA: MIT Press, 1948.

The human use of human beings, New York: Houghton Mifflin, 1950.

Wilde, Oscar, *The importance of being earnest* (1895), London: Methuen, 1966.

Wilden, Anthony, *The language of the self*, Baltimore: Johns Hopkins University Press, 1968; reprinted as *Speech and language in psychoanalysis*, Baltimore: Johns Hopkins University Press, 1975 [includes translation of Lacan, 'Function and field of speech and language in psychoanalysis'].

Williams, Glanville L., *Criminal law. The general part*, London: Stevens & Sons, 1953.

Textbook of criminal law, London: Stevens & Sons, 1978.

Willis, Sharon, 'A symptomatic narrative', *Diacritics 13* Spring 1983 pp. 46–60.

Winnicott, D.W., *The maturational processes and the facilitating environment*, London: The Hogarth Press and the Institute of Psycho-analysis, 1965.

The child, the family and the outside world, Harmondsworth: Penguin, 1964.

'A child psychiatry case illustrating delayed reaction to loss', in Max Schur, ed., *Drives, affects, behavior: essays in memory of Marie Bonaparte*, vol. 2, New York: International Universities Press, 1965, pp. 441–64.

Wittgenstein, Ludwig, *Philosophical investigations*, Oxford: Basil Blackwell, 1953.

'Conversations on Freud', in Wollheim and Hopkins, eds., *Philosophical essays on Freud*, pp. 1–11.

Wollheim, Richard, *Freud*, London: Fontana, 1971.

Bibliography

'The cabinet of Dr. Lacan', *New York Review of Books 21/22* 1979 pp. 36–45.

Wollheim, Richard, and James Hopkins, eds., *Philosophical essays on Freud*, Cambridge: Cambridge University Press, 1982.

Young, Robert, ed., *Untying the text*, London: Routledge & Kegan Paul, 1981.

Young-Bruehl, Elisabeth, *Anna Freud*, London: Macmillan, 1989.

Zeitlin, Froma, 'Configurations of rape in Greek myth', in Tomaselli and Porter, eds., *Rape*, pp. 122–51.

INDEX

Index

Index

consciousness 132, 194, 329
  loss of 193
consent 42, 66–7, 69–70, 73–4, 78,
    79–80, 82, 84, 86, 87, 88, 328, 329,
    332
constitution 204–6, 207, 213, 302–3,
    364
container 247
contract 30, 34, 40, 43, 44, 72, 82, 151,
    156, 157, 164, 167; *see also* pact
convention 156, 159–60, 348
conversation, psychoanalysis and 106,
    107, 115, 353–4
conviction, sense of 77–8, 189, 347
Cordelia 25, 263
Cottet, Serge 322, 324
countertransference 21–2, 167, 236,
    237–40, 322
  and analytic supervision 239
Cranefield, Paul 384
criminology 64
cybernetics 126, 132–3, 134, 339

daimon kai tuché 205, 210–11, 212–13
Dali, Salvador 104
Darwin, Charles 129
Daston, Lorraine 132
Davidson, Donald 337
death 174, 364, 368–9
  and absence 176, 354
  and castration 175
  instinct 134, 191, 229
  in the sciences 294–6
  and waiting 171–2, 174–6
deception 119, 121, 124; *see also* lying
defence mechanisms 304
deferred action 4, 93, 110, 191–2,
    195–206, 213, 236, 242, 270, 290,
    354, 359, 361–2, 363–4, 365–6
déjà vu 365
demand 110–11, 156, 240–1
Dennett, Daniel 133
Derrida, Jacques 3, 6, 174, 238, 239,
    246, 317, 354, 366, 379
Derrida, Jacques, works cited
  'Du tout' 222–3, 226, 227, 370, 371
  'Le facteur de la vérité 223, 247,
    266, 339, 359, 365
  'Freud and the scene of writing' 168,
    318
  Of grammatology 234

'My chances/*Mes chances*' 364
Positions 241–2
'Spéculer – sur "Freud"' 213, 219,
    229, 230, 233–5, 240, 242, 331,
    337–8, 367
'Télépathie' 219, 243–4, 252, 374
Descartes 129, 134, 137
Descombes, Vincent 331, 382
desire 68, 81, 85, 88, 279, 290, 294–6,
    299, 313
  in Lacan's work 110–11, 122, 138;
    for recognition 122, 138–9
  to be an analyst 230–1, 235–6, 238–9
  unconscious 67
destiny 207, 217–18, 272, 364
determinism 95–6, 272, 277
Deutsch, Helene 63, 65, 70, 327–8
developmental stages, Lacan's critique
    of 118–19, 203–5, 363
dialectic 173, 204, 299
  of adult–child sexual relations 79–81
  individual and collective 183
  master–slave 104, 120, 171, 270–2,
    377
  and rape 85
  of seduction 345
  of speech and language 149
  of time in gambling 12, 276, 281
diary 90, 284
Diderot, Denis 125
Didi-Huberman, Georges 323
différance 4, 174, 232, 242, 354
discourse 158
  circuit of 256–8
  confession as form of 383
  Lacan's theory of four 111–12, 358–9
  law of 135
disposition *see* constitution; fate;
    psychoanalysis, causality in
doctor–patient relationship 7, 20–1, 26,
    33–8, 43, 46–7, 287, 291, 378–9,
    379; *see also* authority, medical;
    psychoanalytic practice and
    technique
doctors 5, 19, 22, 24
  as drug 32
  and discussion of sexual topics 18,
    57, 319–20, 326
Dolto, Françoise 114, 204
domination 305
  in discourse 308

407

Index

Index

Index

Index

411

Index

Index

Index

Index

Pascal, Blaise 128, 132, 189, 278–9
passe 231, 240
password 116, 151, 233
past 90, 171, 205–6
pastoral power 297, 311, 313–14
pathological 294–5, 301, 306, 308
Pearson, E.S. 378
performatives 44, 47, 141, 150, 152,
    163–7, 233, 345, 347, 350
Perniola, Mario 331
Perrier, François 335
person
    first and second 143, 153, 154–5,
        235, 241, 247, 347
    third person 139, 154, 162
Person, Ethel 249, 374
pervert 279, 301
Pichon, Eduard 337
phallic
    signifier 110, in *Dora* 52, 53, 58, 246
    stage 85, 279
phenomenology 289
    of time of 173–4, 281
Phidias 315
philology 288, 293–4, 295, 308
philosophy 2, 141–2, 234, 348
physics 130
Pinel, Philippe 286
placebo 31–2
Plato 67, 109, 230, 331–2
Plautus, *Amphitryon* 139
play-acting, limits of 70–1
Poe, Edgar Allan
    The murders in the Rue Morgue 190,
        191
    The purloined letter 130, 133, 136,
        137, 264
    The facts in the case of M. Valdemar
        216
poker 137
Pontalis, J.-B. 202, 203, 337, 354, 355,
    363
Porter, Theodore M. 132
power 32–3, 85, 298–305, 307–8,
    310–11, 315
    juridico-discursive concept of 298,
        303–5
    see also knowledge-power
premonitory dreams 4, 90–3, 365
Prévost, Abbé 376
Prigogine, Ilya 134

primal scene 168, 203, 226, 231, 241,
    262, 265, 290, 371
probability theory, history of 132
promise 5, 44, 150, 156, 159, 164, 235,
    345, 348
    breach of 86, 332
pronouns 142–5, 147, 153ff., 163–7,
    247, 341, 342, 346
prophecies 90–6
prostitute 47, 328
psychical reality 80, 212, 253
    and material reality 67, 219, 368–9
psychoanalysis
    aim of 5
    of author 260–7
    in Britain 2, 113, 371
    causality in 4, 74ff., 207–9, 300
    and communication 149, 151, 344
    as confession 298–9, 382, 383
    and conflict 72, 74
    and constitution 204–6, 207, 302–3
    as a contract 30, 44
    culture of 243–4, 258, 302, 338
    as a discourse 3, 37, 111, 308, 383
    distinguished from superstition 95–6
    as domination 308
    drive and need in 110–11, 121, 139
    epistemology of 126
    eroticisation of 57, 59
    ethics of 7–8, 88, 115, 314
    fictionality of 5, 8, 53
    in France 2, 102–3, 112–13, 227, 258,
        see also Lacan
    as Freud's autobiography 234
    fundamental rule of 36–7, 39–41,
        44–5, 154, 157, 163, 246, 252, 300,
        305, 349, 351
    future of 4
    and gossip 8–9, 10–11, 169, 222, 224,
        245–8
    historicity of 205–6
    history and origins of 4, 9–10, 17, 23,
        25, 27, 29, 75, 235–6, 308, 331,
        original sin of 240, 249, 374
    and hypnotism 31–4, 45
    and intrasubjective 73
    as lexicon of Freud's unconscious 49,
        232
    limits of 222–3, 245, 370
    and literature 261–6
    as obsessional 170–1, 214

416

Index

417

Index

418

Index

Index

Index

Cambridge Studies in French

General editor: MALCOLM BOWIE

Also in the series